THE COMFORTER

THE COMFORTER

Sergius Bulgakov

Translated by Boris Jakim

WILLIAM B. EERDMANS PUBLISHING COMPANY
GRAND RAPIDS, MICHIGAN / CAMBRIDGE, U.K.

© 2004 Wm. B. Eerdmans Publishing Co.

Wm. B. Eerdmans Publishing Co.
255 Jefferson Ave. S.E., Grand Rapids, Michigan 49503 /
P.O. Box 163, Cambridge CB3 9PU U.K.

Printed in the United States of America

09 08 07 06 05 04   7 6 5 4 3 2 1

Library of Congress Cataloging-in-Publication Data

Bulgakov, Sergei Nikolaevich, 1871-1944.
[Uteshitel'. English]
The Comforter / Sergius Bulgakov; translated by Boris Jakim.
p.   cm.
Includes bibliographical references.
ISBN 0-8028-2112-X (pbk.)
1. Holy Spirit. I. Title.

BT121.3.B8513 2004
231'.3 — dc22

2004043413

www.eerdmans.com

Contents

Contents

Translator's Introduction

I

Sergius Bulgakov's *The Comforter* is the most comprehensive and profound book about the Holy Spirit ever written by a Russian theologian, and perhaps one of the most profound books about the Holy Spirit ever written. Bulgakov's stated goal in this book is to continue the work of St. Athanasius, who investigated the christological aspect of the Divine-humanity,[1] interpreting the latter as the dyadic action of the Son and the Holy Spirit, but without considering the relation between the Father and the Holy Spirit. In *The Comforter*, Bulgakov extends Athanasius' conception into "an inquiry into *Divine-humanity* as the work of the Son *and* the Holy Spirit, who in their indivisible Dyad, reveal the Father."[2]

2

The Holy Spirit is often referred to as the Paraclete, in Greek: *paraklētos*. Raymond E. Brown has written the following:

> In its root meaning the Greek term means "called [*klētos*] alongside [*para*]"; and like its Latin equivalent *advocatus* ("called [*vocatus*] to [*ad*]"), it has a forensic or legal use. When people are in trouble, they call in a lawyer or counsellor or *advocate* to stand beside them in court.

1. See p. x of the Translator's Introduction for a discussion of Divine-humanity.
2. See p. 27 of the present edition.

The legal context fits the Johannine history I have described wherein the members of the community had to defend themselves for their christological views. Their help and surety was the Paraclete-Spirit dwelling within them who interpreted correctly the significance of Jesus. . . . Another reason for which the Spirit is "called alongside" is consolation at times of trouble, whence the Consoler or Holy Comforter. In the context of the Last Supper Jesus is going away. Although this makes the hearts of his disciples sorrowful, it is better that he goes away; for then the Paraclete comes (John 16:6-7), and they have the consolation of one who more than makes up for Jesus' departure.[3]

Although Bulgakov does discuss the activity of the Holy Spirit as Advocate, he clearly emphasizes the function of the Holy Spirit as Consoler or Comforter, the One who has been sent to comfort those Christ has left behind: "I will not leave you comfortless" (John 14:18). Indeed, the Russian title, *Uteshitel'*, cannot mean Advocate; it can only mean Comforter. This explains my choice of Comforter (not Paraclete) for the English title.

3

Father Sergius Bulgakov (1871-1944) is the twentieth century's most profound Orthodox systematic theologian. Born into the family of a poor provincial priest, Bulgakov had a strict religious upbringing and entered the seminary at a young age. But owing to a spiritual crisis, in the direction of materialism and atheism, he did not complete his seminary studies. He chose, instead, to follow a secular course of study, which led to his matriculation at the University of Moscow, where he specialized in political economics.

This marked the beginning of his relatively short-lived Marxist period. In 1901, after which he defended his master's thesis, *Capitalism and Agriculture* (1900), he was appointed professor of political economy at the Polytechnical Institute of Kiev. During his years there (1901-1906), he underwent a second spiritual crisis, this time in the direction of idealist philosophy and the religion of his youth.

Influenced first by the philosophies of Kant and Vladimir Solovyov,

3. R. E. Brown, *The Churches the Apostles Left Behind* (New York: Paulist, 1984), pp. 106-7.

and then by the great Orthodox theologian Pavel Florensky, Bulgakov gradually began to articulate his own original sophiological conception of philosophy. This conception was first elaborated in his *Philosophy of Economy,* for which he received his doctorate from the University of Moscow in 1912. Later, in *The Unfading Light* (1917), he gave his sophiological ideas definite philosophical shape. Following this, Bulgakov's intellectual output was, for the most part, theological in character. Indeed, his personal religious consciousness flowered in the following year, and he accepted the call to the priesthood, receiving ordination in 1918.

These years of internal crisis and growth in Bulgakov's personal life paralleled the tumultuous period in Russian political and social life that climaxed in the October Revolution of 1917 and the subsequent Bolshevik ascendancy. In 1918, Bulagkov left Moscow for the Crimea to assume a professorship at the University of Simferopol, but his tenure was short-lived, owing to Lenin's banishment in 1922 of more than one hundred scholars and writers deemed incurably out of step with the official ideology. Bulgakov left the Soviet Union on January 1, 1923, first alighting in Constantinople, and then in Prague. Finally, having accepted Metropolitan Eulogius' invitation both to become the Dean of the newly established Saint Sergius Theological Institute and to occupy the Chair of Dogmatic Theology, he settled in Paris in 1925. Here, until his death in 1944, he was to make his most fruitful and lasting contributions to Orthodox thought.

During the theologically most productive period of his life, Bulgakov produced six books, grouped into two trilogies. The works of the so-called little trilogy, *The Friend of the Bridegroom* (1927),[4] *The Burning Bush* (1927), and *Jacob's Ladder* (1929), are efforts to capture the glory, the uncreated light streaming from John the Baptist, the Mother of God, and the holy angels. The great trilogy, *On Divine Humanity,* consists of volumes on Christology (*The Lamb of God,* 1933), pneumatology (*The Comforter,* 1936), and ecclesiology and eschatology (*The Bride of the Lamb,* published posthumuously, 1945).[5] *On Divine Humanity* is Bulgakov's magnum opus, representing the summation and crowning achievement of many years of philosophical and theological inquiry.

---

4. Published by Wm. B. Eerdmans Publishing Co., 2003, in Boris Jakim's translation.

5. Published by Wm. B. Eerdmans Publishing Co., 2002, in Boris Jakim's translation.

4

The Comforter, the middle volume in the great trilogy,[6] is encyclopedic in its scope and variety. It has historical sections, treating the development of the doctrine of the Holy Spirit in patristics and then the development of the doctrines of procession in the early patristic and later Byzantine periods. It touches upon the place of the Holy Spirit in the Holy Trinity and explores Old and New Testament notions of the Spirit of God and the Holy Spirit. The concluding chapter deals with the mystical revelation of the Holy Spirit, in His gifts and finally in the Pentecost, which is considered to be unending. Throughout this book, we find rigorous philosophical and theological thought illustrated and buttressed by the evidence of Scripture and Church tradition (especially prayer).[7]

Central to Bulgakov's thought in *The Comforter,* as well as in the entire great trilogy, are the concepts of Divine-humanity and Sophia, concepts that are crucial for modern Russian philosophy and theology, starting with Vladimir Solovyov.[8] Divine-humanity is rooted in the Creed of Chalcedon, which defines the dual nature of Christ, divine and human, and expresses the process whereby man cooperates with God, leading to the transfiguration of humanity and fusing the entire human community into a heavenly Church without barriers between dominations. For Bulgakov, this process has its central focus in the Incarnation of Christ and the descent of the Holy Spirit at the Pentecost.

There is much reference to Sophia, both Divine and creaturely, in *The Comforter.* In her divine aspect, Sophia is the "divine world," existent in God and for God, eternal and uncreated, in which God lives in the Holy Trinity. In her creaturely aspect, Sophia can be identified with spiritualized humanity, the community of persons united in Divine-humanity. She is the kingdom of God, the society of those participating in Divine-humanity. It should be noted that, in *The Comforter,* Bulgakov does not present a doctrine of Sophia in relation to the Holy Spirit. Sophia is, rather, the background upon which Bulgakov's pneumatological thought is developed. In other words, *The Comforter* is only implicitly sophiological,

6. The fact that it is the middle volume is perhaps fitting given the mediating function of the Holy Spirit in Orthodox theology.

7. There is a highly significant and nearly unique epilogue, "The Father," which can also serve as an introduction to the entire great trilogy.

8. In many ways the founder of modern Russian philosophy, Solovyov (1853-1900) had a vast influence on Bulgakov's early thought, up to and including *The Unfading Light,* but this influence had begun to wane by the time of the little and great trilogies.

unlike *The Lamb of God* and *The Bride of the Lamb,* in which Bulgakov's sophiological theology is explicitly set forth and reaches its peak of development.

5

An important virtue of *The Comforter* is Bulgakov's treatment of the Filioque question. In fact, his discussion of this question may be the most important twentieth-century contribution to Filioque studies from the Orthodox side. It might be useful to review the disputes surrounding the Filioque question and how they pertain to the Great Schism. (Bulgakov discusses these issues in detail, with much reference to firsthand materials, but he assumes much knowledge on the reader's part.)

The schism between the Eastern and Western churches is traditionally considered to have taken place in 1054. There had been growing misunderstanding and alienation between the two groups, partly due to theological and liturgical differences, and partly due to political rivalries and divisions. Intense disputes over such matters as the ecclesiastical calendar, the use of leavened or unleavened bread, or additions to the Creed (especially the Filioque clause) reached a climax in 1054, when Pope Leo IX and Patriarch Michael Cerularius excommunicated each other.

An important (though undoubtedly not the most important) cause of the schism was the Filioque dispute. The dispute started when the Third Council of Toledo (589) added the so-called Filioque clause, expressing the double procession of the Holy Spirit, to the Nicene Creed. Filioque is a combination of Latin words meaning "and from the Son," the addition to the Creed reading: *Credo in Spiritum Sanctum qui ex patre filioque procedit* ("I believe in the Holy Spirit who proceeds from the Father and Son"). Although this doctrine of the procession of the Holy Spirit from the Father and the Son was accepted by the Western church as a belief by the end of the fourth century, the formula was not authorized for general liturgical use before the early part of the eleventh century. The Filioque addition was assailed vehemently by Photius (c. 810–c. 895), the patriarch of Constantinople for the periods 858 to 867 and 877 to 886. The greatest scholar of medieval Byzantium, he was long considered the initiator of the Schism.[9]

9. A chief reason for this is the fact that, in 867, Photius denounced the presence of Latin missionaries in Bulgaria who, acting as the emissaries of Pope Nicholas I, began to

The Eastern church did not accept the Filioque addition on two grounds: (1) the addition was made unilaterally, altering a creed approved by early ecumenical councils; and (2) the formula reflected a particular Western conception of the Holy Trinity, to which most Byzantine theologians objected. The Filioque clause was probably devised in response to Arianism, which denied the full divinity of the Son. To the Byzantine theologians, however, the clause appeared to compromise the primacy or "monarchy" of the Father. An unsuccessful attempt to reconcile the two points of view was made at the Council of Ferrara-Florence in 1439.

Bulgakov examines the writings of the chief theoreticians on both sides of the dispute, and finds that each of the sides is wrong in its own way: the Orthodox side had unwisely accepted the faulty Catholic problematic. He concludes, however, that the Filioque is not an insuperable obstacle to the reunification of the churches.

6

In *The Comforter*, Bulgakov does much more than develop a theoretical doctrine of the Holy Spirit. He also testifies that the Holy Spirit, Who descended into the world at the Pentecost, continues to abide in the world and to comfort us. The Pentecost is the realized and perfect Divine-humanity: The Divine-humanity is the appearance on earth of the God-Man, who has united in His Person the heavenly and the earthly Adam, but it is equally the descent into the world of the Holy Spirit, Who abides with us forever. The Holy Spirit manifests to the world Christ Who has come, while the Son fills the world with His Spirit. The descent of the Holy Spirit is the fulfillment in man of the Image of God, which is manifested in the world in Christ. His descent therefore clothes man in Christ, in the Divine-humanity.

And the world is full of the radiance of the Holy Spirit. Bulgakov's book too is full of this radiance, and perhaps its greatest virtue is that, through it, the Holy Spirit Himself breathes upon us, its readers.

*   *

---

introduce a text of the Nicene Creed with the Filioque addition. The same year Photius gave an exposition of his objections to the Filioque clause and summoned a council to depose Nicholas.

I have shortened some of the sections in the text dealing with patristic doctrines of the Holy Spirit. I have also eliminated, or shortened, some of Bulgakov's notes. Throughout the text Bulgakov refers to a number of his own works; I give the full bibliographic citation only the first time the work is mentioned.

I have used the King James Version (KJV) of the Bible, since I consider it to be the English-language version that most closely approaches the beauty of the Russian Bible. In a few cases I have modified the KJV to make it conform with the Russian Bible; in particular, throughout I have replaced the KJV's "Holy Ghost" with "Holy Spirit."

Here and there in untwisting some difficult passages I have used the excellent translation into French by Constatin Andronikof: *Le Paraclet*, second ed. (Lausanne: Editions L'Age d'Homme, 1997).

Author's Preface

A book about the Comforter. . . . A theologian will find much to say on this subject, much that is important and necessary, forgotten and not fully understood. But all words about the Spirit will remain poor and dead, deprived of the Spirit itself, of His ineffable sighs and prophetic utterances. The creature cries out and beseeches the Spirit, "Come and dwell within us" (from the Eastern Orthodox prayer to the Holy Spirit). The creature beseeches in the extremity of sorrow; its yearning is unbearable. The Comforter is near; He is in the world, but not with the world — within us but not with us. . . . He is unceasingly accessible and clearly known in His breath, in His mysterious presence. Through the sacraments of the Church He gives us living communion with God. He watches over the Church and guides Her; by His power She is for us a higher reality that is not taken away from us and will not be taken away from us — a joy forever, a light of eternity in this world below.

The Spirit came down from heaven, sent by the Son from the Father, and manifesting the Father and the Son. But in us the Divine is united — "without separation and without confusion"[1] — with the human, which is destined to be deified, to become Divine-human. But how sad and even frightening our plight is: our human side flees the Spirit, is afraid of Him and does not desire Him. On the one side, we have the guardians of the sacred fire, who preserve the piety of the temple but who do not know the piety of the creative life. On the other side, we have those who are wholly ignorant of the sacred fire, who are its malicious blasphemers and de-

---

1. "Without separation and without confusion" is the Creed of Chalcedon's characterization of the union of the divine and human natures in Christ. — Trans.

niers, but who sometimes have some knowledge of the piety of life and the search for creativity. Arrogance and hardness of heart, pharisaic and sadducean, soullessness in the name of spirituality and blasphemy against the Spirit for the sake of the flesh, are harmoniously united to extinguish the Spirit and to denigrate prophecy. On the one side we have a custodianship that seeks to preserve what is vain and false, stagnation elevated to a law of life, and a joyless prosaicness, this disease of pseudo-spirituality. On the other side we have a demonic war against God and humanistic self-divinization, an animal indifference to the spiritual and a submergence in the flesh. The tongues of fire that flash out in the darkness are angrily and maliciously put out and fade powerlessly. The night of the world yawns with the darkness of the void, in the kingdom of the beast and the false prophet.

But even the world itself is repelled by this spiritual void — and it yearns for inspiration. It seeks prophecy, the revelation of the *divine-human about the human,* about the world and man. It knows and preserves the Divine but it does not know and cannot find the Divine-human. And if God does not help, man will not be saved. . . . But God has already saved us, for He came into the world and became Man. And having ascended from the world, He sent from heaven the Holy Spirit; He gave us the gift of the Pentecost. The Holy Spirit abides in the world; He is given to us and woe be to us if we are not in the Spirit. But we pray for and await the new gift of the universal Pentecost, a new answer to unanswerable questions, a new creative activity, a new inspiration that will transfigure life and call us to meet the Coming Christ. Not having the Spirit, we thirst for Him and yearn for Him. Without Him our whole historical epoch is convulsed by a convulsion of death. But mysteriously anointed by the Spirit in the sacraments, with and in the latter we await a new sacrament of life, the gift of the Comforter Who has come and Who abides with us. And in its agony the world knows Comfort and awaits the Comforter, as God's love for the world, and it loves Love.

The world loves Love in her works, in her gifts, which are the gifts of the Holy Spirit. And our insatiable love desires to love Love herself, not her power only, but also her countenance, her hypostatic countenance, which is unknown, unmanifested, unrevealed to us. And our love seeks reflections, manifestations, of this countenance. It seeks, and finds them: in the known and unknown, earthly and celestially glorified countenance of the Spirit-bearer, the Bride and Mother of God, the Virgin Mary, the most glorified Queen of Heaven, Who in Her Dormition did not leave the world but Who — like the hypostatic Love of God, the Holy Spirit — abides both in the world and above the world. We are blind: we cannot see this Glory in the heavens, but we nevertheless await its revelation, its appearance in the world, for Christ will come in His Glory. And it is then that the fullness of Divine-humanity will be manifested: Jesus-Mary, the Logos and the Holy Spirit, revealing the Father. This fullness of revelation has been promised to suffering creation. With elevated minds and purified hearts, let us rise with burning candles before the dawn to meet it — the Divine-humanity.

O COMFORTER, THE SPIRIT OF TRUTH,
COME AND DWELL WITHIN US!
COME, LORD JESUS!

THE SPIRIT AND THE BRIDE SAY, COME.
AND LET HIM THAT HEARETH SAY, COME!
(Rev. 22:17)

The Doctrine of the Holy Spirit
in the Patristic Literature

I. Early Christianity

1. The Post-Apostolic Age

The revelation of the Third hypostasis, the Holy Spirit, not as a gift of the Spirit of God, but as a Divine Person of the Holy Trinity, is expressed by words of fire in the Gospel. Christ Himself announced "another Comforter" (John 14:16), Whom He will send from the Father after His departure from the world; and the name of this Comforter is thunderously proclaimed by Him as part of the Name of the Holy Trinity: "baptizing . . . in the name of the Father, and of the Son, and of the Holy Spirit" (Matt. 28:19).[1]

This baptismal formula is in fact the Christian confession of faith in the hypostatic being not only of the Father and of the Son but also of the Holy Spirit. The doctrine of the Holy Trinity and, in particular, of the Person of the Holy Spirit, is presented in the New Testament as an unshakable dogma of the faith, which it is impossible to deny or diminish by reinterpretation; and it has always been accepted as such by the Church.

The Pentecost was the living revelation of this dogma. The gifts of the Holy Spirit poured forth so obviously and so abundantly upon the

---

1. Throughout this translation I make use of the King James Version, which I sometimes modify to make it conform with the Russian Bible. In all cases I have replaced "Holy Ghost" with "Holy Spirit." — Trans.

Christians in the primitive Church that this dogma was totally self-evident for them, which is indeed attested by the entire content of the Acts of the Apostles as well as by the apostolic writings. The Holy Spirit was life itself for the primitive Church; and if the holy apostles knew Christ in His earthly life, the apostolic Church knew — differently but not less clearly — the "Comforter Himself" living within it. This presence of the Comforter, His action and gifts, were self-evidently obvious not only within the Church but also outside it, for example, even for Simon Magus. And this *divinity* of the gifts of grace and of the Holy Spirit dispensing them possessed an inner self-evidence and immanent certitude that even the person of the Lord Jesus did not have for the disciples of Christ. A long path of the preparation of the disciples was necessary before they were capable of accepting the confession uttered by Peter, "Thou art the Christ, the Son of the living God" (Matt. 16:16), and by Thomas, "My Lord and my God" (John 20:28).

For this required (and requires) a special illumination, whose absence is even forgiven by the Lord: the sin against the Son of man will be forgiven (Matt. 12:32). With regard to the Holy Spirit in the primitive Church, however, people found themselves placed before a certain divine self-evidence, which they could not reject from weakness, lack of reflection, or misunderstanding. They could reject it only by a direct act of the will, filling their hearts with resistance to God, with a "lie to the Holy Spirit" (Acts 5:3). That is why "blasphemy against the Holy Spirit shall not be forgiven unto men . . . neither in this world, neither in the world to come" (Matt. 12:31-32). One can say that the Acts of the Apostles in their entirety are the story of the revelation of the Holy Spirit in the Church, the living disclosure of the dogma of the Holy Spirit. And in the light of this evidence, the New Testament tells us not *Who* He is, the Giver of gifts, but *how* He appears and what gifts He dispenses.

As we move farther away from the Pentecost into the yawning depths of history, as we move farther away from this source of light, it grows dimmer and dimmer. But the post-apostolic age (the age of the so-called "apostolic fathers") still possessed blissful knowledge of the Pentecost. It still possessed the abundance of apostolic gifts directly received by the first generation of Christians; it was still a spirit-bearing and charismatic age. Therefore, in the self-awareness of this age, as it was reflected in the writings of the "apostolic fathers," the revelation of the Third hypostasis, as well as Its gifts, has a factual character that it is sufficient to affirm without dogmatically interpreting. And this is indeed what we find in the early Christian writings. The latter reflect a period of golden childhood, though one that is already fading, approaching its end. The time has not yet come for dogmatic reflection, nor especially for theological speculation. What we have here is a factual attestation of the faith in the Holy Spirit through His gifts. And in this sense one can say that, in the post-apostolic age, as reflected in the epistles of the apostolic fathers, there did not yet exist an express *theology* of the Holy Spirit.[2]

2. The Apologists

In the Apologists we find only an exposition of the rules of the faith, beyond which, at least in pneumatology, they do not go. Their theology, insofar as it is possible to speak of one, is reducible primarily to logology: they confront the theological problem of the Logos, in both its divine and cosmic aspects. Their natural task was to justify their faith, defending it against accusations of polytheism (or at least ditheism) and also revealing the power of the Logos in the world and in human life (they were influenced here by Philo and obviously confused, or even identified, the supra-eternal Logos with the creaturely Sophia[3]). Therefore, "generally speaking, in the dominant thought of the apologists there was no place for a doctrine of the Holy Spirit, and if they nevertheless speak of the latter, one must see in this only traces of the influence of a common Christian tradition little understood by them."[4]

It can be said that the pneumatology of the first two centuries of Christianity staunchly defends the *regula fidei* [rule of faith], bequeathed by the Gospel and the apostolic preaching in the fullness of the living experience of the Church and the life of grace. For this pneumatology, the Holy Spirit is a reality full of grace, unceasingly experienced in churchly communion. Theological thought has not yet posed the problem of the doctrine of the Holy Spirit in the unity and composition of the Holy Trinity, however, or of His place in the Latter. In brief, the pneumatological

2. We do not find it necessary to expound the views of the different authors, but instead refer the reader to existing general works on the history of dogma and patristics. The idea of Trinity is not yet fully developed, as can be seen from the well-known passage in *The Shepherd* of Hermas (*Simil.* V, 2, 5, 6), where we encounter the notion that "the Son is the Holy Spirit"; and instead of the Trinity we get a Dyad, Christ remaining outside it like a witness.

3. See the Translator's Introduction for a discussion of Sophia. — Trans.

4. A. Spassky, *The History of Dogmatic Movements in the Epoch of the Ecumenical Councils* [in Russian] (1906), p. 14.

problem has not yet arisen in the consciousness as a *trinitarian* problem, which it essentially is; for the Holy Spirit can be understood only in connection with the divine triunity. Not only does the second century fail to resolve this problem; it does not even pose it for later centuries, starting with the third.

3. The Patristic Age in Pneumatology

The third century was destined, if not to resolve, at least to pose in all its breadth the trinitarian problem and, in particular, as one of its elements, the pneumatological problem, which concerns not only the role of the Holy Spirit in the creation and in the Divine Providence, but also what He is in Himself, and in the Holy Trinity, as the Third hypostasis.

The dogma of the Holy Trinity arose, then, before theological thought as an extremely difficult speculative problem which surpassed all the accomplishments of religion and philosophy up to that time. It even surpassed the very problematic of the ancient world. This attempt to systematically construct and theologically deduce a trinitarian dogma had no past foundation to rely on: the incipient theology was left to its own powers.

Moreover, it was easy to get lost in the labyrinth of pagan philosophy, in the abundance and variety of its systems. At the same time one could not do without the assistance of this pagan philosophy, which was the indispensable philosophical school for Christian theology, its natural Old Testament. This theologically propaedeutic significance of the philosophy of antiquity can be traced in the history of dogma as well as in the biographies of individual Fathers of the Church. This philosophy was a kind of fate for Christian theology, and one cannot fail to see in this a higher predestination and election. One can say that if, in general, philosophy represents a necessary intellectual culture for theology, then the philosophy of antiquity has unique and supreme significance precisely in this respect.

Therefore, Christian theology assimilated the philosophy of antiquity by natural affinity and selection, in the same manner that Christian art assimilated pagan art; and there thus arose that legitimate or illegitimate, but in any case inevitable, *mixis* or *krasis* [Gk: mixture or synthesis] of philosophy and religion that is so characteristic for Christian theology (and is sometimes even called *"die acute Hellenisierung des Christenthums"* [the acute Hellenization of Christianity]). In its highest achievements, this mixture consists of a transformation of pagan thought into Christian thought. It is

4

a new creation, which indeed is what Christian theology essentially is when it is viewed in the light of the history of philosophy.

But this transformation has not been uniformly successful: hybrid mixtures have sometimes arisen where the sweetness of Christianity was concealed behind the bitter taste of paganism. In a certain sense one can indeed sometimes speak of a Hellenization of Christian theology, of an excessive influence and inappropriate implantation in Christian theology of foreign elements.

Such was the difficulty of the task that confronted Christian theology beginning in the second century, after the age of the "apologists." This too was an apologetics, but no longer a negative one, consisting of the removal of misunderstandings, the refutation of slanders, or a more precise exposition of the "rule of faith." It was instead a positive apologetics, whose task was the spiritual conquest of a strong opponent, the definitive conversion of this opponent to Christianity: instead of the Hellenization of Christianity, there occurred the conversion of Hellenism to Christianity, a task that was triumphantly fulfilled by the Church. "Thou hast conquered, Galilean" — such was the judgment of history uttered by a belated romantic who dreamed of restoring antiquity.

This conquest was attained, however, only through a difficult and dangerous *struggle;* it was not achieved immediately and easily. And we see in the first creative and thus noble and daring efforts of Christian philosophy not only victories but also defeats, not only successes but also failures. At times pagan philosophy infiltrated Christian theology without dissolving in it; and therefore it colored, and even distorted, this theology, having on it an inappropriate and excessive influence. Of course, this influence remained subtle and was not perceived by the theologians themselves. It was chiefly manifested not in specific doctrines but in the *problematic,* in the manner in which problems were approached or posed, which was what determined the paths thought was to take.

As a rule, Christian theology does not introduce into its constructions particular philosophical theories or doctrines of antiquity, but receives them as self-evident premises, which are imperceptibly incorporated in the dogmatics. One can look at this in two ways: On the one hand, pagan philosophy can be considered a kind of natural prophecy of the reason concerning the truths of Christianity; on the other hand, we have a direct philosophical influence. In any case, in various systems of theology we can affirm such an influence of one philosophical system or another. We must say this especially about Platonism, which as a theory of eternal ideas, of the sophianic prototypes of the world in God, has become a permanent part of Christian dogmatics. But we must also mention Stoicism, Neoplatonism, and Aristoteleanism, for they too color various systems of Christian theology, which therefore cannot be fully understood without taking this influence into account.

The trinitarian problem (and the related pneumatological problem) includes several separate but intimately connected problems. The first of these is the problem of divine triunity. The trinitarian dogma, as it is given in the New Testament revelation, combines monotheism (which with Old Testament exclusivity rejects all polytheism) with the trinitarity of the persons of the Holy Trinity, who are of equal dignity and Divinity. They are equal to one another in Divinity and at the same time each is equal in Divinity to the entire Holy Trinity in Its unity and indivisibility. The unity and trinity, the distinction of the Three Persons and Their equal Divinity — that is the aspect of the trinitarian dogma that religious philosophy first encounters in Christian theology. It is in the Christian dogma that this question first arises for human thought. The Christian dogma is remote from all pagan polytheism, which Israel so zealously rejected, being protected from it by the first two Divine commandments, given on Sinai. Of course, both philosophical thought and the religious consciousness consider pagan polytheism to be unsound. But equally alien and inimical to the Christian dogma was the abstract monotheism to which the Judaic dogmatics led. The latter was, of course, incapable of theologically coming to grips with the entire concrete doctrine of God that was already contained in the sacred books of the Old Testament. Therefore, Judaism (just as, later, Islam, which is theologically similar to it) irreconcilably opposes, in the name of monotheism, the trinitarian dogma, considering it a profession of tritheism. To be sure, the task of Christian theology was completely new[5] and exceptionally difficult; and ancient philosophy did not have a ready-made scheme but at best only more or less appropriate means for tackling it.

The trinitarian problem is not exhausted by trinitarity alone as the triunity and consubstantiality of Divinity. It also includes the *differentiation* of separate hypostases in their concrete interrelation, in their intratrinitarian togetherness and mutual determination. According to the trinitarian dogma, the Holy Trinity is not a divine triunity *in abstracto*, but

---

5. To be sure, one can find *vestigia trinitatis* outside of Christianity, for example, in the Hindu trinity. But without going into how nontrinitarian this trinity really is and to what extent it differs from the Christian Trinity, one should in any event remember that Hinduism did not have any *visible* influence on classical antiquity and Christianity.

6

the completely concrete triunity of Father, Son, and Holy Spirit, of the First, Second, and Third hypostases. Trinitarian theology includes the doctrine of *each* of the Divine hypostases and their interrelation. Here, the trinity of Divinity in unity, as well as in the distinction of the three concrete hypostases, must be shown not only as a divinely revealed *fact*, valid by virtue of its facticity, but also as a *principle* owing to which Divinity is not a dyad, tetrad, etc., in general not a pagan Olympus, but precisely a trinity, exhausting itself in its fullness and self-enclosedness. In like manner there arises with respect to the individual Persons the problem of their proper place in the Trinity and the significance of this place for each of them. In particular, in pneumatology the general doctrine of Trinity includes and is complicated by the special problematic of the Third hypostasis, the Holy Spirit. *In concreto,* trinitarian theology is patrology, Christology, and pneumatology, all three. For these concrete aspects of the trinitarian doctrine there are no data or analogies in pagan philosophy.

Thus, it was the task of trinitarian theology to establish two fundamental aspects of the dogma: on the one hand, the concrete triunity of Divinity, where the latter, being the triune absolute subject,[6] includes *three subjects* of equal divinity but distinct personhood; and on the other, the concrete interrelation of the three Persons of the Holy Trinity in their hetero-personal being for themselves and for one another. The unification of these two parts of the doctrine is what determines concrete triadology and, in particular, pneumatology.

The trinitarian problem in this form is conceived only beginning with the third century and, properly speaking, it is examined and solved in the patristic epoch only in the third, fourth, and fifth centuries. In later centuries these questions are addressed only in passing, or on some other occasion: the entire field of attention is occupied by Christology, not pneumatology; and the later epigonic summation (in John of Damascus) does not of course change this relative indifference to the pneumatological problem as such. This problem comes to occupy the center of attention later, in the postpatristic epoch, starting with the ninth century, and it does this in a one-sided and particularly polemical formulation, precisely as the question of the Filioque,[7] with its pro and contra. Therefore, the truly creative period in pneumatology is the patristic epoch of the third to fifth centuries; to sum up the achievements of this epoch is to sum up the achievements of patristic pneumatology.

6. See my essay "Chapters on Trinity" (1928).
7. See the Translator's Introduction for a discussion of the Filioque. — Trans.

Introduction

*   *

One must acknowledge that the third century, despite its remarkable efforts in the domain of trinitarian theology, did *not* solve the problem. On the contrary, it even evaded it, distorting it or substituting another problem for it. The fundamental element of the problematic of the Holy Trinity was ignored, namely, the dogma of the *equal divinity* and *equal dignity* of the Three Persons of the Holy Trinity. This element was replaced by the opposite dogma of their inequality, their unequal dignity and unequal divinity. Instead of a doctrine of the Holy Spirit there arose a doctrine of the revelation of one Divinity in three descending steps, with each successive person having a lesser fullness of divinity and possessing not equal divinity but only partial and gradually decreasing divinity. And this casts doubt on the very existence of the trinitarity, which is by no means a three-step revelation of Divinity. Perhaps it would be more appropriate to speak in this case not of the trinity but of the unicity of Divinity, where the latter is characterized by a three-step modality, the lower stages being included in and subordinate to a single higher monad. In the capacity of a triadology we get a masked monadology. Such a system of triadology is usually referred to by the Latin term "subordinationism," which afflicted, directly or indirectly, all the theological systems of the second century and some of the systems of the third century.

We also find this subordinationism in the second part of the trinitarian problem, in prosopology, the doctrine of the separate persons or *prosopa;* and also, in particular, in pneumatology. If the entire Holy Trinity receives a subordinationistic interpretation, it becomes clear that, in particular, the Third hypostasis, the Holy Spirit, is understood as the *third* and last according to Divinity. But in essence it is not known why it is last, why it is not possible to continue this decreasing self-revelation of Divinity further, beyond the three hypostases. In essence, this substitution and distortion remove the very problem of pneumatology, leaving no place for an orthodox doctrine, but giving instead only its subordinationistic surrogates. Unfortunately, this is the only form of pneumatology that the third-century patristic literature knew.

For this failure of patristic thought with regard to pneumatology we can indubitably blame (besides its lack of experience in this domain and the difficulty of the problem itself) the philosophical influence of antiquity. As we have already indicated, in developing a doctrine as extraordinarily difficult as triadology, theology could not rely solely on its own powers: it needed the aid of the philosophy of antiquity and used the latter as an instrument. But this instrument was a dangerous one, turning out to be poisonous or at least disobedient. It led those who used it much farther than necessary or even where they should not have gone. Imperceptibly, Christian thought wandered to the side or became colored by the pagan philosophical systems. A *syncretism* of pagan philosophy and Christian theology thus arose, a syncretism which later will be overcome slowly and painfully, but never completely.

We can distinguish different forms of subordinationism in the early triadology, depending on which philosophical system of antiquity has the dominant influence. Thus, in Western theology we have the *stoically* colored doctrine of Tertullian and the related theories of Novatian and Hippolytus. In Eastern theology we have Origen's system based on Neoplatonic ideas, which left its ineradicable mark on the whole of Eastern (especially Alexandrian) theology. Finally, we have, rooted in Aristoteleanism, the doctrine of Arius and its arianizing successors, Macedonius, Eunomius, Aetius, and others. As a reaction to subordinationism but parallel to it, in the form of its black shadow, so to speak, negative subordinationism, we can mention various types of modalism, again inspired — directly or indirectly — by antiquity. A closer examination of these different forms of subordinationism will make the above discussion more convincing.

II. Tertullian's Subordinationism and Stoic Philosophy

Before turning to an analysis of the trinitarian doctrine of the third century, let us note that it poses two kinds of problems: (1) the problem of the *immanent* Holy Trinity, i.e., the Holy Trinity in itself, in its eternal being without reference to the world; and (2) the problem of the *economic* Trinity, i.e., the Trinity in relation to the world. The ontological and cosmological aspects of the question in this case not only are not mutually exclusive but are even interrelated. The Holy Trinity is considered here with a primary emphasis on the cosmological or economic aspect; and this emphasis greatly determines the character of the doctrine considered. This predominant cosmologism in the understanding of the Holy Trinity naturally harmonizes with and even leads to subordinationism. In particular, Tertullian's doctrine exhibits features typical of a cosmological understanding of the Holy Trinity, of an economic subordinationism. Such are its fundamental style and its theme: to understand God in His revelation in the world in the capacity of the Holy Trinity. Meantime, the speculative and theological statement of this doctrine, whose dogmatic content is furnished by the Old Testament and New Testament traditions, is determined by premises borrowed from the Stoic philosophy.

The latter is a form of philosophical *monism* with a tendency toward religious and then ethical pantheism. There is one living, rational, fire-like substance, which is the pneumo-corporeal principle, material and life-giving. In this substance, all that is corporeal is spiritual and all that is spiritual is corporeal.[8] This substance possesses the principles of its own self-determination, the properties by which it is concretized in its own being, as well as the possibility of self-differentiation through the relations that arise therefrom. This substance is intrinsically impersonal (we can already observe here the impersonalism that is a fundamental principle of Western theology). Although hypostatic consciousness of self becomes proper to it, this is a secondary, derivative definition, which is ontologically preceded by substantial pre-hypostatic and extra-hypostatic being; substance is primordial here. It bears within itself the reason of the world and all its abundance *(logoi spermatikoi)*. Protomatter *(hulē)*, qualified *(poios)* by form, actualizes these principles in being. In them, substance is revealed in the multiplicity of the world, while preserving its unity.

In these general features, Stoicism approaches the classical systems of dynamic and static hylozoism or monism — the systems of Heraclitus and Parmenides, Spinoza and perhaps Leibniz. From the religious point of view, this monistic pantheism is clearly characterized by naturalistic immanentism, with not an accidental trace of anthropomorphism. By expressing the self-consciousness of being, man thereby also possesses knowledge of God. And through knowledge of the world he learns to know the world reason, *fatum:* he learns *amor fati* [love of fate] as the supreme wisdom.

This general scheme of monistic naturalism appears to have little in common with the dogmatic doctrine of Christianity. On one side we have pantheistic monism; on the other we have an insurmountable distance between God and creation. On the one side we have the impersonalism of a substance deprived of all qualities and definitions; on the other we have the concrete trihypostatizedness of Divinity. On the one side we have the doctrine of the universal corporeality of substance in God and the world; on the other we have the doctrine of God as the Absolute Spirit, etc.

Tertullian assimilates these themes of Stoicism, not only those that

---

8. In this respect Stoicism is most akin to the religious philosophy of occultism as it is expressed in the theosophical and anthroposophical doctrines of our time, with their radial identification of the spiritual and the corporeal.

are appropriate to Christianity but also those that are decisively opposed to it. Among the latter one must include the doctrine of the corporeality of substance as well as the absence of the notion of personhood in Tertullian's ontology. But how can one build a bridge from Stoic impersonalism to the doctrine of the trihypostatic God in the dogmatics of the Christian Church? What saves the situation here is the idea of *economy*, i.e., the cosmological interpretation of the Holy Trinity. There is no place for this interpretation in the Absolute, but it comes into play when one attempts to define the relations between the Absolute and the world. Here one must keep in mind the fact that the creation of the world is by no means a necessity for the Absolute *Itself* in Its self-revelation. Creation is (and here we see a gnostic influence) an *emanation (probolē)* of Divinity into the world, an emanation which then becomes an "economy" and is expressed in the creation of the world and man. At the same time as this emanation and economy in Divinity there also arise personal determinations and, in particular, the Holy Trinity. God is an anthropomorphic spirit.

Tertullian's anthropomorphism has as much a Christian origin (the idea of the image of God in man) as a Stoic one (religious immanentism). Owing to religious immanentism, man has direct self-knowledge of *rerum divinarum*, of the corporeal-spiritual substance, which, being totally sufficient and all-blissful, constitutes space, the world, and all things (*Adversus Praxean*, ch. 5); and this essentially extra-personal or pre-personal substance is God, corresponding in Scripture to the Father: *"Pater tota substantia est"* (ch. 9). The Trinity did not exist; neither did the First hypostasis. Divinity was what existed. "God was alone *(solus)*, but even then He was not properly alone, for He had with Himself His Reason, which He had in Himself. God is a rational entity; and Reason was in Him first, and only then did all things [get their being] from Him. This Reason is His consciousness of Himself *(sensus ipsius est)*. The Greeks call it Logos" (ch. 5). "God did not possess the Word from the beginning *(non sermonalis a principio)*, but He possessed reason *(rationalis)* before the beginning *(ante principium)*. . . . Although God did not utter His Word, He had it in Himself with reason itself and in reason itself, meditating on and organizing what He soon was to express through His Word" (ch. 5).

Of course, this pre-mundane and even pre-trinitarian reason is only a power or attribute of God, not the hypostatic being of the Son. When God said "let there be light," it was then that His Word was truly engendered from Him. "It was then that the Word received His form and adornment, His voice and sound, became the only begotten Son *(unigenitus et unus ex solo Deo genitus),* existing separately from Him" (*Adversus Praxean,* ch. 7, 26). This leads to an Arianizing thesis: "There was a time when the Son, Who made God the Father, did not exist" (*Adversus Hermogenum,* ch. 3). "When God desired to bring substances and appearances to reality in Him, He preferred *(protulit)* the Word, in order to actualize all things *(universalia)* through the Latter, through Whose cooperation they are conceived and predetermined" (*Adversus Praxean,* ch. 5). Logos-Sophia is the mediator or demiurge here, for Tertullian shared the philosophical conviction common to antiquity that Divinity could not enter into direct relations with creation.[9]

Such is also the purpose of the Holy Spirit. He and the Logos are the *"ministri et arbitri"* of the Father (*Adversus Praxean,* ch. 12); the Father confers with Them and They are His agents, acting "by His power and will" (ch. 15). The specific significance of the Holy Spirit is not fully clarified. But fully clarified is the conclusion that follows from the general premises of subordinationism and is characteristic not only for Tertullian himself but also for his followers on this path: this is the proposition that the Holy Spirit, in the capacity of the Third hypostasis originating after the Son, is *less* than the Son, for He originates from the Son. The subordinationism here consists of a three-step progression, expressing a gradual decrease in the fullness of divinity; and the *third* Person in the Holy Trinity is interpreted as having the third place in Its ontological hierarchy. The third Person co-participates in the substance of Divinity, as *gradus, forma,* and *species unius substantiae* [degree, form, and species of one substance]; and in this sense, together with the Son, He partakes in the substance of the Father.

Tertullian also explains their relationship by an ill-chosen physical comparison (a favorite one in patristics): that of source, spring, and river. According to this comparison, the Holy Spirit is placed in a regular subordinationistic dependence not only on the Father but also on the Son. For Tertullian this means precisely *a Patre per Filium* [from the Father through the Son], which is one of the early expressions of the Western doctrine of the Filioque. The Holy Spirit is allocated the third place; and He is conceived, in terms of quantity of Divine substance, as less not only in comparison with the Father but also in comparison with the Son

---

9. Here he commits an error that later becomes a common notion in patristics. Namely, in equating the Logos with Sophia, he makes the Logos itself the sophianic foundation of the world, whereas this mediating place between God and creation belongs not to the Logos, but precisely to Sophia.

(*Adversus Praxean,* ch. 8). This distinction also conforms with the notion of the later appearance of the Third hypostasis: He is considered to have appeared not before the creation of the world, like the Logos, but only after the ascension of Christ; and He is considered to be the continuator of Christ's work on earth and the organizer of His Church. Just as the Logos-Son received from the Father "His form and adornment," so the Son after His ascension, "having asked this of the Father, gave being to the Comforter" (ch. 25).

Tertullian's cosmological subordinationism is so extreme that he proclaims a principle of the future Arianism: there was a time when the Logos did not exist. Does Tertullian not consider this Logos (and *a fortiori* the Holy Spirit) who arises in time a *creation* of the Father? Tertullian evades this apparently inevitable conclusion by means of Stoic philosophy with its monistic impersonalism. Thanks to the universality and unity of substance, the "homoousianism" *(unius substantiae)* of the three hypostases is assured in advance; for in essence there is no other place for all that exists except this one substance, which also possesses the convenient feature that it is easily divided.

This divisibility is conceived according to the type of the inner *distributio* or *distinctio* of temporal and spatial relationships. Divinity is the fundamental substance, of which the Father, the Son, and the Spirit are different aspects, *unius substantiae, unius status, et unius potestatis* [of one substance, of one condition, and of one power]. One must not forget the fundamental impersonalism of Divinity owing to which all the hypostases arise within the limits of this impersonal substance: *nec Pater potuit esse ante Filium* [the Father could not have been before the Son] (*Adversus Hermogenum,* ch. 3); *tres unum sunt non unus* [three are a unity, not one] (*Adversus Praxean,* ch. 35). The trinitarian hypostases are only hypostatized *poiotētes* (in accordance with the postulate of Christian dogmatics), separate species. Here Tertullian anticipates the fundamental theologeme of Western trinitarian theology concerning the hypostases as relations.

As a result of this difference in attributes, the hypostases are, on the one hand, distinguished by them, but, on the other hand, they belong to one substance, are homoousian in character: *tres autem non substantia, sed forma* [three not in substance but in form] (*Adversus Praxean,* ch. 2). They are separated as *alius, alius, alius* [other, other, other], being distinguished not only by their attributes but also by the measure of substance, which is proper, in its entirety, only to the Father, but which belongs to the Son and Spirit only in decreasing parts (the sun, the ray, the light of this ray).

There also result other consequences: the invisibility of the Father and the visibility of the Son, etc. Being only cosmological and economic in nature, this distinction has, evidently, a temporal character, arises with the beginning of time and ends with its end, so that, as a result of this theory, the very existence of the economic Trinity after the end of the present world becomes problematic.

It is this idea of the divisibility of the one substance with the differentiation of the parts or hypostases that thus arise, that enables Tertullian to avoid the purely Arian understanding of the Son as a creature, while preserving all the (relatively) convenient features of cosmological subordinationism in the doctrine of the Son as the demiurge (and of the Spirit as His assistant). From the vantage point of this Stoic monism there can arise a general question: Is there in general a place here for the idea of *creation*, i.e., the appearance of creaturely being from noncreaturely being by virtue of a creative act? Or is there only a series of states or differentiations of one and the same substance, beginning with the appearance of the Trinity and ending with the Divine Incarnation, as the union not of two natures but rather of two states of *one* metaphysical nature? In particular, we find here in Tertullian the idea of the Divine-humanity, the union of the divine and human natures, as the conformity of the proper visible image of the Logos *prior to* the Incarnation with the human body assumed by Him.

In summing up Tertullian's trinitarian doctrine, one must say that it does not at all attain its goal, which is to develop a speculative theology of the trinitarian dogma. Neither his one-sided cosmological interpretation of the Holy Trinity, with a decisive rejection of Its immanent, eternal being, nor his subordinationism, with a sharp departure from the equidivinity of the three hypostases, can be recognized as satisfying the demands of the Orthodox dogmatic consciousness. And as far as the doctrine of the Holy Spirit is concerned (toward which Tertullian apparently should have had, as a Montanist, a marked predisposition), it is the weakest part of his trinitarian theory, both in its fundamental principle and because it is the least consistent and developed part of this theory: Thanks to Its origin (not directly from the Father, but only through the Son and, so to speak, for His needs) the Third hypostasis is put in last place in terms of fullness of divine substance.

At the same time, the Third hypostasis is treated here with an uncertainty which characterizes to some degree the whole of patristic thought, particularly that of the early period. Theology confronts here the *fact* that the Holy Spirit is preached in Church doctrine and manifested in the life of the Church, and that therefore He must be, in one way or another, included in the dogmatic schemata. But there is neither an appropriate speculative idea nor a theological motivation for this. The early logologists, not excluding Tertullian, give the impression that the presence of the Logos, the Second hypostasis, in the self-revelation of Divinity is truly essential for them; and all of them, each in his own way, are convinced of this not only ecclesially and positively but also theologically; and they in fact theologize about this. But as for the Holy Spirit, theologically they do not know what to do with Him and what place to assign to Him in their theological system. In essence, one can say that they are not convinced of the necessity of this; and although they submit to the dogma they could easily do without it in what we can call their binitarian — rather than trinitarian — theology. Therefore, there involuntarily arises in us the thought that, given an external necessity, they could have accepted a dyad, just as they could have gone beyond the Trinity to some larger number. In a word, one must affirm that even the Montanist Tertullian, strictly speaking, does *not* have a pneumatology.

III. Cosmological Subordinationism in Arianism

Arianism has predecessors in the so-called dynamic monarchianism, whose leaders were representatives of unitarianism in triadology and, of course, in Christology. The Antiochene tradition of Aristotelean rationalism through Lucian, teacher of Arius, also touched the latter, whose fundamental ideas about God are colored by Aristoteleanism. In theology Arius represents a direct contrast to the pantheistic monism of the Stoics. The God of Aristotle is completely transcendental to the world in His self-enclosed divine being. Arius taught that "God alone is eternal, unsorrowing, truthful, immortal, wise, good, powerful . . . unchangeable." God is a self-sufficient being Who from all eternity has His own Logos and wisdom, and He is conceived in the spirit of judaistically Aristotelean monotheism. In such a scheme there necessarily arises the old question, posed once by Philo: What is the relation of this transcendent God to creation, i.e., what *mediates* between God and the world? The sophiological problematic was totally foreign to Arius, as it was to the anti-Arian orthodox theology. Therefore, where one should have inquired into the divine principle or foundation of the world in God, one disputed instead about the Divine demiurge or Logos and His properties in relation to God the Creator Himself. This incorrect problematic characterizes both Arius and St.

Athanasius, as it does all further patristic theology, which is not aware of sophiology, although its deductions postulate the latter.[10]

In determining the relations of God to the world, asophianic theology has an irresistible tendency toward subordinationism, as we have already seen and will also see later on. The cosmological problematic also predominantly colors Arius' theology, especially his Christology, which is entirely determined by the cosmological aspect, not the soteriological or some other aspect. Here, he based his theory on wholly other ontological presuppositions than those of Tertullian or Origen. Aristoteleanism with the transcendence and self-enclosed self-sufficiency of Divinity left a place neither for the divisibility of substance, identified with cosmic being, as in Tertullian's Stoic theology, nor for the emanative process, as in Origen's Neoplatonic theology. Between the Aristotelean God-monad and the world there exists a hiatus, an ontological abyss, which can be crossed only by a *salto mortale* [death-defying leap]. Arius made such a leap in his doctrine of the creaturely Son, created out of the non-existent. The Son is created not out of the divine *mē on,* trinely determined in itself, as in the Stoic and Neoplatonic subordinationism, but out of the non-divine and extra-divine *ouk on;*[11] and therefore He does not resemble the Father in any way: the Son does not precisely know the Father and does not see Him perfectly. The Son is changeable; in all things He is separated and alienated from the essence of the Father.[12]

As a creature, the Son appears in time, and therefore the Father also appears in this sense: "God was not always the Father, but there was a time when there was only God, and the Father did not yet exist; it was later that He became the Father. And the Son too did not always exist . . . and there was a time when the Word did not exist. Desiring to create us, God created a certain One and named Him Word, Wisdom, and Son, in order to create us by means of Him." Thus, the cosmological origin and function of the Son are beyond all doubt here. He is created by an act of divine will, or desiring, which has no necessity in itself but is rather an act of divine arbitrariness. True, this creation, in contrast to all other creations, is perfect; it is intended to become the instrument of the creation

---

10. See my book *Agnets Bozhii (The Lamb of God).* [*The Lamb of God* is volume one of the trilogy *On Divine-Humanity,* of which *The Comforter* is volume two. See the Translator's Introduction. — Trans.]

11. For a discussion of these terms see my book *The Unfading Light* (Moscow, 1917).

12. Our information about Arius' doctrine comes chiefly from Athanasius' *Against the Arians.*

of the world, the cosmic demiurge, and then to make His abode in man and become Christ.

For our purposes there is no need to give a detailed account of the well-known Arian heresy. The important thing for us is to indicate this inner logic of cosmological subordinationism, which, here, on the foundation of the Aristotelean doctrine of God, leads to a theological absurdity: the trinitarian dogma is abolished and replaced by a blatant unitarianism, and even one that is disfigured by a dogmatic addition, the doctrine of a creaturely Son. This subordinationistic unitarianism is characterized by a total absence of the doctrine of the Holy Spirit, and even by something that is worse than a mere absence: in order to appease the demands of Church dogma, the doctrine of the Holy Spirit is replaced by the doctrine of a second stage of the divine creation, namely, by the creation of the Third hypostasis through the Second, of the Holy Spirit through the Logos. The Holy Spirit is assigned, both ontologically and cosmologically, the third place in terms of dignity. In essence, Arius could not, of course, be interested in the pneumatological problem. As the final result, those three stages into which Arius divides the Holy Trinity turn out to be ontologically separated from one another by their hetero-substantiality: "Separate by nature, disunited, divorced, and alien to one another are the essences of the Father, the Son, and the Holy Spirit; and they are infinitely dissimilar in all things according to their essence and glories; at least, the Word, with reference to the likeness of glory and essence, is absolutely alien both to the one and to the other, to the Father and to the Holy Spirit."[13]

In the next generation, Arianism's continuators Aetius and Eunomius imparted to the doctrine a repellently rationalistic form. But in the fundamental idea, i.e., subordinationatism, and particularly with reference to pneumatology, they remained faithful to Arius; and if for them the Son is a creature, the Holy Spirit is the creature of a creature. The *unborn* God is one and unique; the Son is a generation and creation, not existing previously and therefore created out of nonbeing, alien to the nature of the Father; and the Spirit is third in both order and dignity and thus third in essence as well.[14]

---

13. Athanasius, *De Synodis*, n. 15.

14. The further development of Arianism leads naturally to pneumatomachianism, with Macedonius traditionally considered as the head of the pneumatomachians (although there is no information about his actual opinions). This question was discussed and partially resolved at the Second Ecumenical Council, at Constantinople (381), about which below.

Thus, in Arianism, despite all its deadness, we find the maximally acute formulation of two problems: (1) the problem of cosmology, whose solution should have been a sophiology (the patristic epoch did not fully understand this problem and provided no solution for it); and (2) the problem of trinitarian subordinationism, in connection with which the question of the consubstantiality (homoousianism) of the hypostases was posed together with the whole trinitarian problem. The further development of this problematic consisted in the fact that the formulation and discussion of the trinitarian problem involved the doctrine not of a cosmological — or rather not only of a cosmological — subordinationism, but of an ontological one. And we find this precisely in the doctrine of Origen, who put his stamp on the whole of patristic theology.

IV. Ontological Subordinationism in Origen's Doctrine of the Holy Trinity

The doctrine of Origen, who is the true founder of Eastern patristic theology, bears distinct traces of the influence of Neoplatonism. His fundamental work *On First Principles (De Principiis)* appeared before Plotinus' *Enneads,* and Plotinus lived after him. However, being a disciple of Ammonius Saccas, whose ideas, according to Porphyry, were expounded by Plotinus, Origen was nurtured on the ideas of Neoplatonism; and he cannot be viewed otherwise than in connection with Plotinus, who represents the supreme achievement of the Greek philosophy (indeed, of natural reason in general) that did not know or at least did not accept revelation.

Origen assimilated the fundamental principles of the philosophy of Neoplatonism and by means of them he constructed a system of Christian dogmatics. This effort was extraordinarily valuable, as well as being full of danger and difficulty. First of all, Origen had to translate the impersonalistic system of Neoplatonism into the language of Christian personalistic, trinitarian theology; and he did this at a time when church theology had very little experience with the problematic of personalism, i.e., in the ante-Nicene and ante-Cappadocian epoch. He did this without express speculation, simply by putting the hypostasis of the Father in place of the Neoplatonic One, the hypostasis of the Son in place of the Neoplatonic Mind, and the hypostasis of the Holy Spirit in place of the World Soul, almost without noticing this substitution. This substitution makes itself felt, however, when it becomes necessary to more precisely define the hypostatic properties as well as the interrelationships of the hypostases.

In general, the Father takes on the features of Plotinus' One and is determined, in the main, apophatically: He is unfathomable, unexplainable, invisible, incorporeal, unchangeable. It is not easy to decide whether He is an essence or higher than essence, and even higher than all that is conceivable. He is unity and uniqueness. He is higher than wisdom, truth, light, and life, all of which come from Him. Meanwhile, He has complete and perfect knowledge of Himself; it is for this reason that Origen rejects the predicate of limitlessness, *apeiron,* in favor of determinateness and knowability. It must be noted that Origen's concept of God the Father coincides with the concept of *God (ho Theos)* or even *auto-Theos,* the first God in the language of Neoplatonism, already presupposing the gradation of Divinity in the second and third god. Neoplatonic subordinationism thus already steals into this first definition. This feature is more fully disclosed in the definition of the relation between the Father and the Son: "Let us try to imagine the power of God *(virtus Dei)* which constitutes the foundations of God's being. . . . Out of this universal and immeasurably great power there arises a *vapor* and, so to speak, a *vigor* which has its own hypostasis *(in propria subsistentia effectus).* Although this vigor comes out of the power itself, like desire out of thought, God's desire itself also becomes God's power. Thus, there arises another power, existing in its quality *(in sua proprietate subsistens),* a certain vapor of the first and unborn power *(primae et ingenitae virtutis)* of God and receiving its being from the latter" *(De Principiis* I.2.9).

Although this emanative conception of the origin of God's second power from the first indubitably introduces a distinction between them in the sense of ontological subordinationism, it nevertheless sufficiently affirms the consubstantiality, the homoousianism, of the two. We thus get an external consonance with Arius, who derived the Son from the Father's desire or will, against which St. Athanasius fought so insistently, affirming, instead, the origin of the Son from God's essence, not from His will. There is of course no intentional inner correspondence here between Origen's conception and Arianism, for he asserts the origin of the Son not from the non-existent but from God, as a "vapor" or a "shining of the eternal light." We therefore find in him the beginnings of a homoousian theology, although its form is imperfect.[15] At the same time he rejects another element of cosmological subordinationism: the temporal dependence of the origin of the Son on the Father; he connects the Son's origin

---

15. To be sure, we do not find the term *homoousios,* but only the idea the term represents.

not to the "economy" of creation but to the eternal being of Divinity it-self. "Just as a light can never be without shining, so of course the Son is not conceivable without the Father. The Son is also called the imprinted image of the Father's substance *(substantiae eius)*, the Word and Wisdom. How can one say that there was once a time when the Son did not exist? For to say this is to assert that there was once a time when truth did not exist, when wisdom did not exist, when life did not exist, whereas in all these things, the substance *(substantia)* of God the Father is thought to a superlative degree. All these things can never be taken away from Him and can never be separated from His essence" (4.28). Relying on the fundamental ontological idea of Neoplatonism, Origen radically overcomes cosmological subordinationism, both that of Tertullian and that of the Arians: The Son is co-eternal with the Father, and He is always born from Him 1.2.2).

However, Origen overcomes cosmological subordinationism only with reference to the creaturely world, clearly and consistently distinguishing creatureliness from the divine principle. But he does not overcome it with reference to the mutual relations of the hypostases, with reference to their equal dignity and divinity. Here, we find in Origen a distinct and consistent subordinationism of the hypostases: The Father is higher than the Son (just as the Son is higher than the Holy Spirit, but about this below). Although the Son is the actualized fullness of the Father's Divinity, He (the Son) presents this Divinity to the world, whose shadow falls on the Son Himself. God (the Father) is the simple one; the Son becomes multiple. God is higher than Wisdom; the Son is Wisdom.[16] The Father is the hidden God; the Son is the principle of self-revelation to the world. The Father is one and simple; the Son is "the idea of ideas and the essence of essences," the principle of all creation,[17] Sophia (?!): "In this hypostasis of Wisdom was (already) contained the whole possibility and image of future creatures; and by virtue of foreknowledge, all was predes-

---

16. Origen also tends to equate the Wisdom of Proverbs (Prov. 8, 9) with the Son. This can be sufficiently explained by the distinctive features of his subordinationism on the one hand and by the absence of a sophiology on the other. The Son thus occupies the place of Sophia in relation to the world and becomes excessively close to the latter. An erroneous interpretation of the text (an interpretation that Origen shares with the entire patristic epoch) characterizes this sophiological lacuna in his theology, owing to which he finds himself defenseless against cosmological subordinationism.

17. Thanks to the aforementioned sophiological tangle and the confusion of the principles of the creaturely and noncreaturely Sophia, Origen, several times calling the Son Sophia, also calls Him a creature (*De Principiis* 1.4; 3.9).

tined and predetermined." "The Son is the beginning of the ways of God, because He contains within Himself the beginnings *(initia),* forms, and species of all creation" (1.2.3).

This confusion of Logos and Sophia leads to the same thing as in Plotinus: acknowledging the eternity of the Son, who is immediately directed toward the world and approaches it, Origen must also postulate the eternity of the world (1.2.10), saving one thing by the other (he could have avoided this logical necessity only by distinguishing the Divine Sophia, the Divine and truly eternal world, from the Sophia of the creaturely world). All this makes the ontological difference between the Father and the Son so profound that one could fear for their consubstantiality if it were not already affirmed higher as an eternal and immanent — and not only economic and temporal — trinity. "The Savior and the Holy Spirit are immeasurably higher than all created things, but the Father surpasses the Son as much (or even more) as He and the Holy Spirit surpass all others. . . . Surpassing in essence, power, dignity, and Divinity many who are greatly elevated (angels and saints), the Son is in no wise comparable to the Father."[18] From this Origen naturally arrives at the idea that prayer in the proper sense of the word *(proseuchē)* can be addressed only to the Father.

This subordinationism extends also to the relation of the Son to the Holy Spirit. All was produced through the Logos, so that the Logos is higher than the Holy Spirit, precedes Him in being *(Commentary on John* 2.6; *PG* 14, cols. 125, 128). The Spirit's relation to the Son is thus similar to the Son's relation to the Father. The Son receives His being from the Father like nourishment, but the Spirit too needs the Son not only for His existence but also in order to be wise, rational, just, and so on *(PG* 10, col. 6). Accordingly, the spheres of action and power of each of the hypostases are distinguished: The Father contains all things; the Son contains only rational entities; the Spirit acts only upon saints. True, these actions of the three hypostases are marked by the spirit of harmony, so that "to participate in the Holy Spirit is the same thing as to participate in the Father and the Son" *(De Principiis* 4.32).

It must be said that, in Origen, we do not find a precise conception of the Holy Spirit as a necessary element of the life of Divinity (or even any definite statements about His Divinity). The schematic inclusion of

---

18. *Commentary on John,* vols. 13, 25; Migne's *Patrologia Graeca* 14, cols. 441, 444. [In the following notes, Migne's *Patrologia Graeca* will be designated *"PG,"* while the *Patrologia Latina* will be designated *"PL."* — Trans.]

the Holy Spirit in Origen's theology is due, first of all, to the Church dogma, and then, of course, to the theory of Neoplatonic trinity. The place and tasks of the World Soul are defined clearly and consistently in this theory, whereas in Origen they are already assigned to a significant degree to the Second hypostasis (which, moreover, he identifies with Sophia), and nothing is left for the Third hypostasis. This confusion of such a mighty intellect underscores to an even greater extent that *absence of pneumatology* which is so characteristic for him, as well as for his predecessors and contemporaries.

In general, subordinationism removes the possibility of pneumatology. And of course Origen could have learned much from Plotinus in the domain of logology, which essentially exhausted the theological interests of the epoch, but not in the domain of the doctrine of the Holy Spirit, which was totally foreign to Plotinus. One must also admit Plotinus' superiority to Origen from the point of view of formal consistency in his overall system. Plotinus developed a system of dynamic pantheism, which, thanks to his marked impersonalism, was liberated from many difficulties. Origen, on his side, replaced Plotinus' Absolute One with the Christian trihypostatic Divinity. This, of course, was the work of a Christian theologian but not of a systematic thinker. When Origen replaced Plotinus' impersonal metaphysical principles with the trinitarian hypostases, the divine persons, his system certainly became more orthodox but by no means more consistent.

This replacement was only a de facto one, not one of substance: it received neither theological nor philosophical justification. Together with Plotinus, Origen introduced into theology the expression "the three hypostases" of the One God.[19] He was aware of the problem of the *consubstantiality* of trinity, but not of the Holy Trinity *itself,* which is why, strictly speaking, he has no triadology (and in particular no pneumatology). Origen did not at all advance the doctrine of Trinity in unity and unity in Trinity; this doctrine remained within the limits of the earlier problematic of logology, i.e., of the Father-Son dyad, formulated by the apologists. Despite his ontologism, Origen not only did not distinguish God and the world in his theology but, in the final analysis, he united them — although, to be sure, not by lowering God to the world but by raising the world into God. In this way, neither the subordinationism nor the cosmologism in the doctrine of the Holy Trinity was overcome. One

19. Origen's (just as Plotinus') use of the term "hypostasis" was not distinguished by any precision, particularly in relation to *phusis* (nature).

can acknowledge only one indubitable achievement here: the problem of trinity was formulated not only with reference to the "economic" Trinity but also with reference to the "immanent" Trinity. The aforesaid does not, of course, diminish Origen's great accomplishment in theology: He is *the creator of the first system* of Christian theology, which includes, although with uneven precision, its fundamental problematic.

V. Homoousianism in the Trinitarian Doctrine of St. Athanasius of Alexandria

St. Athanasius' doctrine opens with a polemic against Arianism; and its theological emphasis is christological and logological. The central element of his doctrine is in part soteriological, inasmuch as only the incarnation of the true God is capable of accomplishing the full restitution and deification of man. The development of this soteriological and christological doctrine is possible, evidently, only on the basis of *homoousianism,* i.e., the acknowledgement of the consubstantiality of the Son with the Father; and this in turn leads to the trinitarian problems, although St. Athanasius does not take them as his starting point, but arrives at them, which is why this part of his worldview is expressed much less precisely than the christological part.

The starting formulation of the trinitarian problem in St. Athanasius is the Neoplatonic and Origenistic position, which had taken firm root in that epoch. He thus takes as his starting point the definition of the Divine First Principle, the Father, as a simple, blessed, and unfathomable substance, surpassing all definition. The only thing that can be said about Him is that He is. The "one principle" of Divinity is higher than substance and human speculation, higher than beauty or goodness. "He is a simple substance in which there are no qualities" (*Ep. ad epis.* 8). In addition, the transcendent Divinity is described (not without some inconsistency) with positive features such as fullness of love and perfection.

The further revelation of the First Principle, in accordance with the Neoplatonic schema, is accomplished in inner self-disclosure, which St. Athanasius explores primarily in relation to the Logos. Here, there spontaneously falls into place, as it were, the distinction between the immanent and the economic Trinity; and affirming with full clarity the eternity of the Holy Trinity, St. Athanasius decisively liberates himself on this point from cosmologism, both Stoic and Arian, in the doctrine of the Holy Trinity. In eternity the Father engenders the Son, Who is the eternal generation of the Father; and "God is the eternal source of His own wisdom." If there could have been a time when the Son did not exist, this means that "the Father would have been without His own Logos and without wisdom, that there would have been light without ray and a source dry and without water."

The Son's generation from the Father is not an act of the free desiring of the Father's will (as, according to Arius, is the creation of a demiurge). This generation pertains to the Father's nature, although it is "desirable" for the Father. The most fundamental definition of the Son for St. Athanasius is that He is from the substance of the Father, or of the same substance as the Father or consubstantial with Him; and as such the Son has all the divine properties, is God. For St. Athanasius, the birth of the second principle from the first is not a work of metaphysical necessity but an act of the proper life of the personal God. Here, St. Athanasius, like Origen, puts hypostatic definitions into Plotinus' impersonal ontological principles, but these definitions are taken only dogmatically, without any special speculative inquiry.

Starting from the radical homoousianism that is characteristic of St. Athanasius, it is not so easy to derive the distinction between individual hypostases; and generally speaking there is no attempt at a theological deduction of the trinitarian dogma in St. Athanasius, which is why his position in the polemic with Sabellianism[20] is insufficiently defensible. In general, in St. Athanasius' thought the balance is dogmatically tilted more toward homoousianism than toward trinitarianism. Innocent of cosmological subordinationism in logology and Christology, St. Athanasius denies that the Son has a demiurgic function. A characteristic problem in his polemic with Arianism arises here. On the one hand, while rejecting cosmologism in the understanding of Divinity, in his own way St. Athanasius, not less than Arius, asserts that there is an insuperable gulf between God and the world, the Creator and creation: "All created things have, in their essence, nothing that is similar to the Creator." "What likeness is there between that which comes out of nothing and the Creator, who creates it out of nothing?"

The opposition between God and the world is taken in all its acuteness. But it is precisely on the basis of this opposition that Arius, following Philo, postulated a creaturely intermediary between God and the world. Of course, this is just an attempt to fill in the gulf between them,

---

20. A form of monarchianism named after Sabellius, who was probably a third-century theologian of Roman origin. — Trans.

but this gulf does not thereby become smaller. In his polemic with Arius, St. Athanasius refers to God's omnipotence, which is sufficiently great to create the world without any mediation; on the contrary, "without delay, all that God desires comes into being." To doubts of an ontological character, St. Athanasius responds only by thus referring to God's omnipotence. To be sure, this scarcely removes the difficulty, since abstract reference to omnipotence is inapplicable to questions of ontology. Moreover, according to St. Athanasius, creaturely being could "not tolerate the unmoderated nature of the Father, His true radiance; and because of the Father's love for humanity, the Logos descends to help creatures" (*Contra Arianos* 2.24). The Logos is the creative principle that contains all the principles of being, and there is nothing in being that is produced not in the Logos and not by the Logos. Here, God's relation to the world is limited to and exhausted by the action of the Logos; no place is left in it for the action of the Third hypostasis. On the other hand, to the Logos is attributed that which is proper to Sophia, that is, the Logos is defined as the divine foundation of the world.[21]

In one way or another, the relation of the Father-Son Dyad, both in eternity and in creation, is sufficiently clarified by St. Athanasius. But his trinitarian problematic (in particular in the critique of Sabellius' doctrine) is usually exhausted by a clarification of the relation of the Two.[22] To be sure, dogmatically, St. Athanasius confesses the Holy Trinity, but *theologically,* his doctrine, though it includes the Dyad, does not in essence include the Trinity; and his trinitarian theology remains predominantly dyadic. Noteworthy in this respect is that aspect of his doctrine where he touches upon the question of the Holy Spirit.

It is significant that in all of his works that are dedicated to logology, St. Athanasius confesses the Church dogma of the Holy Spirit, Whose action he attributes to the Logos. He does not, however, develop any theology of the Holy Spirit. He concerned himself with this problem

---

21. In Athanasius, the confusion of Logos and Sophia (see *De Incarnatione* 42), which is typical for patristic cosmology as a whole, is particularly pronounced, as it is in his doctrine of Wisdom, which he, following Origen and Arius, equates with the Logos. I discuss this in my work on the Mother of God, *The Burning Bush* (the excursus); on Sophia see my *Lamb of God.* One must admit that in this interpretation of the Logos Athanasius does not succeed in overcoming cosmological subordinationatism. Logos is fused with the world to such an extent that in this sense He is ontologically distinct from the Father; and here Athanasius' doctrine takes on traits of Plotinian-Origenistic subordinationism.

22. See *Contra Arianos* 4.9; 4.1; 3.4.

because of the doctrine of heretics (whom he called Tropicists) who denied the Divinity of the Holy Spirit and considered Him a creature. This
led him to expound the orthodox doctrine of the Holy Spirit, relying both
on the testimony of Scripture and on tradition (see his *Letters to Serapion of
Thmuis* I, 3, 4). Affirming the divinity of the Holy Spirit and confessing the
dogma of the Holy Trinity — of the Father, of the Son, and of the Holy
Spirit — St. Athanasius nonetheless constructs his *theology* of the Holy
Spirit solely with reference to the Son, dyadically; so that if in his
christological works we have the first dyad of the Holy Trinity, the Father
and the Son, then here we have the second dyad, the Son and the Holy
Spirit. St. Athanasius virtually does not treat the relation of the Father to
the Holy Spirit (in particular he does not say anything about the procession from the Father, although he cites the appropriate text, John 15:26).
On the other hand, he systematically traces the relation of the Son and
the Holy Spirit: their general interrelationship is expressed in the formula
that, just as the Son is the Image of the Father, so the Holy Spirit is the
Image of the Son (*Letters to Serapion* 3, 4). This Athanasian idea (also encountered in the creed of St. Gregory Thaumaturgus) was a favorite one
in the patristic literature up to and including St. John of Damascus.

To repeat, St. Athanasius' doctrine of the Holy Spirit is not triadic
but dyadic in nature, for it considers only the relation of the Holy Spirit
to the Son. This does not mean, of course, that St. Athanasius excludes in
any way (e.g., subordinationistically) the Holy Spirit from the Holy Trinity; on the contrary, he attests just the opposite many times. He considers
the nature and activity of the Holy Spirit only in relation to the Son, however, and almost completely ignores the Holy Spirit's relation to the Father (and he thus does not specifically consider the question of the procession of the Holy Spirit from the Father and, in general, the question of
procession as opposed to generation). This alone is sufficient to make his
doctrine of the Holy Spirit (or, which in this case is the same thing, of the
Holy Trinity) *incomplete* and to give it a one-sided christocentric orientation. St. Athanasius remains predominantly a logologist or christologist
even in his pneumatology.

This results in another one-sided or incomplete aspect of his
thought: his logology has not only an economic and cosmological character but is also rooted in the immanent, eternal life of the Holy Trinity,
whereas his pneumatology has, preeminently and almost exclusively, an
economic character, is developed with reference to the work of salvation realized by Christ through the Holy Spirit. And to this predominantly
soteriological aspect of St. Athanasius' pneumatology corresponds an-

other one-sidedness of his doctrine of the Holy Spirit: namely, that the latter is not viewed as a Creator in relation to the creation of the world, but exclusively as a giver of grace, completing the work of salvation. That is, the Holy Spirit is viewed not cosmourgically but charismatically. To this corresponds another aspect of St. Athanasius' logology: namely that the Logos, understood rather as Sophia, is a cosmourgic hypostasis to which is attributed the *whole* work of creation, preservation, and providence in relation to the world, i.e., not only that which actually belongs to the Word but even that which, in the later Fathers of the Church and in the Church teaching in general, is attributed to the Holy Spirit. For St. Athanasius, the Holy Spirit realizes salvation by His gifts; the object of His action is only the spiritual but not the natural life of the world. This is indubitably a consequence of the one-sided soteriological christocentrism of St. Athanasius' pneumatology.

This incompleteness and one-sidedness of his pneumatology makes it defective in the sense that it lacks, strictly speaking, a doctrine of the Holy Spirit Himself as the Third hypostasis in the Holy Trinity. This hypostasis has its proper place and hypostatic character in the Holy Trinity with regard to procession and intratrinitarian life in general, and it has its proper place in the life of the world. This soteriological narrowing of the problematic in St. Athanasius remains, however, without influence on further patristic thought. But it represents a characteristic element in St. Athanasius' doctrine as the classic expression of the *dyadic* doctrine of the Holy Spirit and the Son in Their relation to humanity and the salvation of the latter, in Their indivisible duality and unity in the work of salvation, in the action upon man and in man, in other words, in *Divine-humanity*. What makes St. Athanasius' letters remarkable is that in them he, who like no one else in patristics revealed the christological aspect of the doctrine of Divine-humanity, understood and interpreted the work of Divine-humanity as the *dyadic* action of the Son and the Holy Spirit. Such a formulation of this question in St. Athanasius has historical significance. It is to this formulation that we adapt our own problematic in the present investigation, which thus becomes an inquiry into *Divine-humanity* as the work of the Son *and* the Holy Spirit, Who, in their indivisible Dyad, reveal the Father.

VI. The Cappadocians' Doctrine of the Holy Trinity and of the Holy Spirit

The Cappadocian triad — St. Basil the Great, his brother St. Gregory of Nyssa, and St. Gregory the Theologian — play a decisive role in the Eastern trinitarian theology. They have given it a dogmatic formulation that, for the most part, with its strong and weak sides, is the dominant one even today in Eastern theology. Our aim in this section is to expound, succinctly and accurately, the main elements of this doctrine.[23]

First of all, it is necessary to indicate the purely *terminological* achievements of this doctrine, which are not unimportant for theology. The pre-Cappadocian theology did not have categories for the separate expression of personhood and substance, or essence, but confused, both terminologically and logically, the existing terms *hupostasis* and *ousia*, *hypostasis* and *substance*. *Prosōpon*, the Greek term for "person," which as *persona* received the right of citizenship in Western theology as early as Tertullian, seemed suspicious both because of its nearness to Sabellianism and, in general, because of the indeterminacy of its meaning; for it can refer to everything that appears before one's eyes — to profile, mask, appearance, etc. If we do encounter *prosōpon* in St. Gregory the Theologian and St. Gregory of Nyssa, it is only alongside *hupostasis,* as its clarification.[24] The concept "hypostasis" is considered by the Cappadocians not in a personalistic but in a material sense. Decisive here is Aristotle's doctrine of *prōtē ousia* [first substance], i.e., of concrete being in which alone does concrete substance exist and outside of which it is a mere abstraction (*deutera ousia* [second substance]). This concrete reality is established by a particular character of a thing thanks to which hypostasis arises in ousia. Both animate and inanimate objects can be subsumed under this concept of hypostasis: a rock, an animal, a human being, an angel, God. In itself this concept is devoid of personalistic meaning; and if such a meaning is put into it in a de facto manner, in conformity with the Church dogma (as existence *according to itself, kath' heauton*), this meaning has no connection with the category of *hypostasis*. This Aristotelean distinction between ousia and hypostasis with reference to the Holy Trinity postulates for its realization the unity of the Divine substance on the one hand and, on the other

---

23. This doctrine is expounded in more detail in my essay "Chapters on Trinity."

24. St. Gregory the Theologian directed his irony against the Romans (in *Oration* 21) because, due to the poverty of their language, they substituted the term "person" for "hypostasis."

hand, hypostatic properties that would concretize this essence into trihypostatic being; and there must evidently be three such hypostatic properties, in conformity with the number of hypostases.

The first requirement is satisfied by homoousianism, which all three Cappadocians profess steadfastly, although their interpretation of it is perhaps somewhat different from that of St. Athanasius (that is, it is marked by a tendency to homoiousianism): The unity of Divinity as the Divine nature is their fundamental dogmatic presupposition. In his polemic with Eunomius (1.1), St. Basil the Great defends this unity of Divinity by stating that unity is contained in the very idea of substance. The ground for this affirmation had been sufficiently prepared by the development of homoousian theology and the earlier Neoplatonizing Origenism. Rather unexpectedly, the influence of Neoplatonism and Origenism is combined with Aristoteleanism in the Cappadocians' doctrine of the unknowability of divinity, which they were compelled to develop in the struggle against the rationalism of Eunomius (and then Aetius), who considered Divinity to be fully rationally knowable. Against this doctrine the Cappadocians forcefully profess apophatism, the unknowability and, hence, the transcendent character of Divinity.[25]

The substance of God is unfathomable, unnameable, undefinable. God is higher than essence, goodness, beauty, even divinity. Such an assertion of the total transcendence of Divinity is, however, logically overcome in Neoplatonism and Origenism by subordinationism, which makes possible the transition from apophatics to kataphatics, to a positive doctrine of God through the self-revelation of Divinity in the divine world. But given the Cappadocians' rigorous rejection of subordinationism, such a transition is not possible for them. In the Cappadocians' system, Aristoteleanism and Neoplatonism stand side by side unharmonized: That which is impossible in negative theology turns out to be self-evident in kataphatic theology, where ousia is defined in terms of hypostatic properties. Thus, on the one hand, for the Cappadocians the Divine ousia is unfathomable, transcendent Divinity, whereas on the other hand it is a general substance that exists only because it is concretized by hypostatic properties.

But since hypostatized, concrete being represents the only existent being, whereas general nature (the "second" ousia) is an abstraction, there

---

25. In St. Gregory of Nyssa this affirmation is intensified by his skeptically relativistic doctrine of the names of God, which he anthropomorphizes, depriving them of ontological content and thus essentially dooming theology to silence.

arises a new difficulty on the pathways of theological Aristoteleanism: Is the trinely hypostatized substance not divided into three parts, or (which in this case is the same thing) three hypostases? In other words, does one not encounter here the logical phantom of tritheism, which in any case did not afflict the subordinationistic theology? Being, by virtue of the Church dogma, absolutely invulnerable in this respect dogmatically, the Cappadocians were theologically vulnerable from this side in their Aristoteleanism and had to defend themselves against possible attacks (cf. St. Gregory of Nyssa's letter to Ablabius on "Not Three Gods"). According to Aristotle, hypostases (hypostatic properties) not only concretize but also thereby *divide* substance, for only concrete being exists. Therefore, also according to Aristotle, one can rigorously deduce the fact that there are three hypostases, but not their trinity as triunity.

This question has another aspect: *How* do different hypostases have one substance in the capacity of a common nature? In other words, how and to what degree can homoousian consubstantiality (which in St. Athanasius approached identical substantiality, tauto-ousia) be realized here? In the natural world, "hypostases" "fractionate" their ousia (thus, all gold things contain a *part* of gold) as a whole, which exists only for abstracting thought (the substance of Divinity was divided in an analogous manner in Stoic subordinationism). But is it possible, on the basis of Aristoteleanism, to express the dogma not of *common* possession, and not of *separate* possession, but precisely of *consubstantiality?* Although the Cappadocians are, once again, extremely insistent in their defense of the Church dogma, they are not so firm theologically in establishing the *unity* of God's essence in the three hypostases and their consubstantiality.[26] Within the limits of Aristotelean categories, within which the Cappadocians confined their theology, there truly is no place for Divine triunity, for trihypostatic consubstantiality. It remains a philosophically unsubstantiated postulate.

With respect to the one divine substance the trine forms are determined, according to Aristotle, by special hypostatic properties. These properties are taken from the relations of origin in such a manner that

---

26. St. Basil the Great uses the terms "communion" *(koinōnia)* and "communality" *(koinōtēs):* "a certain ineffable and inconceivable communion," "a continuous and indissoluble communion," so that "the difference of the hypostases does not sunder the nature; nor does essential communality lead to the fusion of distinct features." St. Gregory the Theologian also discusses the commonality and co-essentiality of the nature (in *Oration 29*).

the first is designated as fatherhood, the second as sonhood, and the third as procession.

In effect, between these hypostatic properties *(gnōrismata)* and the hypostases themselves there is placed an equals sign such that the Father is unengendered, the Son is engendered, and the Holy Spirit proceeds. The path that is adumbrated here is the one that later was decisively taken (although, to be sure, in its own manner) by Catholic theology. In and of itself, this equation of hypostatic properties with the hypostases themselves is unjustified. One must remember that hypostatization in Aristotle has nothing to do with *personally* hypostatic definitions. The Cappadocians, in effect, apply his scheme to the dogma already given by the Church, but this scheme is totally insufficient to establish the *personal* character of hypostatic being. Nevertheless, it does achieve another goal that the Cappadocians pursue in their problematic: it divides Divinity into three, making it trihypostatic.

This division into three goes, as we have seen, even farther than is needed. That which is required for the trinitarian dogma is not merely *three I's* but a *triune I,* trinity in unity and unity in trinity (to which the Cappadocians ceaselessly bear witness). In this construction, however, the triune I is assured only by the unity of the ousia, not by the unity, even if trinitarian, of the hypostasis. But this is insufficient, for the Holy Trinity is one not only in the ousia, or essence, but also in the trihypostatic subject. And precisely the incompleteness of the doctrine in this respect makes it vulnerable in relation to tritheism. The reason for this is the *reified* but not hypostatic character of the Aristotelean categories, which, in and of themselves, are therefore insufficient for knowing the hypostases and the trihypostatizedness, although, in that epoch, they introduced a certain comparative clarity.

In their theological interpretation of the dogma of trinity (and this is a general feature of the Eastern trinitarian theology), the Cappadocians take as their starting point not the unity of the ousia but the trinitarity of the hypostases, in contrast to Western theology, which takes as its starting point the unity of substance, seeking in it the origination of the three hypostases. The three hypostases are united in the Holy Trinity, which consists of equally divine hypostases. The doctrine of the Cappadocians rejects both subordinationism and cosmologism in the interpretation of the Holy Trinity. The Holy Trinity exists eternally in Itself, independently of Its revelation in the world. This immanent character of the Holy Trinity is sometimes defined entirely in the spirit of Neoplatonism (without its subordinationism), even in the very same words. Elements of Neoplatonic metaphysics are combined here with Aristotle's logical rationalism.

In assessing the achievements of the Cappadocians, one must recognize that they dogmatically established the classic doctrine of the Holy Trinity, which can be accepted as the norm of the Church teaching: It is free of non-orthodox deviations toward monarchianism, and toward subordinationism, both ontological and cosmological; and in this sense it represents a middle, "royal way" of the Church doctrine. The achievements of these "universal teachers of the Church" cannot be overstated here. Moreover, their doctrine includes, in the capacity of its presuppositions, the ripest fruit of ancient speculation — a synthesis of Aristoteleanism, Platonism, and Neoplatonism. The religio-philosophical one-sidedness of each of these positions is overcome; they complement one another, if not always organically.

Such a synthesis cannot be final or complete, of course. It is marked by the limitations of the epoch; and this must be said too about the Cappadocian *theology*, which is far inferior to the Cappadocian *dogmatics*. The weak sides of this theology, already noted in part above, are as follows: First, the doctrine of the Cappadocians is not, strictly speaking, a doctrine of the Holy Trinity as a purely trinitarian doctrine, although dogmatically it aspires to be precisely such. Their doctrine takes as its point of departure the *trinitarity* of the hypostases, of which the Holy Trinity is then composed; but this composition remains unfinished in the sense that its result is *three* united in *one* nature, not a triunity. The unity of the Holy Trinity is thus established not by the trihypostatizedness of the Divine Person, including the trinitarity of the equally divine Persons with one nature, but only by the unity of this nature. As *one*, the trihypostatic Divinity is only the Divine *It*, not the trihypostatic *I*, the Divine triunity. This is the only part of the Cappadocian system where the doctrine of the Trinity is expounded not only imprecisely but even erroneously. *Unity in Trinity* is equally both *Person* (although the *trihypostatic* one, Elohim-Yahweh) and *one nature* (but not only the unity of nature).

Associated with this is a second weak side of the Cappadocians' trinitarian doctrine, a weakness connected with their formal-logical Aristoteleanism: The hypostases, each of which is established by its hypostatic property, remain unconnected among themselves. They are united by the unity of their ousia or substance (with all the obscurity of this definition; see above), but not among themselves. Their relation is only that of a series. They are three, not a trinity; and hypostatic trinitarity is replaced here by ousian unity. This is a result of the formal and mechanical application of the Aristotelean schemata of ousia and hypostasis, where each separate hypostatic property, *gnōrisma,* gives a new hypostasis. The number of these hypostases is defined only de facto, according to the presence of the properties, so that in itself it could be more or less than three. The ontological necessity of precisely three, as a trinity, is not shown and not proved. True, this trinitarity is motivated for the Cappadocians by the three hypostatic properties taken from revelation. Having begun their ontological deduction of trinitarity on the basis of Aristotle, they conclude it on the basis of the dogmatic fact of the revelation concerning the three hypostases; but this conclusion based on revelation cannot replace theological development.

Third, the Cappadocians also desire to constrain the Holy Trinity and theologically justify the triunity of the three by means of the idea of monarchy, the distinction in the Holy Trinity between the Principle without beginning and hypostases that do have a beginning: *aitia* and *aitiatoi.* But this important idea remains theoretically unclarified in its theological significance and, in any case, it must be explicated and defended with reference to subordinationism.

Fourth, owing to their particular formulation of the trinitarian problem, the Cappadocians naturally give a prominent place to the *order,* or *taxis,* of the Divine persons, also in connection with the monarchy of the Holy Trinity. Taking the order of the hypostases from revelation and applying it to the principle of monarchy, the Cappadocians do not give it a theological and ontological interpretation, because their trinitarian doctrine fails to establish a connection between the three hypostases. Meantime, a theory of *taxis* and of its true significance must play a fundamental role in the doctrine of the Holy Trinity.

Turning specifically to pneumatology, it is first necessary to establish the thesis (common to all the Cappadocians) of the divinity of the Holy Spirit. All the Cappadocians did battle with the pneumatomachians, who denied this thesis. The confession of the divinity of the Holy Spirit is a theological feat common to the three Cappadocians, and many of their writings attest to it. It is characteristic of the spirit of that age and of the difficulty of this task that, notwithstanding the ardor of his defense of the Holy Spirit, St. Basil the Great avoided applying the word *God* to the Holy Spirit, for which he was reproached (even by his friend Gregory the Theologian). This is not surprising if we recall that, although the so-called Nicaeno-Constantinopolitan Creed professes that the Holy Spirit is equal in dignity and divinity to the Father and to the Son, it too does not directly call the Holy Spirit God.

One can assume in advance that the absence of a properly trinitarian doctrine of the connection of the hypostases in the triunity (and not just in the trinitarity) of the Holy Trinity will have an impact on the doctrine of the Holy Spirit. In particular, in St. Basil the question of the place of the Holy Spirit in the Holy Trinity arises in the polemic against Eunomius, who expresses the following idea: "The Spirit is third in dignity and order, which is why we believe that He is also third in essence." To this St. Basil answers the following: "If the Spirit is third in dignity and order, what necessity is there that He also be third in essence? For, just as the Son with respect to the Father is second in order, since He is from the Father; and second in dignity, since the Father is the Principle and the Cause . . . and since it is through the Son that God the Father is accessible; but nevertheless He is not second in essence, because in Both Divinity is one; so although the Holy Spirit in dignity and order follows the Son . . . it is not yet clear from this that one can justifiably conclude that the Holy Spirit has another essence."[27] This strange and difficult passage introduces a certain subordinationism "according to dignity and order." This idea can be interpreted in different ways, but in the absence of a trinitarian doctrine it remains ambiguous and unclear.

St. Basil the Great defines the place of the Holy Spirit in the Holy Trinity by two features: first, procession from the Father, according to the principle of monarchy; and second, dyadic interrelation with the Son, which is already familiar to us from St. Athanasius' doctrine. First of all, St. Basil the Great adopts St. Athanasius' basic idea that "the image of God is Christ . . . while the image of the Son is the Spirit, and participants in the Spirit become sons in conformity with what is written: Rom. 8:29." Also: "The Son is the Word of God, and the Spirit is the Word of the Son. For it is written (Heb. 1:3). And since the Spirit is the word of the Son, He is also the word of God."[28] The Holy Spirit, sent from God, is given through the Son. "One can worship the Son not otherwise than in the Holy Spirit; and one can invoke the Father not otherwise than in the Spirit of adoption."[29] "Through the one Son the Holy Spirit is joined with

---

27. *Against Eunomius*, book 3 (the beginning). At the Council of Florence, this passage was read with interpolations related to the Filioque.

28. *Works* III, 163. St. Basil himself is somewhat stumped by the question: "If the Son is the Word of God and the Holy Spirit is the image of the Son, and if the Son is the Word of God and the Holy Spirit is the word of the Son, then why is the Holy Spirit not called the Son of God?" (This doubt is dispelled by the fact that, in this case, one gets a multiplicity of Divinity.)

29. *De Spiritu Sancto* 11.

the one Father and completes the most glorified and most blessed Trinity."[30] "Just as in the Son we can see the Father, so in the Spirit we can see the Son. . . . Just as there is worship in the Son as in the image of God and the Father, so there is worship in the Spirit; since He in Himself shows the Divinity of the Lord. . . . One can see the Image of the invisible God not otherwise than in the illumination of the Spirit" (*De Spiritu Sancto* 26).

Athanasius' general idea of the dyadic interrelation of the Son and the Holy Spirit is shared by St. Basil the Great, who, naturally, develops this idea more fully not with reference to the immanent Trinity but with reference to the economic Trinity, in relation to the world. Here, the action of the Holy Spirit is disclosed precisely in His union with the action of Christ, in the dyadic indivisibility of the entire Holy Trinity. Of particular interest here is the classic text concerning the creation of the world: "In creation . . . conceive the initial cause of all created things, the Father, the demiurgic cause, the Son, and the perfecting cause, the Holy Spirit." "Conceive Three — the commanding Lord, the creating Word, and the affirming Spirit" (*De Spiritu Sancto* 16). In particular, the economy concerning man is accomplished by the Dyad of the Son and the Holy Spirit. The Old Testament economy is accomplished through the Holy Spirit. "The Spirit is proper to the very flesh of the Lord. . . . Every act took place in the presence of the Spirit. The Spirit accompanied the one being tempted by the devil (see Matt. 4:1). The Spirit accompanied the one who worked the miracles (see Matt. 12:28). The Spirit also did not leave the one who rose from the dead (see John 20:22-23). And is the government of the Church not clearly and undeniably accomplished by the Spirit?"

Basil's most remarkable and audacious statement about the combined action of the Son and the Holy Spirit refers to eschatology: "At the time of the awaited-for appearance of the Lord from heaven, the Holy Spirit will not be inactive, as some think, but will appear together with Him on the day of the revelation of the Lord, on which He will justly judge the universe. . . . Those goods prepared by the Lord for the worthy . . . and the crown of the righteous is the grace of the Spirit . . . and the term 'division' means alienation from the Spirit. . . . In hell . . . the assistance of the Spirit is no longer manifested" (*De Spiritu Sancto* 16).

"To the Holy Spirit all things turn that need sanctification. . . . He is the giver of life" (9). Through the illumination of the Spirit are achieved "the abiding in God, likening to God, and the extreme limit of what is desired — deification" (9). In St. Basil's works one can find numerous pas-

---

30. *De Spiritu Sancto* 18.

sages about various aspects of the action of the Holy Spirit, and these
texts are a treasure house of the doctrine of the Holy Spirit. But it would
be fruitless to seek in these texts a complete theory of the place of the
Holy Spirit in the Holy Trinity, a theory not of the spirit but of the Spirit,
not of His gifts but of Him Himself; and the reason for this is the general
state of the trinitarian doctrine in that epoch.

In particular, the fundamental problem of *taxis,* or order, which was
examined by the Cappadocians more throroughly than by anyone else, remains unsolved: What does the *third* place of the Holy Spirit in the Holy
Trinity mean and how should it be understood? The figure used by Basil
to try to explain the procession of the Holy Spirit, namely that "it is the
Spirit from God's lips," adds little to our understanding of the intratrinitarian relationships. Physical comparisons, however widespread they
might be in the patristic literature, do not aid us in understanding the
Holy Trinity (as St. Gregory the Theologian powerfully acknowledged in
Oratio 31).

St. Gregory the Theologian, like his friend St. Basil the Great (although the latter has verbal reservations), professes the divinity of the
Holy Spirit against the heretics: "And so, the Spirit is God? Without any
doubt. And He is consubstantial? Yes, because He is God" (*Oratio* 31). Despite this express profession of the divinity of the Holy Spirit, however, we
do not find anything original in St. Gregory's trinitarian doctrine compared to St. Basil or in his speculations about the place of the Holy Spirit
in the Holy Trinity, except for the inspired and eloquent tone of his discourse.

More than the other Fathers, St. Gregory the Theologian is aware
that new revelations are to be expected in the domain of the doctrine of
the Holy Spirit; and this idea is perhaps the most noteworthy one in his
pneumatology: "There have been in the whole period of the duration of
the world two conspicuous changes in men's lives, which are also called
two Testaments, or . . . two Earthquakes (Hag. 2:6-7). The one from the
idols to the Law, the other from the Law to the Gospel. And now I an-
nounce a third earthquake, namely, from this Earth to that which cannot
be shaken or moved. Now the two Testaments are alike in this respect,
that the change was not made suddenly, nor at the first try. Why not?
That no violence might be done to us, but that we might be moved by per-
suasion. To this I may compare the case of Theology except that it proceeds the reverse way. For in the case by which I have illustrated it the
change is made by successive subtractions; whereas here perfection is
reached by additions. . . . The Old Testament proclaimed the Father

openly, and the Son more obscurely. The New manifested the Son, and suggested the Deity of the Spirit. Now the Spirit Himself dwells among us, and supplies us with a clearer demonstration of Himself. For it was not safe, when the Godhead of the Father was not yet acknowledged, plainly to proclaim the Son; nor when that of the Son was not yet received to burden us further with the Holy Spirit. . . . Instead, the Light of the Trinity [would] shine upon the more illuminated by gradual additions and, as David says, Goings up, and advance and progress from glory to glory" (*Oratio* 31).[31] Let this thought of St. Gregory's even now be the guiding one in the theology of the Spirit!

St. Gregory of Nyssa contended against the very same Eunomius, the Eunomius who thought that the Holy Spirit was a creation of the Son. Gregory of Nyssa too had to insist on the co-eternity and co-divinity of the Holy Spirit with respect to the other hypostases of the Holy Trinity. In general, the line of his thought coincides with the doctrine of St. Basil the Great. One should note that Gregory of Nyssa delineates with greater clarity the relation between the Son and the Holy Spirit, not only in the economic aspect but also in the ontological aspect. The *connection* of the Holy Trinity in its three hypostases (which, strictly speaking, is the trinitarian problem) is delineated by him somewhat more concretely than by St. Basil the Great and St. Gregory the Theologian.

In Gregory of Nyssa, the connection of the three hypostases is based, on the one hand, on the general distinction between the cause and those who are caused *(aitia* and *aitiatoi)* in the Holy Trinity, i.e., on the causal dependence of the Second and Third hypostases on the First hypostasis;[32] and on the other hand on the express, dyadic connection of the Son and the Spirit, which is imprecisely and unclearly expressed in terms of causality (which serves as a pretext to put Gregory in the Filioque party). With reference to the origin of the Holy Spirit *through* the Son, the Letter to Ablabius expresses this as a *mediation* of the Son in the procession of the Holy Spirit. "The mediation of the Son preserves His consubstantiality and does not remove the Spirit from connection with the Father according to substance." It is in this manner that St. Gregory of Nyssa unifies the Holy Trinity and overcomes the divisibility and, so to speak, the disparateness of the hypostases. One cannot say that his conception is clear

---

31. This translation is adapted from that given in *A Select Library of Nicene and Post-Nicene Fathers of the Christian Church,* second series, vol. 7: *S. Cyril of Jerusalem. S. Gregory Nazianzen,* ed. P. Schaff and H. Wace (Grand Rapids: Eerdmans, 1983), pp. 325-26. — Trans.

32. In his work "That There Are Not Three Gods" (*PG* 45, col. 133).

and complete, or that he presents a fully developed trinitarian doctrine. We are in the domain of vague intuition, not clear understanding.

That is the Cappadocian doctrine of the Holy Trinity and the Holy Spirit. The merits of this doctrine are great, for it conclusively affirms and establishes beyond all doubt the supraeternal, immanent character of the Holy Trinity, the equi-divinity and equi-eternity of Its hypostases. This doctrine overcomes subordinationism, both ontological and cosmological. It indicates the distinctive properties of the different hypostases, predominantly in the cosmological and economic aspect. But the *general connection* of the three hypostases in the Holy Trinity remains outside the problematic of the doctrine. Therefore, among other things, despite certain scattered indications (particularly in St. Gregory of Nyssa), the Cappadocians lack not only a doctrine of the Filioque but, and this is much more important, they do not even formulate the problem of the Filioque.

The Cappadocian fathers directly or indirectly inspired the Second Ecumenical Council (381), of Constantinople, which, according to a view held until quite recently, complemented the Nicene Creed as far as the doctrine of the Holy Spirit was concerned. The opinion that the so-called Nicaeno-Constantinopolitan Creed truly belongs to the Second Ecumenical Council has recently been disputed; and this cannot be a historical certainty even for the partisans of this opinion, although, to be sure, how this question is decided *historically* cannot shake the authority of this Creed in church tradition. What is much more important is that we have less information about the Second Ecumenical Council than about any other; and in particular, no information has survived about the discussion of the question of the Holy Spirit at this council. The only direct source is St. Gregory the Theologian's negative characterization of this discussion, and we also have some brief indications from fifth-century historians. Knowing the level of the theological literature and the problematic that predetermined the council's decision, we can come to some conclusion about the course of affairs at the council, which examined this question among a number of other (predominantly christological) heresies.

The council considered the question of the Holy Spirit only in the light of the necessity of totally refuting the pneumatomachians (or "Macedonians"), who denied the divinity of the Holy Spirit. Only *this* question demanded an answer of the council, which had to pronounce its "yes" or its "no." Whatever may be the origin of the Nicaeno-Constantinopolitan Creed, it contains an answer that expressed the actual predominant opinion (although not the one of the overwhelming majority, for there were thirty-six "Macedonian" bishops at the council) and was therefore authorized by the Church. This confession concerning the Holy Spirit reflected the historical conditions of its formation, with regard to what it contains as well as with regard to what it omits.

First of all, it was marked by the same evasiveness that characterized the entire epoch when it considered the question of the divinity of the Holy Spirit (an evasiveness which, as we know, extended even to St. Basil the Great). To the direct question, "Is the Spirit *God?*" St. Gregory the Theologian demanded a direct answer, but only an indirect answer was given. The idea of the divinity of the Holy Spirit is expressed descriptively in the Nicaeno-Constantinopolitan Creed: "the Lord who proceeds from the Father; who with the Father and the Son together is worshipped and glorified." From this divine procession and worship one, of course, cannot fail to conclude that the Holy Spirit is not only a "Lord" (in all the imprecision of this expression) but precisely *God.* But the Holy Spirit is *not* directly called God, as the Son is called God: "The Lord Jesus Christ . . . very God of very God." And this was not an accidental instance of forgetting, but an intentional silence and evasion, for the question concerned precisely this. The Creed's definition concerning the Holy Spirit is therefore deficient. It is incomplete and needs to be completed.

All the definitions of the Holy Spirit in the Nicaeno-Constantino-politan Creed correspond to this task of *descriptively* expressing the belief in the divinity of the Holy Spirit without directly calling Him God. The first and foremost of these definitions is, "Who proceeds from the Father." Here, based on the Gospel text, there is a direct indication of the divinity of the Holy Spirit as proceeding from the Father; but of course this does not represent a formulation of the general dogma of the procession of the Holy Spirit in all its precision and specificity, i.e., in the sense of the Filioque of Western Christianity or in the sense of the *dia tou Huiou* [through the Son] of Eastern Christianity. The problem of the procession of the Holy Spirit only from the Father, or from the Father *and* the Son, or *through* the Son, or in some other manner — was not posed then and thus could not be *directly* solved in the Creed. "Who proceeds from the Father" is by no means a dogmatic formula about the *procession* of the Holy Spirit (in the same way that *homoousios* was the formula of the consubstantiality of the Son). It was, first and foremost, a *descriptive* expression, using Gospel language, of the idea, not expressed directly, of the true divinity of the Third hypostasis, of the Holy Spirit as God. Of all the other possible definitions of the Holy Spirit, the Creed for some reason chooses only one, and the one that is, so to speak, the most Old-Testamental in character: "Who spoke by the prophets." Because it is unique and because of the incompleteness of the definition, this attribute is, to a certain extent, exemplary, especially if we take into account the fact that a New Testament doctrine of the Holy Spirit is wholly absent in the Creed, as is, in particular, any mention of the Pentecost, the Annunciation, or the gifts and actions of the Holy Spirit in the New Testament Church. In short, except for a descriptive expression of the Holy Spirit's equi-divinity, we do not have a *dogma* of the Holy Spirit in the Nicaeno-Constantinopolitan Creed.

We can go further and say that there is no dogma of the Holy Spirit anywhere. *All* the ecumenical councils, from the first to the last, concerned themselves with questions of Christology and thus with the theology of the Second hypostasis. Not one of them occupied itself with the Third hypostasis. *All* the heresies and disputes of the fifth to eighth centuries refer to the domain of Christology, and there is not a single pneumatological one among them, if we do not count the pneumatomachians. The dogmatic creativity of the epoch of the ecumenical councils was never applied to developing a doctrine of the Holy Spirit. His mystery was surrounded by a holy silence.

But the time has now come to consider the Holy Spirit, for all the questions of the dogmatics of the present day chiefly concern pneumatology.

VII. The Western Doctrine of Homoousian Trinitarian Theology (St. Augustine)

The Western theology of the sixth century developed along its own distinctive paths, in parallel to but independently of the Eastern theology; and owing to a poor understanding of each other's language and for general historical reasons, the two theologies had little knowledge of each other. It is therefore not at all surprising that, starting with the fourth century, their paths diverge. Skipping over the trinitarian and, in particular, the pneumatological speculations of St. Hilary and St. Ambrose, who is a predecessor and teacher, as it were, of St. Augustine, let us examine the trinitarian system of the latter.

St. Augustine develops his trinitarian system in various works, but primarily in his main work, *De Trinitate*. The latter represents the most systematic and, in this sense, the most remarkable treatise on the Holy Trinity and, in particular, on the Holy Spirit that exists in the patristic literature. Its distinguishing features are homoousianism, which is its point of departure, and relativism in its conception of trinitarity. St. Augustine is thus the true father of the Western type of trinitarian theology. In other words, his point of departure is not the trinity of the hypostases, as it is for the Cappadocians, but the unity of the ousia *(essentia) (De Trinitate* 1.2). His thought also relies on Tertullian's impersonalistic tradition, but without the latter's subordinationism. The unity of the Holy Trinity in the three hypostases is guaranteed precisely by this unity of substance (1.4.7).

In this one substance the three hypostases are distinguished *"non secundum substantiam, sed secundum relativum"* [not according to substance but according to relation] (5.5.6). The hypostases exist as mutual relations. The initial axiom of Catholic triadology, the doctrine of the hypostases as relations, is expressed precisely here. The Father is defined in relation to the Son as the Engendering One in relation to the Engendered One, while the Father and the Son are defined in relation to the Holy Spirit as *Spirator* in relation to *Spiratus*. This serves as the basis of the Augustinian doctrine of the Filioque. Here too the main principle is the unity of substance: "It must be admitted that the Father and the Son are a Beginning of the Holy Spirit, not two Beginnings; but as the Father and Son are one God, and one Creator, and one Lord relatively to the creature, so are they one Beginning relatively to the Holy Spirit" (5.14.15).[33]

The interpretation of the hypostases on the basis of relations suffers from impersonalism, which is not noticed only because data of revelation of the divine Persons of the Father, Son, and Holy Spirit are substituted for the category of impersonal relations. In themselves the relations do *not* establish the hypostases (which is also clear from the fact that not *all* the relations — *notiones* — have this significance) but only *accompany* and express them. Therefore, modalism, or impersonalism, is not overcome in St. Augustine's doctrine.

Such a monistic theology is characterized by a clearer understanding of the elements that distinguish the trinitarian unity. We therefore find in Augustine discussions about who was the subject of the Old Testament theophanies: an individual hypostasis or the Holy Trinity as one God. His interpretation is different from that of Eastern theology (e.g., in St. Gregory the Theologian): he refuses to see individual hypostases in these theophanies and, evading a decisive answer, nevertheless tends to see in them the appearance of *one* God, existing in the Holy Trinity (*De*

33. This translation is taken from *A Select Library of Nicene and Post-Nicene Fathers of the Christian Church,* vol. 3: *St. Augustine: On the Holy Trinity. Doctrinal Treatises. Moral Treatises,* ed. P. Schaff (Grand Rapids: Eerdmans, 1980), p. 95. — Trans.

Trinitate 2). In like manner, in relation to Wisdom, which Eastern theology tends (even today) to consider a personal attribute of the Son, St. Augustine refers to the original unity of the divinity of all three hypostases: "the Father and Son together are one wisdom, because one essence" (7.2).[34]

Augustine's point of departure in the doctrine of the Holy Trinity gives him a greater grasp than the Eastern theologians have of the problem of the *connection* of the Holy Trinity with respect to the interrelations of the hypostases; the Eastern theologians replace this connection to a certain degree by the mere *juxtaposition* of the hypostases. On this pathway, Augustine makes a true discovery in the trinitarian and pneumatological theology: He is the first to express the idea, wholly foreign to Eastern theology, of the Holy Trinity as Love. Here he clarifies a special significance of the Third hypostasis, namely, that this hypostasis is love itself, the connection of love, *amor* or *dilectio*. He takes as his point of departure an abstract schema of love which distinguishes between *amans, quod amatur, et amor* [the loving one, the loved one, and love] (*De Trinitate* 8.10, 14; 9.11). The Holy Spirit is, in the Holy Trinity, the love of Both, of the Father and of the Son. "And if the love by which the Father loves the Son, and the Son loves the Father, ineffably demonstrates the communion of both, what is more suitable than that He should be specially called love, who is the Spirit common to both?" (15.19).[35] (From this Augustine also draws a conclusion related to the Filioque.)

VIII. The Trinitarian and Pneumatological Doctrine of St. John of Damascus

St. John of Damascus sums up Eastern patristic theology, systematizing it to some extent. Eclectic in content, his *Precise Exposition of the Orthodox Faith* represents an early prototype of a *"summa theologica,"* of a system of dogmatics. As far as the doctrine of the Holy Trinity is concerned, he expounds in general the theory of the Cappadocians, but orders and unifies it to some extent.

His achievement, largely a formal one, consists in the aspiration not only to understand the Holy Trinity in its hypostases but also to under-

---

34. This translation is taken from *A Select Library of Nicene and Post-Nicene Fathers,* vol. 3, p. 107. — Trans.

35. This translation is taken from *A Select Library of Nicene and Post-Nicene Fathers,* vol. 3, p. 219. — Trans.

stand the hypostases in their mutual relationships. Therefore, his doctrine of God considers not only God in general, the Word, and the Holy Spirit (*Precise Exposition of the Orthodox Faith* 1.5, 6, 7), but also the Holy Trinity (1.8); and this latter point has for him a fundamental and guiding significance.

First of all, let us pose a preliminary question: In the doctrine of the *one* God that precedes his doctrine of the Holy Trinity, does St. John of Damascus overcome the impersonalism whose traces we find both in the East and in the West, in the Cappadocians as well as in St. Augustine? It is hard to give a definite answer to this question, inasmuch as it does not explicitly arise in John's thought, which essentially remains within the limits of the impersonalism of antiquity, although one can note that a certain step forward has been made here. In Chapter 5 ("Proof that God is one, not many"), he first refers to the text, "I am the Lord thy God" (Exod. 20:2; cf. Deut. 6:4; Isa. 41:4, 43:10-11; John 17:3), but he goes beyond the unity of God as *Person* to general considerations about the unity of *Divinity*. In the following chapter (6), about the Word, one finds an equally indeterminate statement: "thus, this one and unique God is not without the Word. If He has the Word, He must have a Word not without hypostasis." Here we have a double imprecision: First, it is unclear whether this "one and unique God" is understood as Person or as Divinity, as He or as It. Second, if God is understood here as a Person, is this the one personal God who says about Himself in the Old Testament, "I am the Lord thy God," or is this the First hypostasis, the Father? The concluding words of this chapter, referring to the Father, tend to support the latter.

The deduction of the Holy Spirit (1.7) is marked by the same imprecision: The Holy Spirit, as the breath of the Word, "is not considered an unhypostatic breath" but is a "power contemplated in its proper and particular hypostatic being"; "like the Word, the Holy Spirit exists hypostatically." One must recall here that St. John of Damascus, like St. Basil the Great, is a partisan of the Aristotelean doctrine of hypostasis as individual qualification by a special property, which in itself is by no means personal.[36] Therefore, the question of hypostasis as person is simply absent from his field of vision. Even when he does speak about the individual persons of the Holy Trinity, he, like his predecessors, is merely submitting to revealed doctrine, which is not included in his theological categories.

One should note yet one more special difficulty, which is connected with the eclectic character of St. John of Damascus' theology. His starting point is the apophatic theology of Pseudo-Dionysius concerning the

---

36. For an exposition and critique of this doctrine, see my work "Chapters on Trinity."

unknowability of God, which is overcome by revelation only to a certain degree. St. John of Damascus firmly believes that "what God is by essence and nature is wholly unfathomable and unknowable" (1.4) and that the only thing that can be known here is that "God is." God is therefore defined only "through the negation of all," for He is "higher than all that exists, higher than any being." This, however, does not prevent John of Damascus from affirming, on the basis of revelation, that "God is one," even though this is clearly a positive definition. But clearly absent here is the possibility of giving this *one* God an appropriate definition according to Aristotle's schema and of establishing not only His nature or ousia ("God") but also His hypostasis — by accident. Therefore, on the basis of purely *logical* considerations, the "one God" can be understood only impersonally, as Divinity, which is hypostatized according to hypostatic properties only in three *separate* hypostases.

But three is not yet a trinity as a triunity. St. John of Damascus, like other Fathers, conceives the latter only as ousia, Divinity, not as the personal, trihypostatic God. And this *logical* impersonalism becomes *theological* and taints his system, as is attested by the initial definitions in chapter 8 ("On the Holy Trinity"). In the long definition of the "one God" (taking up a whole page), we find nothing that indicates Personhood. Instead, John of Damascus speaks of "one principle, light, force, one power, one lordship, one kingdom, known and worshipped in three perfect hypostases." He then speaks about these hypostases separately. Clearly, we find here the same general schema that we find in Augustine, and later in Aquinas and the whole of Catholic theology. Divinity, understood impersonally, as divine ousia or essence, is the ontological and logical *prius*, or foundation, in which the hypostases originate and exist. The revealed truth, proclaimed in the Old Testament, that God is the *absolute Person*, "I," in which there is nothing pre-personal, extra-personal, or impersonal, this truth remains unassimilated by the theological consciousness. The result is the erroneous direction taken by the whole doctrine of hypostases considered as relations of origin, the doctrine of dialectic in Divinity, so to speak. (Catholic Hegelianism in theology unexpectedly finds a parallel for itself in the impersonalism of the mystics, that of Eckhart and especially Boehme.) But God, as the Absolute Person, is thereby also the trihypostatic Person, truly One in Three and Three in One. He is not Three in one, but the triunity of the Divine Person and of His life.[37]

---

37. This idea of trinitarian personalism, which overcomes the ancient and patristic impersonalism, is deduced and developed in my work "Chapters on Trinity."

Impersonalistic thought tends to equate the Divine Absolute Subject, the triune trihypostatic I, with God the Father. To a certain degree this veils the impersonalistic conception of Divinity. John of Damascus, too, is not averse to making such an equation, as is attested, in particular, by the following statement: "Of the Father and the Son and the Holy Spirit we speak not as of three Gods but rather as of one God, the Holy Trinity, since the Son and the Holy Spirit are referred to one Cause, but, despite Sabellius' opinion, are not combined and do not merge" (*Precise Exposition of the Orthodox Faith* 1.8). This identification of "Divinity" with the Father is even more evident in John's further affirmation: "When we look at Divinity, the first cause, the monarchy, the unity and identity of Divinity . . . we then imagine one. But when we consider what Divinity consists in, or more precisely what Divinity is and what proceeds from it, what exists eternally from the first cause with equal glory and without separation, i.e., when we consider the hypostases of the Son and the Spirit, we then get *three*" (1.8).

Despite all the imprecision of these definitions, one can nevertheless conclude that, in a certain sense, St. John of Damascus follows Origen in conceiving the Father as the Neoplatonic One, as proto-divinity, proto-will, proto-hypostasis (and not only as the *First* hypostasis). But this is incorrect. God, as the triune trihypostatic Subject, as the Absolute Person, is *not* the Father as one of the three hypostases, even if the First (and on this pathway it is impossible to avoid Origenistic subordinationism); rather, He is the *tri*-une subject in which three are one and one is three. This is, so to speak, the *dynamics* of trihypostatizedness, whereas one usually notices it only in its statics. And only on the basis of this idea can one completely eliminate *hypostatic* subordinationism.

In examining the trihypostatizedness of the Absolute Person, it must be kept in mind that, in itself, in its initial position so to speak, this Person does *not* yet contain hypostatic distinctions (*gnōrismata hupostatika*), but is defined solely by the trine self-positing of I as I-I-I or as I-We-You. The Absolute I is sufficiently revealed for itself as such within the limits of these trinely hypostatic definitions; and, moreover, all of these three hypostatic centers of the one I are equivalent or equi-hypostatic as *I-thou-he,* and are mutually reflected in one another; and only the *secondary,* further revelation of the hypostatic subject in the life of the Holy Trinity, in the concreteness of the Latter, complicates them with hypostatic qualifications, introduces hypostatic differentiation. But the latter does not remove their original hypostatic equivalence, for in this being of theirs as hypostatic centers, centers of *I,* within the limits of the triune absolute I, they preserve their *equi-Iness,* so to speak. St. John of Damascus' equating

of the "one God," i.e., the Old Testament Divine I, with the First hypostasis is therefore *not* correct. This "one God" is not the First hypostasis, just
as He is not the Second or the Third hypostasis; and in general He cannot
be identified with any of the three hypostatic centers. (He is the multiple
and unique Elohim, I-We.)

But in this case to what does this I of the one God who says of Himself, "I am the Lord thy God," refer if it does not refer to the Father, to the
Son, or to the Holy Spirit, to any of the three? Does this not introduce a
fourth hypostasis, as though a super-hypostasis, in Divinity? Of course, it
does *not* introduce such a super-hypostasis, for although this triune Divine I is not the Father, or the Son, or the Holy Spirit in their *differentiation,* it is the Father *and* the Son *and* the Holy Spirit in their *union,* as the
triune inwardly transparent I, existing in three I's. Different in hypo-
stasizedness, they nevertheless remain one, not only with regard to ousia,
with regard to "Divinity," but also with regard to hypostatizedness, like
three lights merging into one. The trinitarian dogma must be understood
more broadly and deeply; it must be understood not only with reference
to the consubstantiality of the three persons but also with reference to
their hypostatic triunity.

The impersonalistic statement of the problem of the one God in St.
John of Damascus guarantees (as in St. Augustine) the *homoousianism* of
the three hypostases; it eliminates ontological subordinationism and
grounds the equi-eternity of the hypostases. As we have seen in Tertullian
and Origen, however, homoousianism alone, in and of itself, does not yet
guarantee the equal dignity of the hypostases and does not overcome
intratrinitarian subordinationism. Nor did the Cappadocians overcome
this subordinationism; they limited themselves to the juxtaposition of
the three hypostases, without attempting to join them into triunity, although they did take a step in that direction in the doctrine of the *monarchy* of the Father.

St. John of Damascus gives special attention to the development of
this idea of the monarchy of the Father, and he bases his trinitarian doctrine on it. What does this idea consist in? In the chapter on the Holy Trinity we read: "We believe in the one Father, the principle and cause of all
things, not begotten from anyone, Who alone does not have a cause and is
not begotten." "If we say that the Father is the principle of the Son and is
greater than He (cf. John 14:28), this does not prove that He has primacy
over the Son in time and essence; and He does not have primacy in any
other respect except with respect to cause, for the Son was begotten from
the Father, not the Father from the Son, and the Father is the cause of the

Son with respect to essence. . . . Thus, when we hear that the Father is the principle and greater than the Son, we must understand the Father as the cause" (*Precise Exposition of the Orthodox Faith* 1.8). "The Father is without cause and is not begotten, for He is not from anyone, but has being from Himself, and of all that He has, He has nothing from another. On the contrary, He Himself is the principle of all things and the cause of the form according to which all things exist by nature. The Son is from the Father according to the mode of generation, and the Holy Spirit is from the Father according to the mode of procession." "Thus, all that the Son has, the Spirit too has from the Father, even very being. And if something is not the Father, it is not the Son or the Spirit; and if the Father does not have something, then the Son and the Spirit do not have it either; but it is through the Father that the Son and the Spirit exist, because the Father exists; and it is through the Father that the Son and the Spirit have all that They have" (1.8). "The Father is the source and cause of the Son and of the Holy Spirit . . . for there is only one Cause — the Father" (1.12).

In order to understand the trinitarian doctrine of St. John of Damascus, and in particular the "monarchy" of the Father and the fact that He is the cause, it is extremely important to establish in what sense he uses this concept of the Father as the *cause* of the other hypostases, especially since this concept becomes exceptionally significant in later theology, both in the Eastern theology and especially in the Latin theology. The simplest, and most natural, interpretation of the proposition that the Father is the *cause* of the Son and of the Holy Spirit, and that from Him They have Their very being — is the *Arian* one: They are *created* by the Father, the Son without mediation, the Holy Spirit through the Son. But to be sure, St. John of Damascus totally rejects this interpretation.

On the contrary, he decisively affirms the equi-eternity of the Three hypostases, something which was already established by Origen. Thus, the birth of the Son "is outside of time and without beginning, for the Son of God was brought into being not out of the non-existent. . . . Rather, He was always with the Father in the Father, out of Whom He was born eternally and without beginning. . . . The Father without the Son would not be called the Father. . . . Thus, it would be impious to affirm about the birth of the Son that it took place in time, and that the being of the Son began after the Father" (*Precise Exposition of the Orthodox Faith* 1.8). "The eternal God engenders His Word without beginning and without end," and even though only the Father is *agennētos,* unengendered, the word *agenētos,* uncreated, "is applicable to the three supra-divine hypostases of Divinity, for they are consubstantial and uncreated" (1.8).

47

The Holy Spirit, with respect to the Father, is also "consubstantial and coeternal." In brief, St. John of Damascus clearly and consistently affirms the equal beginninglessness, uncreatedness, eternity, and consubstantiality of all three hypostases, although he also asserts — following, of course, the Cappadocians — the causelessness of the First hypostasis and, so to speak, the causedness of the Second and Third hypostases, which have Their being from the Father, the First Cause. But what does causality signify in this case? What meaning does this category have here? Not only does St. John of Damascus fail to give this question careful attention, he does not address it at all, as if it were something self-evident. Herein lies the radical imprecision and even the deficiency of his trinitarian doctrine, which had, so to speak, a fatal effect on all later theology.

Causal dependence does *not* signify that the Second and Third hypostases *arise* from the First, for, being equally eternal, they, in general, *do not arise* but eternally are. Moreover, for St. John of Damascus himself, *cause* signifies only origination (the source of "being itself"). If this category of "cause" is to be applied in the doctrine of trinitarian monarchy, it must receive its own *special* philosophical interpretation, but such an interpretation is absent in St. John of Damascus. Therefore, it is unclear what the idea of the one Cause actually signifies. If this is "procession," then how should it be understood? Moreover, into the concept of procession or causality, there imperceptibly creeps a *purely empirical* interpretation; and it is in this form that the trinitarian doctrine is developed and interpreted in the Latin theology (in particular in the doctrine of the Filioque). Nevertheless, St. John of Damascus' clear and consistent exposition of the doctrine of the procession of the hypostases from a single cause has the merit that it leads directly to the main problem of trinitarity, i.e., to the problem of the connection of the Three hypostases amongst themselves, although he leaves this problem for the future to consider.

Turning now specifically to pneumatology, we must first remark that St. John of Damascus considers the hypostatic property of the Holy Spirit to consist in His *procession* from the Father, in contrast to *birth* or *generation,* which is proper to the Son. "But what the form of the distinction [between generation and procession] is, this we do not fathom . . . [but] the generation of the Son and the procession of the Holy Spirit occur simultaneously" (*Precise Exposition of the Orthodox Faith* 1.8). Having full consubstantiality, "it is according to hypostatic properties alone that the three hypostases differ; they are distinguished without separation not according to substance but according to the distinctive property of each" (1.8).

Aside from procession, what for St. John of Damascus is the hypostatic property of the Third Person of the Holy Trinity? It is called "the essential power *(dunamin ousiōdē),* contemplated in its special hypostatic being *(idiazousēi hupostasei),* proceeding from the Father, reposing in the Word and manifesting the Latter. . . . Like the Word, it exists hypostatically *(kath' hupostasin),* lives, has free will and spontaneous movement, is active, always desires the good, accompanies every act of desiring by power" (1.7). St. John of Damascus indicates the immediate hypostatic character of the Holy Spirit, His proper place in the Holy Trinity, by an idea we have already encountered in patristic thought: "The Son is the image of the Father, while the image of the Son is the Spirit, through Whom Christ, dwelling in man, gives to him that which conforms with the image [of God]" (1.13). "We call Him the Spirit of the Son and confess that He was revealed to us and bestowed upon us through the Son" (1.8). St. John of Damascus here does not go beyond the definitions of St. Athanasius, which he briefly reiterates without explanation.

We can see an attempt by St. John of Damascus to understand the Third hypostasis in a *trinitarian manner* in passages where he explains trinitarity by comparisons taken from the natural world. Specifically, he interprets the relation between the Second and Third hypostases as a relation between word and breath. In chapter 7, "On the Holy Spirit: Proofs from Reason," we read, "for the Word there must be breath, for our word too is not without breath. But our breath is distinct from our being; it is the breathing in and out of air, breathed in and out for the existence of the body. When a word is uttered, it becomes a sound, manifesting the force of the word. In God's nature too, simple and uncomplex, we must piously affirm the being of the Spirit of God, for His Word is not more insufficient than our word; but it would be impious to think that in God the Spirit is something that comes from outside, as this is the case with us, who are complex beings. On the contrary, just as when we hear of the Word of God, we do not hold it to be unhypostatic but consider it to exist hypostatically and to have free will, to be active and all-powerful — so, having learned that the Spirit of God accompanies the Word and manifests His action, we do not consider It to be unhypostatic breath," etc. "The Spirit . . . is not disappearing breath, just as the lips of God are not a bodily member; both must be understood in a sense conforming to God." This comparison is supplemented by others, by images of source, river, and sea; rock, branch, and fruit; sun, ray, and heat; rose stem, color, and fragrance.[38]

---

38. In *The Book on Heresies* and the *Dialogue against the Manicheans.*

What can we say about this "deduction" of trinitarity? For us at the present time such explications of trinitarian relations by physical comparisons (in which physical phenomena like sound and breath unexpectedly acquire hypostatic being) scarcely seem valid and, *theologically*, they simply do not hold water (having been invalidated prior to this by St. Gregory the Theologian). From the comparison of word and breath, however, one can extract the idea that the Holy Spirit is the principle of *reality* in the Holy Trinity, that He is the one who *accomplishes*. This accomplishing action of the Third hypostasis had already been clearly explained by St. Athanasius and the Cappadocian fathers. St. John of Damascus' pneumatology does not go beyond this, and it thus has a schematizing significance: it does not introduce new ideas or problems. The theological significance of St. John of Damascus in pneumatology, which significance has gained in appreciation in recent times in the discussions with the Western confessions on the subject of the Filioque but which in essence has been greatly exaggerated, is primarily associated with the formula of the procession of the Holy Spirit from the Father through the Son, *dia Huiou.*

*   *

This represents the sum-total of the accomplishments of patristic pneumatology. Notwithstanding the value of particular theses and remarks, one cannot say that they have any fundamental or decisive significance. The most general impression that we take away from the patristic teaching, from Tertullian and Origen to St. John of Damascus, is that it is marked by a perplexity provoked by the very *fact* of the Third hypostasis as it is given in Revelation and thus proposed to theology as a task that it must explore — a perplexity the Fathers were not always conscious of or able to express. This becomes particularly clear when pneumatology is compared with logology: Whereas the Son-Logos receives His indisputable place alongside the Father as His Word about Himself and about the world, and these two hypostases, so to speak, gaze at one other, the presence of the Third hypostasis does not follow with necessity but rather is a kind of addition with which theology does not know how to deal.

The necessity of the Third hypostasis in the Holy Trinity has not been sufficiently accepted from the theological point of view. Compelled de facto to expound a doctrine of the *three* hypostases, the theology was intrinsically *not* trinitarian; and the sole theological form of trinitarity with which it could operate was the Neoplatonic form, with all its divergences from the Christian form. From this incompleteness of patristic pneumatology, there follows, first of all, an involuntary subordination-ism, owing to which, in the decreasing progression of Divinity, the Third hypostasis is derivative of the Second and after the Second. But apart from subordinationism, the Third hypostasis is coordinated precisely with the Second hypostasis (St. Athanasius and others), by which the Trinity is divided de facto into two dyads, the Father-Son and the Son-Holy Spirit. Meanwhile, the proper place of the Third hypostasis in the Holy Trinity remains undetermined.

On the other hand, the Trinity is understood as the de facto presence and juxtaposition of three hypostases (theology has no answer why there are not more and not less), which differ in hypostatic properties despite their consubstantiality. Their connection is established according to origin, by the causality of the Father, Who is the principle and cause of the Second and Third hypostases. In the Cappadocian conception of causality, the Trinity also consists of two dyads, Father-Son (generation) and Father-Spirit (procession), with the "monarchy" of the Father being the unifying factor. But does it sufficiently unify the Son and the Holy Spirit, so that one gets precisely the Trinity, and not two Dyads with a common principle? One then gets not a trinitarian but a binitarian doctrine.

Another variant of this conception of the Trinity according to origin — the Western, homoousian variant — is based on ousia or nature, out of which the three hypostases arise by differentiation of the relations according to origin. This type of interpretation is essentially impersonalistic in its initial definitions. Of course, here too the fact that there are *three* hypostases — not more and not less — has the force only of a fact, not of a principle. To be sure, the Holy Trinity in its essence can be only a given of Revelation, not a deduction of the autonomous reason. Reason in theology is called to understand this given in its indisputability and self-evidence, however, and not to limit itself to its logical description, so to speak, to a description that can be accompanied by dogmatic distortion (in subordinationism). The problem of *trinitarity* as such remains *unsolved* in the patristic theology, which puts an erroneous or at least a one-sided emphasis on origination when it treats this problem. But outside of the problem of trinitarity the problem of the Third hypostasis as such cannot be posed in a fundamental manner. In essence, these two problems constitute a single problem, that of the (ontological) place of the Third hypostasis in the triunity of the Holy Trinity. The patristic theology bequeathed this problem to future ages.

CHAPTER 1

The Place of the Third Hypostasis in the Holy Trinity

I. Trinitarity and the Third Hypostasis

In order to clarify this question it is necessary to distinguish (of course, in the abstract) the immanent Trinity from the economic Trinity, the supra-eternal life of the Holy Trinity in Itself from Its trihypostatic revelation in creation. Let us first investigate trinitarity in its immanent aspect. Here, Revelation gives us the *fact* of the divine triunity of the Father, Son, and Spirit: Unity in Trinity and Trinity in Unity, the one Name, the one God the Holy Trinity. Not three in unity, but triunity; and not one, but unifiedness in Trinity. This is the divine number, which does not exist in the natural world, but which is a super-number for the latter: the three in one. This super-number refers not to things, which can be counted in their separateness and juxtaposition, but to the Divine Person or Persons, Who has or have one unified, but not common, natural life. This super-number, Trinity-Unity,[1] can be expressed in the language of human discursive thought only as a paradoxical and rationally absurd, for contradictory, union of one and three. This inability of the rational-logical under-

---

1. "Simple, inseparable, consubstantial Trinity; holy unity, lights and light; holy three and holy one, we praise God the Trinity" (from the Great Canon of St. Andrew of Crete, Seventh ode, Glory). "Trinity without beginning, without separation, indivisible unity, receive the penitent that I am" (Third ode, Glory). "One trinitarian divinity" (Fourth ode, Glory). "I am the simple, inseparable, distinctly personal Trinity, and I am the unity united by the substance" (Sixth ode, Glory). "Thou, Trinity, we glorify Thee, unique God" (Fifth ode, Glory). "Trinity Unity, have pity upon me" (Eighth ode, Glory).

standing to accept this super-number manifests the limitation of this understanding: it is not competent to make judgments about the super-rational. Therefore, in its practical relation to the super-number, the rational-logical understanding must *adapt itself*, passing from one to three, and then back from three to one, while simultaneously containing both the one and the other. The speculative reason is still capable of postulating this triunity, which the rational-logical understanding does not have the power to concretize by its operation.

The Trinity is not a simple juxtaposition of three, distinct but united externally (by analogy with three lights that merge into one another). Such a trinity is, first of all, not self-enclosed; rather, it is open for continuation: the juxtaposition presupposes a *series* continuing into (bad) infinity, although it can be broken off at any number of terms, in particular at three. It is solely as such a juxtaposition that trinitarity was conceived by early patristic theology, which thus found itself in a state of perplexity and helplessness before the fact of the Third hypostasis as the end of the series. But the Holy Trinity is not three, but a triunity; and It is not a series but an enclosed whole, which has the fullness of Its being, Its power, precisely in trinitarity. It is necessary to understand the necessity of this *trinitarity* — not more and not less — of the hypostases. And one must take as one's starting point this necessity when considering the Holy Trinity-Unity, as well as the separate hypostases, and in particular when considering the Third hypostasis and His place in the Holy Trinity.

The trinitarity of the hypostases in the Divine Person results, first of all, from the nature of the personal self-consciousness, which is not fully manifested in the self-enclosed, singular I, but postulates thou, he, we, you, i.e., not uni-hypostatizedness, but multi-hypostatizedness, with the latter defined typologically and essentially as tri-hypostatizedness. I presupposes, as its self-affirmation, thou or co-I; and as its confirmation, so to speak, it presupposes he, and is definitively realized only in we (or you); i.e., ontologically it is not unique, although it is one. In creaturely, relative being, I is posited not only in itself but also outside itself; it is extrapolated and thereby limited. Despite its seeming absoluteness, I is not capable of actualizing its I-ness in itself and must, so to speak, become convinced of its own being by looking into the mirror of other I's. Without such a mirror, it disappears for itself, stops being conscious of itself in its I-ness.

But in the Divine Absolute subject, which is *one* and *genuinely unique* according to its own kind, all altero-positings of I cannot be actualized outside of it, because of the absence of all "outside," but must be contained in it itself, so that it itself is for itself simultaneously I, thou, he, and therefore we and you.[2] Furthermore, none of these three positings of I — as I, thou, and he — can be defined solely from a single center, from I alone, which would be only I, I itself, for which the other I's would be only thou and he (and we and you, and even they). They must independently exist for themselves as I, fully equally centered each upon itself, being at the same time thou and he, each for the other.

Thus in the one absolute **I** there exist three I's, as fully equal centers of I, completely transparent for one another and belonging to the fullness of the reality of this Absolute self-**I**, of this genuine triune **I** that has nothing and coposits nothing outside itself — "this one light and three lights," this triunity. These are three hypostases, three personal centers, each of which is an equi-personal **I**, hypostatizing Divinity, the divine nature. But this equi-personal **I** never posits itself in separation from the other equi-personal I's, as unique or even as *one of three I's* (which would transform the trinity into a *community or harmony of three* — a tritheism); rather, it posits itself in the other I's, is coposited with them. And there results a unique but also triune divine *I,* for trinitarity is not only trinity but also unity.

What is the relation of this *unity*-trinity to *trinity*-unity, to the three hetero-personal hypostases? Is this not a "fourth hypostasis," existing in addition to, or above, the three hypostases? No, it is not. There is no "in addition" or "above" here. What there is is the total identity of personal self-consciousness: one is three and three are one, hetero-personally and uni-personally. A static and rational-logical computation necessarily yields either simply three or simply one; or, finally, four, by adding to the three separate I's the trine I; for the rational-logical understanding knows only things fixed in their separateness, not the dynamics of the life of the spirit which overcomes this separateness. The God glorified in the Holy Trinity is *one,* one Divine **I**, the Absolute Subject, the Holy Trinity, which we therefore address as a *person.*[3] But this Person is also three Persons, Who exist for us as such, Who are distinct in prayer, in life, in thought, but Who are never separated from one another and trans-

---

2. Only *they* is excluded, because that would mean that I turns its back to itself, so to speak, transforming itself into they and thus annihilating itself. The pure *they* is only an abstraction from I; it exists only in and for I, but not without I. *They* does not belong to I.

3. For example, in the matins prayer: "We thank Thee, Holy Trinity, for Thou hast not . . . caused me to be lost, but Thou hast shown Thy constant love for human beings."

formed into *three*. The life of this trine, triune subject is love, by virtue of which it is *three*, while being *one* in the divine self-identity. The absolute self-sufficient divine Subject is the unceasing motion, the "perichoresis" of the divine I-ness, which cannot be stopped at some one center, thus breaking the ring of love and transforming the trinity into three or one.[4] God the Holy Trinity, God the Father, God the Son, and God the Holy Spirit are hypostatically equal, for They are equally divine as the divine **I**. They are *not* distinguished in their equal I-ness.

To consider the trine subject and the hypostatic subjects *only* as **I**, in their pure subjectness, however, is to admit an abstraction, for *concretely* in the life of the Holy Trinity all three hypostatic subjects, as well as the triune subject, are mutually defined by an unchanging interrelationship; and therefore, while preserving the equal dignity and equal divinity of their hypostases, they have their defining, distinctive properties, or *gnōrismata*. Therefore, while being equally divine, they are differently divine; and the trihypostatic subject, the trine **I**, is not simply a transparent **I** existent in three centers that are identified, but the Holy Trinity, the Father-Son-Spirit in Their divine triunity. Therefore, the three divine subjects, although equally divine, are not interchangeable: The Father is *not* the Son, *nor* is He the Holy Spirit. The Son is *not* the Father, and so on.

Aside from the hypostatic triunity of the three subjects, which is, so to speak, a priori the Holy Trinity with respect to *one* person, there also exists the Holy Trinity as the trine interrelation or mutual definition of the *three* persons. And just as, with reference to the trihypostatic *subject*, we have established precisely trinitarity, not more and not less, as the determining and exhaustive self-definition of *I* and as the actualization of the self-consciousness of the Absolute Subject, so we must also understand the Trinity in Its interrelation precisely as concrete trinitarity, in the inner necessity and perfection of the number three (once again, not more and not less).

The question arises: Why is God Who exists in the Holy Trinity trine, and not dual or quaternary, etc., in His hypostases? Of course, deduction is incapable of establishing the fact of divine Triunity, which is given by Revelation; but thought is called to fathom this revealed fact to the extent this is possible for human knowledge. We have already seen how ineffective patristic thought was in this respect: it transformed the Third hypostasis into a kind of theological addendum, an "etc." or "and so on,"

---

4. Here I give only a brief summary of the deduction of trinity as the triune absolute subject which I present in my work "Chapters on Trinity."

without inner justification of Its being; or it conceived the Holy Trinity as a double *and*, connecting three separate subjects: the Father *and* the Son *and* the Holy Spirit (the Cappadocians).

Against such a conception of trinitarity as "and-and" or "etc.," it is necessary to set forth the following trinitarian axiom: The Holy Trinity is a divine triunity which is exhaustive and perfect in Its fullness, a triunity of interrelations which is trine and integral in all Its definitions, without any disjunctive or conjunctive "and" connecting the separate hypostases. Every hypostasis in separation, as well as their triunity, must be understood in *trine connection and in trine self-definition*, which form the Whole, the Holy Trinity.

The *connection* of the Holy Trinity — in both the East and the West — is established through origin or origination. In the East, for the Cappadocians and then for St. John of Damascus, the *Father* is the "cause" of the Son and of the Holy Spirit, who originate from Him. In the West, *essence, essentia*, is the principle in and from which the Father-Son, and then the Holy Spirit, originate, although in this origination too the primary place is given to the Father. For this theologeme of origination there is a Biblical foundation, though only in a particular dogmatic interpretation or doctrinal reworking; and it is therefore erroneous to see here a direct Biblical thesis. In fact, Scripture says that the Son is the only begotten Son of the Father, from Whom also the Holy Spirit proceeds. This fact of the fatherhood of the Father and of the sonhood of the Son, as well as of the procession of the Holy Spirit from the Father, is affirmed in Scripture; fatherhood/sonhood is affirmed several times,[5] the procession but once (John 15:26). Concerning the distinction of the hypostases, revelation indicates, essentially, that the Father, the Son, and the Holy Spirit are distinguished hypostatically; and the Father is the Father of the only begotten Son, the Son is the Son of this Father, and there is also the Holy Spirit.

To be sure, the Father-Son relation presupposes generation and birth, although of course in a wholly other sense than earthly birth. But nowhere is it said that this — as if implied — generation, *generatio activa*, expresses the essence of the Father, or that generatedness expresses the essence of the Son and procession the essence of the Holy Spirit, so that

---

5. One should note, however, that the very birth of the Son from the Father is never directly attested in the Lord's discourses. It is only indirectly attested, when He is called "only begotten" (John 1:14, 18); but this signifies not so much birth as uniqueness, exhaustive fullness.

one could place an equals sign between the hypostases and these hypostatic properties (which patristic theology does not yet do but which Latin theology indeed does do). Such an equation is, on the one hand, a logical abstraction, while on the other hand it is a theological deduction and not given by revelation. The judgment that generation and procession signify different modes of the same relation, i.e., origination, and in this capacity can be equated and juxtaposed, this judgment is also a theological deduction.

Thus there results the further opposition between the Father as *anaitios,* not having origination, and the Son and Holy Spirit as *aitiatoi,* having origination. The next step in this generalization is the conclusion that the Father is the cause *(aitia)* of the *origination* of the two other hypostases, and the entire Holy Trinity is interpreted as a *relation of causal origination.* This is the basis of the entire trinitarian theology of the West, which in part also developed here the trinitarian doctrine of the East, where this idea had first appeared, although it did not achieve such complete and consistent development as in the West.

With reference to this doctrine we must first observe that the concept of *origination* is not a Biblical one, for Scripture knows neither *aitia* nor origination, *processio.* The very being of the Father, of the Son, and of the Holy Spirit proceeding from the Father does not yet signify, with reference to divine eternity, their abstract relation according to *origination* or *causality,* in all the imprecision and, what is more important, ambiguity of this expression. One cannot refer here to the fact that, in defining the generatedness but uncreatedness of the Son, both the first and second ecumenical councils also used the non-Biblical expression *homoousios,* because it was accepted by the Church as the authoritative definition of the two ecumenical councils only after prolonged struggle and many efforts at interpretation. Neither *aitia* nor *processio* has the authority of the Church behind it (the doctrine of origination in the Western sense crept only into the definition of the Council of Florence).

The idea of *causality and origination* with reference to the Holy Trinity is not only a product of abstraction but also of a centuries-old hypnosis (especially in the Latin church). It is only by virtue of this abstract-logical hypnosis that unverified and unexamined propositions, without any Biblical foundation, are accepted as indisputable axioms of theology. To interpret "generation" and "procession" as two forms of *origination,* and Fatherhood, with reference both to the generation of the Son and to the procession of the Spirit, as *causality,* is arbitrary and an abuse of an abstraction. Such generalization is legitimate only with reference to phenomena that lie on the same ontological and logical plane and belong to the natural world; it is illegitimate and invalid with reference to the intratrinitarian life: generation is generation, and procession is procession, as relations *sui generis,* and in no wise can they be generalized as different forms of *origination, processiones;* and the Father in His relations to the Son and the Holy Spirit cannot be defined as a *cause.*

In actuality, what does *cause* mean for us? Empirically, it refers to a sequence of phenomena in time, and to be sure, a definition connected with a *temporal* sequence is inappropriate with reference to Divinity. Epistemologically, cause is a category applied by reason to the coordination of empirical phenomena, but of course this category of "transcendental logic" (in the sense of Kant) is, once again, inapplicable to Divinity. Ontologically, cause is *sufficient reason,* the principle *causa aequat effectum* [cause equals effect], or the same proposition in an inverse form: *ex nihilo nil fit* [nothing comes from nothing]; but such a conception of causality is inevitably connected with *origination.* The latter can be conceived as the unfolding or evolution of some principle; such is the whole of cosmic causality, consisting in becoming, i.e., in the actualization of primordial potencies ("evolution"). Or it can be conceived as creation out of nothing; and in *this* sense God can be defined as the metaphysical (but in no wise as the physical or empirical) cause of creation, as its "sufficient reason," *aitia.*

But it is obvious that the application of causality to the intratrinitarian relations in *this* sense leads to Arianism (which, strictly speaking, consists in the fact that it considers the Father to be the *cause* of the Son, Who *arose* out of nothing, while considering the Son to be the cause of the Holy Spirit, created by Him), to the most pernicious kind of subordinationism, or finally to monarchianism. Subordinationism is what we end up with if we understand the origination of the Holy Trinity in the manner of the Stoics or the Neoplatonists: A certain first principle (e.g., Plotinus' One or the first essence of the Stoics) determines itself, positing in itself the second and third principles, which in one sense or another are *not* equi-divine in relation to the first. The consequence of this deduction is invariably cosmism or pantheism, according to which the world, creation, is an *altero-being* of the Absolute. That is the way it is in Neoplatonism (and Origenism), as well as in Tertullian's cosmologism.

Analogous to ancient pantheism are the modern mystical and metaphysical doctrines: that of Jacob Boehme with his *Urgottheit,* in which trinitarity arises through differentiation; and that of Hegel, for whom logic is God before the creation of the world and the world is the altero-being of God. The distinguishing feature of all such theories is their initial impersonalism, with the later *appearance* of the hypostases, i.e., the ontological primacy of ousia over hypostasis. Such impersonalism does not characterize the Cappadocians, for whom the hypostases exist as such; but it does characterize Augustine and the whole of Catholic theology with its initial *deitas,* in which the hypostases exist as relations of origination according to oppositeness.

This Catholic doctrine of originations is nothing else but impersonalistic subordinationism, in which *Divinity, Deitas,* is the initial metaphysical "fund" and, in this sense, the sufficient ground or cause of the hypostases. The latter, in Tertullian's sense, have different shares in this fund: the Father has a full share; the Son has the full share minus the power of engendering; whereas the Holy Spirit's share is not only minus the power of engendering but also minus the power of producing procession. Although in a veiled manner, we have here a special form of ontological subordinationism, in which the true cause is now not even the hypostasis of the Father (for this hypostasis arises from the relation with the Son), but Divinity, *Deitas,* the One in which different relations do not exist.

However, if we pass from impersonalistic subordinationism, for which the hypostases arise or originate in Divinity, to the personalism of the Eastern Fathers, who consider the three hypostases as the initial given, their doctrine of the Father as cause, the "monarchy of the Father," represents a monarchianism that has not been overcome or even fully understood, if any meaning at all can be attributed to the idea of origination from the Father as causality. If the Father truly *causes* the being of the Son and, then, of the Holy Spirit, how can this be understood except in the sense that both the Son and the Holy Spirit are, so to speak, alteropositings of the Father, His self-definitions, who are thus associated with Him by the relation of identity? To be sure, such a view is completely opposed to the true intention of the Cappadocians, who championed precisely the autonomous being and, so to speak, the equi-hypostatizedness of the three hypostases. And if we were in fact to place *causality* at the basis of the relation between the First, Second, and Third hypostases, then monarchianism (of course, modalistic and of the Sabellian type) would be the inevitable consequence, if we exclude the path of explicit subordinationism or Arianism.

But leaving aside these inevitable deviations in the doctrine of trinitarian causality, let us pose the essential question: What meaning, with reference to the trine Divinity, can be assigned to the idea of *cause* and *origination?* If the hypostases are equi-eternal and beginningless, as the holy

Fathers themselves attest, how can one speak of one of the hypostases as the cause of the other two or of their origination from this hypostasis? What real meaning can be assigned to the statement that the Son and the Holy Spirit "have Their being" from the Father (St. John of Damascus)? There is an obvious and essential misunderstanding here. The *principle* in the Holy Trinity, the "monarchy" of the Father, should be retained, but it must be understood in a wholly other sense than *cause* and *origination*.

In the Holy Trinity there is a place neither for causality nor for origination.[6] The trinitarian problem consists not in showing the origination of the hypostases from impersonal (or pre-personal) Divinity, or from the Father as "cause," but in understanding the connection of the three hypostases and, so to speak, the inner structure of the Holy Trinity. One must remember that the three hypostases are *given* a priori, and in no wise require an explanation of their being, a deduction through origination. The problem consists not in the *origination* of the hypostases, who are all equally eternal and equally beginningless, and, in general, do *not* originate, but in their interrelation and connection, which can be defined in different ways, but not according to causality or origination. One must forget the theory of origination and formulate the problem of the Holy Trinity in a different way. What formulation can be proposed?

Scripture directly attests that God is Spirit. This is not only a truth of revelation but also something self-evident for our natural consciousness; the religiophilosophical consciousness as represented by the great philosophical systems and the great natural (pagan) religions cannot conceive Divinity in any other way. Scripture attests not only that God is Spirit, but also that He is a Trihypostatic Spirit: Father, Word, and Holy Spirit. It also attests that God is love (1 John 4:8, 16), which means not only that love is proper to God, for He is loving, but that He Himself is love, that love is His very being. Here we have a definition that is not descriptive but ontological in character. Combining the two definitions, we arrive at the conclusion that God is Spirit-Love. There is no disharmony, or even distinction, between the two definitions, for love expresses the essence of spirit and its life. Thus, we must understand the Holy Trinity as the Spirit whose life is Love.

It is proper to spirit to have a personal consciousness, a hypostasis, and a nature as its self-revelation; and the life of spirit consists in the living out of this personal self-revelation in its nature. In spirit are given: I, as personal self-consciousness; nature, as the source of its self-revelation;

---

6. See my work "Chapters on Trinity," II, sec. 12.

and revelation itself as the life of the spirit in its nature.[7] The distinction between the relative and the absolute spirit consists in the fact that the relative spirit is given for itself in its *nature*. The latter is thus the relative spirit's *given*, one which is not fully transparent, but which is only in the process of becoming transparent; and this spirit's life is therefore a becoming. By contrast, the absolute spirit is wholly transparent for itself in its nature; there is no place for genesis in the fullness of its life. Furthermore, the relative spirit, as unihypostatic, is limited in personal self-consciousness, insofar as it postulates other co-persons for itself; whereas the absolute trihypostatic spirit is self-sufficient and, in this sense, unique (not "one," which is a rational-numerical definition).

But how are self-revelation and life realized in the absolute trihypostatic spirit? In its general scheme, this self-revelation cannot be different from that of any spirit, even a relative one. Every spirit has its own personal self-consciousness; then, the knowledge of its nature or its self-revelation; and finally, life in this nature, the living-out of this knowledge as its own reality and life. In the self-revelation of the spirit there are, therefore, a certain ideal element, the "word," and a real element, the *connection* between this subject (person) and the predicate (the definition of its nature), its own being and life, its *is*. This scheme of self-revelation corresponds to the life of every creaturely spirit in its limitedness, which is due not only to its monohypostatizedness but also to its state of becoming. This limitedness is expressed, first of all, in the fact that nature in the self-revelation of the spirit is for it the *given* and, in a certain sense, an extra-positing, an *object in the subject*, which for this reason does not fully possess it. And therefore its life in this nature is also the given or the *state* of the object, which has place in it or above it, but also does not belong to it in an I-like manner, is for it a kind of "it," not fully hypostatized (whence different forms of the *sub*conscious). Finally, the self-revelation of I is, of course, its love for this its *own*, a love which is its life. But this love is limited in a twofold sense: it is partial according to object and self-enclosed according to the monohypostatizedness of the subject, for which this love is *self-love* that does not overcome the limitedness and self-enclosedness of the subject.

How can this scheme be applied to the trihypostatic, absolute spirit? First of all, in the self-revelation of the Absolute, Divine Spirit there is no place for any *givenness* or extrapositing of untransparent nature: The Divine ousia is thoroughly transparent for the Spirit and in this sense is

7. See my book *The Lamb of God*.

62

Sophia,[8] entirely hypostatized and not leaving a place in itself for anything that is not hypostatically clarified (for any *Urgrund* or bottomless abyss). Second, there is no place here for self-loving monohypostatic limitedness, because the Divine Spirit is the Holy Trinity, because He is not a monohypostatic subject, but a *tri*hypostatic Spirit, Who abolishes in Himself the limits of self-love. In a word, He is not self-love, but Love.

The self-revelation of the Holy Trinity is realized in such a way that God the Father, Who is the initial hypostasis and contains the entire fullness of the divine nature or Sophia as Love, renounces, in His self-revelation, this fullness for or in Himself, and goes out of Himself by the "generation" of the Son.[9] The Son then is the hypostatic self-revelation of the nature of the Father, or the hypostatic Sophia, the self-consciousness or hypostatization of the Divine ousia of the Father; the Son is present before the Father as His Truth and Word, His knowledge of Himself in the Son: "no man knoweth the Son, but the Father; and neither knoweth any man the Father, save the Son" (Matt. 11:27). Not being, of course, the *causal origination* of the Son from the Father, the "generation" is a living interrelation of two hypostases, in which one is revealed and the other reveals. These hypostases do not arise in this self-revelation, but are mutually self-defined through Their relation in the divine ousia.

This *dyadic* interrelation of the Father and the Son is concrete and irreversible: the Father engenders, the Son is engendered, not vice versa. Just as all the hypostases are equivalent in their hypostatic I-ness, so they are concrete and therefore distinct in their ousia-ness. The relation of "generation" precisely expresses — from the side of the Father — the self-revelation of the Father not in and through Himself, but in and through the Son; whereas from the side of the Son it expresses His self-revelation through but not for Himself and thus not in Himself, but in the Father: the Father engenders, the Son is engendered. The Father out of Himself goes into the Son, while the Son out of Himself goes into the Father, but this movement of going out of oneself starts with the Father, proceeds to the Son, and returns from the Son to the Father. The Father is the subject, the Principle; the Son is the predicate, the Word.

This dyadic relation of the Father and the Son can in no wise exhaust the self-definition of the Absolute Spirit, however, for it is characterized not only by self-revelation as self-consciousness, as being in truth, but also by self-revelation as self-life, as being in beauty, as the living-out

8. Cf. *The Lamb of God*, ch. 1.
9. Cf. the deduction of trinity in *The Lamb of God*, ch. 1-2.

of its proper content. The self-revelation of the Father in the Word, Truth, is dyadically united with self-revelation in the Spirit of the Truth, the hypostatic Life of Divinity, which properly is the Love of God for Himself in His ousia as Sophia, or for His own being. This third aspect of the self-revelation, not only in knowledge (ideally) but also in life (really), is the living connection (the copula between the subject and the predicate), the life of Divinity in *Its Own* and in *Itself*. The Father, as the initial hypostasis, is not only revealed in His Ousia-Sophia through the Son, but also *lives* in her by the Holy Spirit. And the Son not only reveals the Father through Himself in His Ousia-Sophia, but also lives in her by the Holy Spirit. And this life in reality, Ousia, as the divine reality of the Truth, or Beauty, actualizes in itself the mutual being of the Father for the Son and of the Son for the Father, not only in the statics of ideal self-definition but also in the dynamics of the life of the one hypostasis through the other. But this dynamics of life is, once again, not only a *state* and in this sense a *given* of external self-definition, for which there is in general no place in the absolute subject. It is also a hypostasis.

This Life of the Father and of the Son has as its source, naturally, the Initial hypostasis of the Father, Who reveals Himself in the Son. This life exists for the Father hypostatically as the Holy Spirit, Who is not generated but "proceeds" from the Father. This distinction between generation and procession is, according to the general testimony of the Church Fathers, a mystery of the Divine life inaccessible to human comprehension. "Procession" expresses a mode of relation to the Father that is different from the Son's relation to Him. The starting point here too is the self-revelation of the Father, which is realized in the Son, but is not exhausted by this. Rather, it is completed by the procession of the Holy Spirit from the very same Father, from the Father of the Son, and therefore with the Son, in the Son, through the Son.

In other words, the relation of the Holy Spirit to the Father *is not only a dyadic one*. If it were, the Holy Trinity would then be divided into two parallel dyads: Father-Son and Father-Spirit, which would not be connected and would be united in the Father only by the unity of "origination." One can therefore say that the Father has two different functions: He engenders the Son and He is the Spirator of the Spirit, Who proceeds from Him. There may even arise the question: Is the First hypostasis the Father only in relation to the Son, while being the Spirator in relation to the Spirit, the one from whom the Spirit proceeds? In reality, this relation is a triadic one, because the Holy Spirit is the Life of the Father *and* of the Son, of the Father in the Son and of the Son in the Father; while for Himself the Holy Spirit is this *And* (or *Is,* the copula of the subject and the predicate).

In other words, in His very being, as the *ontologically Third* hypostasis, not in a dyad but in the Holy Trinity, consubstantial and without separation, the Holy Spirit already presupposes fatherhood and sonhood. This hypostasis completes the self-revelation of the Divine Spirit by definitively overcoming in Him all *givenness;* not only the content of His self-revelation but also His life acquires a hypostatically transparent character, is a hypostasis. Therefore, a complete adequacy between hypostasis and ousia is achieved; all of God's being is personal as well as natural; there is no extrahypostatic nature and no extranatural hypostatizedness. The subject is exhaustively defined by the predicate; and between them there exists just as exhaustive a connection. Natural being is hypostatized in all these elements. There exist *three* hypostases, not more and not less; and these are not three abstract hypostases, but the First, Second, and Third, the trihypostatic interrelationship, the Holy Trinity, the Absolute Spirit.

The Third Hypostasis *completes* the self-revelation of the Divine, Holy Spirit. This hypostasis is in fact the Holy Spirit in the Spirit of God. Among other meanings, this name attests precisely to such a *completing* significance of the Holy Spirit in the self-revelation of the Divine Spirit. And although, of course, both the Father and the Son are Spirit, inasmuch as God is, in general, Spirit, the Third hypostasis is the Holy Spirit par excellence, as the self-revealing *spirituality* of the Spirit. The Holy Spirit in the Divine Spirit is the *Third* hypostasis because, in a certain sense, He is also the *Final* hypostasis.

The self-revelation of the nature of Ousia-Sophia, which is realized through trihypostatic self-revelation and interrelation, is also the self-revelation of Love, for if God is Love, this means that the Holy Trinity is trihypostatic love. In other words, Divine Love is revealed in trihypostatizedness.

The intimate connection of the Holy Trinity is the connection of love. And this love is trihypostatic love: it has three aspects, which are *tropoi tēs huparxeōs* (the essential modes) of the three hypostases. There is, however, a common feature that characterizes love *as such* and thus all the forms of love. This is sacrificial self-renunciation, for the axiom of *personal* love is that *there is no love without sacrifice.* But this sacrificialness is realized in a triple manner in the life of the Holy Trinity.[10] The Father and the Son are in a relation of mutual self-renunciation. The interrelation of the Fa-

---

10. These ideas have already been expounded in *The Lamb of God.*

ther and the Son, in its immediate aspect, is the tragic side of love, the Divine dissonance of sacrificial suffering, without which there can be no reality of sacrifice and no all-reality of love.

The question may arise: Is it possible to speak of suffering in the life of the All-blissful, Absolute God? The answer is that one cannot speak *only* of suffering in the life of God, for that clearly would be incompatible with the fullness and absoluteness of this life, and would signify limitation. However, it is impossible *not* to speak of sacrificial suffering precisely in the Absolute God, as an aspect of the intratrinitarian divine life, an aspect that is overcome and resolved in the same manner that dissonance is resolved in harmony. The latter should not be impoverished in Divinity by reducing it to boring, monotonous unison. The invincible power and fullness of Divine Life are defined by this resolution of dissonance. Love in the Holy Trinity needs to love in a maximally active and exhaustive manner, in the reciprocity of a sacrifice without limit.

But love is not only sacrificial suffering, dying, self-renunciation. It is also joy, bliss, triumph. And if the first axiom of love is that there is no love without sacrifice, the second — and supreme, because final — axiom is that *there is no love without joy and bliss;* and in general there is no bliss other than love. Being tragic, love is also the overcoming of tragedy; and the *power* of love consists precisely in this overcoming. Love is a concrete antinomy: sacrifice and the finding of oneself through sacrifice. And this bliss of love in the Holy Trinity, the *comfort* of the Comforter, is the Holy Spirit. In the whole of the patristic literature only in St. Augustine do we find this schema of love: the loving one/the loved one/love itself, although he says nothing about sacrifice and comfort as the overcoming of tragedy. But he understood the Third hypostasis as hypostatic Love, and this constitutes the undying value of his trinitarian theology.

The Holy Spirit, as the *Third* hypostasis, represents the intratrinitarian completion of the sacrificial love of the Father and the Son, as the joy of this sacrifice, as its bliss, as *love triumphant.* In this lies His significance as the Comforter, not only with regard to the world but also in intratrinitarian life. If God Who is in the Holy Trinity is love, the Holy Spirit is then the Love of love. He is the hypostatic Joy of the Father in the Son and of the Son in the Father; He is Their Joy in Him Himself and His joy in Him Himself and in Them. For both the Father and the Son love not only one another with hypostatic Love, with the Holy Spirit, but They also love hypostatic Love itself, hypostatic Joy itself, the Comforter; and are comforted by Him. He is Their common love, in relation to which even the Filioque comes into play in a certain sense (but not in the Catholic

66

sense): in the sense of the love of the Father *and* of the Son, although in this "and" they do not merge to the point of indifferentiation, to the point of losing their hypostatizedness (as in the Latin schema of the Filioque), but love in conformity with their hypostatic nature.

The Father in His going out to the Son through generation acquires love in the Holy Spirit through His procession. These two moments of the dialectics of love, sacrifice and bliss, are united in the generation of the Son and the procession of the Holy Spirit, which are conjoined. The Son in His sacrificial self-humiliation also "simultaneously" receives the Holy Spirit, who proceeds upon Him from the Father and reposes upon Him, who passes "through" *(dia)* Him as the reciprocity of love, as answering love, as the ring of love. But the Holy Spirit Himself is hypostatic love. It is not only by Him and in Him that the other hypostases love, but He Himself loves. He Himself is love, comprising the whole path of love: sacrificial self-renunciation, the sacrificialness of love, and its bliss. His sacrificial self-renunciation consists in hypostatic self-annulment: unlike the Father and the Son, He Himself by His hypostasis does not reveal and is not revealed. He is only Their revelation, the Holy Spirit, who "searcheth . . . the deep things of God" (1 Cor. 2:10). The Holy Spirit announces not His own, but the Son of the Father. He is a transparent medium, imperceptible in His transparence. He does not exist *for Himself*, because He is entirely in the others, in the Father and the Son; and His own being is a nonbeing, as it were. But in this sacrificial self-dying is realized the bliss of love, the self-comforting of the Comforter, Self-joy, Self-beauty, Self-loving, the peak of love. Thus, in the Love that is the Holy Trinity the Third hypostasis is Love itself, hypostatically actualizing in itself the entire fullness of love.

And again, because of this actualization, this hypostasis is the Love of Love. Thus, the place of the Holy Spirit in the Holy Trinity is defined just as essentially and as unalterably as that of the other hypostases; and there must be no place for any uncertainty here, for any "etc." or "and so on," which we find so often in the ancient pneumatology. The Holy Spirit has a definite place in the life of the Holy Trinity as the self-revealing Spirit. We must now examine the meaning of this definition of the Holy Spirit as the *Third* hypostasis. What does this number signify here?

II. The *Taxis* or Order of the Hypostases in the Holy Trinity

Taxis, or order, in the patristic literature refers to the relationship that exists among the hypostases, in part on the basis of their "origin," and in part on the basis of their "sending" or other features. They are thus defined as First, Second, and Third. [. . .][11]

Taxis should not be interpreted from the point of view of *origination,* either in its Catholic, Filioque-related sense, or in the sense of various forms of subordinationism, Arianizing, Stoic, or Neoplatonic. *Taxis* does not abolish the equi-divinity of the hypostases; nor does it diminish their equi-divinity either with respect to the fullness of their consubstantiality or with respect to their hypostatic being. But the former, the nature, is diminished by the Catholic doctrine of the Filioque, which distinguishes the Son and the Holy Spirit with reference to the fullness of their nature; and it is also diminished by Stoic subordinationism, which distinguishes quantitatively, as it were, the degree of the fullness of Divinity in the different hypostases. A second diminution is introduced by Neoplatonizing Origenism, which, to different degrees and in different forms, infiltrates patristic theology as well as the later scholastic theology, even up to the present day. Do we not see this in different interpretations of the phrase "my Father is greater than I" (John 14:28) (in St. Basil the Great and in other supposedly anti-Arian but actually Arianizing authors)? And do we not see it in the hesitation experienced by the fourth-century doctors of the Church when it came to proclaiming the Holy Spirit God, or in a certain relative diminution of the Holy Spirit in the Filioque (which considered the Holy Spirit to be the one barren hypostasis in the Holy Trinity alongside the two fruitful hypostases)? In general, one can say that patristic and post-patristic theology could not overcome this temptation of subordinationism in connection with the trinitarian *taxis.*

Nor is it overcome by the interpretation of the *taxis* as the *order of origination* of the hypostases from one another, as from their cause, *aitia,* or as from a common source, *divinitas.* The fruitful or productive hypostases are thus superior to the barren hypostasis, which does not produce but only proceeds. In its subordinationism, the Catholic doctrine of the Filioque even has the dubious advantage of a greater consistency in this error, inasmuch as it transforms the Holy Trinity into a three-step ladder

---

11. I have omitted several pages of this excursus, in which Bulgakov summarizes a number of highly technical and complex patristic theories. — Trans.

according to origination: The Father is the cause of the Son and the initial cause of the Holy Spirit *(principium imprincipiatum);* the Son is the derivative cause *(principium principiatum)* of the Holy Spirit; whereas the Holy Spirit is not a *principium* at all.

Orthodox theology, on the other hand, is free of this consistent subordinationism, but is marked by an inconsistent subordinationism. It establishes separate subordinationist relations according to origination between the Father and the Son and between the Father and the Holy Spirit, without knowing what to do with these two dyadic relations and how to unite them in a trinitarian *taxis* of origination. Orthodox theology therefore fails to apply consistently the principle of origination and tacitly divides the *taxis* into two parts, interpreting the first part according to origination and the second according to the mutual revelation of the Son and the Holy Spirit (such, for example, is the theology of St. Athanasius the Great). In effect, Orthodox theology never figures out what to do with the *taxis* of the baptismal formula.

But both the painful success of Catholic subordinationism and the somewhat more comforting failure of Orthodox subordinationism can be explained by the fact that they both rely on an erroneous principle in interpreting the *taxis,* that is, they ground the *taxis* upon mutual *origination,* whereas there is no place for origination in the causal sense in the Holy Trinity. All the hypostases are equally eternal, equally divine, and equally important in their mutual self-definition. Therefore, there is and can be no place for *origination* in the *taxis.*

If, however, one rejects origination as the basis of the trinitarian *taxis* of the baptismal formula (Matt. 28:19), how then should one understand this *taxis?* What other feature can serve as its basis so as to overcome the apparently inevitable subordinationism that is associated with the *order* of the hypostases? And can it be overcome, and should one not in advance refrain from all attempts to overcome it? Can the *taxis* be preserved without the subordinationism, and should one not consider contradictory the very attempt to combine *order, ordo,* with the absence of all *sequence,* i.e., gradation, in this *taxis?*

This question can be answered in the affirmative only if one abandons the criterion of origination and accepts as the guiding principle the *self-revelation* of the Holy Trinity. This self-revelation is accomplished in the three interrelated hypostases. This interrelation is defined as trine: the Father is revealed in the generation of the Son and the procession of the Holy Spirit; the Son is revealed in the generation from the Father and in the reception of the Holy Spirit; the Holy Spirit is revealed in the procession from the Father and the reposing upon the Son. Generation and procession, both in the active and the passive sense, have the significance not of *origination* but of modes of *mutual revelation*. In this trine interrelation, God possesses His nature-ousia and lives by it as by Sophia, in the consubstantiality and unity of His life. This trihypostatic mode of the self-revelation of Divinity, concretely qualified for each of the hypostases, at the same time does not differentiate them with regard to equal divinity, for each of the hypostases is equally necessary in this ring of triune revelation, is — in the sense of its equal essentiality in this self-revelation — the first, and the second, and the last, irreplaceable and unique in its special mode and in all the concreteness of the triunity. The principle of trihypostatic self-revelation overcomes and abolishes all subordinationism.

What meaning can be attached, in the light of the self-revelation of the Holy Trinity, to that which in human thought is expressed as the order or *taxis* of the three hypostases? This *taxis* symbolizes the particular ontological character of this self-revelation: for the Father it is the generation of the Son, connected with the procession of the Holy Spirit; for the Son it is the generation from the Father, together with the reception of the Holy Spirit; for the Holy Spirit it is the procession from the Father and the reposing upon the Son. In these equi-eternal acts or self-definitions of the hypostases there is, of course, neither *before* nor *after* in the sense of time, just as there is neither *first* nor *non-first* in the sense of dignity or equi-divinity. Ontologically, however, there is a connectedness or mutual conditionedness here that includes an *ontological prius* and *posterius* insofar as they can be differentiated in the same concrete act. Precisely the differentiation of the Father and the Son already presupposes their connection in the Holy Spirit; and in this sense one can differentiate the self-definition of Divinity in the first, second, and third positions, those of the First, Second, and Third hypostases. We already know this order as the self-revelation of the Father in the Word, actualized, acquiring reality in the Holy Spirit; or as the self-positing of trihypostatic Love, in which there are the Loving one and the Loved one, the Loved one and the Loving one, and Love itself.

In any interpretation of the *taxis,* however, it remains that the initial hypostasis is the Father, while the Son and the Holy Spirit are the revealed hypostases, their position or participation in the revelation placing them in a mutual ontological order or interrelationship: the Son ontologically precedes the Holy Spirit, just as the Father ontologically precedes both the Son and the Holy Spirit. (This order is not absolute, however: in another sense the Holy Spirit precedes the Son on the basis of the same general concrete interrelation in the Holy Trinity.) In general one can say that the concrete interrelation of self-revelation or love presupposes a definite structure, which is precisely order or *taxis*. And one of the expressions of this *taxis* is what theology calls causality or origination, *processio;* but causality has, illegitimately, come to be accepted as the sole possible basis of the *taxis*.

It is also impossible to deny that *taxis*, which has a definite Principle, *archē*, in the First hypostasis, has a certain *axiological* significance, although it should not imply subordinationism in the ontological sense. The *taxis* differentiates the hypostases according to their place in the divine life, and in this sense it places precisely the First hypostasis, that of the Father, in a special, exclusive position in relation to the other two hypostases. The self-revelation begins from the First hypostasis, Who, in the first position, is the self-revealing God, the subject in the divine trihypostatic self-definition. This does not make the First hypostasis *aitia*, the cause; rather, it is *archē, ho Theos, autotheos,* and so on. These and similar expressions indicate its particular place.

This place and significance of the First hypostasis in the immanent Holy Trinity are, of course, defined differently, in a more differentiated way, in the economic Holy Trinity, in the temporal process. In the latter, the Principle really does acquire a meaning that approximates *aitia* (cause). The Father is the first cause in the creation of the world, and He is also the *One who sends* in the Divine Incarnation.

And so, one cannot fail to see in the Holy Trinity, not causality and a subordinationism associated with the latter, but a certain ontological *hierarchical* relation of the equi-eternal and equi-divine hypostases. This relation consists precisely in the fact that the Father is the *First* hypostasis, whereas the other two hypostases are *not the First.* One cannot go further than this in defining this hierarchism. Does it, however, contain a basis for a *hierarchical* relationship of the Second and Third hypostases as such in terms of sequence? Sufficient grounds do *not* exist for this. Hierarchically, they are united in the dyad of the two not-first hypostases, who have a joint, dyadic relation to the First hypostasis. No further differentiation is possible: they cannot be defined hierarchically as Second and Third. The Second hypostasis is not, in some lower and subordinate sense, first with respect to the Third hypostasis, just as the latter is not second with respect to the Second hypostasis. The expression "Second and Third hypostases" does not define their hierarchical relationship, which, for both of them, exists only with reference to the First hypostasis, for both of them *reveal* the latter, and it is revealed through them. But this self-revelation is accomplished in such a way that the first phase, the ontological *prius,* the generation from the Father of His Word, the content of Divine thought and life, is posited by the Second hypostasis; and only the following phase, the ontological *posterius,* belongs to the procession from the Father of the Holy Spirit as the reality of the word of the Word, the triumph of trinitarian Love. In human language there is a "divine appropriateness" (according to V. V. Bolotov's[12] expression, which is adapted from patristics) in calling the Son not the cause but the "condition" of the procession of the Holy Spirit in the capacity of an ontological *prius.* That is how it is in the immanent Trinity. In the economic Trinity this relation is much more salient: precisely the Son, together with the Father, "from the Father," sends the Holy Spirit.

The ontological relationship of the two hypostases in the self-revelation of the Father through them does not, however, establish a *hierarchical* relationship between them, although such a relationship *invariably* exists in their relation to the Father ("subordination"). Precisely this order or *taxis* of the interrelation of the Son and the Holy Spirit is not stable, but turns out to be reversible. In a certain sense, not only is the Son *prius* for the Holy Spirit, but the Holy Spirit is *prius* for the Word. This depends on the initial point of view: in the *fullness* of the divine self-revelation (in contrast to what we have, so to speak, in its eternal "genesis"), the first place belongs to the accomplishing hypostasis, the Holy Spirit, searching the depths of God, and the second place belongs to the Son. It is in this sense, precisely as the first in the *fullness* of the self-revelation of the divine Spirit, that it is called the *Holy Spirit.* It reposes upon the Son, uniting Him with the Father.

This relationship that exists in the immanent Trinity is also clearly manifested, in its own way, in the economic Trinity: The Holy Spirit initially "moved upon the face of the waters" (Gen. 1:2). And it is the Holy Spirit Who initiates the Divine Incarnation by His descent upon the Virgin Mary; and it is the Holy Spirit Who completes the work of salvation by His descent on the Pentecost, His abiding in the Church, and His accomplishment of the Kingdom of God. Although in different senses, the places of the Second and Third hypostases in the *taxis* are *reversible.* Only the place of the First hypostasis, of the Father, the Principle, has a hierar-

12. Bolotov (1853-1900) was one of the founders of the school of Church history at the St. Petersburg Theological Academy. In the present work, Bulgakov repeatedly refers to Bolotov's seminal "Theses on the Filioque" (1898). — Trans.

chical significance; whereas the "Second" and "Third" hypostases signify not order in the sense of subordination, or hierarchical succession, in which each preceding term is first and in this sense superior to the one that follows it; but only a "co-enumeration," a kind of ontological "and," which expresses a concrete unification of the hypostases. In this case, the trinitarian succession can be expressed without defining the hypostases as "second" and "third" and leaving only the *first* and the two *not-first*. We would then get the following: The First hypostasis, that of the Father, the Principle, is revealed in the *two* not-first hypostases, in the two "Comforters" (according to the expression used in the Gospel of John [14:16]: "another Comforter"), in the Son by or through the Holy Spirit, and in the Holy Spirit Who manifests the Son (again according to the Gospel of John).

The baptismal formula (Matt. 28:19), if we compare it with other Biblical expressions referring to the Holy Trinity, expresses, first of all, the trihypostatic dogma. With reference to the *taxis* this formula does not have absolute significance; it is one of its possible expressions, the most important one, but certainly not unique. In human language the idea of the Holy Trinity must inevitably be clothed in the image of some succession, or *taxis,* of the hypostases. And one specific form of succession has been expressed in the baptismal formula. It is natural that this *taxis* or order has received general acceptance, for the Gospel of Matthew attributes the baptismal formula to the Lord Jesus Christ Himself. This formula has thus received an exclusive authority and the force of law, as it were. One should remark, however, that its real content is the confession of the *trinitarian* dogma, the trinitarity of the persons of the Holy Trinity with the hierarchical *primacy* of the Father, not the affirmation of their unique succession as First, Second, and Third. (Therefore, even this position cannot legitimize the subordinationist use of the notion of *taxis.*) This accords with the fundamental patristic idea that it is a question here not of a number but of an interrelation.

CHAPTER 2

The Procession of the Holy Spirit

I. The First Doctrines of the Procession of the Holy Spirit: *dia* and *et (que)*

The problem of the procession of the Holy Spirit — from the Father alone, from the Father through the Son, or from the Father and the Son — received a completely exclusive significance in the doctrine of the Holy Spirit. This problem dominated pneumatology and at the present time almost exhausts it. In any case, this is the *sole* problem that was actually explored in pneumatology in the course of the last millennium. It is as if no other problem exists.

This is a distortion and one-sidedness of dogmatic thought. Both sides have contributed a sufficient amount of polemical passion in the centuries-old controversy; and instead of continuing it by thinking up new ways to defeat one's opponent, is it not time to return to the *starting* point, namely, to the fundamental *problematic*, in order to subject this problematic itself to a critical examination? For, aside from one or another solution of the problem, it is necessary to ask whether the latter has a right to exist in such a form, whether it might not be a *false* problem, necessarily leading to fruitless logomachy. One must pose — with all possible precision and seriousness — the following question: What are we dealing with and inquiring into, what can and should we inquire into, and what should we not inquire into in connection with the problem of the procession of the Holy Spirit? One must say in advance that this problem has received a distorted Catholic-scholastic formulation, which has been accepted tacitly by the East, starting with Photius, and that this constitutes the decisive victory, continuing to the present day, of Catholic theology over Orthodox theology — a victory more decisive than any gained on the field of patristic citations and scholastic intricacies.

The decisive battle between mono-patrism and the Filioque theory in their dialectical one-sidedness must be fought on the field of a *critique* of, and an inquiry into, the *problematic* itself. The most natural way to conduct this inquiry is by a historical analysis of the relevant doctrines in the patristic and post-patristic epochs. First of all, it must be affirmed that the problem of the *procession of the Holy Spirit* as such simply did not exist for patristic theology and was not posed by it. *Procession* itself, in contrast to generation, is viewed by the Fathers as an ineffable and unfathomable mystery, only indicated but not explained by this word. Therefore, the fact that Catholic theology lumps generation and procession together, as *duae processiones,* is, of course, an arbitrary abstraction and abuse: the two are so individual and distinct that they cannot be counted as *duae,* even if *processiones.* Therefore, the Fathers do not examine *procession* separately, but only in the light of ideas more accessible to us.

One can ask, as a preliminary question: What is the history of the insertion in the Nicaeno-Constantinopolitan Creed of the formula, "who proceedeth from the Father"? What were the direct motives behind this wise and inspired act? There is no historical answer to this question. One can say that this formula appeared spontaneously from the Gospel text (John 15:26) and occupied its proper place. In this respect, its historical origin differs radically from that of the Nicene *homoousios,* which was the result of intense dogmatic struggle and the response to a controversial question posed by heretics.

Nothing leads us to think that this was the case with "who proceedeth from the Father." In and of themselves, these words of the eighth section of the Creed (together with the following words, "who with the Father and the Son together is worshipped and glorified; who spake by the Prophets") served a specific purpose: they described a certain general idea which does not have a direct verbal expression in the Creed. This idea concerned the Divinity of the Spirit: the Holy Spirit is God, an equidivine hypostasis, "Who is the one of the Holy Trinity" (as the Sunday liturgy says). We know that this constitutes the historical deficiency of the Creed, which can and must be corrected and which, of course, is corrected by the catechism. This section of the Creed is clearly *incomplete;* and therefore the Church completes it.

The dogmatic intent of the eighth section of the Creed was to repulse the pneumatomachian doctrine of the creaturely nature of the Holy Spirit and to affirm His equi-divinity, although this intent is realized descriptively and indecisively. The goal was not to expressly establish a dogma of *the procession of the Holy Spirit* with all desirable precision and fullness. This does not, of course, diminish the dogmatic authority of the formula of the eighth section. But what is the content of this formula? This question brings us to a more general question: How was the problem of the procession of the Holy Spirit posed in this epoch and what did it mean? What was the problematic and what were its axioms?

We have already seen that the main goal of the Orthodox doctrine of the Holy Trinity was to overcome subordinationism in its different forms. In Christology, Orthodoxy fought against the Arian heresy and in pneumatology it fought against the "Macedonian" heresy, which denied the equi-divinity of the Third hypostasis and proclaimed the creatureliness of the Holy Spirit. The primary focus of the patristic thought of this epoch was on this heresy, which, not less than Arianism, was set on destroying the foundations of Orthodoxy.[1] Therefore, it is natural that one of the main arguments against subordinationism is the proof of the homoousianism of the entire Holy Trinity and of the Holy Spirit in particular; and this, in turn, naturally finds support in the procession of the Holy Spirit from the Father. Such is the most general conception of the Fathers in connection with procession. This idea is further affirmed and formulated in connection with the fundamental concept of patristic theology, that is, the *monarchy* of the Father as binding and grounding the Holy Trinity in Its triunity. As a result, the question of the procession of the Holy Spirit is, first of all, posed in the sense of His procession from the Father. In connection with this we must mention a particular feature of patristic theology: it desires to be not a dyadic theology, which divides the Holy Trinity into two dyads, but a triadic theology, which establishes concrete trinitarian interrelationships, even if on the basis of the monarchy of the Father. That is why the doctrine of the Holy Spirit is not limited to His relation to the Father, but is extended to His relation to the Son. All these motives are united and interwoven in patristic pneumatology, so that they are not always easy to distinguish. Let us now examine the teachings of individual fathers of the Church.

---

1. This fact is recognized also on the Catholic side, which tries to find the doctrine of the Filioque even among the early Eastern Fathers. We find this in particular in A. Kranich's monograph, *Der Hl. Basilius in seinen Stellung zu Filioque [St. Basil in His Relation to the Filioque]* (Braunsberg, 1882).

1. St. Athanasius of Alexandria

St. Athanasius' predecessors in the doctrine of the Holy Trinity in the West and in the East, Tertullian and Origen, base their theories on subordinationism. Therefore, it is quite natural that, in accordance with the theory of the inequality of the hypostases, their teaching also includes gradation according to origination. Only the Son originates directly from the Father; the Holy Spirit originates directly from the Son and only initially from the Father.[2] St. Athanasius wars precisely against subordinationism, and this in its most extreme form — Arianism and pneumatomachianism. For this reason alone the doctrine of the two-stage origination of the hypostases is alien to him. On the contrary, he forcefully affirms homoousianism, the consubstantiality and equisubstantiality of all three hypostases. "Just as the Son, Who is in the Father and in Whom the Father is, is not a creature but shares in the Father's essence, so the Spirit, Who is in the Son and in Whom the Son is, cannot be ranked among the creatures and separated from the Son. That would be to represent the Trinity as imperfect" (*To Serapion* 1, 21).

Having established the *consubstantiality* of all three hypostases, St. Athanasius considers one other essential problem of triadology, that of the mutual trinitarian relationship of the hypostases, and solves it by distinguishing in the Holy Trinity two dyads, that of the Father and the Son and that of the Son and the Holy Spirit, the uniting link being the Son. The Holy Spirit reveals the Son as His "image," and through this He reveals the Father. St. Athanasius thus unites the three hypostases into the triunity of the Holy Trinity. It is thus clear that the problem of the *origination* of the Holy Spirit as such remains totally *outside* the field of vision of St. Athanasius and his problematic.

2. *St. Basil the Great*

In his general theory of the Holy Trinity, St. Basil the Great seeks to establish the trinitarity of the separate hypostases, connected by the monarchy of the Father. His theory is also characterized by opposition to subordinationism, in the form of late Arianism, i.e., Eunomianism, as well as pneu-

---

2. The Catholic doctrine interprets this feature too in the sense of the later Filioque theory (see, for example, Palmieri's article *"Esprit-Saint,"* in *Dict. de Théol. Cath.,* vol. 1, cols. 774-76), thus exposing its subordinationistic character.

matomachianism (Macedonianism). He naturally encountered the problem of coordinating the three hypostases in the unity of the Holy Trinity and, in particular, of determining the place that should be assigned to the Holy Spirit in the Holy Trinity in the trinitarian interrelation connected by the monarchy of the Father. The essential passage of Epistle 38 (to his brother Gregory) begins precisely with the trinitarian interrelation: "from the Father is the Son, by Whom all things received being and with Whom the Holy Spirit always appears inseparably. One who is not illuminated by the Spirit cannot even conceive the Son."

To be sure, the trinitarian interrelation of the three hypostases, in particular the relation between the Son and the Holy Spirit, is not consistently indicated in the works of St. Basil the Great. This is used by the Filioque partisans to reinterpret various texts in their own favor without taking into account St. Basil's general doctrine or problematic, which in general did not contain the procession of the Holy Spirit in the sense of the Filioque. Thus, the statements of St. Basil that supposedly support the Filioque (if there are any; and I personally do not remark any) are interpreted in a manner that is utterly not in the spirit of St. Basil. One must say simply that, for St. Basil the Great, the problem of the procession of the Holy Spirit from the Father only, or from the Father and the Son, simply does not exist in its later sense; and statements that seem to touch upon this question therefore do not refer to it at all. St. Basil the Great is neutral in the controversy concerning the procession of the Holy Spirit. He touches upon it only within the limits of his own doctrine, which indisputably includes the monarchy of the Father as the "cause" and His union with the Spirit *through* the Son in the trihypostatic connection of the Holy Trinity.

3. St. Gregory the Theologian

Even Catholic theologians cannot find the Filioque in St. Gregory the Theologian except by drawing some suspect conclusions from his theses. His thought highlights two fundamental Cappadocian themes in triadology: the trinitarity of the equi-divine hypostases, which possess their particular hypostatic properties and are united by the unity of the divine nature; and as the coordinating principle, the monarchy of the Father (the trinitarian interrelation of the hypostases is expressed more weakly in his doctrine of the immanent Trinity, whereas in the doctrine of the economic Trinity he tends to follow St. Athanasius).

In general, it is necessary to say that, despite all the loftiness and eloquence of his theological orations, St. Gregory the Theologian does not offer any new elements of the trinitarian problematic or any new trinitarian ideas. He does not give us anything that had not already been offered by his predecessors (especially St. Athanasius) or contemporaries (St. Basil the Great and St. Gregory of Nyssa).

4. St. Gregory of Nyssa

As we already know, St. Gregory of Nyssa does not diverge from the other Cappadocians as far as the trinitarian problem is concerned. He continues the struggle against Eunomius and, in particular, against the pneumatomachianism of the latter — a struggle begun by his brother, St. Basil the Great. And St. Gregory's emphasis here is on proving the equidivinity of the Holy Spirit, which is established for him by the monarchy of the Father and by the interrelation of all three, hypostatically qualified persons of the Holy Trinity. In particular, he affirms that the Third person proceeds from the Father not directly, like the Son, but indirectly, after the Son, but he does not interpret this feature further (whereas Catholic theology interprets it, of course, as implying the Filioque).

*   *

In conclusion, we can say that, to the extent they considered the problem of the procession of the Holy Spirit, the Cappadocians expressed only one idea: the monarchy of the Father and, consequently, the procession of the Holy Spirit precisely from the Father. They never imparted to this idea, however, the exclusiveness that it acquired in the epoch of the Filioque disputes after Photius, in the sense of *ek monou tou Patros* (from the Father alone). On the contrary, for the Cappadocians the problem of procession is connected with the general problem of the trinitarian interrelation of the three hypostases. The Cappadocians never gave a precise formulation to this doctrine, but they also never divided the Holy Trinity into two dyads on the basis of origination, the dyads of the Father and the Son and the Father and the Holy Spirit. On the contrary, they understood this interrelation in a trinitarian manner. They thus expressed, albeit imprecisely, the interrelation of the Son and the Holy Spirit in such phrases as "with the Son and through the Son," "without mediation and by means of," "through the mediation of the Son," etc. And the most typical and general, although not the most exhaustive, expression of this trinitarian interrelation was the formula *dia tou Huiou* (through the Son). This formula was to receive its definitive expression in St. John of Damascus' doctrine of the procession of the Holy Spirit (from the Father through the Son).

Therefore, *dia* became a distinguishing feature of Eastern pneumatology in the fourth century; and it remains such. But the holy fathers, one might say, did not even suspect the possibility of that Filioque usage which, through forcible introjections, operated and operates on the Catholic side. In general, the early Eastern *dia* has no connection with the Catholic Filioque.

5. St. Epiphanius of Cyprus

It is necessary to acknowledge that, of the Eastern Fathers, there is none that could produce in the Filioque partisans a greater sense of triumph than St. Epiphanius. In him we find a whole series of expressions to the effect that the Holy Spirit is from the Father and the Son, out of the Father and the Son, from the Father and out of the Son, from Both, from one and the same essence of the Father and the Son, and so on. And of course, these expressions cannot be weakened by the artificial interpretations that we encounter in Orthodox apologists (e.g., Bishop Sylvester, in his *Dogmatic Theology,* 2.474ff). The external similarity between St. Epiphanius' doctrine and the later Filioque theory is so striking that some interpreters even presume a Western influence here. Such a presumption is totally superfluous, however, for in the fourth century the West did not have a Filioque doctrine in the later sense, just as the East was not opposed to the Filioque, for the problem of the Filioque had not yet been posed by the theological consciousness. The only theologian who might have been influential in this connection was St. Augustine, with his *De Trinitate;* but of course St. Epiphanius could not have been influenced by him, not only because of the distance that separated the Eastern and Western worlds, but also because this work appeared after Epiphanius' death (403).

But in general it is difficult to attribute a *doctrine* of the Holy Spirit to St. Epiphanius, for he considers this problem only in passing. The most important text in this connection is the following: "proceeding from the Father and receiving from the Son, He is not alien to the Father and the Son, but is from *(ek)* the same essence, from the same divinity, from the

Father and the Son" (*Advers. Haer.* 62, n. 4). "The Spirit is from Christ or from Both, as Christ says: He proceeds from the Father and will receive from Mine." Here an equals sign is placed, on the one hand, between the procession of the Spirit from the Father and the reception from the Son and, on the other hand, the procession from the Father and the Son, from Both, etc. This equality is typical of the general imprecision and ambiguity of St. Epiphanius' pneumatology. In actuality, the procession from the Father refers to the immanent Trinity and has an eternal character, whereas the "reception from Mine" refers to the economic Trinity, to the domain of the divine incarnation. To be sure, it is impossible to deny all connection between the immanent Trinity and the economic Trinity, but neither should one identify these relations, as St. Epiphanius does when he simply counts "from Both," from the hypostases of the Father and the Son.

The only thing one can say about St. Epiphanius' pneumatology is that he imprecisely and primitively, without any theological sophistication of the concepts, expresses the general idea of the *trinitarian* interrelation of the hypostases and, in particular, of the trinitarian self-definition of the Holy Spirit, not only with reference to the Father, through procession, but also with reference to the Son. The general intention of his pneumatology thus encompasses much more than just the problem of procession and, in particular, the doctrine of the Filioque. His intention is to unite the doctrine of the Son and the Holy Spirit, of Christ and the Paraclete, into a single trinitarian doctrine.

One can also draw from this a conclusion of a historical character, based on an observation of currents of patristic thought concerning pneumatology: The patristic teaching of the fourth century lacks that exclusivity which came to characterize Orthodox theology after Photius under the influence of repulsion from the Filioque doctrine. Although we do not find here the pure Filioque that Catholic theologians find, we also do not find that opposition to the Filioque that became something like an Orthodox or, rather, anti-Catholic dogma. For the Eastern Fathers of the fourth century, this question was still an open one, one that was not yet ripe enough to be solved; and in certain individual cases they allowed a large deviation toward the Filioque or, in any case, toward *dia tou Huiou*, with all the preliminary ambiguity of this concept. St. Epiphanius is one of the fathers who deviated the most in this direction.

6. St. Cyril of Alexandria

St. Cyril of Alexandria, even more than St. Epiphanius, can present difficulties for the polemicists with the Catholics and lend support to the Filioque partisans, for it is his wont not only to call the Holy Spirit proper, *idios,* to the Son, in all the ambiguity of this expression, but also to speak of the origination *(proeisi)* of the Holy Spirit from the Father and the Son, or even from "Both." Orthodox polemicists try to show, with little success, that St. Cyril is referring only to temporary, "economic" procession. The confusion is aggravated by the fact that there are passages in St. Cyril which speak of procession precisely from the Father. In our opinion, it is impossible to unite these texts into a harmonious whole and to extract a coherent theological theory from all of this.

All that one can say with any definiteness is that the problem of the procession of the Holy Spirit as such did not exist for him. He considered this problem only in connection with the general struggle against the pneumatomachians, who denied the Divinity of the Spirit and considered Him to be a creature, as well as in connection with his personal struggle against Nestorianism. The thesis that St. Cyril is constantly trying to prove is that the divine nature is proper to the Holy Spirit and that He is "proper" to Christ as the God-Man, and not only as a human prophet, i.e., that the Holy Spirit is proper to Christ not outwardly but inwardly. St. Cyril views pneumatology not from within pneumatology itself but from within Christology, and he touches upon the procession of the Holy Spirit only in passing, only with reference to Christology.

St. Cyril does not have a special treatise on the Holy Spirit, and even where we would expect to find one, in his works on the Holy Trinity, he does not make procession a subject of special investigation (*De Trinitate* 7). Most often, he treats it in passing, in commentaries, polemics, letters, and so on. There is, however, one fundamental theme of trinitarian theology in St. Cyril which passes through his works like a scarlet thread: the *trinitarity* of the interrelations of the hypostases of the Holy Trinity. It is in connection with this that he most often touches upon the problem of the "procession" of the Holy Spirit, or rather, the problem of His relation not only to the Father, but also to the Son. The necessity precisely of this problematic, and not some other, is connected with his Christology; and when he speaks of the Son, he often has Christ in mind. His "Nestorian" opponents, dividing the two natures of Christ with their hypostases, thereby separated Jesus from the triunity of the Holy Trinity and disincarnated, as it were, the Logos with the Holy Spirit reposing upon

Him. St. Cyril's intention was to prove that not only the Logos but precisely the Divine Christ, with "His one incarnate nature," is "the One of the Holy Trinity," having one nature and a personal connection with the Father and the Son, and in particular with the Holy Spirit, Who reposes upon Him by virtue of natural unity and hypostatic connection, and not, as was the case with the prophets, in the capacity of a foreign, heteronatural or, more precisely, supra-natural power.

Therefore, it is possible to draw one indisputable conclusion concerning St. Cyril's pneumatology: he strives to fathom the Third hypostasis not only through the First hypostasis but also through the Second, and in this sense his pneumatology is in general characterized by *dia tou Huiou*, in all the indeterminacy and ambiguity of this expression.

7. Didymus of Alexandria

In the works of his that are devoted to the trinitarian problem, Didymus, like the Cappadocians, defends, in the struggle against the Arians and the pneumatomachians, the origination of the Son as well as of the Holy Spirit from the Father, thereby affirming Their divinity and consubstantiality. Didymus does not independently consider the problem of the procession of the Holy Spirit; his main attention is directed at the relation of the hypostases of the Son and the Holy Spirit to the Father. Therefore, one would hardly expect to find anything in his writings that would suggest the Filioque.

8. St. John of Damascus

St. John of Damascus concludes the development of patristics and sums up its results. In particular, with reference to the procession of the Holy Spirit, St. John of Damascus expounds a specific doctrine of the monarchy of the Father, which he combines, however, with a doctrine of the procession of the Holy Spirit from the Father *through* the *Son, dia Huiou,* which thus is the last testament of patristic theology concerning this problem. In order to gain a better understanding of this conception, one must carefully examine the texts. The Holy Spirit, first of all, is referred to as "proceeding from the Father and reposing upon the Son" (*On the Orthodox Faith,* I and 8). As a necessary element of procession, this idea includes the reposing upon the Son. Consequently, this procession is accomplished upon the Son, not independently of Him; it is accomplished in the interrelation of the Two. Further, in the same context, one reads about the mediating function of the Son with reference to the bestowing of the Spirit upon creation (i.e., in the "economic" Trinity): "proceeding from the Father, bestowed through the Son, and (received) by all creation." There follows a series of texts which speak clearly of the supra-eternal procession: "The Father is the Engenderer of the Word and, through the Word, the Originator (Spirator) by procession of the Spirit. . . . The Holy Spirit is the power of the Father, manifesting the hidden Divinity, proceeding from the Father through the Son, as He Himself knows, but not through generation. The Father is the Source and cause, *aitia,* of the Son and the Holy Spirit. . . . The Holy Spirit is not the Son of the Father but the Spirit of the Father, as proceeding from Him, for there is no impulse, *hormē,* without the Spirit. He is also the Spirit of the Son, but not because He is from Him, but because, through Him, He proceeds from the Father, for the Father is the sole cause" (1 and 12).

As we have seen, *dia Huiou* (through the Son) in St. John of Damascus is fully compatible with the idea of the causality of the Father alone. At the same time, he does not reduce this causality exclusively to *temporal* revelation, to the sending into the world (as certain Orthodox apologists try to do). But what does he mean by *dia?* Later commentators have interpreted it in different ways: (1) as cause, where it differs from *ek* (from) only in nuance (in this case a Filioque content is introduced into John's doctrine); (2) as condition; (3) as "modifier of place and time," i.e., as a medium, although with reference to supra-eternal relations, and thus as "how," not "what"; and (4) as a mode of temporal sending.

Each of these interpretations can be justified, but none of them is indisputable. Indeed, there can be no indisputable interpretation, for St. John of Damascus does not have a definite doctrine of the procession of the Holy Spirit. True to his general task, he conscientiously reproduces the doctrine that, as we have seen, is the dominant one in Eastern theology. This doctrine combines two theological, so to speak, postulates: (1) the monarchy of the Father and (2) the *trinitarian* connection of all the hypostases. He gives the first postulate a relatively simple and clear traditional expression, whereas the second postulate is expressed symbolically, rather than theologically, in this *dia,* in the doctrine of the procession of the Holy Spirit from the Father through the Son, as well as of the union of the Father in the Son through the Holy Spirit.

This formula "through the Son," which St. John of Damascus uses as if were self-evident, does require further interpretation, in one sense or another. It can be understood only in the context of a theological doctrine, such as the Catholic Filioque, which for Catholic theologians is the only possible doctrine here, although there is no trace of this doctrine in the works of St. John of Damascus. From the Orthodox side this formula has never received a theological interpretation, and there is no eagerness to accept its authentic meaning. Adduced in its interpretation (predominantly on the Catholic side) is the idea — common to all of patristic pneumatology (starting with St. Athanasius the Great) and shared by St. John of Damascus — that the Holy Spirit is the image of the Son, just as the Son is the image of the Father. To be sure, this idea does not have any direct connection to the Filioque, or "procession" in general, and the only conclusion that immediately follows from this pertains to the *unity* of this divine image, which we in fact find in St. John of Damascus: "three persons but one image *(eikōn),* three distinguishing features but one representation *(mia ektupōsis)*" *(De Trinitate* 2). And as John says in his third oration, about icons, "we know Christ, the Son of God and God, through the Holy Spirit; and in the Son we contemplate the Father."

*   *

Thus, the development of patristic pneumatology with reference to the procession of the Holy Spirit concludes with St. John of Damascus' doctrine of the causality of the Father, who is the "cause of the being" of both the Son and of the Holy Spirit, but also with the participation, in some manner, of the Son in this procession. It is this participation that is expressed by the formula *dia tou Huiou,* in all its ambiguity. And it is remarkable that this patristic formula was included without any discussion or disputation in the solemn confession of faith sent to the Eastern patriarchs in the name of the Fathers of the Seventh Ecumenical Council. This epistle, examined at the council and having the entire authority of the latter behind it, states the following: "I believe . . . also in the Holy Spirit, Lord and Giver of life, *who proceedeth from the Father through the Son (to ek tou Patros dia tou Huiou ekporeuomenon).*" The same Fathers also confessed their faith according to the Nicaeno-Constantinopolitan Creed, as the apostolic, patristic, and orthodox faith.

The only thing that clearly follows from this is that, in the formula *dia tou Huiou,* the holy Fathers saw not an addition or an illegitimate novelty but only a certain *clarification* or unfolding of the idea of the Creed, not more. Otherwise, such a combination of things in the confession of one and the same council would be incomprehensible. Thus, the ancient

Church viewed the eighth section of the Nicaeno-Constantinopolitan Creed as still allowing and thus needing further clarification or dogmatic interpretation; and the addition, *dia tou Huiou,* was in fact such a clarification.

On the basis of this, one can establish a certain gradation or differentiation in the dogmatic definition of the procession of the Holy Spirit: if the procession from the Father, attested by Christ Himself, is a dogma obligatory for the Church, the clarifying *dia* does not possess such force of dogma, but belongs rather to the domain of theology, theological opinions, theologoumena. And lacking definitive Church approval because of its imprecision, this *dia* is not so much a dogmatic definition (which has never been accepted or even discussed by the Church) as a theological testament, which an epoch receding into history bequeathed to the pneumatology of the future. It is not a declaration but a question mark, as it were, and the question is much more replete with meaning than the preliminary answer that has been given.

And this question silently tells us that, when one discusses the problem of the procession of the Holy Spirit, it is insufficient to consider only the procession from the Father, while forgetting or not including the participation of the Son, even if in itself this *dia* remains unclear and even ambiguous. However, it signifies, in any case, that the ancient Fathers did not consider the Nicaeno-Constantinopolitan formula to be exhaustive. Therefore, the opposite opinion, which triumphed later, was, in effect, a new interpretation of *ek tou Patros* (from the Father) as *ek monou tou Patros* (from the Father alone). By the same token, it must be recognized that this interpretation does not accord with the ancient Eastern theology. On the contrary, as we have seen, the overwhelming majority of the Eastern Fathers professed (although in different expressions and with individual nuances) this *dia,* which was the dominant theologoumenon of the Eastern church in the epoch of the ecumenical councils. Although this does not legitimize the premature dogmatization of the clarifying additions to the Creed, it attests to a certain incompleteness of the dogmatic definition.

9. Western Theology: St. Augustine

Western theology, in the person of St. Augustine, takes a wholly different direction in the doctrine of the procession of the Holy Spirit compared to the East. For the latter, the dominant theme of pneumatology is the monarchy of the Father, which is only supplemented by the more or less imprecisely expressed idea of *dia tou Huiou.* By contrast, Western theology interprets the Holy Trinity as a system of inner relations, which constitute It. In pneumatology, this leads to the triumph of the principle of the Filioque. In particular, despite all the efforts of Orthodox apologists to diminish this indisputable fact, Augustine's trinitarian theology is essentially based on the Filioque principle.

The doctrine that the Holy Spirit proceeds from the Father and the Son, or from Both *(de Ambobus),* is confirmed in numerous works of St. Augustine. One can find a systematic exposition of this doctrine in his *De Trinitate,* especially in book XV. This doctrine is in conformity with the general task of Augustine's trinitarian theology, which interprets the Holy Trinity as *relations* arising in *one* nature. The starting point here is not the trinitarity of the hypostases but the unity of the nature: it is not that the three hypostases *have* one nature, but that the three hypostases *arise* in the one nature by an interrelationship. Here, we must mention another feature of Augustine's theology, which, without being stated explicitly, nevertheless permeates his entire theory: the purely Tertullianic (and in general Western) conception according to which this essence or divine nature is equated with the Father.[3] Thanks to this, the system of relations in the Holy Trinity acquires in the Father its stable center, similar, although not identical, to the Eastern principle of the monarchy of the Father. The system of Western relativism turned out to be more favorable than Eastern hypostatic trinitarianism for the posing (if not the solution) of the problem of the hypostases as trinitarian interrelations and mutual definitions. In particular, this trinitarian posing of the problem is applied by St. Augustine also to the relationship between the Father and the Holy Spirit, which he supplements and complicates by the problem of the participation of the *Son* in this procession, the problem of the Filioque.

To this general tendency to conceive the relations of the hypostases in a trinitarian manner is added a special theme in the doctrine of the Third hypostasis, which constitutes an original contribution of St. Augustine to general pneumatology. This is the doctrine of the Holy Spirit as intratrinitarian love — love between the Father and the Son. Although from this conception there do not follow any indisputable conclusions concerning the procession of the Holy Spirit, Augustine affirms that if the Holy Spirit unites by a hypostatic love the Father and the Son, then the Holy Sprit proceeds from Both.

Augustine elucidates the procession of the Holy Spirit from the Fa-

---

3. See *De Trinitate* 4.20.29; *PL* 42, col. 908.

ther and the Son from different points of view. First, he indicates that the Holy Spirit is *bestowed* not only by the Father but also by the Son, that He is Their *donum commune* (*De Trinitate* 5.14-15); and being realized in temporal sending, this property of the Holy Spirit that He is their common gift has a supra-eternal basis. This results from the fact that the Spirit is bestowed by Christ upon the apostles: "We are so taught that He proceeds from the Father. And when He had risen from the dead, and had appeared to His disciples, 'He breathed on them, and saith unto them, Receive ye the Holy Spirit' (John 20:22), so as to show that He proceeded also from Himself" (*De Trinitate* 15.26).[4]

According to Augustine, the general basis for the procession of the Holy Spirit also from the Son consists in this being given to Him by the Father: "As the Father has in Himself that the Holy Spirit should proceed from Him, so has He given to the Son that the same Holy Spirit should proceed from Him . . . if the Son has of the Father whatever He has, then certainly He has of the Father, that the Holy Spirit proceeds also from Him" (*De Trinitate* 15.26).[5] Further, in *De Trinitate* 5. 14, bearing the heading "The Father and the Son the Only Beginning (Principium) of the Holy Spirit," we read: "it must be admitted that the Father and the Son are a Beginning of the Holy Spirit, not two Beginnings; but as the Father and Son are one God, and one Creator, and one Lord relatively to the creature, so are they one Beginning relatively to the Holy Spirit."[6] One cannot say that this analogy between the relation of the trihypostatic God as the one Creator in relation to creation and the Father and Son as the one *principium* of the Holy Spirit is, in and of itself, very convincing (if only because, in the former case, we have the entire Holy Trinity in relation to creation, whereas in the latter we have only the Dyad of the Father and the Son in relation to God the Holy Spirit, i.e., these relations are, essentially, not identical and therefore do not admit explanations through one another or even only analogies between one another). There is adumbrated here the later thesis of the Catholic Filioque, but it is not developed further, in the sense of the Florence formula and future hypotheses of the same theology, which attribute the procession from Both to unity of na-

---

4. This translation is taken from *A Select Library of Nicene and Post-Nicene Fathers of the Christian Church*, vol. 3: *St. Augustine: On the Holy Trinity. Doctrinal Treatises. Moral Treatises*, ed. P. Schaff, reprint (Grand Rapids: Eerdmans, 1980), p. 95. — Trans.

5. This translation is taken from *A Select Library of Nicene and Post-Nicene Fathers*, vol. 3, p. 225. — Trans.

6. This translation is taken from *A Select Library of Nicene and Post-Nicene Fathers*, vol. 3, p. 95. — Trans.

ture, not to Their hypostatic differentiation. Augustine here does not go beyond the general formula: "God the Father alone is He from Whom the Holy Spirit principally proceeds. And therefore I have added the word principally, because we find that the Holy Spirit proceeds from the Son also. But the Father gave Him this too" (15.17).[7]

In general, it is hard to reduce Augustine's doctrine of the procession of the Holy Spirit to a totally coherent theologeme. The foundations of the future theology of the Filioque are visible even here, however, although they are still very far from having received a systematic expression. The basic idea of Augustine's pneumatology, i.e., the procession of the Holy Spirit from the Father *and* the Son, is not a random and episodic idea for him; rather, it is his central idea, which permeates his entire theology, and one cannot diminish this fact with artificial interpretations. Historically it is even more important to note that Augustine is not alone here, but is the progenitor of the *entire* Western theory of the procession of the Holy Spirit. It should also be noted that he expounds this conception not polemically but positively and with a certain naive immediacy as the only possible and self-evident doctrine of the procession of the Holy Spirit "from Both." Thus, in Augustinism we find already defined the Western type of doctrine of the procession of the Holy Spirit from the Father and the Son in contradistinction (but not yet in opposition) to the Eastern *dia Huiou*. The two theories exist simultaneously and in parallel, mutually ignorant of each other, so to speak, until the time comes for their mutual recognition, collision, competition, and, finally, rejection.[8]

To this one must add that the Augustinian theory of the Filioque was received in a natural and elemental manner in the West, without the participation of doctrinal theology, without new efforts to understand and prove this theory theologically. It was simply professed to be a self-evident theory and the only one that was possible. A whole series of Western writers, including popes who are venerated as saints by the Eastern church, confess the procession of the Holy Spirit also from the Son; and it is even more striking that there is virtually no disagreement with this theory.

The true homeland of the dogmatic doctrine of the Filioque, not

---

7. This translation is taken from *A Select Library of Nicene and Post-Nicene Fathers,* vol. 3, p. 216. — Trans.

8. H. B. Swete, *History of the Doctrine of the Procession of the Holy Spirit* (Cambridge, 1876), p. 153: "After the death of S. Augustine Western Europe appears to have generally adopted the Augustinian view of the Procession almost without being conscious of the change thus made in its theology."

only theological but also ecclesial, is the Spanish church, which in its struggle against Arianism desired to magnify and affirm the divinity of the Son by attributing to Him participation in the procession of the Holy Spirit. Isidore, the Bishop of Seville (circa 600), already decisively confesses this doctrine: "The Holy Spirit is called God because He proceeds from the Father and the Son, and therefore He is called the Spirit of both."[9] The doctrine of the Filioque also finds its way into liturgical texts and council decrees. It is here that the custom of reading the Credo at liturgy with the addition of the Filioque originated. Without going into the disputed history of individual council decrees,[10] one can in any case affirm that, at a number of local councils, confessions of faith with the Filioque were read and approved. Later, this doctrine, with the acceptance of the addition of the Filioque, was championed by Charlemagne, who at the Council of Aachen (809) not only legitimized it dogmatically but even turned to Pope Leo III for permission to include the Filioque in the Credo (although this time the request was denied). Nevertheless, in the course of the centuries, this doctrine became self-evident for the Western church prior to its incorporation in the Creed.

From the dogmatic point of view it seems important to ask whether this difference between the Eastern and Western churches was felt as such, and whether it immediately led to dogmatic disputation. It must be recalled that this difference already existed in the epoch of the ecumenical councils, but this did not prevent contact between the Western and Eastern churches, or their meeting together in the ecumenical councils. It must be noted that there were particular instances when this difference was clearly felt by the two sides; and it is interesting to see what reaction this evoked. The first such case refers to the epoch of the monothelitic disputes, when, in the West, Pope Martin summoned a Roman council in 659, which anathematized the monothelites. Although at this council the Creed was read without the Filioque, the monothelitizing circles of Constantinople learned that Martin had expounded the doctrine of the procession of the Holy Spirit from the Son as well as from the Father.

This fact is known to us from a fragment of a letter of St. Maximus Confessor addressed to Marin of Cyprus (655). Here, Maximus attempts to rehabilitate the Pope and to expound the Western doctrine in an Eastern spirit: "They cited in their justification utterances of the Latin fathers

9. *Etymologiae* 7.3; PL 82, col. 268.
10. See a review of the question in Palmieri's article "Filioque" (*Dict. de Théo. Cath.*, vol. 15, 2, cols. 230-59).

as well as of Cyril of Alexandria (in the commentary on John). By this, they revealed that they do not see the Son as the cause, *aitian*, of the Holy Spirit, for they know that the Father alone is the cause of the Son and Spirit, of the One by generation and of the Other by procession; rather, they only show that the Holy Spirit proceeds, *proienai*, through Him, indicating thus the kinship and unchangeability of the substance."[11] This adaptation of the Western theologoumenon attests that the Orthodox confessor St. Maximus did *not* acknowledge it to be a heretical divergence, capable of leading to the separation of the churches. This tolerance is apparently explained by the fact that a certain dogmatic ambiguity remained in connection with this question.

A century and a half later (809) an episode occurred that once again posed the problem of the Filioque, this time in connection with the dispute between the Frankish monks on the Mount of Olives and the Orthodox monks, with brother John of the Monastery of St. Sabba at their head.[12] The dispute was provoked by the fact that the Western monks read the Creed with the Filioque. The Western "heresy" was noticed, and the incident evoked a polemic (not preserved) between Pope Leo III (who was a partisan of the Filioque, although he was opposed to inserting it into the Creed), and the Orthodox monks along with the patriarch of Jerusalem, Thomas. Whatever the case might have been, however, it remains a fact that at the beginning of the ninth century "the Jerusalem affair did not become a pretext for breaking relations with the western church over the Filioque" (Bolotov, thesis 24). Bolotov adds (thesis 25) that, however sharp and decisive Patriarch Photius' pronouncement against the Western "heresy" might have been, he and his successors maintained contact with the Western church, without having received (and evidently not having demanded) from it an explicit conciliar renunciation of the Filioque; and therefore "it was not the question of the Filioque that caused the separation between the churches" (thesis 26).

What does this historical fact signify *dogmatically?* To be sure, the mutual tolerance of East and West, whose relations were repeatedly poisoned by rivalry and lust for power, can — with reference to a question of such major doctrinal importance — be explained neither by a spirit of conciliation nor by indifference. The reasons for this tolerance are more profound; they are dogmatic in nature. The fact of the matter is that the

11. *Epist. ad Marin, Cypr. Presb.*, PG 91, col. 136.
12. The original text of the message sent by the Frankish monks to Leo III can be found in Swete, *History of the Doctrine of the Procession of the Holy Spirit*, pp. 227-29.

definition of the doctrine of the Holy Spirit in the eighth section of the Nicaeno-Constantinopolitan Creed, which is universally accepted and has the authority of the Church behind it, is incomplete, and this is the case in different respects. We have already mentioned that a direct confession of the divinity of the Holy Spirit is absent in the Creed.

But we have the same incompleteness when it comes to the Holy Spirit's relation to the other hypostases: the eighth section contains only a definition of the relation of the Holy Spirit to the Father, namely, through procession: "who proceedeth from the Father." But it does not say anything about the relation of the Holy Spirit to the Son. And this incompleteness is essential and organic, for the general doctrine of the Holy Spirit in the Holy Trinity must contain not only a definition of the relation of the Holy Spirit to the Father but also a definition of the relation of the Holy Spirit to the Son. The Gospel text pertaining to the procession of the Holy Spirit from the Father, cited in the eighth section of the Creed, cannot therefore receive a *limiting* or even *prohibitive* interpretation in relation to later dogmatic investigation; on the contrary, it presupposes such dogmatic investigation. And although this incompleteness of the eighth section was never explicitly formulated, it was always felt and attempts were made to do something about it. The Church did not have a dogmatic definition of the Holy Spirit in His relation to the Son, however; such a definition was (and remains) a dogmatic *unknown;* and we therefore have in this domain only particular theological opinions, formulated in two theologoumena, Eastern and Western: *dia* and *que.*

It must be noted that these dogmatic seekings did not concern only the doctrine of the procession of the Holy Spirit, for the general question of the relation between the Second and Third hypostases is much broader and can also be posed in another plane (as St. Athanasius does, for example). "Procession" is only one of the possible ways of posing this general problem. But historically it transpired that this general problem of the relation of the Holy Spirit to the Son — in the East in particular and often random utterances and in the West in more insistent and dogmatic pronouncements — tended to be posed only with reference to the procession (or nonprocession) of the Holy Spirit from the Son. This exclusive posing of the problem was never subjected to critical verification and dogmatic investigation, but was accepted as self-evident — of course, by analogy with the Creed's definition concerning the procession of the Holy Spirit from the Father. But since the Church had never formulated a dogmatic definition on this point, it was natural to have a panoply of significantly divergent views or theologemes. The problem of the relation of the Holy

Spirit to the Son in the epoch of the ecumenical councils remained in the stage of theological investigation, and the existence of two types of theological opinions on this issue did not provoke a separation of the churches, or even the kind of breach that occurred because of the christological disputes. The time had not yet arrived for dogmatic definition in the domain of pneumatology; this was still a period of dogmatic seekings, which were much less intense than in the christological domain and therefore did not serve as a pretext for the separation of the churches.

This state of affairs changes, however, beginning roughly with the ninth century. The normal development of dogmatic creativity and the natural maturation of dogma are disrupted and complicated by facts of another order, which, strictly speaking, have no connection with dogmatic divergences concerning the Holy Spirit. One of these external facts is the ambition and rivalry of the Western and Eastern hierarchs, complicated by two catastrophes: first, by the conquest of Byzantium by the Crusaders, who by their violence and crimes provoked a long-lasting hostility between West and East; and second, by the fall of Byzantium and the prolonged absence of any cultural continuity in the East. The latter thus became incapable not only of conducting a spiritual polemic against the West but also of collaborating with it theologically. There was also a fact of the inner life of the Church that led to a long-lasting separation between West and East: the Roman papacy with its universalistic pretensions. As far as the doctrine of the Holy Spirit was concerned, the papacy dogmatized the Western theologoumenon, the Filioque, giving it the significance of a universally obligatory dogma and incorporating it in the Western creed (at the threshold of the second millennium). A particular opinion was thus transformed into an arbitrary affirmation, *hairesis*. The whole East, accused of heresy, was thus forced into a posture of necessary defense against dogmatic coercion. The East in turn proclaimed the rejection of the papal dogma of the Filioque as an accepted church dogma, even though this anti-Filioque dogma had not been accepted anywhere, not in the East, not in the West, and not at any ecumenical council. It has and continues to have only the status of a theological opinion, at best that of a theologoumenon. Such a state of affairs launched an unhappy and little-productive epoch in the history of the dogma of the Holy Spirit, defined by the struggle between the Western theory of the Filioque and the Eastern theory of the anti-Filioque. In terms of the history of the Eastern church, this can also be defined as Photianism and anti-Photianism. Divine Providence permitted the most delicate and mysterious problem of theology to be thrown into the abyss of struggle for power. And we still await the time when these complicating themes will lose their virulence and the questions will be posed in a substantive way.

II. The Second Epoch in the Doctrine of the Procession of the Holy Spirit. The Greco-Latin Polemic: Photian (Anti-Latin) Theology against the Latin Filioque

1. Patriarch Photius' Doctrine of the Procession of the Holy Spirit

The ninth century is the beginning of a new epoch in the doctrine of the procession of the Holy Spirit. The peaceful coexistence of two variants of the doctrine of the procession — Eastern and Western, the Greek *dia* and the Latin *que* — comes to an end, and there begins an epoch first of polemical opposition and then of dogmatic separation.

Outwardly, this epoch begins with the polemic initiated by Patriarch Photius in his encyclical of 866 to the Eastern bishops and especially in his famous treatise, *Logos peri tou Hagiou Pneumatos mustagōgias*, written around 885.[13] This treatise presents an argument in support of the anti-Latin polemic, but its dogmatic significance should not be exaggerated. Its polemical orientation makes it one-sided, more anti-Latin than Orthodox, despite the presence of strong arguments against the Filioque. The main weakness of the polemical (as opposed to positive) Eastern theology is its total acceptance of the Latin *problematic,* which, of course, is more important than the non-acceptance of the doctrine itself. In this sense, Photius is the first of the Eastern theologians who *latinized* in the doctrine of the procession of the Holy Spirit; and his treatise represents the first, bloodless victory of the Latin theology over the Eastern theology.

Photius launched the latinizing polemic against the Latin theology, and that is how it stands to the present day. This feature of Photius' theology has been remarked neither by the Latin nor by the Eastern side, however. Following Latin theology, Photius considered the problem of the procession of the Holy Spirit from the point of view of the *source of His*

13. This work was published by Cardinal Hergenroether; see *PG* 102. Hergenroether added his own *Animadversiones historicae et theologicae,* which remain the most detailed critical study of this question, although they are one-sided, to be sure. He also wrote an unsurpassed, though highly tendentious, three-volume study of Photius. Photius' treatise has been translated into Russian with the title *Discourse on the Mystery of the Holy Spirit* (*Dukhovnaya Beseda,* 1866).

origination; and he diverged from the Latin theologians only by a different interpretation of this source. As a consequence, we get the Photian *either/or* antithesis: either from the Father alone *(ek monou tou Patros)* or from both the Father and the Son. In the person of Photius, Orthodox theology accepted the former alternative as expressing the true Orthodox doctrine.

This, of course, came at the cost of distorting the Orthodox tradition. As we saw above, the holy Fathers had not posed the problem of the procession of the Holy Spirit as such — from the Father alone or from the Father and the Son. They considered this problem in a more general and complex context: either in connection with the doctrine of monarchy in the Holy Trinity or in connection with the doctrine of the interrelationship of the hypostases, particularly the Second and the Third. From this there appears the *dia* in all its ambiguity and indeterminacy, together with all the locutions akin to it: *emmesos, idios, ek Patros kai Huiou, ex amphoin,* etc. In the Latin-Greek polemic these expressions acquired a new interpretation, one that the Eastern Fathers did not give them. The sole focus here was on the relationship between *dia* and *ek,* or *que;* on whether *dia tou Huiou* was equivalent or not to *ek tou Huiou.* That was what served as the content of the dogmatic disputes of the thirteenth to fifteenth centuries.

Photius posed this problem in essentially the same way, although in a preliminary manner. It is extremely strange and astonishing that the highly learned Patriarch Photius, who of course knew the Greek Fathers better than did many of his predecessors and contemporaries, did not know that the patristic doctrine of the procession of the Holy Spirit, with its *dia* and other additional definitions, was essentially different on this point from his own. His anti-Latin *ek monou tou Patros* is the Latin Filioque with a minus sign. It is, so to speak, a non-Filioque or an anti-Filioque, whereas the patristic doctrine is neither the one nor the other, but a third thing, although the expression given to it is embryonic and frequently contradictory. For Photius, the Fathers are Photians, which they in fact were not; and for a long time this stylization was accepted as true, until a more attentive study of the patristic texts (first in the thirteenth to fifteenth centuries and then in the nineteenth century) put an end to this error. But Photius not only claimed to expound the generally accepted Eastern doctrine, but he even maintained that the Western Fathers Ambrose and Augustine shared his view. Only reluctantly did he admit the possibility that their opinions diverged from his own on this point. He also attributed views similar to his own to a number of Western popes, including Leo the Great, Vigilius, Agatho, Gregory, Zacharias, Leo III (on the basis of the latter's rejection of the addition to the Creed, even though he accepted the Western dogma),

Benedict, and John VIII ("our John"). But history attests that all these popes professed the Western doctrine of the Filioque, although they did not yet include it in their solemn confessions of faith (just as at the Seventh Ecumenical Council the general confession of the Fathers, proclaimed by the Patriarch Tarasius and including the *dia,* was accepted by both East and West, although this did not prevent them from being united in the general confession of the Nicaeno-Constantinopolitan Creed).

Photius' historical characterization of the status of the problem of the procession of the Holy Spirit in the East and in the West was erroneous and tendentious, whatever the cause of this might have been: a deficiency of historical knowledge or dogmatic bias. And this erroneous characterization served as a further temptation to impart to this dogmatic question that one-sided, purely Latin formulation that it received in the West, partly before Photius, but definitively and decisively after Photius, as anti-Photianism.

The antithesis of Latin anti-Photianism, which in the further development of scholastic theology evolved into a consistent and integral doctrine, and anti-Latin Photianism, which was received in the East as the worthy heritage and definitive generalization of patristic theology, without of course being such — this antithesis has been the sad lot of pneumatology for centuries and continues to hold sway even at the present time. It began to seem that Photianism and anti-Photianism exhausted all the possibilities of pneumatology, and the only option was to choose between them. But in reality this is not only incorrect, it is also a *fatal,* centuries-old misunderstanding, which it is time to overcome. But let us now turn to the fundamental theses of Photius' doctrine.

Together with his opponents, Photius understood the problem of the procession of the Holy Spirit exclusively as a problem of causality; and it is to this central problem that all of his arguments against the Filioque refer. We first have the problem *in abstracto* (*Logos . . .* 3): "If from one cause *(aition),* the Father, both the Son and the Spirit originate . . . and if the Son is also the one from whom the Spirit proceeds . . . then would it not be consistent to spread the fable that the Spirit is also the one from whom the Son proceeds (4)? On the other hand, if to the Son is not alien the ineffable simplicity of the Father, whereas the Spirit has two causes and originates by a double procession, does not complexity follow from this?"[14] To this is added the argument that the *personal properties* of the Father and of the Son are abrogated in the procession of the Holy Spirit

14. *PG* 102, cols. 281-83.

from Both: the distinctive property of the Father was communicated to the Son, and "the two divine hypostases merged into one Person" (9). There thus occurs "a sundering and division of the indivisible," insofar as one of the properties, the procession of the Holy Spirit, is communicated by the Father to the Son, whereas the other property, generation, is not communicated by Him to the Son (10).

Photius' principal and decisive argument against the Filioque refers to the violation of the principle of monarchy: "If two principles *(aitia)* are represented in the Holy Trinity, then where is the realm of monarchy? And if we admit these two principles in the Holy Trinity, then should we not also admit a third?" (12). This would be a "polyarchic principle" (13). "And finally, if together with the Father as the principle and cause, there is also the Son as principle and cause, how then can one avoid admitting different principles in the Trinity — one without beginning and founded upon itself and the other subordinate while also serving as a principle?" (14, cf. 42)?

This argument of two principles is, of course, the most essential one in Photius. Against this principle, Catholic theology puts forward the doctrine of *una spiratio duorum,* and distinguishes between *principium imprincipiatum* and *principium principiatum.* This dogma, scarcely an adornment of Latin theology, is also permeated with anti-Photianism. To be sure, the persuasiveness of Photius' argument depends on his understanding of procession as causal origination, a view that is fully shared by his Catholic opponents. But this argument must be verified not only against the Western Filioque but also against the Eastern *dia.*

Further, Photius presents a series of particular theses in the domain of the doctrine of the Holy Trinity. First of all, there is the argument concerning the *personal character* of the hypostasis of the Father: if the Father is the cause of those who originate from Him not with respect to nature but with respect to hypostasis (and no one has ever attributed this property to the hypostasis of the Son), then "by no means can the Son be the cause of any of the persons of the Holy Trinity" (15). If one admits that the Son is also a cause of the Spirit, it will turn out that either the Son participates in the hypostasis of the Father or He completes the person of the Father, which is acknowledged as deficient before it is thus completed (31). "The Son thus receives a Paternal portion; the dread Mystery of the Trinity is divided into a dyad" (16). In general, "the distinctive properties of the hypostases are mixed" (18); and "the hypostasis of the Father is completely dissolved in the essence" (19). The following argument concerns the essence of the entire Holy Trinity (ch. 17, 36, 64; cf. ch. 46): "All that is not common to the almighty consubstantial Trinity belongs to only one of the three: the procession of the Holy Spirit is not common to the three; thus, it belongs to one, and only one, of the three."

Further, Photius notes the consequences that can follow from the Western doctrine of the Holy Spirit Himself. First, he asks whether anything is added to the Spirit as a consequence of His procession not only from the Father but also from the Son (31), and whether the Spirit's difference from the Father is greater than the Son's (32). That is to say, the Son will be closer to the essence *(ousias)* of the Father, and therefore the Spirit will take the second place after the Son in the consubstantial kinship with the Father; we thus get a new Macedonianism (32). Further, from the participation of the Son in the procession of the Spirit, does it not follow that from the Spirit too there proceeds "something else," so that we get not three, but four or more hypostases (37-38)? And in general the Holy Spirit is diminished before the Son: "The theomachic language not only calls the Son greater than the Spirit according to hypostasis, but it even distances the Spirit from proximity to the Father" (41).

Such is the essential content of Photius' treatise. It stays within the confines of polemic and does not contain a positive doctrine of the Holy Spirit, and in particular of the relation between the Second and Third hypostases, to which so much of the patristic literature is devoted, particularly in the theology of *dia*. The problem is reduced to the causal origination of the Holy Spirit either from one hypostasis or from two hypostases; and this formal abstraction permits one to see in Photius the founder of the scholastic orientation in pneumatology, which has triumphed in the West. As the most important themes in Photius' theology, one must identify two problems: (1) the problem of monarchy or diarchy in the Holy Trinity and (2) the problem of the relation of divine hypostasis and nature to the procession of the Holy Spirit. The accusation of diarchy made by Photius against the Filioque partisans merits attention, of course, and it certainly produced alarm in their ranks, although fairness compels one to admit that this difficulty has by no means been overcome in the Eastern theology, even in St. John of Damascus. Also, the problem of unity and difference in the Holy Trinity with reference to hypostasis and nature is only outlined, not explained, by Photius.

But in any case, *habent sua fata libelli* (books have their fate), and the fate of Photius' *Mystagogy* turned out to be exceptional in the sense that the impression produced by it and the attention devoted to it do not at all correspond to the actual merits of this work, which is far from being classical in its genre, but is rather second-rate. Photius' work has been criticized in its entirety and its particulars, in its chapters and arguments, both in the Latin literature and in the Greek Uniate literature, from Patriarch John Beccus and Hugo Eterianus to Cardinal Hergenroether and the present-day Catholic theologians. This is a clear sign that the opposing sides occupy the same territory, and the principal task of modern thought should be to shift the problem to new ground, thus overcoming both Photianism and anti-Photianism, in both their Western and Eastern variants. It is a remarkable fact that the defenders of the Orthodox dogma after Photius could not make much use of his work, inasmuch as it quickly became outdated, both in its patristic and in its theological parts. The Orthodox had to confront opponents who were much better armed than Photius, and they had to find their own answers to the patristic and theological arguments of these opponents.

That is how the matter stood in the thirteenth century and later. The significance of Photius' treatise is much greater for church history than for theology, and in general this significance must be acknowledged as negative, not positive. First of all, his treatise solidified the scholastic interpretation of the problem of the interhypostatic relations in the Holy Trinity as relations of causal origination. Second and most important, in later centuries the East considered Photius to be the true enunciator of the Orthodox doctrine of the procession of the Holy Spirit from the Father *alone*, although in actuality this formula is, as we have seen, by no means proper to patristic theology.

In general, one can say that the imposing title of Photius' thoroughly rationalistic and scholastic treatise, *Mystagogia*, is totally unjustified.

2. The Latin-Greek Polemic in the Thirteenth Century in Connection with the Council of Lyons of 1274

Photius' treatise launched the wholly specific polemic between the Latins and the Eastern Latinizers on the one hand and the Latinophobes and the partisans of Photius (the Photianizers) on the other. This polemic became extremely bitter and one-sided: the whole of pneumatology was reduced to the problem of accepting or not accepting the Filioque. The authentic patristic tradition of the doctrine of the Holy Spirit was distorted by being thus narrowed; and in the works of the holy Fathers one sought only arguments for or against the Filioque. In attempting to refute Photius' *Mystagogy*, the Latins and Latinizers composed a mountain of treatises, which did not leave unanalyzed a single one of Photius' propositions, so that, at least quantitatively, these responses immeasurably exceeded Photius' small treatise.[15]

The main thrust of the polemic was directed against two of Photius' propositions: (1) that the Latin Filioque is a novelty not grounded in church tradition and (2) that it introduced two principles into the Holy Trinity and abrogated the monarchy. One must say in advance that the first problem, that of showing the erroneousness or at least the one-sidedness of Photius' patrological assertions, was solved exhaustively and incontrovertibly by his opponents. A careful study of the patristic texts showed that Photianism did not at all conform with patristic theology with reference to the problem of the procession of the Holy Spirit, or in general with reference to the problem of the place of the Holy Spirit in the Holy Trinity; and in this sense, as the Latins could justly affirm, Photianism itself is a theological novelty. The second problem, however, the dogmatic one, led Catholic theology and dogmatics astray, and the false paths that they took resulted in the dogmatic definition of the Council of Florence and all the intricate conceits of the Filioque theology. This theology, it is true, began with St. Augustine, but in Photianism it found a spiritual stimulant for itself, as it were, and became a kind of anti-Photianism. In general, the fruits of the Latin-Photian dispute contained the poison of schism for both sides; and we hope against hope that theology can finally find a way out of this impasse.

This vast polemical literature, only part of which has been published, still awaits monographic investigation, without which it cannot be amenable to exhaustive survey. Such an investigation is, of course, not part of our task, and therefore we must limit ourselves to the most general characterization of the material. In the formation of this literature one can observe two waves, corresponding to two attempts at union, both of them fruitless: the second Council of Lyons, in 1274 (the union with Emperor Michael Paleologus); and the Council of Ferrara-Florence (1438-1439). Each of these events generated an extensive literature with the exacerbation of theological passions and polemical intensity, which, though abating to some extent, has continued with interruptions even to our own day.[16]

---

15. The most exhaustive refutation of Photius is given, of course, by Hergenroether in his *Animadversiones,* which in this sense are unsurpassed, despite the fact that they are dated. Despite all the erudition displayed in them, however, they are theologically barren.

16. The best guide to this polemic is Krumbacher, *Geschichte der Byzantinischen Literatur,* second ed. (1897).

From the Latin side, the earliest polemical treatises against Photianism belong to Archbishop Anselm of Canterbury (twelfth century): *De processione Spiritus Sancti contra graecos* (PL 158); and to Hugo Eterianus: *De haeresibus quos graeci in latinos devolvunt* (PL 202). Against Photius, Anselm tries to prove that the Holy Spirit proceeds from the Father and the Son not as two principles but as one. He tries to clarify his conception by a figure, namely, that, even though God is three persons, He is one Creator in relation to creation. Likewise, Hugo Eterianus (circa 1170) attempts to show in his bulky treatise that, if the Holy Spirit proceeds from the Father and the Son, He has not two, but one *principium*.

On the Greek side, the defense of the Latin doctrine of the procession of the Holy Spirit begins in the twelfth century, with the treatise "Six Dialogues between a Greek and a Latin" by Nicetas, Archbishop of Thessaloniki, in support of the unional tendencies of Emperor Manuel I Comnenus (excerpts from these dialogues have been published in *PG* 139, cols. 169-220). After a dialogic discussion pro and contra, the author arrives at the conclusion that the Western *e filio* (from the Son) and the Eastern *di' Huiou* (through the Son) are identical, although he comes out against an addition to the Creed. This free and substantive discussion of the question shows that, at that time, Photianism had not yet become the official Orthodox doctrine, and that the question remained open for discussion, at least if the imperial court gave permission.

Opposed to this was Andronicus Camateros,[17] a high official who, commissioned by the same Emperor Manuel, wrote a "Sacred Compendium," the anti-Latin part of which contains a dialogue about the procession of the Holy Spirit, as well as a collection of patristic passages attesting against the Latin doctrine. We know this part from the refutation of John Beccus,[18] who, step by step, interprets all of these passages in his own way.

The conquest of Constantinople by the Crusaders, whose violence evoked a natural fury on the part of the Greeks, was also reflected in an anti-Latin polemical literature in the thirteenth century which has not come down to us.[19] In the second half of the thirteenth century, however, there is manifested once again a pro-Latin reaction, expressed in the literary activity of Nicephorus Blemmida: he wrote two works in defense of Latinism, although he publicly opposed the Latins. This work cites a series of patristic testimonies favorable to Latinism.

---

17. See Krumbacher, *Geschichte der Byzantinischen Literatur,* p. 90.

18. PG 141, cols. 395-612: *Adversus Andronicum Camaterum.*

19. Krumbacher, *Geschichte der Byzantinischen Literatur,* p. 93.

The most important and interesting part of the anti-Photian polemic belongs not to the West, but to the East — to the Byzantine literature of the thirteenth century, i.e., the epoch of the Second Council of Lyons. Its most important representative is, of course, the Constantinople patriarch John Beccus, distinguished both by his theological gifts and by the moral courage with which he professed his convictions. Twice, by his imprisonment and by his confinement, did he attest his fidelity to them. It is a remarkable fact of his life that he began as an *opponent* of the union with the Latins that was being prepared by the emperor of Constantinople. He was imprisoned for this, and it was precisely the question of the procession of the Holy Spirit that for him was the chief stumbling block. In prison he obtained works of the Latinizers on this question, in particular the work of Blemmida; and they made upon him an impression so great that he became as ardent a defender of the Western doctrine as previously he had been an opponent of Latinism. After the triumph of Latinism in the Lyons union (1274), Patriarch Joseph, who was hostile to the union, withdrew into a monastery; and Beccus, as a partisan of the union, ascended to the patriarchal throne in 1275. He was patriarch (with interruptions) until 1282. After the death of Emperor Michael Paleologus, the latter's son Andronicus persecuted the adherents of the union and, of course, Beccus as well. But Beccus did not change his convictions to conform to the will of the emperors like the majority of his contemporaries and, first of all, like his main antagonist, George (Gregory) of Cyprus, who later supplanted him on the patriarchal throne. Beccus was sent into exile, condemned at a council, and then sent into a new exile, where he died in confinement. Out of the darkness of this confinement there reaches us the courageous voice (in polemic and apologia) of this man of conviction, who, in intelligence and character, stood head and shoulders above his rivals and contemporaries.

The works of John Beccus are gathered in volume 142 of Migne's collection (the Greek series) and comprise sometimes short and sometimes extensive treatises devoted to the apologetics of union, with the predominant attention given to the question of the procession of the Holy Spirit. Beccus shows himself here to be a skillful polemicist and an expert in the patristic literature. In any case, with his collection of patristic opinions, he demolishes the stylized mythical conception that characterizes Photius' *Mystagogy*. And strictly speaking, it is Beccus who definitively establishes the fact of the patristic *dia*, although his own interpretation of this *dia* is excessively dependent on his adherence to the Latin theology. If one were to compare the power of Beccus' patristic argumentation with that of the Latin polemicists, his superiority is incontestable, although he employs the one-sided scholastic method that was dominant in this domain: he collects the patristic texts that support his tendency without reference to the context of the given Father's doctrine, i.e., he suffers from the patristic talmudism which leads the partisans of the Filioque to boast of having found six hundred passages in the Fathers that supported them (to be fair, the opponents of the Filioque do not lag far behind them). As a way to familiarize the reader with the existing state of affairs, however, such compendia had their significance; and one can say that Beccus reveals to his contemporaries, and of course not to them alone, the true status of the question of the Holy Spirit in the patristic literature.

Among the most interesting of his works one can name the following: (1) "On Church Peace"; (2) "On the Union and Peace of the Churches of Ancient and New Rome" (*PG* 142, cols. 16-157), where after bemoaning the long-lasting schism, Beccus considers the dogmatic obstacles to union, chiefly the dogma of the procession of the Holy Spirit, with a polemic against Photius among others; (3) "On the Procession of the Holy Spirit," an analysis of patristic doctrines and, in particular, of the question of the *deutereuein* of the Son and the *taxis* of the Holy Spirit in connection with the doctrine of *dia;* (4) a letter addressed to a deacon of Constantinople, Agallianos Alexios, (from prison) on the same theme; (5) three epistles to the archdeacon Constantine on the same theme; (6) three epistles to Theodore, Bishop of Sugdaea, also on the themes of union with Rome; (7) objections, constituting a polemical commentary, to Andronicus Camateros (cols. 396-613) concerning patristic testimonies about the procession of the Holy Spirit; (8) a refutation of Photius' *Mystagogy* (cols. 728-864), a very important treatise representing a critical commentary (abundantly used by Hergenroether in his *Animadversiones*); (9) three personal apologia (including his *Testamentum*); and finally (10) the *Epigraphae,* a systematic collection of the sayings of the holy Fathers on the question of the procession of the Holy Spirit, divided into thirteen sections (proofs of the equivalence of *dia* and *ek*).

A central place in the history of the question of the procession of the Holy Spirit can be assigned to the polemic between Beccus and Gregory of Cyprus (formerly a unionist). From both sides the polemic is conducted in an excessively virulent tone, with abundant anathemas (especially on the part of Patriarch Gregory) for a mere difference of theological opinions; but this polemic does represent a dogmatic summation of the pneumatological developments of the eleventh to thirteenth centuries. Of primary significance here is Gregory's treatise on the procession of the Holy Spirit

(*PG* 142, cols. 269-300), to which Beccus responded with his own treatise (*PG* 141, col. 896). Both treatises chiefly comprise a polemic on the subject of various patristic texts (of Cyril of Alexandria, the Areopagite, the Cappadocian Fathers, et al., without citations). This polemic cannot be expounded without a special monographic investigation, and it essentially consists of a boring, picayune, and rather fruitless logomachy. Chronologically, this polemical brawl is preceded by Gregory's "Exposition against Beccus" (*PG* 142), his "Epistle" to Emperor Andronicus Comnenus, and his "Confession of Faith" (*PG* 142, cols. 247-52). Beccus again responded (*PG* 141, cols. 864-96), also with patristic texts.[20]

Patriarch Gregory expounds the "foreign" dogma of the Latinizers as follows: "The Holy Spirit proceeds from the Son as well as from the Father, and the Son, just like the Father, is the Cause of the Holy Spirit" ("Scroll of Faith"; Russian translation published in the periodical *Khristianskoye Chtenie* [*Kh. Ch.*] [Christian Readings], vol. 1, p. 345). The Holy Spirit "has His origin from the Father and is proud of Him as the Cause of His being together with the Son" (*Kh. Ch.*, vol. 1, p. 349). With regard to "the writings of certain fathers" which state that the Holy Spirit proceeds from the Son and through the Son, Patriarch Gregory expresses his fundamental conception (which is often repeated in the Filioque polemic), namely, that these writings "manifest the Holy Spirit's shining forth and appearance therefrom [from the Son and through the Son], for it is indisputable that the Comforter eternally shines forth and is manifested through the Son like the light of the sun through a ray; and it is not at all the case that the Holy Spirit originates *(huphistatai)* through the Son and from the Son, and receives His being through Him and from Him" (cap. 3; *Kh. Ch.*, vol. 1, p. 356). "The expression 'through the Son' indicates only the origination of the Holy Spirit into eternal shining forth, not simply into being" (cap. 3; cf. cap. 9; *Kh. Ch.*, vol. 1, p. 360). It is difficult to say what the precise meaning of this "eternal shining forth" is in comparison with and in contradistinction to "procession." Gregory is seeking to formulate here a theologoumenon about the relation of the Father and the Son to the Holy Spirit, but, constrained by the schemata of causal origination, he does not find such a theologoumenon and, instead of formulating his theology in clear concepts, he seeks refuge in empty phraseology.

---

20. This entire polemic was translated into Russian by Professor I. E. Troitsky with the general title, "On the History of the Disputes Concerning the Question of the Procession of the Holy Spirit" (in *Khristianskoye Chtenie*, 1889, vols. 1-2). All the quotations in this section are taken from this translation.

John Beccus demolishes without difficulty his opponent's theory, which is based on the distinction of "origination . . . into eternal shining forth, not simply into being." "I cannot understand in what manner this subtle and wonderful theologian contrives to distinguish the origination of the Spirit through the Son into eternal shining forth from His origination simply into being. . . . What else can the origination of the Spirit through the Son into eternal shining forth be except the origination of His hypostasis from the Father through the Son?" ("Answer to the Scroll," cap. 5; *Kh. Ch.*, vol. 1, pp. 586-87). "Let it be the case, as you say, that the procession of the Spirit from the Father through the Son signifies His shining forth from the Father through the Son . . . but . . . why do you use the preposition 'through' *(dia)?* It indicates mediation. But in what sense do you understand this mediation? Do you conceive the Son here as an instrument in this shining forth, invented by you, through Him of the Spirit from the Father? Or, to avoid the blasphemy that would follow from this, would you find it necessary to consider Him the natural mediator in the case of this shining forth? If the Holy Spirit is naturally manifested through the Son, and according to you this is the same thing as His proceeding through the Son, then can it be that even after this you will resist being reconciled with those who say that the Holy Spirit proceeds from Both?" ("Answer to the Scroll," cap. 6; *Kh. Ch.*, vol. 1, pp. 587-88; cf. cap. 7; *Kh. Ch.*, vol. 1, pp. 588-89). "Therefore," concludes Beccus, "I do not see how this eternal shining forth of the Spirit through the Son is different from eternal origination . . . and in what manner can the Spirit be conceived as eternally shining forth through the Son if He will not be conceived as having origination through the Son?" ("Answer to the Scroll," cap. 9; *Kh. Ch.*, vol. 1, pp. 591, 592). In this polemic, Beccus has the upper hand.

We find that the opposite is true with regard to another problem, that of the procession of the Holy Spirit from hypostasis or essence, *logoi phuseōs* or *logōi hupostaseōs.* Gregory of Cyprus attacks his opponents for their assertion "that the one essence *(ousia)* and Divinity of the Father and the Son is the cause of the origination of the Spirit. This was never said or thought by anyone of any intelligence, for it is not the common essence and nature that is the cause of the hypostasis, since, in itself, this common essence is incapable of generating or originating indivisibles, but the essence with properties *(hē de met' idiomatōn ousia)* is" ("Exposition of Faith" 6; *Kh. Ch.*, vol. 1, p. 359).

He also attacks them because they "put forward as a dogma that the Father and the Son together, and not as two principles and two causes, are the causes of the Holy Spirit; and that the Son acts in common with the Father to the extent that this common action can be expressed by the preposition 'through' *(dia)*. And it is by the difference and strength of the prepositions that they determine the difference between the causes of the Spirit, conceiving the Father to be the cause in one manner and the Son to be the cause in another manner. They thus introduce multiple causes of the Spirit" ("Exposition of the Faith" 7; *Kh. Ch.,* vol. 1, p. 359). Finally, Gregory of Cyprus censures those of his opponents "who insist that the Father is the cause of the Holy Spirit not hypostatically but naturally, and who thus conclude that the Son too must necessarily be the cause of the Holy Spirit, for He has one nature with the Father" ("Exposition of the Faith" 8; *Kh. Ch.,* vol. 1, pp. 359-60).

Gregory returns to this question in his treatise on the procession of the Holy Spirit. He points out that "although the Spirit, considered to proceed from the essence of the Father, is considered to proceed also from the essence of the Son, nevertheless He is thereby not considered to proceed also from the hypostasis of the Son." "It would be another matter if one could unite the Son with the Father also according to hypostasis as they are united according to essence; the Holy Spirit then would also in fact proceed from the hypostasis of the Son. . . . And since, according to hypostasis alone, He [the Son] is separated from the Father . . . how does it follow that we must consider the Holy Spirit to proceed from the Son on the basis that He [the Spirit] is from the Father, and that the Father and the Son have a common essence?" (*Kh. Ch.,* vol. 2, pp. 391-93). "We consider the Father to be the principle and cause not because we recognize that the Son and the Spirit proceed from His essence, but on the contrary because He is the natural principle and cause of those who have essentially arisen from Him . . ." (*Kh. Ch.,* vol. 2, p. 294; cf. 301); "and the Son is distinguished from the Father by the fact that He is from the Cause, and on this point He is united with the Spirit, Who is also from the Cause, since He is from the Father, and He is not at all the Cause of the Spirit, and the Spirit is not from Him" (*Kh. Ch.,* vol. 2, pp. 308-9). In the final analysis, "the procession of the Holy Spirit signifies nothing else but the very mode of His origination *(tropon autou tēs huparxeōs)*" (*Apologia; Kh. Ch.,* vol. 2, p. 548).

In response to Gregory's argument that the Holy Spirit proceeds from the Father not naturally but hypostatically, and that consequently, in proceeding from the Father, He does not proceed from the Son, Beccus asserts that to theologize in this manner is to go "contrary to the tradition of the holy fathers," who admitted both of these affirmations ("Response to the Scroll," 12; *Kh. Ch.,* vol. 1, p. 596). Not responding substantively to his opponent's argument, Beccus unleashes a patristic diatribe whose general conclusion can be expressed in the following words: "the prepositions *dia* and *ek* are used as identical in meaning; and having become convinced of this, we have made peace with those who say that the Holy Spirit proceeds from the Father and the Son, with love and respect accepting His procession from the Father through the Son" (*Kh Ch.*, vol. 1, p. 585; cf. 593).[21]

What are the results of the dogmatic controversy in the thirteenth century concerning the procession of the Holy Spirit? They are negligible, if not entirely negative, for no agreement or even clarification of the problem was achieved. Rather, there was mutual embitterment; and let it be added that, often, the decisive factors here were not dogmatic arguments but career considerations, which only Beccus was free of. On the one hand, a patristic scholastics arose, which specialized in counting the various passages in the Fathers pro and contra, usually outside of their dogmatic context. True, as a result of this reexamination, significant fluctuations and distinctions were found in the nuances of thought of the Fathers, whose views had previously been interpreted in a simplistic and stylized manner (we see this in Photius). Beccus' achievements are noteworthy here, but all this did was produce a special technique of fending off texts by counter-texts, a sad art which continued to evolve with increasing sophistication but also with increasing sterility. The general question of how one should read and interpret the patristic doctrines as a whole, in their historical context, had not yet been posed.

The fundamental dogmatic importance of this polemic consists in the fact that the problem of the procession of the Holy Spirit received a definitive interpretation in the sense of *causal origination,* and the dispute concerned only whether the Son participates in the causal origination of the Holy Spirit. That which had been sketched out by Photius was here accepted by both sides as self-evident in the problematic. No one felt the need to subject this problematic to critical investigation and verification, and it was inherited in its entirety by the polemicists of the fifteenth century, as well as later. The problem of the Holy Spirit was thereby robbed of its soul and schematized to the extreme; pneumatology (as well as

21. On the contrary, Gregory says the following: "We condemn those who say that the preposition *dia* (through) is everywhere in theology equivalent to the preposition *ek* (from or out of), and who therefore insistently assert that to say that the Holy Spirit proceeds through the Son is the same as to say that the Holy Spirit proceeds from the Son" ("Exposition of the Holy Faith against Beccus," *Kh. Ch.,* vol. 1 [1889], p. 357).

triadology in general) was transformed into a sort of etiology. The two sides occupied opposite poles in this etiology, and they were totally incapable of understanding or accepting one another: Where one said "yes," the other, just as justifiably, said "no," and the only thing that was possible was to *choose* between the one assertion and the other. No life of thought, no *dialectic,* can be detected in this static opposition; and the *choice* of the one proposition or the other, associated with the condemnation and rejection of the opposite proposition, is inevitably marked by a *schismatic* spirit, which permeated this controversy from the outset; and this is true for both sides, each of which considered itself to be the defender of the truth. A schismatic spirit is, of course, what least befits pneumatology.

In the fourteenth century, into the Latin-Greek polemic concerning the procession of the Holy Spirit, there enters the productive writer St. Gregory Palamas, whose unpublished treatises[22] on this subject are known only from fragments of his works cited by writers polemicizing against him.[23] As far as one can judge on the basis of these excerpts, the treatises of Palamas do not contain any new arguments.

*   *

This whole polemic on the question of the procession of the Holy Spirit was raised in connection with the council of union, that is, the Council of Lyons of 1274, during the papacy of Gregory X (XIV according to the Western count). At the council itself, however, there were no discussions, and the Greek representatives attended only to attest their submission to Rome and to proffer the confession of faith of Emperor Michael Paleologus, which was to become the confession of the whole Greek church. Here, besides the acceptance of the primacy of the papacy, the primacy of the Roman church, and its decisive importance in the entire universal church, the council also proclaimed the doctrine of the procession of the Holy Spirit from the Father and the Son: "*Credimus et Spiritum Sanctum, plenum et perfectum verumque Deum ex Patre Filioque procedentem* [We believe also in the Holy Spirit, full, perfect, and true God, who proceeds from

---

22. Among these are (1) *Liber demonstrativus primus, quod non ex Filio, sed ex solo Patre procedit Sp-s S-s;* (2) *L. secundus ex eodem argumento;* (3) *In inscriptiones-epigraphas — I. Vecci.* Beccus' work thus found a critic only a hundred years after its appearance; and this critique was followed about a hundred years later by the anti-critique of Bessarion (*PG* 161, cols.137-244).

23. For example, the talented fourteenth-century writer Cydonius, whose work *Adversus Gregorium Palamam* (*PG* 164, cols. 837-64) influenced Bessarion.

the Father and the Son]."²⁴ In the name of the council, after it had concluded, the pope published the following dogmatic definition (canon I), in
which the Latin doctrine of the procession of the Holy Spirit receives, for
the first time, an official expression: "*Spiritus Sanctus aeternaliter ex Patre et
Filio non tanquam ex duobus principiis, sed tanquam ex uno principio, non duabus
spirationibus sed unica spiratione procedit*... [the Holy Spirit eternally proceeds
from the Father and the Son not as from two principles but as from one
principle, not by two spirations, but by one spiration]."²⁵ This is held not
only by the Roman Church, but also "by the orthodox Fathers and by both
the Latin and Greek Doctors." And therefore "*sacro approbante consilio,
damnamus et reprobamus qui negare praesumpserint, aeternaliter Spiritum Sanctum ex Patre Filioque procedere, sive etiam temerario auso asserere, quod Sp. Sanctus ex Patre et Fiilo, tanquam ex duobus principiis, et non tanquam ex uno,
procedat* [with the approval of the council we condemn those who presume
to deny that the Holy Spirit eternally proceeds from the Father and the
Son, or who have the temerity to assert that the Holy Spirit proceeds from
the Father and the Son as two principles, not as one principle]."

But this union from above, with all its dogmatic definitions, did not
withstand the first test. All it took was a change of emperors on the
throne of Byzantium, Michael Paleologus being replaced after his death
by his son Andronicus who opposed the union, for the union to disappear
without a trace. And its few sincere adherents in the hierarchy, with John
Beccus at their head, were expelled and imprisoned, whereas the insincere
ones, like George of Cyprus, rushed to attest their fidelity (now pleasing
to the powers-that-be) to Orthodoxy. Meanwhile, the masses, who had always been indifferent or hostile to the union with the Latins (after the
horrors of the Crusader violence), annulled this pseudo-ecumenical council together with the union that it had proclaimed. This attempt at union,
provoked not by religious but by utilitarian and political motives (the fear
of new Crusades), was thus doomed to failure.

3. The Latin-Greek Polemic in the Fifteenth Century and the Council of Ferrara-Florence (1438-39)

The next wave of dogmatic excitement arrives in connection with a new
attempt at union. It is initiated by the emperor John Paleologus, and is

24. Denzinger, *Enchiridion,* ed. 10, n. 463.
25. Denzinger, *Enchiridion,* ed. 10, n. 460.

connected with the hope of receiving, by means of the union, military assistance against the Turks. In contrast to the Council of Lyons, the Council of Florence featured long debates, in particular concerning the question of the procession of the Holy Spirit.[26]

These debates opened, as the Greeks wished, with a discussion of the question of the legitimacy or illegitimacy of the addition of the Filioque, "and from the Son," in the Western creed irrespective of whether it was essentially true or not. Although, to be sure, this addition revealed an illegitimate self-assertion of the West in relation to the East and constituted an autocratic imposition of power by the Roman throne (so that, more than anything else, it is essentially a question here of this imposition of power), nevertheless, for a *dogmatic* discussion of the question of the procession of the Holy Spirit, such a state of affairs must be recognized as abnormal and even unnatural. Approximately the first two months (from October to the beginning of December 1438) of council sessions in Ferrara (fifteen in all) were consumed by dogmatically fruitless debates about the addition to the Creed. The Orthodox attempted to adduce as much historical and patristic evidence as possible in support of the external inviolability of the Creed, whereas the Catholics attempted to prove that the addition was only a clarification. After the Council shifted to Florence, substantive debates about the procession of the Holy Spirit began in March 1439. On the Greek side, these debates were led by Bishop Mark of Ephesus, while on the Latin side they were led by the Dominican provincial John of Ragusa. Eight sessions were devoted to this question (from March 3 to 24); Mark was absent at the last two sessions, which allowed John to dominate them.

26. The documents concerning these debates, and in general concerning the history of the council, are not fully satisfactory. The official protocols, established by the secretaries in both Latin and Greek, have been lost. The most important source is the detailed history of the council in Greek, composed on the basis of the acts and containing excerpts from them, which is included in volume 9 of Harduini's collection and in volume 31 of Mansi (we cite from Mansi); we can only conjecture about the author. These materials are supplemented by the Latin-language materials collected by the Vatican librarian O. Giustiniani, as well as by the work of a participant of the council, the Greek, Sylvester Syropoulos: *Vera historia unionis non verae inter Graecos et Latinos, sive consilii Florentini exactissima narratio* etc. [True history of the un-true union between Greeks and Latins, or an exact account of the Florence Council] (the author's tendency is sufficiently clear from the title). Of the secondary literature, one should first of all mention Hefele, *Die Conciliengeschichte*. In Russian, there is Gorsky's *The History of the Florence Council* (Moscow, 1847), a brief and documentary, though not completely unprejudiced, account. Finally, there is Fromann, *Kritische Beiträge zur Geschichte der Florentiner Kirchenvereinigung* (Halle, 1872).

The most significant part of the debates was devoted to an examination of the patristic evidence, with each side attempting to support its thesis with relevant texts. The Catholic side used texts of St. Epiphanius (from *Ancoratus*) and St. Cyril, as well as certain passages from the works of St. Basil the Great; the Orthodox side used contrasting texts from the same Fathers as well as from St. Maximus the Confessor (for some reason texts from St. John of Damascus were not used). More than a little time and attention were expended on mutual accusations of falsification and interpolation (three sessions were consumed by a debate concerning an interpolation at the beginning of the third book of St. Basil the Great's *Against Eunomius*). The debates were far from systematic, and the application of the patristic texts was based on the established methodology of patristic scholastics, where one considered not the overall doctrine of the given Father but certain separate, and sometimes random, expressions and even slips of the tongue. It is natural that this method of what one can call the patristic talmud could never yield any positive results. Both sides came to a dead end.

In particular, texts of St. Epiphanius, St. Basil the Great (*Against Eunomius,* books 5 and 3, etc.), St. Cyril, St. Theodoret, St. Athanasius the Great, St. Gregory the Theologian, and St. Dionysius were examined as well as certain formulas of the ecumenical councils and their definitions (of the first, second, and third councils), and finally the epistle of St. Maximus. Less attention was devoted to Biblical texts (in the session of March 17, Mark of Ephesus started with a Biblical exegesis but quickly went over to patristics). There was no mention at all of Photius or of the polemical literature of the thirteenth century, although its influence can, perhaps, be felt in the ready use that was made of patristic texts by both sides. The two opponents, Mark and John, had at their disposition roughly equal resources in this essentially fruitless logomachy; although John surpassed Mark in scholastic sophistication and subtlety, this superiority was a purely formal one and did not have a decisive significance.

These debates did not have any theological content or significance. The opposing sides once again stated their opinions and mutual accusations, and departed with new misunderstandings and newly embittered. But what is most remarkable here is that, in the most essential thing, they were much closer to each other than they suspected: they shared the same point of view on the *problematic* of the procession of the Holy Spirit. Specifically, both sides understood this procession as the origination of the Holy Spirit, His *huparxis* or *to einai,* and differed only in their understanding of the sources of the origination. And both sides did not know and did not wish to know other interhypostatic relations besides origination. The whole controversy stands or falls with the validity or lack of validity of this assumption, but the two sides did not debate it. The debates never ascended to the general theme of the Holy Trinity and the intratrinitarian interrelations of the hypostases; they began with the well-trodden paths of the Filioque controversy and ended there. Their entire content is therefore reducible to the question of whether the procession of the Holy Spirit has *one cause* or a *double cause;* Mark of Ephesus sees this one cause in the hypostasis of the Father, whereas John tries to prove that the procession of the Holy Spirit from both hypostases does not shake the unity of His cause. In essence, the problem of pneumatology, impoverished and scholastically depleted to the extreme, is reduced solely to this. To be sure, this problem was never posed in this way in the patristic literature. The chief victory of the Catholics over the Orthodox in this controversy, before and now, has been won precisely in connection with this *problematic of origination.* Without noticing it, the Orthodox have accepted this problematic as the only possible one; and they view their Orthodoxy as consisting only in a specific type of doctrine of the procession of the Holy Spirit, i.e., from the Father alone. And here, Mark of Ephesus, in advance and without any struggle, laid down his arms before his foes; and at the Council of Florence the question of the procession of the Holy Spirit remained unclarified. Indeed, if anything, it was obscured even more.

We will not examine the further negotiations between the Latins and Greeks that were held not in general sessions but in private conferences, for this does not present any dogmatic interest. The Latin formula of the procession of the Holy Spirit had triumphed and was accepted by the Greeks. Or rather, it was imposed on them.

The wave of dogmatic excitement after the Council of Florence, never recognized by Byzantium, can be felt up to the very fall of the latter, and even afterward. The dogmatic polemic continues in a written manner; the chief participants are Cardinal Bessarion and Mark of Ephesus, who are now hostile opponents. The chief subject of this polemic remains the question of the procession of the Holy Spirit. This polemic has never been the subject of a special monograph,[27] and so a complete scholarly understanding of the issues involved cannot be achieved. One can state in advance, however, that this polemic does not present any independent

27. About Bessarion we have the valuable Russian-language monograph of L. Sadov, *Bessarion of Nicaea* (St. Petersburg, 1883). This work contains an account (far from exhaustive) of Bessarion's polemical theology.

dogmatic value. Bessarion is clearly more talented and more learned, and has a better literary style than his opponent, Mark of Ephesus. One cannot fail to remark the strong influence of Latin dogmatics (both sides refer to Thomas Aquinas, whose *Summa* had already been translated into Greek). Their works have been published in Migne's series (*PG* 160 and 161).

The polemic of the fifteenth century, more than that of the thirteenth century, reinforces the view that patristic texts are nearly equal to the Holy Scripture. This flagrant exaggeration is common to the two warring sides. In particular, it is shared by Bessarion, who thus encounters a peculiar difficulty: his knowledge of patristics, not only Eastern but also Western, is so profound (something one cannot say about the Eastern theologians) that he cannot fail to notice the radically different ways in which the Eastern and Western traditions view the procession of the Holy Spirit — *ek* and *dia*. At the same time, he cannot fail to acknowledge that there are not only contradictions but even divergences among the Fathers. He thus faces a peculiar apologetic problem: that of clarifying and smoothing over this difference, of eliminating it through interpretation.

The opposing side accepted this same principle of the unanimity and infallibility of the Fathers. But as the original patristic texts became better known through in-depth investigation (in this respect the thirteenth century and especially the fifteenth century had made great advances compared to the ninth century, that of Photius), it became less possible to reach any firm and indisputable conclusion. In actuality, there was no unanimity or even agreement of the Fathers concerning the procession of the Holy Spirit, for the simple reason that for most of them this problem did not exist (and certainly not in its later formulation). And if they did consider it, it was always as part of a particular dogmatic complex. We can thus affirm that *there was no unanimous and uniform harmonious patristic doctrine of the procession of the Holy Spirit.* The numerous separate formulas that existed could be interpreted in diverse ways. This long-lasting polemic turned out to be fruitless, and the polemicists found themselves at a hopeless impasse. And this duel by means of patristic texts continues to the present day and is just as hopeless. There is only one positive result: the selection, study, and comparison of the original texts have convinced us that different patristic opinions and utterances exist on this subject, and that there is no unified tradition. But in any case, *dia* has triumphed in the East (with the total absence of Photius' *ek monou*) and *ek* or *que* has triumphed in the West. But the very idea of equating patristics with the infallibility of Scripture is not only a scholastic exaggeration, but even an outright heresy.

Nevertheless, the recognition of the fundamental verbal difference between the East and the West, expressed in the formulas *ek tou Huiou* and *dia tou Huiou, Filioque* and *per filium,* raised the question of the true meaning of the two locutions. And, of course, the interpretations of Bessarion on the one hand and of Mark of Ephesus on the other turned out to be different to the point of oppositeness, with each trying to obliterate the nuances of the other. According to Mark of Ephesus, "the Son is engendered from the Father and the Spirit proceeds from Him; and the Son does not participate in the procession and the Spirit does not participate in the generation; or thanks to their common origination, *hama tou proodou,* and the one together with the other, as the fathers teach, about the Spirit it is said that He proceeds through the Son, *di' Huiou,* i.e., with the Son, *meth' Huiou,* and like the Son, but unlike Him not by the mode of generation; whereas, about the Son it is not said that He is engendered from the Spirit too, because the name of the Son is relative, *schetikon,* so that it does not seem that the Son is of the Spirit" (*PG* 160, col. 16). Thus, for Mark, *dia* equals *meta,* "through" equals "with."

In Bessarion's interpretation, the distinction between *dia* and *ek* consists in the fact that "*ek* signifies the equality of that about which we are speaking; it does not signify the order *(taxis)* of the one in relation to the other. . . . By contrast, *dia* signifies order, but in no wise equality" (*PG* 161, col. 398). That is why, in considering the equality or rather the identity of the originating power of the Father and the Son, the Fathers, both Eastern and Western, say that "the Holy Spirit proceeds from the Father *and* the Son, and that He is and originates, *einai kai proienai,* from the Father and the Son. By this, they wish to show the identity of Their power in the origination (of the Spirit), that, in one and the same process of procession, the Holy Spirit originates from Both" (col. 397; cf. 443). "Most of the Eastern fathers (like John of Damascus) focused their attention on order, whereas most of the Western fathers focused their attention on equality, but in essence they mean the same thing and do not contradict one another" (col. 400). One cannot deny the cleverness of this thesis, but it is not confirmed by an examination of patristic texts or by an analysis of instances of the use of one preposition or the other.

In any case, this controversy attests that the use of the one preposition or the other does not yet make the theology transparent or self-evident. It still requires interpretation, and the attempts at interpretation in the polemic between Mark and Bessarion would seem to merit special attention. But the dogmatic lessons of this polemic were forgotten at the Bonn Conference of Orthodox and Old Catholics.[28] This conference tried to find a formula that could be used against the Filioque in the doctrinal Catholic interpretation, clothed in all the compulsoriness of dogma, as well as against the Photian *ek monou tou Patros,* which was not acceptable for the West, for it contradicted its tradition. The way out was found in John of Damascus' *dia tou Huiou,* which was proclaimed to be identical or equivalent to the Filioque, and to express the true meaning of the latter. And so, a formula of conciliation was found. But it must not be forgotten that this formula, though with the opposite dogmatic coefficient, was the one proclaimed in Bessarion's theology and, what is more important, not only at the sessions of the Council of Florence,[29] but also in the dogmatic definition decreed by this council.

Although *dia* was used by the Fathers and, in particular, by St. John of Damascus, the last representative of the Eastern patristic tradition, it is by no means dogmatically self-evident. On the contrary, it requires a dogmatic interpretation, which it has not yet received. Therefore, the Bonn formula too lacks a definite dogmatic meaning; and one can say that it defines the unknown through the unknown. In any case, the men of the Florence period were theologically more acute and perspicacious, inasmuch as they perceived here a problem that was yet to be solved, not an imaginary certainty. Therefore, although the Bonn acceptance of John of Damascus' formula has a practical significance in that it rejected the dominant Filioque, it does *not* represent a dogmatic definition, for it is not accompanied by any theology and does not even make an attempt at theological interpretation. But at the same time it accepts without critical analysis the fundamental ideas of John of Damascus' theology concerning the single causality of the Father, i.e., the very point that needs analysis more than any other. It has significance only insofar as it excludes both the one-sided Photianism of *ek monou* and the anti-Photianism of

28. Attended by a number of German Old Catholic, Greek and Russian, and high Anglican theologians, this conference (held in 1875) attempted to settle the dispute regarding the procession of the Holy Spirit. On the basis of the teaching of the Fathers before the division of the Eastern and Western churches, the conference judged the Filioque to be an unauthorized and unjustifiable interpolation. The Bonn Conference has not, however, been sanctioned by any ecclesiastical authority. — Trans.

29. See *The History of the Florence Council* (n. 26 above), vol. 7, pp. 144-45, 147, 156. In particular, in his opinion Patriarch Joseph directly states that "through the Son means the same thing as from the Son" (p. 156), and this equality became authoritative in composing and discussing the dogmatic formula (p. 159).

the exclusive Filioque, thus making a place for the indeterminacy of *dia*. But it would be erroneous to consider this indeterminacy a dogmatic achievement.

The dogmatic polemic between the Latinizers and the adherents of the Eastern view is conducted on the ground of the Latin problematic. This fact expresses the definitive victory of the Latin theology, a victory that, to the present day, still affects the Orthodox dogmatics. Typical problems of Thomism are discussed. Thus, for example, Mark of Ephesus argues against Thomas Aquinas concerning whether the hypostases differ according to oppositeness *(schesin-antithesin)* or contradictoriness *(anti-phantikōs)*. Distinction by means of the abuse of the negation *mē* is transformed into contradiction, so that this method establishes "all the divine persons." This method also establishes the distinction between the Son and the Holy Spirit: to be the Son and not to be the Son are opposed as a contradiction.[30] Mark of Ephesus attempted to tear out of Aquinas's hands his own weapon, but in reality he only parodies Aquinas.

In turn, Bessarion attempts, in his post-Florence works, to prove the fundamental thesis of Latin theology concerning the procession of the Holy Spirit from the Father and the Son as one principle. He displays here a great literary mastery (far outshining his opponent) and a considerable knowledge of Greek patristics; but in general his thought revolves within the confines of Thomism and the Latin Filioque doctrine in general. In attempting to prove the *unity* of the principle from which the Holy Spirit proceeds, Bessarion, following the Western theologians, leaps from hypostasis to ousia, and vice versa. Here is the general scheme of his thought. Having defined the personal property of the First hypostasis as fatherhood and not as the origination of the Holy Spirit (which is only added on to this personal property), Bessarion is compelled to attribute this origination to the properties of the divine nature. But nature in the Holy Trinity is one both for the Father and for the Son. It follows that "the Holy Spirit is from the essence of the Father and the Son, and draws His principle from Their essence" (col. 369). But essence is inseparable from hypostasis, in this case from the hypostasis of the Father and the Son. Thus, he arrives at the conclusion that the Holy Spirit proceeds also from the hypostasis of the Father and the Son. But given the unity of the divine nature proper to the three hypostases, does not the Holy Spirit proceed also from Himself, inasmuch as the same one essence belongs also to Him? This problem is solved by the following argument: such a self-

30. See Marci Eugen, *Capita syllogistica, adv. Latinos* (PG 161, cap. VI, 53, 73).

procession would contradict His hypostatic property, just as engendered-ness would contradict the hypostatic property of the Father and engendering would contradict the hypostatic property of the Son. Therefore, the Holy Spirit too, to Whom procession is proper, does not engender and does not cause to proceed. Bessarion, like all of Catholic theology, hides behind the notion of "personal property" in order to avoid the consistent application of his own logical principle.

In addition, Bessarion distinguishes between the participation of the two hypostases in the origination of the Holy Spirit: the Father is the first cause, or the principle "from which" *(ex hou ē huph' hou)*, whereas the Son is the principle "through which" *(hōi)*. This is an idea proper to Latin theology, which distinguishes *principium imprincipiatum* and *principium principiatum*. The origination of the Holy Spirit from the two hypostases is explained by the participation of all three hypostases in the creation of the world, but this is not a good analogy: the world is created by the tri-une God, and each of the hypostases creates it in His own special way, in accordance with His hypostatic property. But this is the *action* of God in extra-divine, creaturely being, which is different from the eternal trihypo-static interrelation.

The question of the sending of the Holy Spirit into the world is also examined in this light. Bessarion's Orthodox opponents (and following them, theologians of the present day) attempt to reduce all the texts which attest the relation of the Second and Third hypostases solely to the actions of the "economic" Trinity in the world, separating them from Their eternal, "immanent" interrelation and thus introducing a certain trinitarian occasionalism. By contrast, in Latin theology, whose representative in this case is Bessarion, such actions are directly and invariably atttributed to relations of origination: the Son sends the Holy Spirit because the Latter originates from the Father and the Son.

*   *

Such is the dogmatic sum-total of the Florence conflict. The union proclaimed at this council was rejected in a de facto manner without further discussion (the conqueror already stood at the gates of Byzantium), and the dogmatic results of the council turned out to bear very little fruit. These results had significance only insofar as they revealed the actual status of the question of the Filioque in the East and in the West, as well as the irreconcilable disharmony of the two sides. It appears that, on both sides, *all* possible arguments pro and contra had been exhausted; and if I am not mistaken, later developments did not add and could scarcely add anything new to this disharmony, which remains unreconciled. In this one cannot fail to see one of the strangest paradoxes in the history of dogma, a hopeless dogmatic impasse in which each side, with apparent justification, considers itself right, while of course considering the other side to be wrong. In this controversy, all the paths have been taken and all the issues have been examined, but we are as far from mutual understanding as ever. Looking at this failure from outside and examining it in a formal manner, one would be compelled to say that one of the sides is in a state of heresy, and is even hardened in its heresy. In order to find a way out of this impasse, one must raise oneself above this antithesis.

The external victory was won by the West. First of all, the Western dogmatic definition was accepted, in which for the first time the fundamental propositions of Western theology were expressed with total precision and clarity. Second, the most gifted representatives of the East went over to the side of Western theology. Chief among these was Bessarion, to whom, in terms of learning, culture, and talent, belonged the first place in the Eastern delegation (and his acceptance of the Western theology was due, of course, to inner conviction, not to self-seeking; this was an indisputable victory of the West over the East). But here one must also add Isidore of Kiev, George Scholarius (although, later, he returned to the Eastern side), Mitrophanes Mammas, and others. On the side of Greek theology remained only Mark of Ephesus, who by no means represented a theological force that could rival his Western opponents, or Bessarion. The prolonged decline of Eastern theology was manifested here on the background of the intense activity of Western theology.

Third and most important, the opponents fought with unequal weapons also in the sense that the Western theologians already had a developed Filioque doctrine, whereas the Eastern theologians did not have a corresponding theory of their own, but based their doctrine on the de facto tradition. But the latter, when it was examined carefully, was by no means as unanimously accepted as supposed, and the most acute of the Eastern theologians understood that the ground was shifting beneath their feet. Theology, even if erroneous or one-sided, inevitably defeats the absence of theology, and in the dispute between East and West concerning the procession of the Holy Spirit the victory was won by theology. This victory of the theological doctrine was also accepted as a dogmatic victory, and the force of dogma was given to the doctrinal definition. Instead of uniting the Eastern and Western churches, this dogmatic definition, essentially premature and perhaps unnecessary, separated them even more. It introduced an actual *dogmatic* divergence, to which was attributed, because of the importance of the subject, a capital dogmatic significance. Those who hitherto had been schismatics, now turned out to be heretics for one another. Such are the deplorable and negative results of the Council of Florence. In order to draw a general dogmatic conclusion, it is necessary to familiarize oneself with the Florence dogma as it relates to the Western doctrine of the procession of the Holy Spirit.

4. The Western Doctrine and the Florence Dogma

As we know, differences between the West and the East concerning the doctrine of the procession of the Holy Spirit always existed in the patristic theology. But in the eleventh to fifteenth centuries, under the influence of a schismatic spirit and with the decline of ecclesial love, these differences hardened into dogmatic disagreements; and the ultimate result, a totally negative one, was the new Western dogma of the Filioque. Fortunately, the East did not establish an analogous dogma; but, as has happened repeatedly, the place of dogma was occupied by the *rejection* of the Catholic dogma, by its anti-dogma, as it were. To be sure, both the dogma and the "anti-dogma" were premature and polemical by their very essence. It is true that the dogmas of the ecumenical councils too were formed in the battle against and rejection of heresies, and in this sense the polemical spirit was not alien to them either. But there is a quantitative difference here, which becomes a qualitative one: at the ecumenical councils it was a question of expelling false teachers and rejecting obvious heresies which sought to destroy the Christian faith (Arianism, Eutychianism, Macedonianism, Monophysitism, etc., and even iconoclasm, in a certain sense), whereas here we have an unfinished theological dialectic and the different traditions of the *two parts* of the Church.

As long as there was mutual love, accompanied to be sure by a certain degree of mutual unfamiliarity, this difference was not malignant. But when love dried up and one heard the thunder of mutual anathemas, these doctrinal divergences (together with other insignificant differences) turned out to be convenient pretexts for mutual hatred. The crimes of the Crusaders in the East, which for centuries poisoned the relations between East and West, the arrogance of the West, coupled with that of the East, and finally the progressively increasing papal power with its pretensions, expressed in particular in the addition to the Creed — all this transformed the pneumatological dogma into a weapon of mutual warfare.

And the question of this dogma, apart from its direct meaning, became a means of bringing the opposing side to its knees or of asserting one's own independence. That was the case in Lyons as well as in Florence. And the dogmatic definitions concerning the procession of the Holy Spirit, which did not exist officially prior to these councils, now appeared as supposedly unional formulas, although they were actually schismatic ones. At the very origin of these formulas there was a sin against love; premature and therefore unnecessary, they were a dogmatic misfortune for the Church, which separated into two parts, East and West. And sorrowfully, these formulas became associated with the pseudo-dogma of papal primacy and infallibility. For it was primarily a question of this primacy, and one must await "a time pleasing to the Lord" when this association will finally be abrogated and the dogmatic problem, posed substantively, will be subjected to critical analysis. One can already notice signs of the coming of this time, as well as a new awakening of a substantive interest in this question, beginning with the Bonn Conference. And the inspiring words of Professor V. V. Bolotov that divergences concerning the Filioque are ceasing to be an *impedimentum dirimens* [an obstacle that divides], these words can serve as a slogan for our time.

The dogmatic definitions of the Western church concerning the procession of the Holy Spirit comprise the following theses:

(1) The procession of the Holy Spirit from the Father and the Son not as two principles, but as one principle, *unica spiratione* (the Second Council of Lyons and the Council of Florence).

(2) This procession signifies the origination of the Holy Spirit, i.e., the reception by Him of "essence and substantial being" from the Father and the Son as one principle.

(3) The Father gives everything to the Son by engendering Him except the capacity of being the Father; and consequently He gives Him the capacity to originate by procession the Holy Spirit. The difference between the Father and the Son with respect to the procession of the Holy Spirit is that between *principium* **sine** *principio* and *principium* **de** *principio* [principle without principle and principle from principle].

(4) Although the eternity of all three hypostases in God is proclaimed, the initial principle for understanding the Holy Trinity is the impersonal and, as it were, pre-hypostatic divine principle, denoted as *unus Deus, una substantia, una divinitas;* and this principle, in or by itself, grounds not only the unity of the trihypostatic God but also the very being of the hypostases (*solus Pater ex substantia sua genuit Filium*

[the unique Father from His substance engendered the Son]). In this impersonal substance, *"omnia sunt unum"* [all is one] (it is characteristic here that the very term *omnia* is in the neuter, or impersonal, form); and only the opposition of relations (according to origin) establishes the difference of the hypostases.

None of these definitions represents anything new for Latin theology. Their formulation began with Hugo Eterianus and Anselm, and their systematic development was achieved by Thomas Aquinas. But they now take on the significance of dogmatic definitions; and that which was merely doctrine now acquires the force of dogma.

Let us examine Aquinas's ideas on this subject. At the basis of his theory, we find Augustinian impersonalism, by virtue of which the hypostases appear first as relations in the initial unity of divinity and as relations of origination. According to this relativism, the Persons are relations such that fatherhood is the Father, sonhood is the Son, and procession is the Holy Spirit. Aquinas writes that "the divine Persons differ from one another only by relations. But relations cannot distinguish the Persons except to the extent they are opposite. . . . The Father has two relations, of which one refers to the Son, while the other refers to the Holy Spirit; but not being opposite, they do not establish two persons but pertain to the person of the Father alone. If in the Son and the Holy Spirit one could find only two relations, each of which refers to the Father, these relations would not be mutually opposite, nor would those two relations by which the Father refers to them be mutually opposite. From this it would follow that, just as the person of the Father is one, the persons of the Son and the Holy Spirit would be one, as having two relations, opposite to the two relations of the Father. . . . It is therefore necessary that the Son and the Holy Spirit be mutually related by opposite relations" (*Summa Theologica*, Qu. 36, a. 2). Here, with full certainty, the doctrine of the Filioque is a logical consequence postulated from the doctrine of the hypostases as relations of origination; and the source of this doctrine is not revelation but scholastic theology with its erroneous conclusions, so that one wishes to say to it: hands off!

By the same universal means, where the hypostases are considered as relations of opposition, Aquinas postulates the following theorem of the Filioque doctrine: the Holy Spirit proceeds from the Father and the Son not as two principles, but as one. "The Father and the Son are one in everything in which they are not divided by their opposed relations. Thus, since in that which is the principle of the Holy Spirit, they are not opposed relatively, it results that the Father and the Son are the one principle of the Holy Spirit" (Qu. 36, a. 4).

The impersonal relativism of this doctrine leads to the following general conclusion: "the relation *in divinis* is not an accident as it were, inherent in the subject; it is the divine essence itself and therefore substantial, *subsistens*, just as the divine essence is substantial, *subsistit*. Consequently, just as divinity is God, so divine fatherhood is God the Father, who is a divine person. *Persona igitur divina significat relationem ut subsistentem* [the divine person thus signifies relation as the substantial; the emphasis is Aquinas's]" (Qu. 29, a. 4). This conclusion signifies impersonalism: In the impersonal and pre-personal *Divinitas*, persons originate from relations in the capacity of substantial accidents, the ontological priority belonging to this *Divinitas*, whereas the persons appear in the capacity of accidents, although substantial ones. This is a radical *deformation* of the trinitarian dogma. The latter does not establish any priority for nature or hypostasis. Ontologically, both possess a primordial equi-eternity, alien to any origination of the one principle from the other given their indivisible and eternal conjugacy.

Thomas Aquinas's doctrine became the general guide for Catholic theology, both in its grounding of the Holy Trinity on two processions, of the intellect and of the will, and in its impersonalism in the doctrine of the hypostases as relations. Numerous dogmatic works of Catholic theology were to follow, but we can obviously not examine all of them. We shall instead focus on a single representative work, which is also a typically scholastic one: M. J. Scheeben's *Handbook of Catholic Dogma*.[31] Scheeben considers the hypostases to be "uniquely and essentially conditioned by the fact that they are with respect to one another in an eternal relation of origination" (p. 831); and "the plurality of persons is produced and can be produced only through the production of the others from the first" (p. 839). "Inner divine productions are true productions, and from this it follows of itself that these productions must essentially be conceived as the communication of the divine nature from one subject to another, and thus precisely as the production of other subjects. . . . This production is directed at communicating the perfection of the producing subject to the other subject and at the possession of the latter; and since this production emplaces in the product *all* perfection, its own essence and nature, its products must truly be the recipients, bearers, and possessors of the di-

---

31. M. J. Scheeben, *Handbuch der katolischen Dogmatik* (Freiburg im Breisgau, 1878; repr. 1925).

vine nature and essence, or divine hypostases and persons" (p. 855). Such is Scheeben's understanding of the Holy Trinity as productions of producing nature. This easily accommodates the production of the Third hypostasis. Thus, triadology, like pneumatology, takes on the character of a doctrine of *origination or production*.

Turning now to a critique of the Filioque theology, we cannot fail, first of all, to be struck by the fact that it has resurrected Tertullian's triadology, although in a concealed form. True, it is not directly affirmed here that the Father is greater than the Son, Who, as *derivatio* or *partitio*, is only part of Divinity; or that the Son is greater than the Holy Spirit for the same reason. The principle of the origination of the hypostases from one another leads here, however, to quantitative subordinationism. But an analogous principle is concealed in the Filioque doctrine. Let us look at this doctrine's scheme of hypostatic "productions": the Father, in producing the Son, communicates to Him the fullness of the divine nature, together with the capacity to originate through procession the Spirit, although without the capacity to generate, for this capacity does not conform with His personal property; the Father and the Son communicate to the Holy Spirit the same fullness of the divine nature, but without the capacity to generate or to originate through procession, for this capacity does not conform with His personal nature. As a result of such *derivatio*, we get a hypostatically decreasing progression of Divinity: the Father = the fullness of the nature, Deitas; the Son = Deitas minus the power to generate; the Holy Spirit = Deitas minus the power to generate and the power to originate by procession. Although these differences are motivated by hypostatic properties, this does not change the fact that the hypostases are unequal, i.e., not equally divine. And this affirms not only hierarchical but also ontological subordinationism, thus distorting the trinitarian dogma. This subordinationism is expressed in the Filioque doctrine, which states that, although both the Father and the Son constitute the principle of the Holy Spirit, they do so in different senses: the Father is the principle without beginning, *principium imprincipiatum*, whereas the Son is the principle that has a beginning, *principium principiatum*. This distinction, which serves as a defensive weapon in the hands of Catholic polemicists, can mean only one thing: hypostatic subordinationism of the ontological type, grounded upon the conceptions of Tertullian and Origen.

It is also necessary to note that, in the construction of the Filioque dogma, the triunity of the Holy Trinity is destroyed, and the Holy Trinity is sundered into two dyads. This is precisely what the Catholic side accused the Photian doctrine of, and not unjustifiably, at least with regard to the extreme applications of the principle of *ek monou,* inasmuch as the latter excludes the trinitarian interrelation of the hypostases: The Trinity consists here of two Dyads: Father-Son and Father–Holy Spirit. We get an angle, not a triangle:

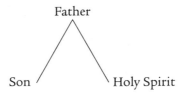

not

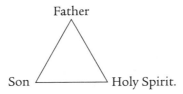

Monou here is the elimination of the line Son — Holy Spirit. The Catholic sundering of the Holy Trinity is of another kind, however: here we have, first of all, the Father-Son Dyad and, second, the Father-and-Son — Holy Spirit Dyad. How these dyads are linked into a triunity has never been shown and, I think, never can be shown. The position of the Filioque theology is made even more difficult by the fact that, according to it, the hypostases are determined for one another by the relation of origination according to opposition. The Holy Spirit must, it is ceaselessly repeated, originate from the Son in order to be distinguished from Him and to exist for Him as a hypostasis. But what do we in fact see? We see that this postulate is not realized in the Filioque dogma. If the Holy Spirit originates from the Father and the Son, and not in Their hypostatic difference as Two but in Their unity, *una spiratione,* then the required opposition of origination arises not between the Father and the Holy Spirit, or between the Son and the Holy Spirit, but between the Father-Son bi-unity and the Holy Spirit. From this it must be concluded that the Holy Spirit does not exist as a hypostasis either for the Father or for the Son. This is the absurd conclusion we are brought to by the doctrine of hypostatic originations according to opposition, at least in its Filioque application. The Holy Trinity is divided into two dyads: the Father-Son dyad and the Father-and-Son — Holy Spirit dyad.

This brings us to the very heart of the Filioque dogma: the Holy Spirit proceeds from the Father and the Son not as from two causes, but as from one cause: *unus spirator, una spiratione.* This postulate can be realized only by a conceptual device which (with reference to Bessarion) we can define as a "leaping" from hypostasis to nature and vice versa. In reality, that unity which is sought for the Father and the Son in the unity of origination by procession *(spiratione)* is nothing else but the divine *nature,* one and identical in the trinitarian Divinity. But, first of all, how can the nature, which is submerged in its own depths, extrahypostatically (so to speak) "produce" a hypostasis if hypostatic being is transcendent for it? Here we find a particularly pronounced manifestation of the impersonalism of Catholic triadology, where the nature is the first principle of the Holy Trinity, and the hypostases arise in it and through it by means of differentiation. On the other hand, if from the surface, where the hypostatic differences between the Father and the Son exist, one submerges oneself into the depths of pre-hypostatic or sub-hypostatic nature,[32] how then can one distinguish there the two different hypostases of the Father and the Son, and confess the procession of the Holy Spirit from Their bi-unity? Is there not imposed upon us the analogous and parallel conclusion that the Son is generated — in the divine nature — from the Father and the Holy Spirit by *one generation,* not in that in which They differ but in that in which They are identical?

The logical chain of conclusions is broken off at the point of this leaping from the hypostases to the nature: From the unity of the nature one cannot see the hypostases; and it is absolutely impossible, taking refuge in hypostatic nondifferentiation, to declare triumphantly that the bi-unity of the hypostases is thereby proved. Such an assertion is logically arbitrary. To this one should of course add that not only is it impossible to separate the hypostases from the nature in reality, but it is also impossible to separate them logically from the nature, just as it is impossible to separate the nature from the hypostases. The argument of the unity of the nature as hypostatic nondifferentiation could be used (of course, without any positive result) in all three ways: it could be used to prove the origination of the Father from the Son and the Spirit, the origination of the Son from the Father and the Spirit, and the origination of the Spirit from the Father and the Son. But, in essence, none of this can be proved, because there does not exist any nonhypostatic nature in which the difference be-

---

32. The possibility of such a submergence is, of course, in fact excluded by the inseparability and ontological identity of nature and hypostasis.

tween the hypostases would be abolished. The nature, truly, is one and identical in the consubstantiality of the three hypostases, but it is also thoroughly hypostatized, Trinity in unity or unity in Trinity, by the *one* trihypostatic subject, by the three persons of the Holy Trinity. That is why the Filioque postulate, the postulate of *from the Father and the Son as one principle* in Their hypostatic nondifferentiation, contradicts the very essence of the trinitarian dogma.

The fundamental defect of the whole of the Catholic triadology, and of the Filioque doctrine in particular, is that it considers the hypostases as relations, and in particular relations of origination by opposition. This impersonalistic doctrine affirms that the hypostases originate thanks to differences in one Divinity, which in turn have their basis in relations of opposition: *in divinis omnia sunt unum* [in divinity all is one] where *relationis oppositio* is absent. The hypostases themselves *are* relations: the Father is fatherhood; the Son is sonhood; the Holy Spirit is procession. This assertion is a theological absurdity, exposing this impersonalism. In itself, a relation is a predicate, not a subject; and it cannot become a subject. A relation arises and exists only where the things that are related exist; it is grounded by them and arises between them. It does not ground them. The concocted Filioque argument that the Holy Spirit must necessarily proceed from the Father and the Son in order to exist for the Son, differing from Him by a relation according to opposition, abolishes the very existence of hypostasis as such. The argument in support of the Filioque based on the necessity of the hypostatic differentiation of the Son from the Spirit is erroneous.

This brings us to the final generalization of the Filioque theology, to the doctrine of hypostatic processions or productions, which lies at the basis of this theology and to which the Catholic triadology can be reduced. This doctrine has also infected the Eastern theology, so that the argument now is not about the substance of these productions but only about their interpretation. But this doctrine of the hypostases as productions and of the Holy Trinity as a system of productions or originations is arbitrary and, in the final analysis, erroneous.

The fact of the matter is that the hypostases, supra-eternal and equieternal, do not have any *origin*. For their being they do not need relations of origination, and in particular those according to opposition. They are subjects of relations, as related to one another, but they are in no wise these relations themselves. The being of the hypostases — in the ontological sense — is immanent to the nature, inasmuch as the spirit is hypostatic nature, the indissoluble, ontological unity of nature and hypostasis. In the absolute subject, without relation to nature, hypostasis as personal consciousness of self is trinitarian or trihypostatic. The trihypostatic subject is *one*, but it is also *three* persons in *hypostatic* (and not only natural) interrelation.[33] In this sense, all three hypostases are equally without beginning, and in this equi-beginningless being of theirs, they do not know origination from one another; they exist supra-eternally. And in this sense the theology of hypostatic originations or productions is defective and erroneous, both in part and in whole. The Filioque doctrine, which is entirely a theology of originations, must be rejected as such. The dogmatic hypnosis of this dogmatic prejudice, which has lasted for a millennium and half, must be dispelled, both in the Western theology, which is the source of the infection, and in the Eastern theology, which has been infected.

On what authority do the Western theologians speak of *duae processiones* or *productiones*, arbitrarily generalizing under this name the generation of the Son and the procession of the Holy Spirit? And, first of all, who told them that these concretely hypostatic relations can be understood and generalized as originations or productions, as if they were two forms of causal dependence? Neither generation nor procession is origination, for the latter is not known by the equi-eternal, equi-divine, co-beginningless hypostases. And there are no grounds at all to *count* generation and procession as *two* originations or productions, and then to abstract them into "relations of origination by opposition." Finally, one must proclaim in a loud voice that fatherhood, sonhood, and procession are not modes of origination. In general, they refer not to origination but to the concrete interrelations of the equi-eternal hypostases. This deceptive mirage of theology generated and continues to generate its illusions, and the first of these is a false problematic: imaginary equations with solutions through imaginary roots. The whole of the Filioque theology is such a mirage, as is the whole of the anti-Filioque theology, which is much closer to the former in substance, in its initial premises and its problematic, than it differs from it in its solutions.

The understanding of the Holy Trinity as a system of originations or productions results in its sundering into dyadic interrelations and the abolition of the fundamental principle of trinitarity: the hypostasis of the Father is defined only in relation to the generation of the Son, and vice versa; the hypostasis of the Holy Spirit is defined only in relation to the Father from Whom It proceeds (and by the Catholics, in relation to the Son as well). But the Father is the Father not only as the Engenderer of

33. See my work "Chapters on Trinity": the deduction of the absolute subject.

the Son but also as the Spirator of the Spirit ("who proceedeth from the Father," as the Nicaeno-Constantinopolitan Creed says); and the Son is the Son not only as the Engendered One, but also as the recipient of the reposing of the Holy Spirit; and the Holy Spirit is the Spirit not only as proceeding from the Father, but also as reposing upon the Son. Each hypostasis establishes for itself not only a double relation to each of the other hypostases but also a trinitarian one; and these relations are in no wise relations according to "origination" or opposition. The principle of production or origination must, in general, be eliminated from the doctrine of the Holy Trinity.

5. General Conclusions Pertaining to dia tou Huiou and Filioque

From the point of view of positive dogmatics, this millennium-and-a-half logomachy pertaining to the procession of the Holy Spirit was totally fruitless. Despite immense efforts of thought, the problem of the procession remained in a nebulous dogmatic state, and the efforts of scholastic theology as well as the inquiries of patristics and exegetics produced nothing. New patterns were woven and mountains of diverse texts grew, but the only result was that each side, clenching its teeth in an exertion of the will and of course in good faith, would not abandon its point of view, while, at the same time, being powerless to convince its opponent. Efforts to defeat one's opponent not by the power of conviction but by forcing him to submit to tradition also did not, and could not, lead to anything, for the patristic sources are not inexhaustible. On the contrary, they have already been exhausted, but without yielding the expected answer in the sense of a clear, uniform, and indisputable solution of the problem. And the problem remains in a hopeless state of "suspended animation."

The practical results of the Filioque dispute are also totally negative. The dogmatic question became a weapon of domination and self-defense. This started with Photius, with his first pneumatological treatise. And it continued on the part of powerful and proud Rome; and at both councils of union, Lyons and Florence, the Filioque became a symbol of papal absolutism or of the rejection of the latter (which is why the question of the insertion of the Filioque in the Creed became, in Florence, more important for the Greeks than the very content of the dogma). Even if other dogmatic divergences had been contaminated with the lust for domination and schismatic tendencies, they were never identified to the same degree with questions of dogma. But this primacy of schismatism in such a dogmatic question as that of the Holy Spirit condemns this dogmatic controversy to sterility, for where there is no will to union but there is instead a will to make others submit, the heart can never be filled with "it seemed good to the Holy Spirit, and to us" (Acts 15:28). There is nothing in the history of dogma that contradicts this scriptural text more than these disputes about the Spirit. But if six to seven centuries ago these disputes and divergences excited a logomachy akin to athletic strife and a mutual embitterment in the struggle for power, at the present time the ashes of indifference cover the coals of the once-raging fire; and although the old accusations of heresy are still heard, the two sides do not really believe them any more. And the judgment of the dispassionate Russian historian V. V. Bolotov, whose voice can be considered the testimony of conscience, both scholarly and dogmatic, has already been rendered: the Filioque does not constitute an *impedimentum dirimens* [an obstacle that divides] for the re-unification of the divided church.

It is remarkable that this Filioque dispute killed all interest in the theology of the Holy Spirit. We have already observed that, in the epoch of the ecumenical councils, which concerned themselves with questions of Christology, the dogma of the Holy Spirit was totally undeveloped and even remained outside the scope of consideration. The definition of the eighth article of the Nicaeno-Constantinopolitan Creed contains no more than a recognition of the divinity of the Third hypostasis and of His equi-divinity with respect to the two other hypostases (and, as we have seen, the formula here is an indirect one). This definition can in no wise be considered an *exhaustive* dogma of the Holy Spirit. But it remains in this form during the entire following epoch, so that the Filioque disputes turn out to be an obstacle to true pneumatology, for they lack spirit. Waged in the icy emptiness of scholastic abstraction, these disputes were never extended or generalized in the direction of true, substantive pneumatology. To be sure, they often included such vital questions as the sending of the Holy Spirit into the world, from the Father and the Son, or from the Father through the Son, but these questions were examined not in and of themselves but only as *arguments* in favor of one or another scheme of the procession of the Holy Spirit, that is, they were treated in such a meager, one-sided, and distorted manner that it would be better if they had not been treated at all. (Of course, this did not prevent the development, past and present, of particular doctrines of grace, of the action of the Holy Spirit in the Church, of salvation, of the Church, and so on, but this development was invariably oriented toward particular questions of dogmatics, and was not connected with a general doctrine of the Holy Spirit.)

To this one must add the following. Each side in this dogmatic dispute attacked and anathematized the other for distorting the most important dogma concerning the Holy Spirit. Therefore, it would have been natural to expect that the existence of such a grave heresy, of such a fundamental dogmatic divergence, would permeate the entire life of the two churches and their entire doctrine. Over the course of many years, I have sought traces of this influence, and I have attempted to comprehend the *life*-significance of this divergence and to find out *where* and *in what* it is manifested *in practice*. And I must admit that I have not been able to find this practical life-significance; and, more than that, I deny that there is any such significance.

Evidence for the practical significance of this divergence cannot be found anywhere in the patristic teachings regarding the actions of the Holy Spirit in the world, the "sending down" of the Holy Spirit, the gifts of the Holy Spirit, the sacraments, grace, etc. It is as if the initial dogmatic divergence is simply forgotten. One could say that the Fathers adhere not to a dogmatic but to a practical Filioque doctrine, in the sense that no one disputes or can dogmatically dispute the "sending down" from the Father of the Holy Spirit through the Son or by the Son. Christ Himself attests to this, and He even does so in the most fundamental of all texts: "But when the Comforter is come, whom I will send you from the Father, even the Spirit of truth, which proceedeth from the Father, he shall testify of me" (John 15:26; for other texts, see below).

What we get is a strange dogma, one without dogmatic power. Of course, in the West (not only in Catholic circles but also among Protestants and Anglicans, who, despite the Reformation, have inherited the Filioque dogma from Catholicism), there exists the conviction that the denial of the Filioque diminishes the Son, whereas its acceptance magnifies Him. Historically, this is an echo of the battle against Arianism in Spain and Germany, one of the indirect consequences of which was the acceptance there of the Filioque as an additional argument in support of the equi-divinity of the Son. But this argument too represents, indubitably, a dogmatic misunderstanding: in order to refute Arianism and to recognize the equi-divinity and consubstantiality of the Son with respect to the Father, one has absolutely no need of the Filioque. The Filioque partisans themselves can and must now acknowledge this, for the source of the Filioque for them is not in Christology.

To be sure, one can find a religio-psychological and, further, a dogmatic source of the Filioque doctrine also in that special feature of Western Christianity which we can call its *christocentrism*. This feature of Western Christianity, not only its special gift, but also its one-sidedness, provides the religio-psychological basis for the possibility of the dogma of the pope as the vicar of Christ, with the idea of the Church clearly centered here on the Second hypostasis (and this is equally, or perhaps even more so, the case in Protestantism). This leads to a loss of dogmatic and practical equilibrium in the understanding of the Second and the Third hypostases, an equilibrium which precisely constitutes the essence of the dogma of the Church: the Church is the Body of Christ, living by the Holy Spirit. But this ecclesiological feature, which perhaps is the de facto source of the Filioque, is not identical with the Filioque dogma itself as such. In its ultimate and authentic meaning, the Filioque dogma — we affirm this one more time — remains outside of life and scholastically abstract; and in this practical sense it is, as it were, not a dogma at all, for dogmas have not only cognitive but also practical significance.

But another question arises in connection with this: Does this dogma exist even theoretically? Is it not an imaginary dogma, a non-dogma, a dogmatic misunderstanding, and this in both of its versions — in the theory of the procession from the Father and the Son and in the theory of the procession from the Father alone? That is the decisive question to which we are inevitably led by the very history of this dogma. The whole Latin-Photian controversy, with its manner of posing the problem, thus leads to an *imaginary dogma,* which derives from an *imaginary problem.* And this necessarily leads only to a dogmatic misunderstanding.

In what do the misunderstanding and imaginariness of the problem consist? They consist in understanding the *procession* of the Holy Spirit as an *origination* or *production;* this is associated with an analogous understanding of the *generation* of the Son. The two are grouped together as two modes of origination or production, *duae productiones* or *duae processiones.* Each of the two sides in the controversy expounds in its own manner this doctrine of productions — and in particular the doctrine of the procession of the Holy Spirit. Moreover, this origination is understood in the sense of the causal origination (or *"productio"*) of one hypostasis from another as from its cause *(aitia, causa)* or principle *(archē, principium).*

None of the participants in the controversy attempted to thoroughly examine this doctrine of the causal origination of beginningless and uncaused (supra-causal) divine hypostases, a doctrine which involves an obvious logical and ontological contradiction: namely, that the uncaused has a cause and the beginningless has an origin. In the East, this conception of the Holy Trinity as bound by causal origination from the Father received the right of citizenship thanks to a doctrine that considers the Father to be *anaitiatos* (uncaused) while being the *aitia* (cause) of the other hypostases, who are *aitiatoi* (caused). (This is one of the variants, actually the weakest, of the general theory of the Father's monarchy, which is by no means exhausted by this variant.) This idea of *aitia* with reference to the Holy Trinity was first conceived by St. Basil the Great. Reproduced by St. John of Damascus, it was then received by later theologians without critical examination as clear and self-evident, whereas there is no concept more difficult to understand.

Generalized in the concept of "cause" or origination (production), the generation of the Son and the procession of the Spirit were counted as **duae** *processiones,* two forms or particular cases of the general concept of causality. This generalization, which was of primary importance, was also received as self-evident, as not subject to critical examination. Furthermore, in the West the Holy Trinity was considered as a system of two originations or productions, of the intellect and of the will, *processio intellectus* and *processio voluntatis.* This imparted a fixed anthropomorphic form to the conception of the Holy Trinity, which was based now not only on causality but also on a certain inner necessity of the self-grounding of the absolute — a kind of causal modalism. And theology was so hypnotized by this centuries-old idea that it never allowed itself to inquire into the validity of this fundamental premise that determined the whole of triadology. But the mere initiation of such an inquiry will immediately convince one that this premise is *false,* and that all the dogmatic conclusions based on it are therefore false. From imaginary problems there can follow only imaginary dogmas, dogmatic illusions, which do not correspond to dogmatic reality or, therefore, to anything in life.

And first of all, does this generalization (**duae** *processiones*) have any basis in Scripture, in direct Revelation? Can we find anywhere in Scripture the linkage of the generation of the Son and the procession of the Spirit as two forms of origination, *duae processiones?* Indisputably, we cannot. There is no Biblical justification for counting and accepting them as two variants: one *and* one. On the contrary, they should be examined in their particular concrete quality, which is not subject to abstract numerical generalization and the identification contained in the latter. On the basis of this generalization, the hypostases can further be considered as relations of origination or, according to the Eastern conception, as "personal properties," of which we can count three. Such a "count" is a grave coercion and a dogmatic arbitrariness, which has a major impact on the general doctrine of the Holy Trinity.

This counting, in the capacity of two similar units, of two concretely different forms of "origination," leads to a further abstraction: the First hypostasis is thus understood not as the concrete image of the Father, the Engenderer of the Son and the Spirator of the Holy Spirit, but as the "Principle, Source, and Cause" (St. John of Damascus), from which the Second and Third hypostases get Their very being *(auto to einai),* Their existence *(huparxin).* The category of causal origination is thus applied to the eternal being of the hypostases. Of course, none of the fathers dispute the equi-eternity and equi-beginninglessness of all three hypostases, and they therefore reject the chronological understanding of this origination, accepting only the ontological understanding.

This only displaces but does not eliminate the difficulty, however, which has never been subjected to critical examination: What can *causal origination in eternity* signify? Can one in general speak here about cause, *aitia* (with the group of derivative concepts, *anaitios, aitiatos*)? This is a rationalistic category that is valid only with reference to this empirical world, but is not applicable to the *Ding an sich,* to Divinity. What does *cause* signify here, and is Divinity subject to causality? If we ask if the application of the concept of *cause* and *causality* to Divinity has a justification in the Bible, in the Gospel, in revelation, we must answer: Absolutely not! We find in the Bible only concrete definitions of the hypostases and their interrelations; and therefore the philosophical and theological concept of causality that appears in the theological literature has a Biblical foundation neither in its form (unlike *homoousios,* which, though absent in the lexicology, could, as far as its content is concerned, be confirmed on the basis of the Bible and, in this capacity, affirmed by the Church) nor in its substance.

This concept appears imperceptibly in the patristic literature, especially in the Cappadocians and St. John of Damascus. Although in individual passages of these Fathers this concept received a rather extreme expression as the doctrine of the acquisition of being itself from the Father as cause, it was never logically polished by them, but was used descriptively for the most part, alongside other expressions, which refer to the Father as root *(rhiza),* source *(pēgē),* principle *(archē),* and cause *(aitia).*[34] In general, antiquity did not put any emphasis on the category of causality, an emphasis that is so characteristic of modern philosophy, especially starting with Kant. It is remarkable that in the *Philosophical Chapters* of St. John of Damascus (where he expounds Aristotle's theory of categories,

---

34. Here is an example of many such patristic definitions: "The Holy Spirit proceeds from the Father as the principle *(archē),* cause *(aitia),* and source *(pēgē)* of Divinity" (John of Damascus, *De recta sententia,* n. 1, *Contra Man.,* n. 4).

which he places at the basis of the highly important doctrines of hypostasis, ousia, etc.) *there is a total absence* of a theory of the category of causality, which remained for him, so to speak, at the level of popular usage, not philosophical examination.

In general, if we examine the application of this category to the doctrine of the Holy Trinity, where the word "cause" is invariably used as a logical trope alongside others, and not as a strict logical definition, we will arrive at the conclusion that, in describing the interrelations of the hypostases by the concept of causality, the doctors of the Church were attempting to express, first of all, the *monarchy* of the Father. A narrowly causal interpretation of the patristic etiology is proper not to the Fathers themselves, despite the imprecision of their words, but only to the epoch of post-patristic, scholastic epigonism, that is, in connection with the Photian-Latin dispute. In his critique, Photius reduced the question of the procession to the alternative: two causes or one; and in his *ek monou* he thus affirmed *one* of the different meanings of the patristic doctrine. The anti-Photian doctrine of the West took this path even farther. The Filioque doctrine is a *doctrine of causality in God,* and it entrained into its orbit also the anti-Filioque doctrine, which became nothing more than a variant of the same causality.

But is this theory of the causality or causal origination of the hypostases justified? Is it the only possible theory? Or is it a deviation from the true path in the doctrine of the Holy Trinity? Does this theory not inevitably lead to the conception of the hypostases as relations, which appear in an apersonal, precausal divine essence. The problematic of the long-lasting Filioque dispute has never been subjected to critical examination; and therefore both Catholicism and Orthodoxy consider that the doctrine of the Holy Trinity is a doctrine of the causal *origination* of the Son from the Father, and of the Holy Spirit from the Father alone, or from the Father and the Son. But as we showed above, patristic theology (prior to Photius) never posed this question of the causal origination of the Holy Spirit by procession from the Father *alone (ek monou),* or from the Father and the Son. And even when the Fathers speak of this procession, they always consider it in a fuller context, in connection with the doctrine of the unity and the monarchy of the Holy Trinity, and of the interrelations of the hypostases. But this doctrine is never reduced to a definitive, logically articulated theory of hypostatic origination. Nor, of course, was this question discussed at the Second Ecumenical Council, where the eighth article with the definition "who proceedeth from the Father" was introduced into the Creed. This was an argument in favor of the equi-divinity of the Holy Spirit in the Holy Trinity, i.e., here too, this doctrine was considered in a fuller context, not by itself. This explains the existence of *different*, not always harmoniously conjoined definitions. This also explains the existence in the patristic literature of *different* definitions concerning the procession of the Holy Spirit: from the Father, through the Son, from both, and from the Father and the Son. And none of these definitions has the significance of exclusive causality.

The Father is called Unengendered in relation to the Son, but this is only a negative definition. The Father is called principle, source, cause, initial hypostasis, for from Him the Son is engendered and the Holy Spirit proceeds. But this does not signify that the Father is the cause of Their origination *(auto to einai)*, for the hypostases do *not* originate. They exist eternally. The interrelation of the hypostases, as the interrelation of the Father, the Son, and the Holy Spirit, should be understood not on the basis of their origination but on the basis of their concrete self-definition. The Trinity of hypostases is already given in its being in the very interior of the absolute hypostatic (i.e., trihypostatic) subject by the manifestation of the absolute I as I, Thou, He, We, You. It is in vain that Catholic theology attempts to ground the hypostases through their origination from relations. On the contrary, it should be affirmed that the three hypostatic centers of the triune Subject are already given apart from their hypostatic qualification as the Father, the Son, and the Holy Spirit. The entire problematic of originations, particularly with reference to the Holy Spirit, is connected with the impersonalistic presupposition of the primacy of the divine nature with respect to the hypostases, and the latter must therefore originate in the nature. On the contrary, existence as subjects, i.e., independently of the nature, is proper to the three hypostases, although, to be sure, such an opposition or distinction is possible only *in abstracto*, not *in re*.

The generation of the Son and the procession of the Holy Spirit cannot be generalized and counted as *two* "originations." Rather, these are two images of God in these two images of love. The Father is the Subject of this self-revelation, the Principle, the "Cause"; whereas the Son is the One Who gives Himself for this revelation of the Father. He is the One Who reveals the Father, the One Who Speaks, the Word. Generation here should by no means be understood in the anthropomorphic sense of origination or production, for this aspect of generation belongs only to temporal being, to being that has an origin. It must be understood as a spiritual image of the love of the Engendering One and the Engendered One, but by no means as the image of the originating one and the originated one.

The Father, the one from whom the procession occurs *(proboleus)*, and the Spirit, Who proceeds, *spirator* and *spirans,* are also two images of mutual, self-revealing love; and the procession is not an origination. The Father, revealed in the Son, goes out of Himself in His love; and this love is for Him the hypostatic Spirit. The *Spirator,* the One Who breathes out the Spirit, loves the Spirit by the Spirit Himself; whereas the Spirit proceeds *Himself,* giving Himself, His hypostasis, for the service of Love, in order to be Love itself. The hypostasis does not arise in the procession; rather, the mutual service of love and the images of supra-eternal love are realized in the procession by the fact that the Father loves, whereas the Spirit is the hypostatic love of the Father. And the monarchy of the Father, the procession from the Father, is the very foundation of this relation, for there is only One Who Reveals Himself — the Father. And He is also the Engenderer and the Spirator; and this constitutes the difference between Divine fatherhood and earthly fatherhood, which, although it is in the image of the heavenly fatherhood, is not identical to the latter. And the Father is not a double cause, the Engenderer on the one hand and the Spirator on the other. Rather, He is the unique Paternal hypostasis: the Father as the Engenderer and Spirator. He is the truly unique *pēgē, archē, aitia* of the entire Holy Trinity. To count the Engenderer and the Spirator, or generation and spiration, as *duae processiones* is to double and fragment the one, trihypostatic, triune act.

In this interpretation, the Father is also the *principle* (and in *this* sense also the source, root, and cause) in the Holy Trinity. He is the source hypostasis, for *He* reveals Himself in the other hypostases, is their subject, in relation to which they are predicate and copula. He is the ontological and logical center of the union that forms the three hypostatic centers of the Divine triunity. It is absolutely impossible to diminish this primordiality and centrality of the First hypostasis or to attribute this centrality to a second hypostasis as well (as in the Latin interpretation of the Filioque) without disrupting and complicating this triunity. And in this sense — but of course *only* in this sense — it is possible to accept even *ek monou tou Patros* (from the Father alone) insofar as it signifies in a positive form the negation of diarchy or bicentrism in the Holy Trinity.

But when we understand this *ek monou causally* (as both Photius and his opponents did) and thus reduce the Holy Trinity to a system of causal relations, we transform this formula into a doctrine that is just as one-sided and erroneous as the Filioque. This doctrine sunders the Holy Trinity into two unconnected dyads according to the causal relation of the hypostases. Or these dyads are connected solely by the unity of the principle with which each of the two causally produced hypostases is causally correlated, but there is no intrinsic connection between them. The Filioque attempts to connect the Second and Third hypostases by a relation of causal origination, but this attempt is unsuccessful, for the two dyads, the dyad of the Father and the Son and the dyad of Father-Son and the Holy Spirit, remain separate. In a word, the *causal* interpretation inevitably destroys the triunity of the Holy Trinity; and in this respect *ek monou* and Filioque are completely equivalent. This triunity exists outside all causality by virtue of the trihypostatic character of the Divine Person, in which all three hypostases are present independent of any origination. None of the hypostases is *produced* by any other, such as the Father, the Son, or the Holy Spirit; but each defines, qualifies, or "produces" Itself: the Father is the image of Paternal sacrificial love, the Son is sacrificial Filial love, the Holy Spirit is the exultant love of the Holy Spirit.

In order to show definitively the impermissibility of "originations" or "productions" in the Holy Trinity, it is necessary to add that these different qualifications of the hypostases — the fatherhood of the Father, the sonhood of the Son, and the spirithood of the Holy Spirit — are *eternal* and therefore absolutely unalterable self-definitions of the hypostases: in the Holy Trinity there is "no variableness, neither shadow of turning" (James 1:17). Therefore, one cannot conceive any change in the hypostatic self-definition: the Father cannot become the Son, and the Son cannot become the Father, etc. But this is a result not of unalterable relations of origination which would introduce into the life of the Holy Trinity the principle of *necessity* with its mechanical unalterability, but of the divine freedom of autonomous being, *aseitas,* which has unalterable validity for all three hypostases. All the hypostases supra-eternally posit themselves in defining themselves; and the self-definition of each of them includes and presupposes not only a distinct and personal but also a trihypostatic self-definition. In other words, it is both personal and trinitarian.

Thus, to the doctrine of origination or production, i.e., to the causal interpretation of the Holy Trinity, it is necessary to oppose divine trihypostatic aseity. All the hypostatic self-definitions are also *natural* ones, for hypostasis does not exist outside nature, just as nature does not exist outside hypostasis. The identity of hypostasis and nature is so exhaustive that even their very differentiation and thus their opposition can be realized only *in abstracto.* Even though, in reality, hypostatic nature and natural hypostasis are identical, it is also true that nature is not hypostasis and hypostasis is not nature. Despite their ontological conjugacy, there is also an unalterable ontological difference between them. One should not be troubled by this apparent contradiction between the simultaneous identification and differentiation of nature and hypostasis. Here, thought is dealing with divine things, and the dumfounded reason lays down its rational weaponry of the laws of identity and contradiction, antinomically unites contradictory things, and posits an "excluded" middle between the contradictory judgments. One of the properties of such antinomic judgments is their irreversibility: if we say that a hypostasis is identical to its nature, which it possesses, we cannot say, conversely, that the nature is identical to the hypostasis, by which it is possessed, although in fact there does not exist in God any nonhypostatic or nonhypostatized nature. But we remark here that, in the trihypostatic Divinity, each of the hypostases, and the entire Holy Trinity in its triunity, are equally natural, i.e., have nature wholly and indivisibly; and in this sense they are all nature. But nature, belonging to each of the hypostases, cannot be equated with only one of them.

Because of this inseparability of hypostasis and nature, the hypostatic definitions are self-definitions according to the nature too. Thus, the fatherhood of the First hypostasis actualizes itself not only in a personal center but also in a natural self-definition, in the concretely hypostatic living-out of its nature. The same thing can be said about all three hypostases. Therefore, the hypostatic aseity is not only a *subjective* self-consciousness, limited to the domain of the divine subject, but also an *objective* or natural self-positing. If to hypostasis, in particular to the hypostasis of the Father as such, it is proper to generate and thus to express its Paternal self-consciousness and self-positing, such "generation" extends to the entire being of the First hypostasis. In other words, the Father generates not only from Himself, but also *ek ousias tou Patros* [from the essence of the Father], as defined by the First Ecumenical Council.

Analogously, the Holy Spirit proceeds from both the hypostasis and the essence of the Father. The Filioque doctrine plays upon this: "*ex uno principio* — not in that in which the Father and the Son differ, but in that in which they are one, namely, in the one nature." The error that is committed here consists in the fact that the nature is conceived separately from the hypostasis as a certain common property or common possession — in this case the undivided common possession of the Father and the Son. But in reality there is no *common* possession of the nature on the part of the hypostases. What there is, is separate or unique possession: the Father and the Son have the divine nature integrally each by Himself and for Himself, but They do not possess it jointly.

Furthermore, all three persons of the Holy Trinity have this nature as the triunity of the Holy Trinity. Therefore, two possibilities are given in the general relation of the hypostases to the nature: each of the equidivine hypostases enjoys full unique and personal possession, according to its hypostatic image, of the nature; or the entire Holy Trinity fully possesses the divine nature according to the image of triunity. Therefore, the one nature, equal to itself, equally belongs both to the entire Holy Trinity and to each of the hypostases (here once again we have the antinomy of the identity of different things and the difference between identical things). The case that is imagined by the Filioque doctrine is not given here, however, and is even excluded *ex hypothesi*, so to speak: that is, the case where the hypostases of the Father and the Son, in their bi-unity, have common possession of the nature as a certain common fund, from which as from one principle, they draw the Holy Spirit, without being distinguished from each other. But the nature is not a fund, but always a hypostatized being, and there can be no place here for common possession, because this idea signifies the *separation* of hypostatic being and natural being, to which is thus attributed the possibility of belonging — in different combinations — to one, two, or three.

This introduces a *tritheism* in the definition of the relations between the trihypostatic being and the nature. The result achieved is totally opposite to that which is adumbrated in the Filioque doctrine: in order to avoid the hypostatic differentiation of the two in the procession of the Holy Spirit, one has recourse to the nature, in whose darkness no hypostatic suns shine. But this presupposes such a separation of the nature from the hypostases, such an extrahypostatizedness of the nature, that the hypostases become separate co-participants in the one nature, in the common possession. Thus, the goal is not attained and the dogma of divine consubstantiality is abrogated. The nature does *not* exist in Divinity as an independent principle, in which the difference of the hypostases is abolished and two are as one. The ray of each hypostasis penetrates down to the very bottom of the nature and totally hypostatizes it. That is why it is impossible to posit *two* hypostases that would be *one* in nature, that would lose, as it were, their individual hypostatic personhood: two hypostases, that of the Father and that of the Son, are and abide *as two according to the nature as well*. If one wishes to insist that the Holy Spirit proceeds from the Father and the Son, then one should affirm that this procession is from two principles, not from one; and Photius' "diarchic" counterargument acquires new force.

Returning to the question of aseity in the hypostatic self-definitions, we must say that it equally concerns both the hypostatic being and the natural being of each of the hypostases. Consequently, the Paternal hypostasis is the Father both hypostatically and naturally in Its interrelation with the other hypostases, in generation and procession. But one can say the same thing about the Son, Who is self-defined both naturally and hypostatically as the Son, that is, He is engendered. And the same thing can, of course, be said about the Holy Spirit, Who is self-defined both naturally and hypostatically in His procession. But besides this there is also the triune nature of the consubstantial Trinity, which is substantially identical with the nature of each of the individual hypostases, while differing from this nature modally, as it were, according to the mode of its hypostatic possession. This difference refers, of course, not to its ousian essence but to the mode of its possession by the Holy Trinity in the triunity and by each individual hypostasis.

The Holy Trinity is the *trinitarian* act of the self-definition of the hypostases; and each of the elements of this trinitarity, despite the aseity and equi-divinity of the three hypostases, is *correlative* to the other two hypostases and in this sense is conditioned by them. The *fullness* of natural being, as self-revelation, is given only in the trinitarity of the hypostatic self-definitions. Naturally too, the Holy Trinity exists only *trinely*, "consubstantially and indivisibly," which is why each of the individual hypostatic modes of natural being does not simply exist, but coexists in its indivisibility with the others. Therefore, in general, none of the hypostases in its separate personal being can be understood except in trinitarian conjugacy. This leads to a general thesis, which is a kind of axiom concerning the Holy Trinity: *the three hypostases, in their character, are not single and not double, but trine.* They must be understood not on the basis of themselves alone, but on the basis of their trinitarian union; they are defined and shine not only with their own light, but also with the light reflected from the other hypostases. It follows that all three hypostases must be understood in a *distinctly personal as well as trinitarian* manner; and any doctrine that transforms the Holy Trinity into a system of originations and dyads is fundamentally deficient.

Therefore, all three hypostases must be considered in the context, so to speak, of these distinctly personal but also trinitarian interrelations — and first of all the hypostasis of the Father. Of course, it is not by accident but in full conformity with the *trinitarian* self-definition of each of the hypostases that it is said about the *Father* with reference to both the Son and the Holy Spirit: "who proceedeth from the Father." This means that the Father is the Father not only with reference to the Son but also with reference to the Holy Spirit, not only as the Engenderer but also as the

Spirator. Heavenly Fatherhood is defined by generation and spiration, but it is not limited to this. In contradistinction to earthly fatherhood, it necessarily includes the procession of the Spirit upon the Son: "This is my beloved Son" (Matt. 3:17). If we were to apply this to multihypostatic being, for human beings too the complex of fatherhood is not exhausted by generation but also includes a relation of the active love of the engendering one to the one engendered, which in the creaturely world is analogous to the hypostatic Paternal love for the Only Begotten Son.

Analogously, the hypostasis of the Son is defined not only by His relation to the Father, the relation of the Engendered One to the Engendering One, but also by Their mutual love. And this love is precisely the Holy Spirit, Who not only reposes upon the Son but also passes *through* the Son. He is the *union* of the love of the Father and the Son. Finally (and most importantly here), the hypostasis of the Holy Spirit necessarily includes this trinitarian (not double) definition: the Holy Spirit can be understood only in relation to the Father *and* the Son; however, contrary to the Catholic doctrine, this relation concerns not that in which the hypostases are not distinct and do not exist separately, but that in which they are distinct and hypostatic. In the triangle, which is the geometrical symbol of the Holy Trinity, the determinants are not the lines but the three points connected by these lines. Each point or apex of the triangle has a complex relation to the other two points, implies or contains them as it were. And in *this* (but only in this) sense, the Filioque represents a self-evident premise of the doctrine of the Holy Spirit. This doctrine cannot eliminate or forget the interrelation of the Third hypostasis not only with the First but also with the Second: the Holy Spirit is such not only for the Father but also for the Son. One can say that the Father engenders the Son even as the Son is engendered from the Father, with the necessary presence and thus the participation of the Holy Spirit; and that the Holy Spirit proceeds from the Father, or the Father draws out of Himself in procession the Holy Spirit, with the necessary presence or participation of the Son. If one uses Bolotov's expression "condition" (despite all its inadequacy), one can say that, in the Holy Trinity, the Son is the condition of the Holy Spirit, even as the Holy Spirit is the condition of the Son. The three hypostases are concrete trihypostatic interrelations.

The Church Fathers were always conscious of this truth, that is, the trinitarian inter-definition of the hypostases, and attempted to express it in different ways, for the most part descriptively, in search of the most precise formula, although this, as it turns out, was never found. And this led to the multiplicity, and apparent imprecision, ambiguity, and even contradictoriness of patristic propositions on the interrelation of the three hypostases. Without mentioning the constant and confounding question of the "origination" of the hypostases from one another, we cannot fail to see one fundamental fact, which is the most characteristic fact for the patristic literature on this question: not only is there no fixed dogmatic definition on this subject, but there is even a great diversity in the expression of this one general idea, a diversity which one attempts in vain to smooth over by artificial reinterpretations. Most striking at first glance are the different nuances in the expression of the general interrelation of the trinitarian hypostases, especially the relation of the Holy Spirit to the Father and the Son, nuances which we find in the writings of different Fathers or in the writings of the same Father but in different passages; however, these differences almost never led to misunderstandings or conflicts among the Fathers themselves.

This mutual tolerance and even permissiveness, as it were, is most striking in the doctrinal difference between East and West concerning the Trinity and, in particular, concerning the doctrine of the procession of the Holy Spirit. Both "theologoumena" (as Professor Bolotov calls these opinions), the *dia* and the Filioque, enjoyed the same right of citizenship prior to the Latin-Photian dispute. This difference was not felt to be a fundamental divergence, for unity of thought, precisely concerning the trinitarian character of the definition of each of the hypostases, appeared to be more essential than *particular* differences in the definition of this trinitarity. The general idea was self-evident, as it were, whereas the particularities were evidently viewed not so much as dogmatic definitions or even as "theologoumena" but as dogmatic hypotheses, attempts to descriptively express an idea that had not received or, at that point, had not even sought for itself a precise dogmatic definition. The axis of the trinitarian dogma, its generally accepted initial truth, was the recognition of the *monarchy* of the Father, of the primary and central significance of the Paternal hypostasis, which was accepted by representatives of all the orientations. By contrast, the question of the *origination* of one hypostasis from another, in particular the question of the procession of the Holy Spirit from the Father alone or from the Father and the Son, and whether He proceeds from one cause or from two causes, had not yet been placed at the center of attention (though it had been adumbrated); and the problem had not yet acquired the one-sidedness that came to characterize it later.

Thus, the state of the theological doctrine of the Holy Spirit in the patristic epoch, both in the West and in the East, is comparable to the state of logology in the ante-Nicene epoch or to that of Christology in the ante-Chalcedonian epoch, when different and widely divergent theological tendencies and theologoumena peacefully coexisted, the difference being that pneumatology (in contrast to logology and Christology) has still not had its council of Nicaea or Chalcedon — for the Second Council of Constantinople, which only fleetingly considered, on the basis of the Gospel, the relation of the Holy Spirit to the Father but did not consider at all His relation to the Son, cannot be regarded as such a council. There has not yet been an ecumenical council devoted to the doctrine of the Holy Spirit, and no dogmatic formula pertaining to the Holy Spirit has been found that would be obligatory for the entire Church. The Latin-Photian dispute was, in general, a dogmatic misfortune for the Church, owing to its schismatic spirit; and a particular misfortune was the fact that both sides, the Eastern church and the Western church, felt themselves to be in possession of the true dogma of the procession of the Holy Spirit — either from the Father alone or from the Father and the Son. And both of these theological opinions, or doctrines, acquired the significance of dogmas in the consciousness of the two adversaries.

More blameworthy here is the Western church, which not only erected an entire dogmatic construction for its theologoumenon, a construction that was erroneous in its premises and false in its conclusions, but which even stamped it with the seal of papal infallibility (which is why, in practical terms, the Filioque is, first and foremost, a dogma about the pope, something which Professor Bolotov has pointed out in his theses[35]). In the East, the analogous significance of a false dogma has been acquired by Photius' doctrine, which represents a sort of novelty for the Eastern church and is infected by a similar schismatic spirit.

This spirit grew in intensity, as did the internal schism between East and West, which culminated in the mutual anathemas of the unhappy year 1054. But these contradictory theological opinions never acquired the force of a dogma of the universal Church. In particular, for the East, Photianism cannot pretend even to that simulacrum of dogmatic authority which is possessed by the Filioque for the West by virtue of its inclusion in the papal infallibility. Here, the East could never tie up the loose ends and resolve the divergences and often the contradictions of the patristic opinions, which were by no means easy to adapt to the Photian

---

35. Having established that the Filioque is not an *impedimentum dirimens* separating the East and West, Bolotov poses the question: "What sundered the communion of the one catholic Church? I answer without evasion: It was sundered by the Roman papacy."

pseudo-dogma. And here, as we showed above, the question of the procession of the Holy Spirit was usurped, in both the East and the West, by the question of *origination*. But this question cannot exist with reference to the equi-eternal hypostases.

One must accept a fundamental fact, both historical and dogmatic, that, in and of itself, has a much greater dogmatic significance than the false dogmas of the procession: namely, that "the Greek fathers and Augustine followed quite different paths in theology and arrived at far from identical theologoumena" (Bolotov). Furthermore, "Photius and his successors continued relations with the western church without receiving (and evidently without demanding) from it the explicit conciliar renunciation of the Filioque" (thesis 25). This mutual tolerance toward different theological opinions, which would certainly have been inappropriate and even impossible with reference to fully established dogmas, accorded with the correct *dogmatic instinct* of the Church, which precisely defines the limits of what is acceptable and possible. And this centuries-old mutual tolerance indubitably attests that the Church did not have a definite dogma *then,* even as it has not established one in later epochs.

The authentic tradition of the Church, which on this subject was expressed with dogmatic restraint and discreet imprecision, must be our guide now too, for nothing of essence has changed in this question and nothing decisive has occurred. As before, our guide must be the following proposition: *there does not yet exist a definitive dogma of the procession of the Holy Spirit,* either with regard to the meaning of the procession or with regard to its mode. This is either because the time has not yet come for such a dogma or because the only answer that can be given to the imaginary question concerning the procession understood as *origination* is an imaginary dogma; and the Church does not dogmatize imaginaries. And if, in the ancient Church, *different* theologoumena had the right to exist, in particular the *dia* and the Filioque, now too they retain this right, though not as dogmas but only as theologoumena, theological opinions and hypotheses, as different forms of theologizing. But these *different* opinions must not be stigmatized as heresies, from the one side or the other. It was precisely this idea that was expressed by Professor V. V. Bolotov when he had the courage to proclaim that it was not the Filioque that divided the Church, just as now it is not an *impedimentum dirimens* [obstacle that divides] for the union of the churches; that is, in and of itself, *the Filioque is not a heresy.* And so, according to the competent and impartial judgment of an Orthodox historian of the Church, there is one less phantom impediment, which is perhaps the most frightening one, to the reunification of the churches. But Bolotov himself remained enshrouded in the mist of imaginary problems and imaginary dogmas concerning the procession of the Holy Spirit as *origination*.

If we dispel this mist and expose the true character of this imaginary dogma, we can with even greater confidence affirm the absence of heresy where there are only different attempts to express the inexpressible, to describe the indescribable. For heresy begins here only when power is gained by the schismatic spirit, which transforms theological opinions into "abstract principles," into one-sided convictions, and in this sense into heresies (inasmuch as the precise meaning of "heresy," *hairesis,* is, first and foremost, one-sidedness). "Filioque," "through the Son," "from Both," *"ek monou tou Patros,"* and other suchlike formulas can and must be understood (as they were understood by the ancient church) not as mutually contradictory or mutually exclusive expressions but as equivalent in some sense, as having the same meaning or at least as imbued with the same idea. This can be done if we emancipate the dogmatic doctrine from the imaginary problematic of *procession as origination.* The general and fundamental idea of the dogma of the Holy Spirit and of His "procession" consists in the fact that His relation to the Father is defined on the basis of the "monarchy" of the Father; the Holy Spirit's relation to the Father is that of the Revealing One to the One Being Revealed, and not merely as the Revealing One but as the Co-Revealing One (together with the Son). The definition of the Holy Spirit that follows from this inner interrelation is therefore not dual but trinitarian. This definition can be dogmatically *described* starting from different points, and these different dogmatic descriptions coincide in substance, inasmuch as they refer to one and the same Divine being.

In particular, it is possible to justify even Photius' interpretation of the formula "who proceedeth from the Father" as "who proceedeth from the Father alone [*ek monou*]" if, instead of associating this idea with imaginary origination, one understands procession itself as the fundamental interrelation between the Father, Who is revealed, and the Spirit and the Son, Who reveal. "From the Father *alone*" expresses the idea of the "monarchy" of the Father as the initial principle in the Holy Trinity, as the only one who is revealed. Of course, this *ek monou* does not by any means have the limiting and exclusive significance that was given to it by Photius; it is compatible with the recognition of another interrelation between the Holy Spirit and the Son, based on the procession from the Father.

Further, one can understand, justify, and accept the *dia tou Huiou,* as well as even the Filioque with its different variants ("from Both," "proper to the Son," etc.), together with *ek tou Patros* and even *ek monou tou Patros,* if one in general considers that the relation of the Holy Spirit *to the Son* is indicated here. This relation is not rejected; it is just not indicated in the text, "who proceedeth from the Father." The relation of the Holy Spirit to the Son is by no means excluded, but is presupposed by His relation to the Father. And all the formulas of the procession, if only the latter is not understood as origination, represent only different forms of the trinitarian definition of the Third hypostasis — not only in relation to the Father but also in relation to the Son. As different *descriptions* of this interrelation, these formulas can all be admitted in parallel if only one does not attribute to them a literal dogmatic significance. The general meaning of these formulas can be expressed as follows: The Third hypostasis must be understood simultaneously not only in relation to the First, according to the principle of the monarchy of the Father, but also in relation to the Son (just as the hypostasis of the Son must be understood not only in relation to the Father but also in relation to the Holy Spirit).

This leads to a practical conclusion: The dogmatic divergence concerning the procession of the Holy Spirit, due to an erroneous understanding of procession as origination, attests above all that this question has not sufficiently ripened for dogmatic *definition,* which is something that remains perhaps for the not so near future. That is why these dogmatic divergences, in and of themselves not representing an *impedimentum dirimens,* must not serve as a pretext for mutual accusations of heresy, inasmuch as they can be harmonized or at least considered not to exclude one another. Not imaginary heresy, but the schismatic spirit and false dogmatism sustain that separation of which the ancient church was free.

The dogmatic divergence is further complicated by the Western insertion of the Filioque into the Creed; this addition bears the stamp of Roman absolutism, although it is also retained by confessions that have broken off from Rome (Anglicanism, Protestantism). At the present time there is a tendency to consider this divergence in the Creed an attribute of the Western and Eastern rituals in the context of their different liturgical traditions. Originally, the insertion of the Filioque appeared in the West spontaneously and imperceptibly. It became militantly tendentious only after it had become a weapon of the schismatic spirit on both sides. It was used as a means of battle and separation. But even if we do not dispute that this addition infringed to some extent on the formal inviolability of the Creed that had been accepted and confirmed by a series of ecumenical councils, initially it was only a kind of interpretation or gloss.

We cannot in all sincerity insist on the purely formal inviolability of the Creed once we know that, in essence, the dogmatic teaching was complemented by the later decrees of the ecumenical councils themselves, although they formally affirmed this inviolability. What is important, of course, is the meaning of the addition: Can it be understood as an ecclesiastically admissible theologoumenon, which is how it is currently understood by the Old Catholics and the Anglicans? Thus, if one extracts from the Filioque addition the thorn of dogmatic irreconcilability, one must take into account the fact of a centuries-old *liturgical* tradition, which, if only by virtue of its antiquity, has acquired a sacred character and a kind of inviolability. Thus, tolerance could have been extended even to the Western addition, which would have become liturgical in character and lost its dogmatic acuteness.

Opposed to the schismatic spirit is churchly love; and love, according to the Apostle, "beareth all things" (1 Cor. 13:7). Dogmatically, the "question" of the procession must yet be a subject of further investigation. But in and of itself the divergence expressed by the two traditions, Filioque and *dia tou Huiou,* is not a heresy or even a dogmatic error. It is a difference of theological opinions which was dogmatized prematurely and erroneously. *There is no dogma of the relation of the Holy Spirit to the Son,* and therefore particular opinions on this subject are not heresies but merely dogmatic hypotheses, which have been transformed into heresies by the schismatic spirit that has established itself in the Church and that eagerly exploits all sorts of liturgical and even cultural differences. (That is why, in the most deplorable epoch of the schism, from the eleventh century onward, there were dozens of mutual accusations of heresy.)

The best evidence for this is the fact that, *in practice,* the two sides, West and East, do not differ in their veneration of the Holy Spirit, despite their divergence regarding the procession. It seems highly strange that such a major dogmatic divergence would have no practical impact, whereas normally a dogma always has a practical significance, determines the religious life. In this case, even the most extreme zealots of the schismatic spirit have not been able to apply the imaginary dogma to life or to indicate its practical consequences. One can say that neither the Western church nor the Eastern church knows the living heresy of the Holy Spirit, but such knowledge would be inevitable if there were a dogmatic heresy. It might appear unexpected and strange that such a long-lasting dispute, to which such a crucial importance has been attributed, is based not on reality but on a dogmatic phantom and misunderstanding: Can it be that innumerable theologians on both sides who fought for their truth were in error, were victims of a terrible exaggeration? Yes, they were in error, but it was not they themselves, as theologians, who were in error, in their effort to find a satisfactory theological theory or doctrine; rather, it was the schismatic spirit living in them that was in error. The dispute over the Holy Spirit, the hypostasis of intratrinitarian Love, unfolded in an atmosphere of *un-love,* of *active schism,* and it was thus doomed to sterility. The dogmatic controversy concerning the Spirit was deprived precisely of spirit, and its result was therefore sterility and emptiness.

*   *

The Filioque dispute includes and discloses an important aspect of the doctrine of the Holy Trinity, namely, the special, *dyadic* union of the Second and Third hypostases in its relation to the monarchy of the Father. Both the Western Filioque and the Eastern *dia* justly indicate the special *connection of bi-unity* between the Second and Third hypostases, a connection one should never forget about when discussing the Holy Trinity. But, unfortunately, in the Western theologoumenon the logical accent was shifted to the union of the Son with the Father in the spiration of the Holy Spirit, thereby postulating a false dyadic union. Meantime, although the Eastern theologoumenon, *dia,* never expressed the idea of the dyadic union of the Son and the Holy Spirit with all the precision and fullness that could be desired, it nevertheless suggested a possible way to understand this union.

The idea of the monarchy of the Father, which constitutes the very foundation of the trinitarian doctrine, was understood erroneously, that is, it was understood with reference to origination or production, an imaginary concept. Its true meaning, protecting this idea from the otherwise inevitable admixture of ontological subordinationism, is that the First hypostasis is the One that is Revealed, while in relation to this hypostasis the other two are its bihypostatic Revelation. This implies, of course, a certain *hierarchism,* a voluntary hierarchism of the self-renouncing love proper to each of the hypostases of the Holy Trinity; each has its proper mode of concrete hypostatic love, *ho tropos tēs huparxeōs.*

In this trinitarian mode of love, according to its meaning, there is only one *subject,* the *center of revelation,* and this constitutes the "monarchy" of the Father; and He is the center in relation to the *hypostases of revelation,* the Son and the Holy Spirit. These two hypostases not only differ as different modes of this revelation, Word and Spirit (the predicate and the copula, so to speak), but they are also united as the bi-une mode of this Paternal self-revelation; and in relation to the monarchy of the Father

149

they represent a certain *dyad,* in which one cannot think of one of the hypostases without thinking of the other.

This dyadism expresses a truth that is formulated differently by the Filioque and by the Greek *dia.* The Son cannot be separated in hypostatic self-definition from the Spirit, or vice versa. And neither can He be separated — hypostatically or dyadically — from the Father. This dyadic character of the relations of the Son and the Holy Spirit to the Father as the "Principle" is falsely expressed by the doctrine of two originations or productions from the Father: through generation and through procession. The two revealing hypostases, in their dyadic union as well as each separately, are correlated with the Father as their Principle as far as His self-revelation is concerned; and here the two are united as the unique but bihypostatic revelation of the Father.

Thus, one can say that the "being" of *each* of these two hypostases, in all the originality of their *tropos huparxeōs* [mode of being], depends not only on the Father but also on the other co-revealing hypostasis. Therefore, with regard to the Son, one must say that, in being generated from the Father, He receives upon Himself from the Father the reposing of the Holy Spirit; and consequently in His "being" He is inseparable (although personally distinct) from the Holy Spirit. The being of the Son in all the originality of the Second hypostasis depends *a Patre Spirituque* [on the Father and the Spirit]. Likewise, concerning the Spirit one can say that He proceeds from the Father not in a general and abstract manner, but precisely upon the Son; consequently, we get *dia tou Huiou* or Filioque. This *"que"* ("and"), which Latin theology introduces in only *one* place, actually occurs in all places where the *trinitarian* definition of each of the trinitarian hypostases must be expressed. This trinitarian definition is not a relation of "origination," however, but the complex and concrete interrelation of the Revealed hypostasis and the Revealing hypostases.

It is this bi-unity of the Second and Third hypostases that is indicated by scriptural texts in which the Spirit is called Christ's: "the Spirit of truth" (John 16:13), "the Spirit of the Son" (Gal. 4:6), "the Spirit of Christ" (Rom. 8:9). These texts attest the dyadic connection of the Son and the Spirit, the fact that They are inseparable, although personally distinct. This is also attested in cases of a reverse character, which involve the reposing of the Holy Spirit upon the Son and Their inseparability in this sense. One should not forget that the God-Man received the name "Christ," and that this name tacitly includes the name of the Third hypostasis: *"Anointed* by the Holy Spirit." We find this in the narrative concerning the descent of the Holy Spirit upon Jesus at the Epiphany, as well as in Jesus' direct application to Himself of Isaiah's messianic prophecy: "The Spirit of the Lord God is upon me" (Isa. 61:1; Luke 4:18). Also pertinent here is the whole series of texts where the Lord says that He expels demons by the Holy Spirit.

CHAPTER 3

On the Spirit of God and the Holy Spirit

God is spirit and spirituality is the very essence of God. In addition, spirituality in God is expressly associated, as it were, with the Holy Spirit, the Third hypostasis. The spirituality of the Holy Spirit as the Third hypostasis is identical to the spirituality of God, but at the same time it *hypostatically* differs from it in some sense. One can say that the Holy Spirit is also the spirit of God, but one cannot say, conversely, that the spirit of God is the Holy Spirit, for God is spirit in His entire trihypostatic being, not only as the Third hypostasis, but also as the First and Second. Spirituality is proper to the First and Second hypostases not less than to the Third. The Father and the Son are spirit to an equal degree as the Holy Spirit; but it is the Holy Spirit Who manifests the spirituality of the Holy Trinity as the Trihypostatic God.

And thus we have here the equality-inequality, the identification-distinction between the spirit of God and the Holy Spirit. The Holy Spirit *actualizes* the spirituality of God, without retaining it, exhausting it, or even defining it, for His own spirituality is that of the Father and the Son. Ontologically we have here the interpenetrability but also the inconfusibility of the Father and the Son and the Holy Spirit, of the entire Holy Trinity, which is spirit, *one* spirit, not doubly or triply spirit. And at the same time, each of the hypostases has its own spirituality, or more precisely, it possesses its own spirituality in its own way; but at the same time it actualizes it in the Holy Spirit. In this sense, the Holy Spirit is a hypostasis that is both one and trine. He manifests and bears within Himself the trinitarian transparence of the substance of the spirit. The Holy Spirit is the spirit of God; the spirit of God — the spirit of the Father and the spirit of the Son — is the Holy Spirit, Who is not only the Holy Spirit as the Third hypostasis but also the spirit of God.

This transparence of the trihypostatic spirit makes His trinitarity imperceptible and indistinguishable, even though the latter constitutes the very foundation of His being. There can be no monohypostatic spirit; for the spirit is not a unihypostatically but a trihypostatically or multihypostatically revealed spirituality. The Holy Spirit exists by virtue of the Father and the Son, as *Their* mutual love and as very Love for Them. In this sense, the Holy Spirit does not belong to Himself, is not His own, but is the Spirit of the Father and the Son, for in general to be one's own, self-enclosed and limited, is not proper to the nature of the spirit. But at the same time, as a hypostasis, the Holy Spirit is personal, that is, He is the Spirit contained within Himself, the Third hypostasis. These definitions can obviously not be encompassed by a discursive scheme based on the rational law of static identity. They transcend this law, for here we have a *dynamic identity,* expressed by a series of static nonidentities or identities of the nonidentical. Based on this fundamental property of dynamic identity with static difference, an essential fact becomes clear: following Scripture, we say about the *spirit of God* and the Holy Spirit that they are different and the same. When we speak about the spirit of God, we do not yet speak about the Holy Spirit. However, here we cannot in essence distinguish the spirit of God from the Holy Spirit, the Third hypostasis; and even less can we oppose the one to the other.

The spirit of God is the triunity of the three hypostases in *the separateness of Their Persons.* The Holy Spirit is Their *hypostatic* union in the Third Person. If one can say, on the basis of the principle of the monarchy of the Father, that the entire Holy Trinity is the Father Who reveals Himself in the Son and the Spirit, one can also speak about the divine triunity of the Divinity revealed in the hypostasis of the Holy Spirit. In the first case the Father is *autotheos* or *ho Theos,* God the Subject; in the second case, one can say about the Third hypostasis that it is the Spirit of the spirit, *to pneuma* (with an article), in relation to *Theion pneuma,* a predicate (or even copula) that has become its own subject. In the fullness and perfection of His self-revelation, God is the Third and final hypostasis, which in this sense is, as it were, also the First hypostasis.

This character of the relation that exists between the Divine spirit and the Holy Spirit is manifested both in the interhypostatic interrelations of the Divine Persons and in Their interrelation in the one Divinity, or the Divine Sophia.

The Divine Sophia possesses being not only for the hypostatic tri-unity but also in herself, as the glory and revelation of Divinity. She, the Divine Sophia, is, of course, also a *spiritual* principle, the spirituality of the trihypostatic spirit. She exists inseparably from the divine trihyposta-tizedness but *not* indistinguishably from it. She possesses aseity or auton-omous being as the divinity or spirituality of the hypostatic spirit. In her, this hypostatic spirit is revealed in itself and for itself in its proper spiritu-ality, but this revealing principle, the spirituality in the spirit, the "hypostatizedness" of the hypostases, has also its own being according to itself, as the Divinity of God. In this sense, God is also spirit as the Divine Sophia. And in this spirituality of hers, the Divine Sophia, in her final fullness, receives the seal of the Holy Spirit.

And about her one can also say that, in general being spirituality, she is also a revelation of the Holy Spirit. This revelation includes, as its onto-logical *prius* or precondition, the entire content of the revelation of the First hypostasis in the Second, which content is manifested and realized by the Holy Spirit; and in *this* sense it is the Holy Spirit. God reveals His spirituality in the Divine Sophia, not only in the Word but also in the Holy Spirit, in the Third hypostasis. But He reveals it not only in her her-self, but also outside of her, in creation, in the creaturely Sophia. In other words, the *direct* revelation of the hypostatic God to creatures, of the Di-vine Sophia to creation, is an action of the Holy Spirit ("grace"); and this revelation has as its content the Word, Who in Himself shows the Father. The spirit of God, who is also the Holy Spirit, is not his own, not a spirit self-enclosed in his own content. He is the Spirit of Truth, the Spirit of Wisdom, the Spirit of the Father and of the Son, the Spirit of the Holy Trinity.[1]

With these theological considerations we wish to establish an im-mensely important fact: the apparent failure to distinguish two different senses of the term "spirit of God," as Divinity in general and as the Holy Spirit, is a fundamental, general, and typical feature of the Holy Scripture.

---

1. On the basis of the foregoing discussion, we establish the following principle of dogmatic exegesis. In all cases where the "spirit of God" is mentioned, one should under-stand the revelation and action of the God who is in the Holy Trinity, without differenti-ation of the individual hypostases — the revelation and action of the Trinity as a unity. But this general understanding can be combined with a more particular one, with refer-ence to the Third hypostasis, to the Holy Spirit as such a hypostasis, which specially ex-presses the spirituality of the Divine Spirit in the fullness of His self-revelation. This ex-pression does not have to be accompanied by any definite relation to the Third hypostasis itself, however, but can designate solely its action or manifestation.

The expression "spirit of God" is used *promiscue,* and it is difficult, if not impossible, to determine its precise meaning except in certain particular cases. It can mean God Himself, the Holy Trinity, the Third hypostasis, the Holy Spirit, or the action of God in the world, and this sometimes in the broadest and most indeterminate sense. One can say that in general whenever it needs to indicate the action of God in the world or His revelation to Creation, Scripture speaks of the "spirit" of God. This apparent imprecision of the sacred writers is capable of causing confusion and even of producing offense if one does not take into account the above-indicated interrelation among the spirituality of God, the spirit of God, and the Holy Spirit.

I. In the Old Testament

The dogma of the Holy Trinity is, of course, contained in the Old Testament; however, it remains partially hidden and as if undeveloped, so that only in the light of the New Testament revelation do the pertinent texts acquire their full significance and lose their apparent incomprehensibility. The Old Testament displays clear traces of the doctrine of the trihypostatic God (see Isa. 6:3) and even hints, as it were, at the distinctly personal being of the hypostases, at least that of the Son (Ps. 2:7; Ps. 110:1-4) and thus, indirectly, that of the Father. As for the Third hypostasis, even hints are absent, but at the same time a great deal is said about the spirit of God (see Isa. 63). This constitutes a fundamental fact of the Old Testament revelation concerning the spirit of God, namely, that *this revelation does not know at all the hypostasis of the Holy Spirit but knows very well the action of the spirit of God.* There naturally arises the problem of the correct dogmatic exegesis of the pertinent texts: Is it a question of God as spirit in general or is it a question (though in a hidden manner) precisely of the Holy Spirit? But in this case there is no *either/or* alternative, for the two terms are compatible: if God is spirit, every one of His actions is spiritual, is a manifestation of spirit; but at the same time God's spirituality finds its revelation precisely in the Third hypostasis, in the indivisible unity of this hypostasis with the other hypostases. Therefore, the distinction concerns not the essence of the matter but only the logical accent or the express intention of the particular text. It concerns the idea that the text predominantly expresses: the hypostatic being of the Holy Spirit, the revelation of God in theophany, or the communication of express gifts. Naturally, different texts have different meanings. Let us present a brief survey of these texts.

Our attention is first drawn by Genesis 1:2: "the Spirit of God moved upon the face of the waters" of the first creation. This, of course, expresses God's general creative action upon the formless primordial matter, the initial chaos, unmanifested in its content, the *tohu vabohu*. Insofar as in general the creation of the world is the work of God Who is in the Holy Trinity, there is no obstacle to associating this spirit of God with the action of trihypostatic Divinity in the world. But at the same time, since the place of the Third hypostasis in creation is defined precisely as that of the *accomplishing* hypostasis, one can see here a direct indication of the action of the Holy Spirit as the *Third hypostasis.*

Nevertheless, and this must be underscored, here it is directly more a question of the *action* of the Holy Spirit than of His hypostasis: the spirit of God is considered apart from His hypostatic definition, as if extrahypostatically (although not nonhypostatically). And this separation between the action of the Spirit and the knowledge of His hypostasis, the possibility and presence of such a nonhypostatic revelation of the Spirit, is the primary and primordial fact in the revelation of the Holy Spirit, which can be observed at the very beginning of the being of the world, or in its *first* creation, which will be followed by the second creation, the Six Days.

This movement of the Spirit of God over the earth (in the liturgical symbolics this corresponds to the movement of the covering over the sacred gifts during the recitation of the Creed) is already the *first* Pentecost, not one which is effected upon man, but one which *anticipates* the coming of man into the world. To continue this parallel, let us note that neither the first nor the second Pentecost knows the *Holy Spirit Himself* in His hypostatic being; they only receive His power, both in the fructification of the world and in the human souls inflamed by the tongues of fire. Genesis 1:2 is, in general, the most important testimony about the Spirit of God in the Old Testament revelation that refers to the time *before* God's first covenant with man and even *before* man. However, this earth was precisely that dust of the ground out of which was created the human body for the breathing into it of the breath of life from God (Gen. 2:7).

The next Old Testament text concerning the Spirit of God concerns antediluvian humanity's blasphemy against the Holy Spirit. Antediluvian humanity had extinguished the spirit in itself to such a degree that it was said about it, "My Spirit must not for ever be disgraced in man, for he is but flesh" (Gen. 6:3; translation taken from the *Jerusalem Bible*). Exegetically, we have here the same double meaning: "My Spirit" can refer either to Divinity and His spirituality in general or to the Spirit Himself, the Third hypostasis. But even in the second case the accent lies precisely upon the *spirituality* of the Spirit, not upon His *hypostasis*.

The Spirit of God in general, without further specific definition, is mentioned in a number of texts of a messianic character. These texts can also be interpreted in the general sense of divine action and inspiration, and acquire a more precise meaning only in the light of the New Testament revelation, precisely with reference to the Holy Spirit. Here we may mention Isaiah 11:2, "and the spirit of the Lord shall rest upon him," and Isaiah 61:1, "the Spirit of the Lord God is upon me; because the Lord hath anointed me." The authentic interpretation of this text is given by the Lord Himself in Luke 4:18. Not as indisputable is the exclusive application of Isaiah 42:1 to the Third hypostasis: "Behold my servant. . . . I have put my spirit upon him" (cf. Matt. 12:18); the same goes for Isaiah 48:16. But the direct and immediate meaning of even these texts does *not* necessarily include a revelation of the Third hypostasis, but concerns above all the general effect of inspiration from God.

Apart from these texts of messianic import, there are a number of expressions where the "Spirit of God" is synonymous with the concept of God. Among these we find: "the spirit of God hath made me" (Job 33:4); "by the word of the Lord were the heavens made; and all the host of them by the breath [spirit] of his mouth" (Ps. 33:6); "thy spirit is good; lead me into the land of uprightness" (Ps. 143:10); "whither shall I go from thy spirit?" (Ps. 139:7); "thou sendest forth thy spirit, they are created" (Ps. 104:30); "until the spirit be poured upon us from on high, and the wilderness be a fruitful field" (Isa. 32:15); "thou gavest also thy good spirit to instruct them" (Neh. 9:20); "yet many years didst thou forbear them, and testifiedst against them by thy spirit in thy prophets: yet would they not give ear" (Neh. 9:30); "I will pour my spirit upon thy seed, and my blessing upon thine offspring" (Isa. 44:3); "this is my covenant with them, saith the Lord; My spirit that is upon thee, and my words which I have put in thy mouth, shall not depart out of thy mouth, nor out of the mouth of thy seed" (Isa. 59:21); "a new heart also will I give you, and a new spirit will I put within you. . . . I will put my spirit within you, and cause you to walk in my statutes" (Ezek. 36:26-27; 37:5, 14); "they . . . vexed his holy Spirit. . . . Where is he that put his holy Spirit within him?" (Isa. 63:10-11); "neither will I hide my face from them: for I have poured out my spirit upon the house of Israel" (Ezek. 39:29); "my spirit remaineth among you: fear ye not" (Hag. 2:5). Joel 2:28-32 occupies a special place among these texts: "And it shall come to pass afterward, that I will pour out my spirit upon all flesh . . . and also upon the servants and upon the handmaids in those days will I pour out my spirit," and further. In and of itself this text can be placed in the series of texts that refer to divine inspiration. But apart from its direct historical significance, this text has also received an express interpretation that relates it to the descent of the Holy Spirit at the Pentecost (Acts 2:17-18); and thus this prophecy acquires a more concrete meaning with reference to a specific event. Even here, in this exclusive and, in its own way, unique text, we have an indication of the revelation of the Holy Spirit, but not of the manifestation of His hypostasis. Here it is said that "they were all filled with the Holy Spirit" (Acts 2:4), but it is not said that they saw His Face, which was of course not manifested in the vision of the tongues of fire.

Apart from these texts of a general significance, we also have in the Old Testament a number of testimonies about the communication of various *gifts* of the Holy Spirit of a special character. These testimonies have, of course, a major dogmatic significance: they represent a sort of Old Testament Pentecost, in anticipation of the New Testament Pentecost. The Old Testament speaks of various gifts of the Spirit: artistic gifts (or creative gifts in general), as well as the gifts of government, waging war, kingship, priesthood, and, finally, prophecy.

II. In the New Testament

Among the multitude of texts in the New Testament that refer to the Holy Spirit, one should first identify those that are naturally absent from the Old Testament, that is, those that refer to His *hypostatic* being. Only in the New Testament do we have a clear revelation of the Holy Trinity and of Its three distinct hypostases: the incarnate Son revealed together with Himself also the Father, as well as the Holy Spirit as the hypostatic Paternal love reposing upon Him. Therefore, in the New Testament we have a differentiated revelation of the Holy Spirit and of the spirit of God with His gifts. It is true that, thanks to the accomplished revelation of the Holy Spirit as the Third hypostasis, the particular manifestations and revelations of the spirit of God and of divine grace are naturally interrelated with the Holy Spirit and receive His hypostatic coefficient, as it were. One must first identify passages that indisputably refer to the Holy Spirit, insofar as the general character of the texts enables us to do this.

Let us begin with the Synoptic Gospels, and in particular with the Nativity (for our purposes, this includes the Annunciation). The angel Gabriel tells Mary: "The Holy Spirit shall come upon thee" (Luke 1:35).

And in Matthew 1:18, we read: "before they came together, she was found with child of the Holy Spirit"; further, the angel of the Lord appears to Joseph in a dream and tells him, "that which is conceived in her is of the Holy Spirit" (Matt. 1:20), whence the formula of the Nicaeno-Constantinopolitan Creed: "incarnate of the Holy Spirit and the Virgin Mary." According to church tradition, these texts refer to the *hypostasis* of the Holy Spirit; however, there can arise a purely grammatical doubt, although one that does not have decisive significance: in these texts the expressions *pneuma hagion* and *ek pneumatos hagiou* lack an article.[2]

But this is not the case in the narrative concerning the Baptism of the Lord, which speaks of the descent of the Holy Spirit from the heavens in the form of a dove: *to pneuma* (Mark 1:10; cf. 1:12); however, we find *pneuma theou* in Matthew 3:16 (but also *hupo tou pneumatos* in 4:1) and *to pneuma to hagion* in Luke 3:22; cf. 4:1: *plērēs pn. hagiou,* but *en tōi pneumati.* Also relevant here is John's testimony about the descent of the Holy Spirit seen by him: *to pneuma katabainon,* followed soon after by *en pneumati hagiōi* (John 1:32, 33).

Also relevant is the narrative in Luke 2:25-26 about the righteous Simeon, upon whom was the Holy Spirit *(to pneuma to hagion);* it was promised to him by the Holy Spirit *(hupo tou pn. hagiou)* that he would not see death before he had seen the Lord's Christ; and he came "in the Spirit" *(en tōi pneumati)* into the temple.

Further, different modes of the reposing of the Holy Spirit upon Jesus are attested: "Jesus being full of the Holy Spirit *(Pneumatos Hagiou)* returned from Jordan, and was led by the Spirit [*tōi Pneumati*] into the wilderness" (Luke 4:1). Further, in the preaching in Nazareth it is said, "the Spirit of the Lord [*Pneuma Kuriou*] is upon me" (Luke 4:18). About the healings it is said, "I cast out devils by the Spirit of God [*en Pneumati Theou*]" (Matt. 12:28), which is connected with the Lord's words about the blasphemy against the Holy Spirit, *kata tou Pneumatos tou Hagiou* (12:32); "in that hour Jesus rejoiced in the Holy Spirit" (Luke 10:21).

Also pertinent here are John the Forerunner's words about Christ, namely, that Christ will "baptize you with the Holy Spirit [*en Pneumati Hagiōi*], and with fire" (Matt. 3:11; cf. Mark 1:8; Luke 3:16; John 1:33). Also,

---

2. According to H. B. Swete (*The Holy Spirit in the New Testament* [London: Macmillan, 1910], pp. 395-98), in general, *pneuma hagion* is encountered significantly more frequently in the New Testament than *to pneuma to hagion* or *to hagion pneuma,* the ratio being 54:34. In particular, the absence of the article is encountered after the preposition *ek,* especially in Matthew 1:18, 20.

about John himself it is said by the angel Gabriel that "he shall be filled with the Holy Spirit [*Pneumatos Hagiou*], even from his mother's womb" (Luke 1:15). Finally, of essential importance here is, of course, the baptismal formula of Matt. 28:19: "baptizing them in the name of the Father, and of the Son, and of the Holy Spirit."

Turning now to the Gospel of John, it is necessary to say first of all that this Gospel is pneumatological *par excellence*. Having been written by Christ's beloved disciple, who received into his home the Spirit-bearing Mother of God and was adopted by Her, this Gospel is filled with knowledge of the Holy Spirit and revelation about Him in a wholly special, exclusive sense. The revelation concerning God the Word, logology, is marvelously united here with the revelation of the Holy Spirit, pneumatology. And here the revelation concerning the Third hypostasis has a twofold character: first, a direct character, as a doctrine of the Holy Spirit (encountered throughout the Gospel) and of the Comforter (in Jesus' Last Discourse); and second, an indirect and hidden character, which gives us a glimpse of the *dyadic* connection of the Second and Third hypostases, so that logology becomes also pneumatology. Let us examine separately these two forms of the revelation concerning the Holy Spirit in the Gospel of John, beginning with the dyadic and hidden revelation.

Let us begin with the *prologue*, which is usually viewed as only a logology, a doctrine of the Logos in God (the Father), as if the Holy Trinity were only a dyad. As might be expected, however, we have here a hidden, though intelligible, doctrine of the Holy Spirit as well, and thus a doctrine of the entire Holy Trinity. "In the beginning was the Word [the Second hypostasis], and the Word was with [*pros*] God [*ton Theon*, the First hypostasis], and the Word was God [*Theos*]. The same was in the beginning with [*pros*] God" (John 1:1-2). What does this "with," this *"pros,"* signify here? In the usual interpretation of this text, it seems to signify nothing. But in this sacred text, full of such significance, is it possible to treat with such neglect a preposition that expresses the relation between the Father and the Son? This is an essential and hypostatic relation: the Holy Spirit as the hypostatic love of the Father and the Son. Therefore, this text refers precisely to the *entire* Holy Trinity, although in a hidden manner.

The dyadic union of the Son and the Holy Spirit is indicated here — also in a hidden manner — in the following verse: "All things were made by him; and without him was not any thing made that was made" (John 1:3). This verse, referring to the creation of the world, indicates not only the demiurgic significance of the Second hypostasis but also the accomplishing significance of the Third hypostasis: the ideal "all things" of the

Logos "were made," received reality and life in the Holy Spirit. Here, the action of the two hypostases is defined dyadically, one in or through the other: "All things were made by him."

Verse 4 has a similar dyadic significance: "In him was life; and the life was the light of men." What does the expression "life" signify here? It has a specific hypostatic significance and refers to the Life-giving Spirit, who reposes upon the Son and, with Him, constitutes the Dyad of the self-revelation of the Father, while abiding "in him." And this hypostatic life, revealing itself in union with the Word, this divine-human Dyad, is "the light of men" and thus of the entire creaturely world, which arose out of the darkness of nonbeing: "And the light shineth in darkness; and the darkness comprehendeth it not" (1:5).

About this dyadic light it is said further, now in connection with the Divine Incarnation: "That was the true Light, which lighteth every man that cometh into the world" (1:9). In the Gospel of John as well as in the prayers of the Church,[3] the *light* refers to Christ; but in the ecclesiastical literature it also frequently refers to the Holy Spirit[4] ("the light of Tabor"). Further, the prologue treats one of the basic themes of the Gospel of John: *glory* and glorification, which is, of course, a manifestation of the Third hypostasis, together with *grace* (and truth). "And the Word was made flesh, and dwelt among us (and we beheld his glory, the glory as of the only begotten of the Father), full of grace and truth" (1:14). And the glory is, of course, the reposing upon Him of the Holy Spirit. Further, the prologue speaks of the "fullness" of grace, i.e., of the Holy Spirit, reposing upon Him: "And of his fullness have all we received, and grace for grace. For the law was given by Moses, but grace and truth came by Jesus Christ" (1:16-17). Here, the communication of grace to the world through the sending down of the Holy Spirit is defined as the work of Christ. And this is confirmed and attested by John: "I saw the Spirit descending from heaven like a dove" (1:32); "the same is he which baptizeth with the Holy Spirit" (1:33).

We arrive at the conclusion that the prologue of the Gospel of John cannot be understood only as a logology; rather, it contains a complete trinitarian theology, including a pneumatology, though the latter is expressed almost tacitly, in a mere breath, as it were (according to a common patristic simile, like the breath from God's lips, speaking the supra-eternal Word).

---

3. "O Christ, true light, illuminate and sanctify all men who come into the world," etc.

4. See, for example, the "Hymns" of Symeon the New Theologian.

The narrative in John 2 of the first miracle, the transformation of water into wine at the marriage of Cana of Galilee, can be allegorically interpreted in the sense of a manifestation of the power of the Spirit (for it is said that here Christ "manifested forth this glory," i.e., the Holy Spirit [2:11]). But the Holy Spirit is already the direct subject of the conversation with Nicodemus in John 3, where Jesus speaks of being born of the Spirit (3:5-6, 8); also, the Forerunner says in John 3 that "God giveth not the Spirit [*to pneuma*] by measure" (3:34). From this is concluded that "the Father loveth the Son, and hath given all things into his hand. He that believeth on the Son hath everlasting life" (3:35-36). Do these words not refer to the Father's hypostatic love for the Son and to eternal Life in the Holy Spirit?

We find a new revelation of the Spirit in the fourth chapter of John, in the conversation with the woman of Samaria. At the beginning of this conversation, Jesus speaks of the living water that He will give, which in those who drink it will become "a well of water springing up into everlasting life" (4:14). This is clearly a reference to the Holy Spirit, as we see from the commentary in John 7:38-39: "He that believeth on me, as the scripture hath said, out of his belly shall flow rivers of living water. (But this spake he of the Spirit; which they that believe on him should receive: for the Holy Spirit was not yet given; because that Jesus was not yet glorified.)" Further, the Gospel of John speaks of the worship of the Father "in spirit and truth" (4:23), because God seeks such worshippers, for "God is a spirit: and they that worship him must worship him in spirit and in truth" (4:24). Here the Gospel speaks simultaneously of God Who is in the Holy Trinity as Spirit and of the express hypostatic spirituality of the Holy Trinity in the Holy Spirit through the revelation in Spirit and Truth.

The fifth chapter of John, which contains Jesus' discourse about eternal life and resurrection, includes a series of testimonies, albeit indirect, about the Holy Spirit. It speaks of the "works" of the Father and the Son (5:19-20), which in general are accomplished by the Holy Spirit. It also speaks of resurrection and quickening (5:21), which (as we see from a comparison with other texts, e.g., Rom. 8:11) are also accomplished by the Holy Spirit. Finally, it speaks of Life, which, according to the Prologue, also signifies the hypostasis of the Spirit. "For as the Father hath life in himself; so hath he given to the Son to have life in himself" (5:26). This Life is, of course, not a mere "property," which can be communicated (or fail to be communicated); rather, it is hypostatic Life itself, the Holy Spirit, who proceeds from the Father and reposes upon the Son. But, in conformity with the intratrinitarian distinctions, Life is also the principle that is expressly proper to the Third hypostasis; and John 5:26 refers precisely to the procession of this hypostasis upon the Son and to its reposing upon Him.

This same fifth chapter refers mysteriously to the Holy Spirit when it speaks of *bearing witness:* "If I bear witness of myself, my witness is not true. There is another that beareth witness of me; and I know that the witness which he witnesseth of me is true. Ye sent unto John, and he bare witness unto the truth. But I receive not testimony from man" (5:31-34). Who is this "another" who bears witness and whose witness is not from man, and in particular not from John? This is, of course, the hypostatic Holy Spirit; and the very expression "another that beareth witness" is clearly meant to remind us of an analogous expression: "he [the Father] shall give you another Comforter" (John 14:16), alongside Christ. In conformity with this, after the Resurrection and in preparation for the Ascension, when His own earthly testimony was about to come to an end, the Lord assigned the function of witnesses to the apostles, to whom He said: "ye shall receive power when the Holy Spirit comes upon you, and ye shall be witnesses" (Acts 1:8; the King James Version has been modified to conform with the Russian Bible). The text of Luke confirms that of John by also speaking of the Holy Spirit as "another," as a "witness" *(marturōn).* In connection with this, the Father's own testimony at the Epiphany is recalled: "And the Father himself, which hath sent me, hath borne witness of me" (John 5:37). John 8:13-18 once again speaks of bearing witness, and about *two* witnesses, but this time they are the Father and the Son.

The sixth chapter of John, which contains the eucharistic conversation, once again refers to the Eternal Life received from the Son (6:40, 47, 54), and to the "raising" (6:54) — a set of ideas that includes, besides the action of the Son, the action of the Spirit. And it is even directly said about the Spirit, "It is the spirit *(to pneuma)* that quickeneth; the flesh profiteth nothing: the words that I speak unto you, they are spirit, and they are life" (5:63), i.e., they have the Holy Spirit (cf. Rom. 8:2; 2 Cor. 3:6). And it is not by chance that Simon Peter testifies before Him in the name of the apostles: "Thou hast the words of eternal life" (John 5:68), i.e., from the Holy Spirit. Here, the word of the Word and the spirit of the Spirit are united in the ministry of Christ, the Spirit-bearing Incarnate Word.

The seventh chapter of John contains the text, already mentioned by us, concerning the rivers of living water, representing the Holy Spirit, which those who believed in Christ were to receive from Him after His glorification (7:38-39). In the eighth chapter, a pneumatological significance can be attributed to the verse "ye shall know the truth, and the truth shall make you free" (8:32) when it is compared to the text of the apostle Paul: "where the Spirit of the Lord is, there is liberty" (2 Cor. 3:17).

The ninth chapter, which is about the healing of the man blind from his birth, contains a testimony about the light, and this testimony is in the most decisive form: "As long as I am in the world, I am the light of the world" (9:5); cf. John 12:35-36. Does this passage, clearly parallel to John 1:4-9, signify that the word "light" here refers solely to the Son? We do not see the necessity of such an interpretation, for Christ lighted the world not only by His own light of truth, that of the Word of God, but also by the light of the Holy Spirit reposing upon Him and revealing the Son in Him. He lighted the world not monohypostatically, so to speak, but dyadically, precisely as *Christ*, the incarnate Son, anointed by the Holy Spirit; and only in this fullness can we understand Christ's words about the light.

Christ's words to Martha prior to the raising of Lazarus must be understood in a similar dyadic sense with reference to the incarnate Word, Christ, anointed by the Holy Spirit: "I am the resurrection and the life" (John 11:25). Her answer must be understood in the same dyadic spirit: "I believe that thou art the Christ [the Anointed by the Spirit], the Son of God" (11:27).[5] About the raising itself, Christ says, "if thou wouldest believe, thou shouldest see the glory of God" (11:40), i.e., the manifestation of the Holy Spirit (just as in the Synoptic Gospels we have the testimony that Christ expels demons by the Spirit of God). The voice from heaven, heard during the arrival of the Greeks, likewise signifies a manifestation of the power of the Holy Spirit, this time with reference to Christ's own resurrection: "I have both glorified it [His name], and will glorify it again" (John 12:28).

Thus, we see that the first twelve chapters of the Gospel of John (except perhaps the tenth) present a doctrine — sometimes implicit and sometimes explicit — of the Third hypostasis, a doctrine which permeates the entire theology of the Theologian Evangelist. One can say that this theology has as its object the Incarnate Word and the Holy Spirit in Their dyadic union.

But this theme, hitherto only subordinate, becomes the central and dominant one in chapters 13-17 of the Gospel of John, i.e., in the Last Discourse of the Lord Jesus. This divine leave-taking melts our hearts with unearthly music in divine love, which pours forth in this discourse like a

---

5. One cannot fail to see a parallel to this text in Peter's confession: "Thou art the Christ, the Son of the living God" (Matt. 16:16; cf. John 6:69).

Pentecost of the Word. The Lord departs from the world and leaves His disciples behind, but He will soon return to the world and will never again leave His disciples; that is the fundamental antinomy of this discourse. The Lord pronounces this discourse not as the Christ sent into the world but as the Paraclete, the Intercessor before the Father, and as the Comforter. Although Christ Himself is leaving the world, He is sending into it "another Comforter, *allon paraklēton*" (John 14:16), Who will abide with us forever and Who, being identified with Christ in some sense, will take His place. Therefore, about this coming it is said, "I will not leave you comfortless: I will come to you. Yet a little while, and the world seeth me no more; but ye see me: because I live, ye shall live also" (14:18-19).

Christ's Last Discourse is not only an exceptional and abundant source of revelation concerning the Holy Spirit as the hypostatic Comforter; it also includes an exceptionally clear doctrine of Their dyadic bi-unity, bi-identity, bi-Comforterhood. In the divine dyad the two hypostases are made transparent in divine love; and in the Last Discourse this identification reaches such an extreme that its true subject is not the Son, Who speaks, and not the Spirit, about Whom He speaks, but *Their* bi-unity, in which the Father is revealed. The discourse speaks about the trinitarian mystery, and the Holy Trinity is glorified in Christ's last earthly speech, in this miracle of miracles, this Gospel of Gospels, the sweetest word of the Sweetest Lord.

By its design the Last Discourse is a complex symphonic composition, in which the dominant theme with its subthemes is repeated and developed in different combinations and variations, in conformity with an internal, not always easily accessible, unity. We will not attempt to give a detailed analysis of this divine symphony; rather, we will trace its dominant theme: the doctrine of the Third hypostasis as the *Paraclete*. The Lord pronounces here this name for the first time, as a new revelation. (The same apostle John applies the expression *parakleton* — advocate — to the Lord Jesus Christ in 1 John 2:1.)

The entire symphonic complexity of the Last Discourse is centered on the promise to send down the Holy Spirit; and in this sense this discourse is nothing else but a *promise of the Pentecost*. In this sense, this discourse is perfectly parallel to the Savior's conversations with His disciples, recorded in the Acts of the Apostles, before His final departure from the world in the Ascension: Appearing to them for forty days, the Lord spoke to them about the "kingdom of God" (Acts 1:3), which, in general and in particular in this context, signifies the coming of the Holy Spirit. Having "assembled" them, He "commanded" them to "wait for the promise of the

Father" (1:4), that is, for the baptism with the Holy Spirit (1:5). The Last Discourse concerns both the Lord's preparation for the passion and His departure from the world and His glorification. The passion, the glorification in the resurrection, the ascension, and the sitting at the right hand of the Father with the sending down of the Holy Spirit are therefore considered as a single, complex act as well as separately (in different parts of the discourse).

Let us examine in detail the promises concerning the Holy Spirit in this discourse and, first of all, the direct testimony concerning the Comforter. The Third hypostasis receives this name here for the first time; in fact, He simultaneously receives two names: "Comforter, which is the Holy Spirit" (John 14:26), and "Paraclete," which can also mean "advocate," *"advocatus"* (cf. 1 John 2:1: "we have an advocate . . . [before] the Father [*paraklēton pros ton Patera*], Jesus Christ"). The work of the *first* Paraclete, of the Advocate Christ, consists, first of all, in advocating the sending down of the "other" Paraclete, the Holy Spirit: "And I will pray the Father, and he shall give you another Comforter, that he may abide with you for ever" (John 14:16). The *sending down* of the Comforter is represented here as a work of the Father in response to the Son's prayer and thus as a work of Both of them, of the dyadic union of the Father and the Son (which leads to a particular interpretation of the Filioque). In the same way, the sending down of the Holy Spirit is understood only in connection with the Son, by Whom and instead of Whom He is sent: we thus have another dyadic union, that of the Son and the Holy Spirit. The Holy Spirit too is an Advocate, Who gives us the grace of prayer: "the Spirit [*to pneuma*] itself maketh intercession [*huperentunchanei*] for us with groanings which cannot be uttered" (Rom. 8:26).

But besides this purely soteriological meaning, the "Paraclete" signifies precisely the Comforter, who brings *comfort* to the apostles and to the entire world by His descent, for through Him is given the abiding of Christ "always, until the end of the world." As we have seen, in the Last Discourse Christ speaks *four* (or more precisely five) times about the coming and sending down of the Comforter, so that it becomes the dominant theme of this discourse, as it were. And each time we have a new development of this theme in a different aspect. First, Christ speaks dyadically about the coming of the Comforter, that is, His coming is related to the departure of the Son: *"another* Comforter, that he may abide with you for ever" (14:16). This "another Comforter" *(allon Paraklēton)* dyadically unites the Spirit with the Son with reference to the sending down into the world and the action in the world; the coming of the Spirit replaces the departure of the Son, and the two are identified, as it were: "I will not leave you comfortless: I will come to you. Yet a little while, and the world seeth me no more; but ye see me" (John 14:18-19). Here, the Holy Spirit, also dyadically, is called "the Spirit of Truth," *to pneuma tēs alētheias;* and the Truth, of course, is Christ: "I am the way, the truth [*hē alētheia*], and the life" (John 14:6).

Next, Christ says about the Holy Spirit, also in a dyadic sense, that "the Comforter, which is the Holy Spirit, whom the Father will send *in my name* . . . shall teach you all things, and bring all things to your remembrance, whatsoever I have said unto you" (14:26). In His third reference to the Comforter, Christ speaks of the sending down of the Comforter in a more complex dyadic combination: "when the Comforter is come, whom I will send unto you, from the Father, even the Spirit of truth, which proceedeth from the Father, he shall testify of me" (15:26). Here, Christ is referring both to the dyadic relation of the Holy Spirit to the Father ("which proceedeth from the Father") and to the dyadic relation of the Spirit to the Son ("whom I will send unto you, from the Father"), which represent two definitions of the Holy Spirit: (1) in the most *primordial* self-revelation of the Father in the Holy Spirit and (2) *within* this self-revelation of the Father, in the Son *and* the Holy Spirit. In the framework of the second definition, the dyadic interrelation of the Son and the Holy Spirit is determined by the fact that the "Spirit of Truth" manifests the Son: "he shall testify of me."

Next and fourth, the coming of the Comforter is directly related (also, to be sure, dyadically) to Christ's departure: "but if I depart, I will send him unto you" (16:7). And His work will be to "reprove the world of sin, and of righteousness, and of judgment: of sin, because they believe not on me; of righteousness, because I go to my Father, and ye see me no more; of judgment, because the prince of this world is judged" (16:8-11).

Finally, the coming of the Holy Spirit (although without the name "Comforter") is referred to a *fifth* time in this discourse, also in the same dyadic interrelation with the Son, Whom He reveals: "when he, the Spirit of truth, is come, he will guide you into all truth: for he shall not speak of himself; but whatsoever he shall hear, that shall he speak; and he will shew you things to come. He shall glorify me: for he shall receive of mine, and shall shew it unto you. All things that the Father hath are mine: therefore said I, that he shall take of mine, and shall shew it unto you" (16:13-15). This passage, even more decisively than the preceding ones, attests that dyadic interrelation of the Son and the Spirit in the self-revelation of the Father according to which the Son manifests the content of this revelation whereas the Spirit actualizes it: "he shall not speak of himself; but whatsoever he shall hear"; "he shall receive of mine, and shall shew it unto you."

The centuries-old disputes about the Holy Spirit's procession as origination infinitely obscured and distorted the true meaning of these texts. This is because some wished to find in these texts testimony confirming the procession of the Holy Spirit also from the Son, whereas others desired to weaken their true meaning by various exegetical intricacies. But if one removes this false problematic (for nothing is said here about the procession of the Holy Spirit), the meaning of the texts becomes simple and clear. In the self-revelation of the Holy Trinity, the Father is revealed through the Son by the Holy Spirit; and the inner character of this self-revelation is such that the Father directly manifests Himself to the Son, Who is the image of His hypostasis, while the Son is revealed in the Life-giving Holy Spirit, Who, in this sense, is, according to St. Athanasius, the "image of the Son." In this self-revelation of the Holy Trinity, we have: triadically, the Father through the Son in the Holy Spirit, or the Father through the Holy Spirit in the Son; dyadically, the Father in the Son, the Father in the Holy Spirit, the Son in the Holy Spirit, and the Holy Spirit in the Son. That is why "all things that the Father hath are mine [the Son's]," and "he [the Holy Spirit] shall take of mine" and "he shall glorify me." The intratrinitarian definition of the place of the Third hypostasis in the Last Discourse is given fully and exhaustively: both triadically and doubly dyadically.

Besides these direct testimonies, the Last Discourse also contains indirect testimonies concerning the actions and manifestations of the Third hypostasis. There is, first of all, the testimony concerning the Glory, which begins and ends the Last Discourse. Glory is the action of the Holy Spirit, His revelation and illumination, both in the Holy Trinity and in the world. That is why it is said, "He [the Comforter] shall glorify me" (John 16:14). In the Holy Trinity, Glory, the accomplished trihypostatic revelation, is the Divine Sophia, which the Son of God is deprived of by His kenosis, but which is restored to Him in His glorification (see John 13:31-32; 17:1-5). This glorification includes the Resurrection, the Ascension, and the Sitting at the right hand of the Father, all this being accomplished by the Holy Spirit. For the apostles, this glorification (17:22-24) is requested by the Son from the Father, and it too is accomplished by the action of the Holy Spirit, as is their sanctification by truth (17:17). But the action of the Comforter-Spirit is, of course, also "joy" (15:11), which is "full" (16:24), as well as peace ("Peace I leave with you, my peace I give unto you" [14:27]; cf. John 20:19, 21, 26)[6] and works accomplished in the Divine Spirit. The abiding of the Father in the Son and of the Son in the Father, which is accomplished in the Holy Spirit, results in works: "Believe in me that I am in the Father, and the Father in me: or else believe me for the very works' sake. . . . He that believeth on me, the works that I do shall he do also . . . because I go unto my Father" (John 14:11-12). But even more important are the testimonies of the Spirit in love, for, in the trinitarian God-Love, the Holy Spirit is hypostatic Love. It is in this light that one should understand the *new* commandment, much repeated, of love for one another (13:34; 15:17).

The commandment of love was proper to the Old Testament as well, as a commandment of the law on which "hang all the law and the prophets" (Matt. 22:40; cf. Mark 12:29-31; Luke 10:27). But the *new* commandment, by which "shall all men know that ye are my disciples, if ye have love one to another" (John 13:35), refers to *ecclesial* love, in the Holy Spirit; and the keeping of the commandments is only a consequence of love: "If ye love me, keep my commandments" (14:15, 21, 23; 15:10). This love is here traced back to its highest source, to Divine, intratrinitarian love, which, hypostatically, is the Holy Spirit. This most sublime content is proper to the following text: "my Father will love him, and we will come unto him, and make our abode with him" (14:23). In this "we" is concealed the hypostasis of love, the Third or connecting hypostasis. Also important in this connection is John 14:20: "At that day [at the Pentecost and also at the Parousia] ye shall know that I am in my Father, and ye in me, and I in you." This "in" signifies, once again, the Holy Spirit; cf. 15:4: "Abide in me, and I in you." This abiding is also in the Holy Spirit: "As the Father hath loved me, so have I loved you: continue ye in my love" (15:9); and this love is the Holy Spirit: cf. 16:27.

A similar meaning can be attributed to *union,* of course, in the Holy Spirit: "That they may all be one; as thou, Father, art in me, and I in thee, that they also may be one in us . . . that they may be one, even as we are one . . . that they may be made perfect in one" (17:21-23). "And the glory which thou gavest me I have given them; that they may be one, even as we are one" (17:22). (This passage is made remarkable by a trait that cannot be en-

6. Cf. the context: "Then said Jesus to them again, Peace be unto you: as my Father hath sent me, even so send I you. And when he had said this, he breathed on them, and saith unto them, Receive ye the Holy Spirit" (John 20:21-22). Cf. Luke 24:36, as well as Romans 14:17: "the kingdom of God is . . . righteousness, and peace, and joy in the Holy Spirit."

countered anywhere else in an analogous form: the unification or rather the identification of the abiding in Glory and the abiding in union; both are given by the Holy Spirit.) And the high-priestly prayer concludes with the most sublime passage concerning love in the Holy Spirit: "that the love wherewith thou hast loved me may be in them, and I in them" (17:26). This love of the Father for the Son is in fact the Holy Spirit, Who is inseparably (dyadically) united with the Son and Who brings the Son.

There is yet another text that, though it speaks directly about the Holy Spirit, refers to His gifts, rather than to His hypostasis. We mean John 20:22-23: "when he had said this, he breathed on them, and saith unto them, Receive ye the Holy Spirit: Whose soever sins ye remit, they are remitted unto them: and whose soever sins ye retain, they are retained." It is a question of a specific hierarchical gift in the Church. This is, as it were, a consecration of the apostles to the rank of hierarchs, accomplished by the High-Priest Christ while He is still on earth, in anticipation of the Pentecost of the entire Church. In the First Epistle of John too, it is a question of the spirit of God rather than of the hypostatic Holy Spirit: see 1 John 3:24; 4:1, 13; even 5:6 (we refrain from using the *comma Johanneum*, 5:7-8, because of the uncertain nature of this text).

In the inspired Revelation of John, all is said in the spirit (1:10), but little is said directly about the Third hypostasis. The Spirit speaks to the churches (2:7, 11, 17, 29; 3:6, 13, 22), although here one can see only the action or inspiration of the spirit, not His hypostasis. The most important and solemn passage concerning the Holy Spirit in the Church concludes with "And the Spirit and the bride say, Come" (22:17)[7] and the answering call of "him that heareth": "Even so, come, Lord Jesus" (22:20).

The book of the Acts of the Apostles, a history of the evolving Church, occupies a special place in the New Testament writings. It begins with the Pentecost, the visible descent of the Holy Spirit upon the apostles and His palpable action in the Church. Although this is the clearest revelation of the Third hypostasis that we have, here too, even in the manifestation of the cloven tongues of fire, we know the Holy Spirit only in His gifts and actions. That is why the Acts of the Apostles do not teach us more about the hypostasis of the Holy Spirit than do the other books of the New Testament. Wherever in the Acts of the Apostles it is said that the Holy Spirit (or simply the Spirit, *to pneuma*: 6:10; 10:19; 11:12, 28; 16:7; 20:22; 21:4) "witnesses" (5:32; 20:23), "was given" (8:18), "descended" or "poured

---

7. One should also take special note of the words of Revelation 22:17: "let him take the water of life freely."

out" (10:44-45), is "received" (19:2), "speaks" (11:12; 21:4, 11; 28:25) — this refers not to the Holy Spirit in His hypostatic being but to His grace-bestowing action, to the gifts of the Holy Spirit. It is precisely this character of the revelation of the Holy Spirit and concerning the Holy Spirit that is attested by that text of Joel's prophecy (2:28-32) to which the sacred historian refers (Acts 2:16-21). But just as the Old Testament did not in general have a hypostatic revelation concerning the Holy Spirit but knew only the spirit of God, so the Acts of the Apostles attest precisely to the *gifts* of the Holy Spirit, to the "cloven tongues like as of fire" (2:3). But these tongues do not yet manifest the very source of the flame, the Divine hypostasis of the Spirit. "And they were filled with the Holy Spirit" (Acts 2:4), said about the apostles, is therefore synonymous with "I will pour out my Spirit" (2:17).

Numerous sayings about the Holy Spirit in the apostolic epistles have a similar meaning. These sayings refer to the actions of grace and to the gifts of the Holy Spirit, that is, in general, to the divine action upon man, just as in the Old Testament, although more concretely. Only in certain exceptional cases is it possible to determine that what is meant is precisely the distinct hypostasis of the Holy Spirit, and not the action of Christ, of the Holy Trinity, or of God in general. Such a predominantly hypostatic conception of the Holy Spirit can be found in the following texts: 1 Peter 1:2 (trinitarian blessing); 1 Peter 1:11 ("the spirit of Christ which was in them"); 1 Peter 1:12 ("that have preached the gospel unto you with the Holy Spirit sent down from heaven"); Romans 8:11 ("if the Spirit of him that raised up Jesus from the dead dwell in you, he that raised up Christ from the dead shall also quicken your mortal bodies by his Spirit that dwelleth in you"); also 8:14-27; 1 Corinthians 2:10 ("God hath revealed them unto us by his Spirit: for the Spirit searcheth all things, yea, the deep things of God"); also 1 Corinthians 2:11-14; 12:3-11, 13; Ephesians 3:5, 16; Philippians 1:19 ("the supply of the Spirit of Jesus Christ").

In summing up, we can say that even the Pentecost, as it is represented in the Acts of the Apostles and other New Testament writings, *does not yet give us knowledge of the Third hypostasis itself,* but reveals only its gifts and its actions upon human beings. The Pentecost is the manifestation of the tongues of fire, not of the Fire itself. The gifts and actions of the Spirit are known in the Old Testament as well, but to a different degree and in a different manner. A general question arises: Is the baptism with the Holy Spirit (see Acts 1:5), promised by Christ to His disciples before the Ascension, this descent of the Holy Spirit through which the disciples will receive the power to become witnesses of Christ (see 1:8) — is this descent, this Pentecost, the *already accomplished* coming of the Comforter Spirit Himself, promised in the Last Discourse? Or is it only the anticipation, only the prefiguring, of the Comforter Spirit in the "vision" of the tongues of fire? Was this the fire itself or was it only a subjective sensation, a visual projection, so to speak, of the spiritual shock experienced by the disciples ("they were all filled with the Holy Spirit" [2:4], but *without* the article: *pneumatos hagiou*)?

A direct effect of this descent of the Spirit was the gift of tongues, which the apostle Paul describes as only one of the *gifts* of the Holy Spirit ("to another divers kinds of tongues" [1 Cor. 12:10]) among a series of gifts. The discourse of the apostle Peter immediately after the Pentecost does *not* refer to the hypostasis of the Holy Spirit, although it does begin with a reference to the prophecy of Joel about the pouring out of the "spirit upon all flesh" (Joel 2:28). But this reference is not the subject of the apostle's discourse, but is only the proof that he has the right to preach. Moreover, the event that had just occurred does not, clearly, cover the *entire* content of the prophecy, with regard either to the pouring out of the Holy Spirit "upon all flesh" or to its overall eschatological perspective. It is impossible to deny that the Pentecost is the fulfillment of the promise to send down the Comforter.

A comparison of the promises about the Comforter with the actual content of the event of the Pentecost, however, necessarily leads to the conclusion that here we have only the *beginning* of the fulfillment of the promises, not the perfect fulfillment. This beginning differs from the Old Testament pouring forth of the gifts of the Holy Spirit not so much qualitatively as quantitatively: it is characterized by a greater abundance and continuity of possession of these gifts in the Church. Meanwhile, the qualitative difference refers not so much to the revelation of the Holy Spirit as to the Incarnation of Christ, which finds its completion in the Church. In this sense the content of the Pentecost is more christological than pneumatological in nature, and it is directly expressed not in the preaching about the Holy Spirit but in the preaching about Christ and His resurrection.

We must strongly affirm a certain fact, which is established by a simple analysis of the totality of the Biblical texts that are pertinent here, of both the Old and the New Testament (and in particular the second chapter of the Acts of the Apostles): None of the revelations about the pouring forth of the Holy Spirit, either in the Old or in the New Testament, contain the manifestation of His hypostasis. The Holy Spirit is revealed not personally but impersonally (if one can use this expression), as a certain *action* of the entire Holy Trinity, or of the Father and of the Son, Who send *grace*. And where Scripture appears to speak of the hypostatic action of the Holy Spirit, a closer examination of the texts demonstrates that it is a question only of the grace-bestowing *action* of the Holy Spirit, not of the Holy Spirit Himself or of His personal presence. In particular, precisely this meaning can be attributed to the general formula of the eighth article of the Nicaeno-Constantinopolitan Creed: "who spake by the prophets." This means, of course, that the Holy Spirit "inspired the prophets" by His illumination, but by no means does it signify that the Holy Spirit proffered His *personal* word through the prophets, who in that case would only be His instruments. This entire article of the Creed is an extended affirmation that the Holy Spirit is a hypostasis which has its *personal* being in Divinity, but nothing is said about this personal being in its manifestation and revelation.

This becomes even more evident if we compare this silence, this absence of the personal revelation of the Holy Spirit, with the fullness of the personal revelation of the Son that is contained in the Gospels and other New Testament books, as well as in the Creed. And even if we compare it with the meager but nonetheless personal revelation that we have of the Father Himself and about the Father in the Son and through the Son, we must conclude that we know more about the hypostasis of the Father, which is transcendent in the Holy Trinity and which is revealed only through the other hypostases, than about the Holy Spirit in His hypostatic being. We cannot fail to be amazed by the fact that, with a single exception,[8] nowhere does the Bible speak of the Third hypostasis in the first person. Rather, it always speaks of the Third hypostasis in the third person, i.e., impersonally. The person of the Holy Spirit remains enshrouded in mystery; He is unknown, unrevealed. Is this a mystery that will be revealed in the future age, an as yet unaccomplished revelation, in the same way that the Old Testament did not know the *personal* revelation of the Son? Is it the case that the manifestation of the Person of the Holy Spirit cannot be encompassed by the "kingdom of grace," but can be realized only in the "kingdom of glory"? Or does this silence derive from a special personal property of the Holy Spirit as the Third hypostasis? Here,

---

8. This exception occurs in Acts 13:2: "As they ministered to the Lord, and fasted, the Holy Spirit said, Separate me [*moi*] Barnabas and Saul for the work whereunto I have called them." This unexpected and, of course, extremely important case of the use of the first-person pronoun with reference to the Holy Spirit does not differ in content from other cases of His guidance described in The Acts of the Apostles.

on the basis of the results of exegesis, we must affirm that we do not have a Biblical revelation of the Comforter Himself, as a Person, even as we do not know His hypostatic revelation in the history of the Church. The Comforter has not yet been manifested *personally,* although He has been sent to the Church in His New Testament gifts at the Pentecost.[9]

9. This absence of a personal revelation of the Third hypostasis is reflected in liturgics and prayer. Almost no prayers are directly addressed to the Holy Spirit (virtually the sole exception is "Heavenly King"), whereas an enormous number of prayers about the *sending down* of the Holy Spirit are addressed to the Father and the Son. One should also note the absence of a liturgical development of the feast of the Holy Spirit (after the Pentecost).

CHAPTER 4

The Dyad of the Word and the Spirit

I. In the Divine Sophia

The first part of this trilogy, *The Lamb of God* (ch. 1:4),[1] expounds a doctrine of the Divine Sophia considered as the self-revelation of the Holy Trinity, of the Father in the Son by the Holy Spirit, but primarily with reference to the *Second* hypostasis, the Lamb of God. It is now our task to examine this doctrine with reference to the Third hypostasis, the Holy Spirit. When one speaks of the Divine Dyad, of the Second hypostasis and the Third hypostasis in their dyadic union, this in no wise signifies that the triunity of the Holy Trinity is diminished in any way, or that It undergoes separation or sundering. On the contrary, the inner structure of the Holy Trinity includes not only the distinctly personal hypostases in their triunity but also their dyadic interrelations. The trinitarian character of the Dyad is fully affirmed through the principle of *monarchy,* which is established by the dyadic self-revelation of the Father as the "Principle," the Divine Subject. But His Predicate or Self-revelation, the Divine Sophia, is actualized as the bi-unity of *two* hypostases: the Word uttered by the Father, upon which reposes the Holy Spirit, Who proceeds from the Father.

This bi-unity, this intradivine "and" or "*dia* (through)" about which the Eastern and Western theologians dispute, is precisely the Divine Sophia as the self-revelation of the one Father. In this bi-unity, the personal revelations of the Second and Third hypostases are coordinated. In the depths of the consubstantial and indivisible Trinity, in Its triunity, one can distinguish, on the one hand, the First or Revealed hypostasis

---

1. See Translator's Introduction for information about this trilogy. — Trans.

and, on the other hand, the other two hypostases, the Dyad of the Son and the Spirit, the supra-eternal hypostatic self-revelation of the First hypostasis. This hypostasis must first be expressed in a negative form, by showing that, for the fullness of the self-revelation, it is insufficient to have just *one* of the hypostases, either that of the Son or that of the Holy Spirit. The Divine Sophia is not *only* the Son, just as she is not *only* the Holy Spirit; rather, she is the bi-unity of the Son and the Holy Spirit as one self-revelation of the Father. The true definition of the Divine Sophia is established by her identical relation to the self-revelation of *Both* the Son and the Spirit, in their dyadic interpenetration. All the misunder-standings concerning the relation of the Divine Sophia herself to the hypostases of the Word and Spirit, as well as concerning Their connection in the "procession" of the Holy Spirit *from* or *through* the Son, are rooted in an insufficient attention to the true character of this intratrinitarian Dyad, which really exists but which is usually sought in the wrong place.

This negative characterization serves to establish that the dyad can-not be reduced to a unity or sundered in half. On the other hand, its *posi-tive* definition signifies that the two hypostases are united through the self-revelation of the Father in the Divine Sophia *without separation and without confusion*. The one cannot be revealed without the other, just as they cannot be united to the point of complete fusion or identification.[2] The inseparability and inconfusibility of the hypostases of the dyad sig-nify at the same time the perfect concreteness of their interrelation, in which there can be no mutation or replacement: the first cannot take the place of the second, or the second the place of the first. To be sure, this concreteness must not have the slightest trace of subordinationism. The concreteness does not diminish their equal divinity, linked to their sepa-rate hypostatizedness; it refers, rather, to the equal necessity and irreplaceability of the hypostases in the divine self-revelation of the Fa-ther. This can be shown on the basis of the personal properties of the hypostases: it is proper to the Second hypostasis to be the Word of all words and the ideal objective content of the self-revelation, whereas the Third is *not* the Word, although It does not exist without the Word. Like-wise, the Word does not possess that power of quickening and accom-

2. The Ante-Nicene triadology and logology approached such a fusion or identifi-cation of the two revealing hypostases, in effect establishing not a trinitarian but a binitarian form of the Holy Trinity. This was due to a lack of development of the doc-trine of the Holy Spirit, which in effect was viewed as an *attribute* of the Second hypostasis.

plishment which is proper only to the Third hypostasis. And in this sense the Holy Spirit reposes upon the Son, Who receives this reposing, but not vice versa. In the interrelation of these two hypostases there can be no reversibility, for the latter would signify the abolition of their personal properties, that is, it would mean hypostatic nondifferentiation together with the denial of the inseparability and inconfusability of the Second and Third hypostases.

To characterize the hypostasis of the Holy Spirit the patristic literature likened the Second hypostasis to the lips and the Third to the breath out of the lips, or the Second to the word and the Third to the air moving as the word sounds. However poor and unsatisfactory this natural simile may be in clarifying the hypostatic character of the Word and the Spirit, it nevertheless correctly establishes this feature of Their *dyadic* union, which is inseparable and inconfusible, and also concrete and determinate. In effect, this dyadic union is *necessary* for the very realizability of the self-revelation: a word that is unspoken does not sound, although it preserves its conceptual content; a sound that does not contain a verbal idea is not a word, but only a vibration of the air.

Likewise, in the depths of the trinitarian self-revelation the Divine Sophia, as the all-ideal or all-verbal all-reality, the divine world, *entitas entium* [the entity of entities], cannot be realized through the Word alone, or through the Spirit alone. Expressing this crudely, we can say that there is no word in the Word for the Word Himself, for it is spoken *not* by the Son but only by the Father. It is the Father's Word. However, not only is there no word for the Son, Who does not say it, leaving this to be done by the Father; there is also no word for the Father, for the Father also does not say it Himself, leaving this for the begotten Son. *Both* are silent in mutually sacrificial love; and the Word Himself becomes mute in this sacrificial silence *between* the hypostases of the Father and the Son. The Word, begotten and born, becomes kenotically mute, as it were, does not speak itself. In *this* sense, it is as if *it does not exist* — if one can use this admittedly crude expression (and, in general, human language does not have words strong enough to describe this) — *prior to* the self-revelation of the Spirit and *outside* of Him.

Both the Father and the Son, each in His own way, seek longingly as it were the Word that is begotten and born but hidden in the silence of kenosis: it is as if the dyad of the Father and the Son exhausts itself in this birth of the Word, which seemingly cannot be realized (that is why this first dyad, that of the Father-Son, cannot be the complete self-revelation of the Father). But the self-revelation of the Holy Trinity is not exhausted by the Second hypostasis alone; the latter cannot realize this self-revelation by itself. It is completed by *another* form of the self-revelation of the Father: by the procession of the Holy Spirit upon the Son. The Holy Spirit, the Comforter, is the triumphant love of the accomplished sacrificial self-revelation. In the Third hypostasis, in its self-revelation, the Word *sounds and is spoken*. The Father recognizes the Word, raised from the sacrifice of silence, born and begotten; and the Son recognizes Himself as the Father's Word. The Holy Spirit is Life triumphant over the kenotic sacrifice, resurrection from the death of kenosis, the triumph of life-giving Love.

Above, the First Dyad was considered, so to speak, *before* the Holy Spirit entered the Holy Trinity; now we will consider this Dyad *after* the Holy Spirit's entry into the Holy Trinity. It is true that for eternity there is neither *before* nor *after*, for *before* and *after* coexist there; but *before* is the foundation or *prius* for *after*. In the Second Dyad, that of the Son and the Spirit, the kenosis of birth and the triumph of procession are united by one eternal and trinitarian act. The procession of the Holy Spirit does not occur by virtue of some metaphysical necessity or divine *fatum*. It is the hypostatic movement of Love. The Holy Spirit proceeds onto the Son, to *repose* upon Him; and the presence of the Son is the necessary condition of this procession. In this sense, the Holy Spirit is precisely the *Third* hypostasis, which cannot be conceived as the Second (even less can it be conceived as the First). The doctrine of causal originations, in both the East and the West, actually knows *two* second hypostases, insofar as it sunders the Holy Trinity into two unconnected dyads: Father-Son and Father-Spirit (or in the Catholic doctrine: Father-Son – Spirit). But the Holy Spirit is not the Second but precisely the *Third* hypostasis in the Holy Trinity, which reposes upon the Son, realizes the Word for the Father and the Son, and quickens the Son and therefore the Father. The Third hypostasis is the *being* of God in God Himself. And therefore if God is spirit, the Third hypostasis bears, par excellence, the name God spirit: the Holy Spirit.

The trinitarian self-revelation in Divine life, or Sophia, contains two inseparable acts: self-depletion, which is the kenosis in birth; and self-inspiration, which is the glory of the procession. In other words, it contains dying and resurrection, self-depleting ideality and self-accomplishing reality. These are the two forms of Love: its sacrifice and its triumph, "perfect joy": the Father Who has depleted Himself by engendering and the Son, immersed in ideality, Who has depleted Himself by being engendered; and in this and above this there is the life-giving Spirit, the *breath* of Divine love in its fullness, in its triumph. By the Holy Spirit the Father loves the Son not as being engendered but as already born. The first movement of the Holy Spirit proceeding from the Father is toward the Son, upon the Son, in relation to the Son, as the Father's hypostatic love. And the reverse movement of the Holy Spirit is from the Son, through the Son toward the Father, as the Son's hypostatic love for the Father, completing the circular movement of the Spirit from the Father *through* the Son *(emmesōs)* or, to put it differently, from the Father *and* the Son. But in this circular movement of the Holy Spirit, besides the hypostatic movement toward the Son from the Father and toward the Father from the Son, besides the Father's love (for the Son) and the Son's love (for the Father), there is also the very movement of love, which is precisely the hypostasis of the Holy Spirit. This hypostasis entirely dissolves in trihypostatic love. For the Father loves not only the Son but also the Holy Spirit, and He loves Them by the ecstatic love of "procession"; and the Son loves not only the Father but also the Holy Spirit; and He loves Them by a triumphantly ardent love ("I and my Father are one" [John 10:30]). The Father loves Himself in the Son while the Son loves Himself in the Father, but Both love hypostatic Love itself. The Father "proceeds" into this Love, and the Son "reposes" in It, embracing and receiving It as His own being in the Father. And this hypostatic Love, in turn, loves the Father and the Son, Whose hypostatic unity It is, the hypostasis of Love. The human understanding is given the capacity to know these aspects of the being of the Spirit only discursively, by successively passing from one definition to another, for it knows love only as a state or attribute of a hypostasis, not as a hypostasis in itself.

This transcendence of Love as a *hypostatic* principle expresses a special mystery of the Third hypostasis, its inaccessible and unrevealed character. Love in us is the definitive overcoming of the selfhood with which, for us, even hypostatic being itself is connected. That is why we consider love to be nonhypostatic, only a *state* of a hypostasis or, more precisely, of hypostases (at least two, if not more). But the Third hypostasis is *hypostatic* Love, although deprived of all selfhood. Like the first two hypostases, the Third hypostasis has, in its own hypostatic life, its *own* kenosis, which consists precisely in hypostatic *self-abolition*, as it were: By its procession from the Father upon the Son, the Third hypostasis loses itself, as it were, becomes only a *copula*, the living bridge of love between the Father and the Son, the hypostatic *Between*. But in this kenosis the Third hypostasis finds itself as the Life of the other hypostases, as the Love of the Others and as the Comfort of the Others, which then becomes for it too its own Comfort, its self-comfort. In a word, just as birth has both a passive and an active side, so does procession: it is spiration and procession, hypostatic depletion and self-acquisition, kenosis and glorification. The character of the Third hypostasis, of Love, is expressed in this "in-between" being, with the inclusion in it of the hypostases who love and who are loved. That is why its hypostatizedness is, as it were, a non-hypostatizedness, a complete transparence for the other hypostases, a non-selfhood. In this sense, Love is *Humility:* Before this special "impersonality" of the Third hypostasis, the first two hypostases appear as personalities with selfhood, as it were, as subject and object, or subject and predicate, for which the Third hypostasis is only a copula and is deprived, as it were, of its own content. To be sure, one cannot speak of "selfhood" in the limited creaturely sense with reference to the Divine hypostases, since each of them has its own kenosis of love. It is possible, however, to distinguish different *modes* of this love and, in particular, to see that, in the Third hypostasis, the kenosis is expressed in a special self-abolition of its personality.[3] The latter disappears, as it were, while becoming perfectly transparent for the other hypostases, but in this it acquires the perfection of Divine life: Glory.

This hypostatic character of the Third Person of the Holy Trinity leads to an important consequence for the *inseparability* and *inconfusibility* of this Person with the Second hypostasis in the Dyad of Divine self-revelation. This inseparable and inconfusible character derives, first of all, from the *hypostatic* being of the Second and Third persons of the Holy Trinity. The hypostases are not confused, for they are "distinctly personal" as personal centers. The inconfusibility of the Second and Third hypostases in the Dyad of the revelation of the Father also follows from the fact that each of these hypostases reveals the Father *in its own way:* the Second as the Word or the Idea of ideas, as *content;* the Third as the actualized reality of this content, as *beauty.* In the Third hypostasis, God not only *knows* Himself as the absolute Truth or the Word of all and about all, but He also *lives* in this hypostasis and *feels* it, with the reality of the felt truth being beauty. The latter is not a particular content of the Third hypostasis, a content which is already given to it in the Word, but its being or actualization, not "what," but "how." There exists here an absolute adequacy of interpenetration, which, however, never becomes the *identity* of the two modes of revelation, of the logical and the alogical, of ideality and

---

3. In the creaturely world, this self-abolition has an analogy in the self-determination of the Spirit-bearing Mother of God: "Behold the handmaid of the Lord; be it unto me according to thy word" (Luke 1:38).

reality. Nevertheless, the ideality is real and the reality is ideal, full of content. Reality has nothing to say about itself except the ideality that exists in it, whereas the ideality cannot, by itself, include in its content precisely that which makes it reality.

The inconfusibility of the two hypostases of the divine self-revelation is correlative with their inseparability. The latter corresponds to their mutual transparence or mutual penetration. Without this mutual fulfillment, neither of them is the self-revelation of Divinity in all its fullness. Of course, since each of the hypostases is equally divine, each hypostasis, in its own being, is already God: God the Father, God the Son, God the Holy Spirit. However, since Divinity in its self-revelation, or in Sophia, is an intratrinitarian trihypostatic act, the latter is accomplished by the harmonious action of all three hypostases, which presuppose and actualize one another, while revealing one another. Each hypostasis lives and is revealed not only in itself but also outside itself, in the other hypostases; and each would be one-sided and incomplete if all it had was its own being, its own selfhood (of course, one cannot even for a moment entertain such a blasphemous idea).

This mutuality is expressed in the depths of the Holy Trinity by the fact that there is a Revealed hypostasis, the Father, and that there is a Dyad of Revealing hypostases, the engendered Son and the proceeding Holy Spirit. The inseparability of these two hypostases is based not only on the fact that both of them have a common "principle" in the Father but also on the fact that both of them *together* reveal Him in the Divine Sophia, by a unified concrete act determined by their interrelation. This interrelation is expressed in a specific order or *taxis,* where the Son is the Second hypostasis and the Holy Spirit is the Third hypostasis, not vice versa. Ontologically (but not chronologically, of course), the Third hypostasis is *after* the Son, since it presupposes Him for its being. The Holy Spirit "proceeds" from the Father *onto* the Son, *through* the Son; He reposes *upon* the Son, is correlative with Him in a determinate, concrete manner. The Holy Spirit cannot even be conceived without a relation to the Son, or, for that matter, to the Father, for all the hypostatic relations are trinitarian in character. And that is why the Son cannot be conceived without a relation to the Holy Spirit Who reposes upon Him; the Son is not revealed outside of this interrelation with Him.

When we say "Son," our thought adds "and the Spirit," and vice versa. This "and" unites the two hypostases in one revelation of the Divine Sophia. *Sophia is one, but there are two sophianic hypostases,* which reveal one subject, but in a double manner: uni-dyadically, without separation and without confusion. One hypostasis does not repeat the other, but manifests it: the Word is accomplished by the Holy Spirit and the Spirit quickens the Word. Divinity contains the Word and the Spirit reveals Him: "for the Spirit searcheth all things, yea, the deep things of God" (1 Cor. 2:10). By the Spirit the Father inspires Himself in His own Word, and this self-inspiration is divine life, Beauty. Inspiration is not object-less and empty; it creatively reveals the "deep things of God." Divine life is an act of divine self-inspiration, and in this *sense* a cognitively creative act, in the Word through the Holy Spirit. To be sure, here one must not think of creative activity in the creaturely sense, which is marked by par-tiality, limitedness, becoming, imperfection. In God, all things are actual and actualized in the Holy Spirit. But inspiration and creative activity have a *theme*, and this divine theme is God's own Word, accomplished by the Holy Spirit and inspiring, so to speak, God Himself to creatively posit Himself: the Father as Spirator "breathes" the Holy Spirit upon the Son, that is, He is inspired by His own divine theme. The Son Himself be-comes, both for Himself and for the Father, the revelation of Divinity, while the Holy Spirit is this very inspiration.

This supra-eternal interrelation in the immanent Trinity becomes ac-cessible for us in the economic Trinity, that is, it becomes accessible christologically. The Holy Spirit Himself is not Truth, but the "Spirit of Truth," the "Spirit of Wisdom." "The Spirit of truth . . . will guide you into all truth: for he shall not speak of himself; but whatsoever he shall hear, that shall he speak: and he will show you things to come" (John 16:13). "He shall glorify me; for he shall receive of mine, and shall shew it unto you" (16:14). Christ's apparent self-identification with "another Comforter" in the Last Discourse has the same meaning: "A little while, and ye shall not see me; and again, a little while, and ye shall see me" (16:17, 19).

This dyadism of the Son and the Holy Spirit is particularly evident in the Wisdom of Solomon, which seems to equate the "Spirit of Wis-dom" with Wisdom itself.[4] This results in a fundamental difficulty of the doctrine of the Divine Sophia, a difficulty that remains insurmountable for many: how can it be affirmed about Sophia that she is the revelation both of the Son and of the Holy Spirit, or more precisely the revelation of the Son *and* the Holy Spirit? The error here is that one seeks a rationalistic *identification* of Sophia with *one* of the hypostases of the Holy Trinity, al-though Sophia is in no wise a hypostasis; and there is amazement when

---

4. See the Biblical excursus in my book *The Burning Bush: An Essay in the Dogmatic Interpretation of Certain Features in the Orthodox Veneration of the Mother of God* (Paris, 1927).

one says that the Wisdom of God as the self-revelation of the Father is the dyadic unity of the revelation of the *Two* revealing hypostases.

Sometimes this idea of dyadic unity is expressed in a cryptic, short-hand manner that hinders immediate understanding of the true interrelation of the hypostases. Thus, the Nicaeno-Constantinopolitan Creed says about the Holy Spirit: "who spake by the prophets." In many passages in the Old and New Testaments, prophecy as the pronouncement of truth is represented as an express act of the Spirit of God ("all scripture is given by inspiration of God" [2 Tim. 3:16]; and prophecy came from "holy men of God [who] spake as they were moved by the Holy Spirit" [2 Pet. 1:21]). One gets the impression that the *word* of truth is pronounced precisely by the Holy Spirit; and dyadic self-revelation and divine inspiration thus appear to be effected by the Third hypostasis alone. But it is necessary to expand and clarify this shorthand expression: It is not the Holy Spirit but the Son of God Who is the *word* of truth. Christ is the Truth, but the Holy Spirit inspires with this word, manifests this word, in general manifests Christ. That is why the expression "who spake by the prophets," which occurs in the eighth article of the Creed after the detailed doctrine of the Son, must be understood *in its full context:* According to the Last Discourse, the Holy Spirit "shall not speak of himself; but whatsoever he shall hear" (John 16:13); and He inspires us to hear precisely this inner word, without which "prophecy" is impossible, even as the hearing of the word is impossible without the inspiration by the Holy Spirit. That is why the expression "who spake by the prophets" must be understood in the sense of the *accomplishing* action of the Third hypostasis inspiring the prophets, but not with reference to the *content* of this word, which is from the Word. That is why one should not regard the divinely inspired character of the sacred books as a mechanical dictation of words of truth which the prophet passively transcribed. It signifies rather the inspiration of the prophet himself by the word of truth which he found in the depths of his human essence by the action of the Third hypostasis.

Sometimes this kind of shorthand expression of the doctrine of the *dyad* of the Word and the Spirit is even more cryptic. For example, consider the story in Genesis of the creation of the world, in which we have the action of all three hypostases: of the initial hypostasis, the Father, and of the two accomplishing hypostases, the Son and the Spirit. The external accent lies on the action of the Holy Spirit as the accomplishing "let there be." But each time there is added a word representing the object of "let there be" (light, firmament, etc.); and that is why the creative "let there be" contains the sacred monogram of the *dyadic* revelation of the Holy Trinity in creation.

The Divine Sophia is the eternal Humanity, the heavenly proto-image of creaturely humanity. As a consequence, this humanity too is both dual and one on the basis of the inseparability and inconfusibility of the two Divine hypostases; and it is the case that the unity and the duality are equally true. The Divine-humanity is known by us on the basis of the creaturely humanity, which bears the image of the former. And this image of the creaturely humanity is one, insofar as the creaturely proto-man Adam is one, but it is also dual, as the unity of the male and female principles: "in the image of God created he him; male and female created he them" (Gen 1:27). These male and female principles in which is imprinted the image of the Divine Sophia, of prototypical humanity, are the differentiation and unity — expressed in the language of creaturely being — of the Logos and the Holy Spirit in Sophia. From the image we ascend here to the Proto-image and understand it. Of course, here we must set aside the specific qualities of the male and female principles according to which they exist in the creaturely world in the images of the male and female *genders*. One must instead understand them as images of one and the same spiritual principle, Sophia, in the fullness of its self-revelation, in the image of the Second and Third hypostases.

The Holy Spirit reposes upon the Logos, and the Logos abides in His bosom. The Holy Spirit is life, and love, and the reality of the Word, even as the Logos is, for Him, the determining content, word-thought and feeling, Truth and being in Truth — as the Beauty of self-revealed Truth. All these interrelations have a *parallel* (not more and not less than a parallel) in that bi-unity of the human spirit in which the male, solar principle of thought, logos, is united with the female principle of reception, creative accomplishment, beauty. The human sophianic spirit is a male-female androgyne, although, in fact, every individual human being is only either male or female; that is, despite this androgynism of the spirit, every individual human being experiences being according to only one of these principles, in relation to which the other principle is only complementary. And this androgynism is the *fullness* of the image of God in human beings, just as, conversely, a human being in whom one of these principles would predominate to the point of the virtual absence of the other would be a spiritual freak, strictly speaking, no longer a human being.[5]

5. By contrast, in the angelic world of pure spirits the image of God is expressed in each spirit in particular, and not in its integrity, as in the human race, where the male

We already know that, in the Divine Incarnation, this differentiation of the male and female principles corresponds to the incarnation of Christ in the male image and the most perfect manifestation of the Holy Spirit in the image of the Spirit-bearer, the Ever-Virgin Mary, so that the image of the perfect Divine-humanity[6] in its fullness — both in heaven and on earth — is not the Son only, but also the Son and the Virgin, the supra-eternal Infant in the bosom of the Mother of God. This also indicates the heavenly bi-unity of the Son and the Holy Spirit.[7]

The inseparability and inconfusibility of the two revealing hypostases in the Divine Sophia find a new expression in this polarization and mutual dependence of the two principles which in the life of the Spirit correspond to the male and female principles and which in the doctrine of the Church are symbolized by the wedding of Christ and the Church, the Holy Spirit. By its personal character, each of these hypostases conditions, manifests, and actualizes the other, but cannot be absorbed or abolished by a fusion with the other. There is established here this absolute *correlativeness* of the two hypostases of revelation. The Father is revealed by both of them: by the hypostasis of generation, the Word, and by the hypostasis of procession, the Holy Spirit, in their unity in the Father. The two hypostases are mutually transparent in their being; but at the same time each of them has an irreducible hypostatic nucleus, a distinctly personal I.

This personal differentiation of the hypostatic divine I's is overcome and abolished, as it were, by the trihypostatic act of self-renouncing love, in which these personal centers are self-identified in the one trihypostatic

---

and female principles are united but distinct (see my book *Jacob's Ladder: On the Angels* [Paris, 1929]), although this condition is overcome by their communality and love. But in the world of fallen spirits, where precisely love has been extinguished, we see the image of sterile one-sidedness: Lucifer is an example of bad maleness, whereas Lilith, "Babylon," the great whore, is an example of bad femaleness.

6. See Translator's Introduction for a discussion of Divine-humanity. — Trans.

7. Here and there in the Church literature we find the image of the Spirit as a female hypostasis. For example, we find this in the fourth-century Syriac writer Aphraates. The Semitic languages lack a neuter gender, and *ruach,* the word for wind or spirit, is feminine; therefore, the ancient Semitic literature, prior to any appreciable influence of Greek theology, speaks of the Holy Spirit in the feminine gender. The ancient Syriac translation of John 14:26 in fact says, "The Holy Spirit, the female Comforter, shall teach you all things." And so, in conformity with the more ancient usage, Aphraates uses feminine adjectives for "life-giving" and "holy" in the doxology, "glory and honor to His Son, and to His Spirit, life-giving and holy." It is also noteworthy that, in the ancient Gospel of the Hebrews, cited by Jerome and Origen, the Lord speaks of the Holy Spirit as His Mother.

I of the Holy Trinity, although they are not extinguished in it. This differentiation of the persons is also necessarily preserved in the mutuality of the bihypostatic revelation; the two hypostases are mutually transparent not in their hypostatizedness as such but precisely in the forms of their personal revelation, or (if one can express it in this way) not in their character as subject but in their character as predicate. The Word is transparent for the Spirit and the Spirit embraces the Word reposing in His bosom; but the Word and the Spirit are not non-hypostatic in their revelation but are, in themselves, persons. Here too, however, there is a distinction in their hypostatic mutual being. In itself, the hypostasis of the Word is expressed by the fact that it is engendered by the Father. This hypostasis is the Subject of the Word-Predicate. It possesses in itself its predicate, the word; and its hypostasis is thus self-evident, as it were. But this cannot be said about the Third hypostasis insofar as it is the *Spirit of the Second hypostasis* ("the Spirit of Truth"). In its content it is correlative with the Word. It becomes transparent for the Word, becomes, as it were, only the *form* of the Word's being, or the copula connecting the subject and the predicate. The hypostasis of the Spirit is "eclipsed" here in its transparence for the Word, is identified with the Word, as it were.

The hypostasis of the Spirit does not have its own Face, as it were, but is only the Face of the Son in His *Glory*. But its supra-eternal kenosis is also glorification, *Glory*, which is not only the *glorification* of the Son but also Glory in Itself. However, in the light of this Glory we can discern the glorified Face of Logos-Christ but not the proper Face of Glory itself, which remains invisible both in its kenotic self-renunciation and even in the glory of the glorification of the Logos. We see the sun in light, as the source of light, but we do not see the light itself in and through which the sun is visible for us; we do not see it at the same time as the sun or apart from the sun.

The Third hypostasis is *the hypostatic revelation not concerning itself.* At the same time, it is also not the *transcendent* Paternal hypostasis; the latter remains *outside* of revelation, as the subject of revelation. The Third hypostasis is contained *within* the revelation of the Father, as a kind of sacred mystery of this revelation; it is a *Mystery* about itself. It is revealed in the other hypostases by its action, as the *spirit of God*, but not in itself, as the hypostatic Holy Spirit. Hypostatic Love is submerged in love and shows itself, testifying *not* about itself but about Another: "He [the Spirit] shall glorify me: for he shall receive of mine, and shall shew it unto you" (John 16:14). That is why, in speaking about the sending down of the Comforter, the Son also speaks about it in this manner: "A little while, and ye shall not see me;

and again, a little while, and ye shall see me" (16:17) — "me" in the Holy Spirit, Who manifests not Himself, but the Son and the Father in the Son ("All things that the Father hath are mine: therefore said I, that he shall take of mine, and shall shew it unto you" [16:15]). The Spirit Himself does not have anything that He can call "mine," so that it is as if He does not exist, although it is precisely in this "non-existence" that the mode of His existence is manifested — in His inseparability and inconfusibility with the Son.

This inevitably imparts a *practical* Filioque character to the theology of the Holy Spirit with reference to His relation to the Son. If one does not reduce this theology to a rationalistic theory of "origination," one must necessarily understand it dyadically: A theology of the Holy Spirit cannot be realized without the Son, for the Spirit is His very being as the Son. The Son *is* the Son by the Holy Spirit, and the proper "is" of the Holy Spirit is the being of the Son: without separation and without confusion. The Spirit is the transparence of the revelation, while the Son is that which *is* in this transparence, its content. The Spirit is Life; the Son is the One Who lives by this Life. Logos becomes an abstract idea if it does not acquire real concreteness in the Spirit; but without the Word that it contains this concreteness would be a formless void. Sophia is the revelation of the Son and the Holy Spirit, without separation and without confusion.

II. In the Creaturely Sophia

The created world is established in being by God at the "Beginning," that is, in the Divine Sophia, as her creaturely image, or the creaturely Sophia (see *The Lamb of God*). In creation there is nothing that does not belong to Sophia, except nothing itself, which is the sole beginning of creation (see *The Unfading Light*[8]). It is by the creative act that nothing appears; it is established by God as a being in its own right, as an extradivine being: *ouk on* becomes *mē on* and receives the power of being. The world arose and exists by the *will* of God: "thou hast created all things, and for thy pleasure they are and were created" (Rev. 4:11). The Book of Genesis attests to this with archaic and lapidary grandeur: "In the beginning God created the heaven and the earth" (1:1). We will not complicate our discussion by considering "heaven" here (see instead my book *Jacob's Ladder*). The creation of the angelic choir, which is meant here, is the initial act of God's

---

8. *The Unfading Light: Contemplations and Speculations* (Moscow, 1917) is Bulgakov's chief *philosophical* work on sophiology. — Trans.

creation, and the sole act of His creation which is complete and self-sufficient. These are the hypostatized ideas of creation, the heavenly "project" of the latter, which can be understood only with reference to the *world*, or the "earth." The latter has its own *history* of creation, something the angelic world lacks.

The creation of the world is invariably interpreted in Christian dogmatics as the action of the trihypostatic God Who is in the Holy Trinity, an action in which it is necessary to distinguish the actions of each of the hypostases — of the Father, the initial cause, of the Son, the demiurge, and of the Holy Spirit, the accomplishing cause (according to St. Basil the Great's formulation). These and other patristic formulas express in a characteristic manner the participation of all three persons of the Holy Trinity in creation. This idea represents one of the particular applications of the dogma of the Holy Trinity, but the modes of the participation of the separate hypostases are yet to be clarified. Of course, there can be no doubt that the whole of creation bears the imprint of the trihypostatic God. In particular, it is said about the Word that was with God (= the Father) that "all things were made by him: and without him was not any thing made that was made" (John 1:3); even as it is said about the Holy Spirit that "all the host of them [of the heavens] by the breath of his mouth [was made]" (Ps. 33:6; cf. Ps. 104:30).

One cannot fail to notice that Genesis speaks about God simply as the Creator (Gen. 1). Although the *pluralis maiestatis* Elohim is used, its predicate is singular, and the plural pronoun occurs only in Genesis 1:26: "let us make man." In general, by comparing different texts about creation, one gets the impression that God (the Father) creates by His Word and Spirit, so that both of these hypostases acquire an instrumental significance, as it were, act in creation as means that the Father has at His disposal, as His "hands," according to the patristic expression. It is the Father Who properly is the Creator; it is He Who possesses the will to creation; it is He Who is the Proto-will in creation. He is the beginning (*archē*) not only in the Holy Trinity; He is also the beginning in creation, where He is revealed by the Word in the Spirit. He is the *Will of Love,*[9] and

9. In the Catholic theology there has existed since Augustine an erroneous identification of will and love, *voluntas sive amor*, precisely with reference to the character of the *Third* hypostasis. But will and love are, of course, not identical. In God-Love, however, which is the entire Holy Trinity, one can distinguish in the characters of the individual hypostases also the First Principle of Love, which is proper precisely to the Paternal hypostasis.

in this sense He is the Father in creation as well ("Our Father" in the Lord's Prayer; "thou, O Lord, art our father" [Isa. 63:16]). Strictly speaking, it is He Who is the hypostatic Creator of the world, that Divine I that addresses the world with the creative word: *let there be all things.*[10]

But how can we understand the participation of the Second and Third hypostases if we consider that they do not participate *hypostatically* in the creation of the world, which is the work of the Father, Who is inseparably and consubstantially united with Them? They both participate in the creation *sophianically*, through their self-revelation in Sophia, who is also the self-revelation of the Father in the Holy Trinity, the divine world. Sophia is not a hypostasis, although, belonging to the hypostases, she is hypostatized from all eternity. In herself, however, she is the objective principle of divine being, by and in which God the Father not only reveals Himself in divine being but also creates the world. Sophia is the revelation of the two hypostases through which the self-revelation of the Father is realized. Both the Second hypostasis and the Third hypostasis therefore participate in the creation of the world through this revelation, not by hypostatic directedness toward the world, but by their revelation in Sophia. They are the divine foundation of the world, which has its hypostatic Creator or Principle in the Father.

The creation of the world by the Father in and through Sophia is expressed with perfect clarity in Chapter 1 of Genesis. Here, all the acts of creation are accomplished by God the Father, Who commands as if from a transcendent "outside," from the height of His Divinity, by His sophianic Word: "let there be" this or that form of creation. "Let there be *(fiat)*" is repeated eight times, with reference to each of the works of creation (Gen. 1:3, 6, 9, 11, 14, 20, 24, 26); six times it is accompanied by "and it was so" (Gen. 1:7, 9, 11, 15, 24, 30). And to each of these acts of "let there be" and "it was so" corresponds a word referring precisely to this act of creation.

These are the words of the Word which are contained in the Divine Sophia and are called here to creation in the creaturely Sophia, in the world. These are those words of the Word about "all things" by which "all things were made"; but they are spoken here *not* by the hypostatic Word, Who seems to be mute here, in the creation of the world, although He speaks in the eternal Sophia. They are spoken by the creative hypostasis of the Father, Who repeats, as it were, the words of the Word already spoken eternally in Sophia. God the Father, Who engenders the Son from all eternity, is mute from all eternity, for He speaks Himself only in the Son. But

---

10. See the epilogue to the present work: "The Father."

God the Father, as the Creator, in creation *Himself* speaks these words spoken from all eternity in the Son, transmitting them to creation as commands. It is in this sense that the Word acts in the world not as the world-creating hypostasis but as the Word about the world and pronounced in the world by the Father. "All things were made by him; and without him was not any thing made that was made" (John 1:3). It is not said that the Word Himself is the creator, but only that He is the foundation and content of the creation called into being by the Father. In the creation the hypostatic Word remains His own hypostasis *outside* or *above* the world, as it were, although by His content He determines the world's being and its *all*-multiplicity as *all*-unity. He is the logos and logic of the world, while remaining hypostatically transcendent to the latter. He is united with the world only in Sophia, that is, not as the *hypostatic* Logos but as the *spoken pan-logos*. In short, the world is directly created according to the will of the Father by the Word in Sophia.

This idea is developed in the first chapter of Genesis in a series of creative pronouncements by God, corresponding to the six days of creation: "Let there be light. . . . Let there be a firmament in the midst of the waters. . . . Let the waters . . . be gathered . . . and let the dry land appear. . . . Let the earth bring forth grass. . . . Let there be lights in the firmament of the heaven. . . . Let the waters bring forth . . . the moving creature. . . . Let the earth bring forth the living creature." All this represents a shorthand monogram for the fullness of the entire creaturely world prior to man. And only with the creation of *man* do we have not only an act of *sophianic* creation, which defines his place in the cosmos, but also an act of *hypostatically* divine creation, which is expressed in God's counsel (of course, in the Holy Trinity): "Let us make man in *our* image, after *our* likeness" (1:26). Man's *hypostasis*, eternal and creaturely, uncreated and created, is formed with the participation of the integral trihypostatic person of the Holy Trinity. But man's *substance*, creaturely humanity, is sophianically created by the Father according to the general order of creation: "So God created man" (1:27).

But if we know the participation of the Logos in creation only as the *action* of the Logos, as His revelation in Sophia, the participation of the Holy Spirit is analogous: He participates in the creation of the world not hypostatically but by His action, not as the Holy Spirit but as the spirit of God moving upon the face of the waters. His action in creation corresponds to His revelation in Sophia. In her, His action is, above all, reality, life, beauty, or glory. And the first action of the Holy Spirit in creation is that in the void of nothing reality arises (in *ouk on* there appears *me on*) as a certain preliminary actuality: i.e., precisely the *earth* as the ontological *place* of future creation, and then different species of being. This action of the Holy Spirit, the hypostasis of reality, is expressed in the words "let there be" and "it was so," repeated a number of times in the Genesis account of the creation. We can also see the express action of the Spirit in the actualization of the generative power of the earth and water as the maternal womb, the proto-reality which has been seeded with the words of the Word, the ideas of creation actualized by the life-giving force. This is described in the following passages: "Let the earth bring forth grass . . . and the earth brought forth grass" (Gen 1:11-12); "let the waters bring forth . . . the waters brought forth" (1:20-21); "let the earth bring forth the living creature" (1:24). In addition, the revelation of the Holy Spirit in beauty is spoken of in the refrain concluding each day of creation: "And God saw the light, that it was good" (1:4); "and God saw that it was good" (1:10); etc. This is repeated for all the days except the second (1:4, 10, 12, 18, 21, 25, 31).[11]

The express action of the Holy Spirit which clothes creation in beauty and glory must also be considered to include the first, preliminary manifestation on earth of the glory of the creation, the transfigured earth: this first manifestation is the planting of paradise. Genesis speaks of this briefly, using an anthropomorphic, mythological image: "God planted a garden eastward in Eden; and there he put the man whom he had formed" (2:8). Eden with its tree of life directly corresponds to the future city of God on the transfigured earth, also with "the tree of life" (Rev. 22:2). This is the initial transfiguration of the world, which was given by God but which was to be extended to all creatures through man, who was put "into the garden of Eden to dress it and to keep it" (Gen. 2:15). But afterward, just as man himself in his fall was deprived of the glory of God (Rom. 3:23), so the rays of heavenly light that had shined over the creation in Eden have faded on earth and will not shine again until the coming of the times and seasons of its transfiguration.

The most important and characteristic passage referring to the action of the Holy Spirit in the creation is certainly Genesis 1:2: "the earth was without form, and void [*tohu vabohu*] . . . and the Spirit of God moved upon the face of the waters." What is characteristic here is, first of all, the place that is assigned to the action of the Holy Spirit (likened to the sitting of a bird in its nest) — prior to the individual acts of creation. These

---

11. The final time this is in a generalized form: "And God saw every thing that he had made, and behold, it was very good."

acts make the individual forms of creation appear out of chaos, formless confusion, the "earth." In other words, what we have here is the reverse relation of the Second and Third hypostases: first the action of the Spirit and only then the action of the Word. The *proto-reality of being*, proto-matter, the earth, are produced by the action of the Spirit, which causes all the sophianic seeds of being implanted in this proto-reality to sprout. Here, at the very threshold of the creation of the world, there is manifested the express relation of the Holy Spirit to what is usually considered to be diametrically opposite to Him — His relation to *matter*. Here, one finds already adumbrated the special *theme* of the life of matter as a reality that is to become permeated with the Holy Spirit and *spiritual* in this sense, that is, a reality that is to achieve its transfiguration as the "new earth" (together with the "new heaven"), where the *tohu vabohu*, the chaotic formlessness and void, will be overcome. Reposing "maternally" upon the Word, the hypostasis of the Spirit manifests its maternal character in the revelation of Sophia during the creation of the world: it manifests itself as the maternal womb in which the forms of this world are conceived. Here we already have that mysterious cryptogram of the Divine-Maternity in which is born the God-Man, the supreme purpose and goal of the entire creaturely world. In this spirit-bearing chaos, the *tohu vabohu*, we have the image of the creaturely Sophia, considered not in her verbal or ideal content, but in her reality, life, and being.

But how should one more precisely understand this movement of the Spirit upon the void and the darkness? Is this the Holy Spirit or the spirit of God, the Third hypostasis or only its action in sophianic revelation? The general idea of the moving Spirit is expressed with archaic naturalism in anthropomorphic-mythological language, and it does not easily lend itself to the interpretation that it was actually the Third hypostasis that, in its hypostatic descent, organized the *tohu vabohu*, forming cosmos out of chaos in a kind of supramundane Pentecost. On the contrary, the seeds of this organization had already been implanted in the chaos itself, as its life-giving force, in conformity with the sophianic proto-image of the world. That is why it is not necessary to think that the chaos could truly be the "place" of the hypostatic presence of the Holy Spirit Himself, and not only of His force acting in creation. And in this sense we have yet once more with regard to the Holy Spirit the confirmation of the general idea that, in the creation of the world, there actively participates the supramundane hypostasis of the Father, which introduces, so to speak, the Son and the Spirit into the world at its creation, although not in Their *hypostatic* revelation, but only by Their action, which is given eternally in the Divine Sophia. But Sophia is not a hypostasis but a "hypostatized-ness." Therefore, we again arrive at the conclusion that the world is created by the hypostasis of the Father in and through the Divine Sophia by the action of the two hypostases that reveal her.

This idea requires clarification. We are saying that God the Father creates the world by and in Sophia, who is not a hypostasis but a hypostatizedness; she is the objective principle of divine self-revelation and life. Here we must remember that, since Sophia is hypostatized by the hypostases from all eternity, she does not exist separately from them. That is why when one says that it is the Father Who creates the world by Sophia, this cannot mean that the Son and the Holy Spirit do not participate hypostatically in creation but bring to it only Their sophianic revelation. Such a *separation* of hypostasis from hypostatizedness in Sophia is inconceivable and inadmissible. It is perfectly admissible and even necessary, however, to introduce a distinction in the self-revelation of Divinity to the effect that it is predominantly realized either relative to hypostasis or relative to hypostatizedness, i.e., relative to its sophianic definition; and accordingly we have either hypostatic (more precisely, hypostatically sophianic) or sophianic (more precisely, sophianically hypostatic) revelation, with the emphasis placed on the one or the other, on hypostasis or on hypostatizedness.

In the creation of the world, we have the following interrelationship: the hypostasis of creation, the Principle or Subject of the latter, is the Father, Who creates the world in the Holy Trinity, that is, inseparably from the Second and Third hypostases, by a trinitarian act in the Divine Sophia. This does not mean that Sophia, the objective principle of creation, separated herself from the hypostases and became extrahypostatic. But the hypostases do *not* appear here in their personal differentiatedness; rather, they kenotically conceal themselves, as it were, in the hypostasis of the Father. The Divine Subject, the I who creates the world, is, as a Person, precisely the hypostasis of the Father, with which the two other divine I's are indistinguishably united here. This I of the Father acts and commands in the creation of the world, whereas the other I's are included in Him, without being abolished but also without being manifested. They participate in the creation of the world not by Themselves but by Their Own, i.e., in the Divine Sophia. Three hypostatic flames are lit in a row, one behind the other; and therefore they are seen as a single flame; and this single flame is the I of the Father. It overshadows, as it were, the divine I's of the Second and Third hypostases, which are kenotically concealed in Him and which are *not* actualized hypostatically in creation.

This is also the case as far as divine providence is concerned. In the Old Testament, where in general God is revealed unihypostatically, this one hypostasis, which conceals the Divine triunity, is that of the Father; and in this sense it is sometimes said that the Old Testament is "the revelation of the First hypostasis." In turn, the New Testament discloses the Second hypostasis, which reveals the hypostasis of the Father ("he that hath seen me hath seen the Father" [John 14:9]), while veiling it to a certain degree. The hypostasis of the Father becomes accessible only through the hypostasis of the Son; and in this sense one can say that the New Testament is preeminently "the revelation of the Second hypostasis." Nevertheless, in the Old Testament too, where the world-transcending hypostasis of the Father is the divine subject of all the divine revelations, it participates in creation only through the hypostases that reveal it, the hypostases of the Son and the Holy Spirit. Concealed in the Father, these two hypostases act in His name, as it were, and hypostatically they remain unknown to creation. In this sense, one can and must say that Jehovah, the God of the Old Testament Who appears to man, Who speaks with him, and reveals His Name to him, is the Divine Logos, Who, nevertheless, kenotically diminishes Himself, conceals His Face in the light of the hypostasis of the Father, speaks, as it were, with the voice of this hypostasis and in its name,[12] and appears in the theophanies and the doxophanies (the manifestations of Glory). These latter are, properly speaking, manifestations of the Divine Sophia, "sophiaphanies," correlative to the divine Person Who is the Son concealed in the Father, or the Father speaking in the Son, a certain hypostatic unity of Son-Father. In the New Testament, by contrast, the Son is *sent* into the world by the Father in His own hypostasis. "Descending from heaven," He now realizes kenosis not with regard to His own hypostasis, which, on the contrary, now separates itself from that of the Father, becomes independent, and appears in its own right, but with regard to His own divine life and glory.

Likewise, as far as creation and providence are concerned, the Father acts in relation to the Holy Spirit, in different manifestations and actions of the Third hypostasis. In *this* sense the Father *sends* the Holy Spirit into the world even prior to the Pentecost (just as the Logos is present in the world, into which He is sent by the Father in theophanies prior to His hypostatic incarnation). In the Old Testament, this action of the "Spirit of God," which consists in the communication of His various gifts, is accomplished only by the *sophianic* revelation of the *non*-hypostatic manifes-

12. See my book *The Lamb of God,* p. 216.

tation of the Holy Spirit. These gifts necessarily presuppose the Holy Spirit's hypostatic participation, however, inasmuch as the *action* of the Third hypostasis is inseparable from the Accomplisher of this action.

One can therefore say that, without any exception, in those cases in the Old Testament when God (= the Father) sends down His Spirit, He acts through the hypostasis of the Holy Spirit and with the personal participation of this hypostasis, for no gift of the Spirit can be considered to be *extra*-hypostatic, to be separated from the hypostasis of the Spirit, to be anywhere other than in the Divine Sophia. That is why all these particular and small pentecosts, which are to be united in the one hypostatic Pentecost of the Holy Spirit, cannot be conceived separately from Him. Consequently, throughout the Old Testament it is the hypostatic Holy Spirit Who is revealed in His gifts, but He is revealed *non*-hypostatically. His proper hypostasis (like that of the Son) is kenotically concealed in the hypostasis of the Father, by which the Holy Trinity addresses the world; and in the sun of this hypostasis, the hypostasis of the Holy Spirit becomes invisible, indistinguishable, and virtually nonexistent, as it were. In the Old Testament this does not prevent the works of the Holy Spirit from being done by the hypostatic Holy Spirit according to the will of the Father, however; and the *spirit of God* never acts and does not exist apart from the hypostatic Holy Spirit.

Such is the general interrelation of the three persons of the trinitarian Divinity in the creation and in the government of the world, with the primacy of the hypostasis of the Father, but also with the necessary participation of the Revealing hypostases. Let us return to the question of the actions of the Holy Spirit in the creation. In the creation of the world, the latter has a double definition: fullness and perfection on the one hand, and development and incompleteness on the other. As for the first aspect, it must be remembered that the creative words, God's decrees concerning the world, are not just pronounced once as God's creative command, "let there be" this and that; on the contrary, they resound in the world for all time, are its foundations. It is necessary to add that, in the initial plan of creation, considered as the combination of the logoses of its being, as the words of the Word, the fullness of creation is already realized: "All things were made by him; and without him was not any thing made that was made" (John 1:3). The same idea can also be expressed in these terms: "God ended his work which he had made; and he rested on the seventh day from all his work which he had made" (Gen. 2:2); "he . . . rested from all his work which God created and made" (2:3). In an anthropomorphic form this unquestionably expresses the idea that creation already possesses a fullness to which nothing can be added, which is why God rested from His work.[13]

But on the other hand, the world, created in fullness, is called to undergo a process of becoming; and these tasks of the becoming of the world are included in the very acts of creation, where the earth and the water receive the commands: "let the waters bring forth," "let the earth bring forth" (certainly, not in a single but in a prolonged act), "be fruitful, and multiply, and replenish the earth," and so on. The world is created for time and in time. And in itself and especially in man, the world has a *history*, is being completed, but is not yet complete. Thus, the world simultaneously has both the statics of its fullness and the dynamics of its becoming; and, clearly, the two mutually condition each other.

This dual foundation of the world also corresponds to the dyadic character of God's self-revelation in the Divine Sophia, who is the foundation of the creaturely Sophia. In its creation the world contains the entire fullness of the logos-seeds of being; *all* is said about it and in it. The theme of the world is fully *given* and only needs to be developed. In the fullness of its being and in its connectedness as a multi-unity, the world is an image of the Logos, in Whom there cannot be *more or less* and nothing can be added or taken away. All the meanings of the world are initiated in it, although they are not yet manifested. This male element of meanings and Meaning corresponds to the revelation of the Logos as the sophianic Word. This static immobility of fullness does not yet determine the being of the Logos in the creaturely Sophia, however. The Logos is *being accomplished*, is receiving the life-force of being from the Holy Spirit reposing upon Him. In the Divine Sophia this accomplishment is a single, supraeternal act in which there is no place for *more or less*, no place for becoming. By contrast, in the creaturely Sophia there is a place for such an accomplishment, which is becoming and knows *more or less* for itself. In the entelechy of the world, the given and the proposed, that which is accomplished and that which is not yet accomplished, can always be distinguished, as well as the transition from the one to the other — becoming.

This dynamics of life corresponds to the domain of the Holy Spirit in the creaturely Sophia, to His life-giving force. He is thus the cosmourgic hypostasis about which it is said that "in him was life; and the life was the light of men" (John 1:4); for only in the life of the world, in its becoming, does there shine forth the light of its meanings, of the Word. It

13. This does not refer to Divine Providence, about which it is said, "My Father worketh hitherto, and I work" (John 5:17).

is by the power of the Holy Spirit, "the giver of life,"[14] that *life* is bestowed upon the world. Furthermore, the very *being* of the world — the creative womb, the proto-mother, identified in the creation of the world with proto-matter — depends on the Holy Spirit in this sense. The force of the Spirit is the earth from which all things have their being, the leaf of grass as well as man. It is a certain silent being in which, nevertheless, the words of the Word are spoken and resound. This is not that absolute, transcendent Silence (Greek: *Sigē*) of the Father, Who is revealed only outside Himself, in the other hypostases, and Who in this sense is not in the world, for He is above the world.

No! In the creaturely Sophia, the Spirit is a hearing and perceiving silence, in which the Word born from all eternity is born again for creation, as it were. In the creaturely Sophia, this Spirit is resonance, breathing, accomplishment, life; this Spirit is *natura naturans,* which, through the word implanted in it, engenders *natura naturata,* or becomes it. This Spirit is the *being* that contains *all* things in itself, although it does not add anything to this all from itself. This Spirit is the world in its extra-divine aseity. This Spirit is the meonic darkness of being just before dawn, the earth invisible and void, as if *prior to* the Word that will flame up in it, casting His seed in it; this Spirit is the perfect accomplishment of the transfigured world. This Spirit is the natural energy of the world which can never be extinguished or interrupted in the world, but always bears within itself the principle of the growth of creative activity. This Spirit is "our mother, the moist earth,"[15] out of which all things grow and into which all things return for new life. This Spirit is the life of the vegetative and animal world "after their kind." This Spirit is the life of the human race in the image and likeness of God. This Spirit is that life-giving principle which pious paganism, without knowing Him, worshipped as the "Great Pan," as the Mother of the gods, Isis and Gaia. This Spirit is that which the impious paganism of our own day confesses as living and life-giving matter in the blindness of its "hylozoism," or attempts to capture in a test tube as the "life force." This Spirit is the world itself in all its being — on the pathways from chaos to cosmos.

But is this not a pantheism, an impious deification of the world, leading to a kind of religious materialism? Yes, it *is* a pantheism, but an entirely pious one; or more precisely, as I prefer to call it in order to avoid

14. Words from a prayer to the Holy Spirit. — Trans.
15. "The Mother of God is our mother, the moist earth." Is it not appropriate to recall here this penetrating vision of Dostoevsky (in his novel *Demons*)?

ambiguity, it is a *panentheism*. True, one should not profess pantheism as the sole, exhaustive conception of the world, for that would truly be pagan cosmotheism, the worship of creation instead of and in the capacity of the Creator. It is even less possible to reject it totally, however, for it is a dialectically necessary moment in the sophiological cosmology. The world and we in it "live, and move, and have our being" (Acts 17:28) in God. "Thou takest away Thy Spirit, they die, and return to their dust. Thou sendest forth thy spirit, they are created; and thou renewest the face of the earth" (Ps. 104:29-30; the King James Version has been modified here to conform with the Russian Bible).

What *other* energy, if not divine energy, gives life to the world? In their fear of pantheism, do not some critics introduce an independent, extra-divine and nondivine principle of the world which exists alongside Divinity: "Nature was created by a white god and a somber black god acting together." Is this not manicheanism or dualism? The falsehood of pantheism is not that it recognizes a divine force acting in God's creation and constituting its positive foundation, but only that this divine force in the world is *equated* with God Himself, Whose action or energy it is. God is a personal being, whereas the world is impersonal. God has in Himself His own supramundane life, which is only revealed in the world but is scarcely exhausted by the latter. Finally, the world possesses a creaturely aseity, given by God, by virtue of which it is just as impossible to *identify* the Creator and creation as to *separate* creation from Him.

This entire misunderstanding, which leads to insurmountable contradictions from the point of view of abstract and anti-sophianic theism, is completely resolved in the light of sophiology. The divine foundation of the world (its "pantheism") is determined not by the fact that the personal God Himself is present by His Personality in the world and thus is identified with it, but by the sophianicity of this foundation: God creates the world by and in Sophia; and in its sophianic foundation the world is divine, although it is at the same time extra-divine in its creaturely aseity. In this sophianic foundation, it is necessary to distinguish its logoses or the forms of its being from its being itself, which is aptly expressed by the Latin word *natura* (the feminine future participle from the verb *nasci*: "destined to give birth to all she contains").

And this ontic foundation of the world that corresponds to the action of the Third hypostasis in the Divine Sophia we define as the active presence of the Holy Spirit in the world, the natural grace of the latter, so to speak. This is precisely that spirit of God that is sent or taken away by God and that is the life of creation, according to Psalm 104. This life-giving force is present in all creation and is, so to speak, the *grace of creation:* it is by this force that plants grow, animals live, minerals have their slumbering being, and human life is sustained, above all as a natural process of birth and multiplication. The life-giving principle of life in the world is also a formative principle. The ideal seeds, the logoses of being which come from the Logos, are actualized in creation by the Holy Spirit as forms. In this capacity they are clothed in beauty, which is actualized idea, transparent in its formedness. All the *forms* of being, the *meanings* that clothe the latter, are — as creations in beauty — the artistry of the Holy Spirit, Who is the Artist of the world, the Principle of form and the Form of forms. . . . For us, the form and formation of the ideal principle of being represent something that is self-evident and given, but nothing in the world is self-evident and nothing in the world is without a creative principle. In the proto-matter of the world, in the chaotic *mē on,* the *tohu vabohu,* which, however, is full of all the seeds of being, an organism of forms is formed; it is "hatched," as it were, clothed in Beauty. The beauty of the world is an effect of the Holy Spirit, the Spirit of Beauty; and Beauty is Joy, the joy of being. . . .

> The soul of the Divine creation
> Is nourished by eternal joy.[16]

Of course, this action of the natural grace of creation, this blowing of the Holy Spirit in the creaturely world, this continuous "movement" of the Holy Spirit "upon the face of the waters" of creation, is the *positive* force of being. This force is manifested in the overcoming of the power opposed to it, the creaturely "nothing," which receives its own force of being by a creative act of God. This *mē on* rages as the *elemental* power of creation, as "seething chaos,"[17] Achamoth, "the dark face of Sophia." If it is not illuminated, this dark face can even become an opposition to the light, darkness in the process of being actualized, anti-Sophia, the "minus of being." That is why the life of creation is not only an idyll, the blossoming of being, but also the "struggle for existence," the struggle between life and death. *Nothing* is conquered but not convinced by life; the chaotic element is restrained but not tamed; and "contradiction" (Heraclitus) or "war" (also Heraclitus) is the law of being, not only in the life of individu-

16. From Schiller's "Ode to Joy" in Tyutchev's celebrated translation into Russian. — Trans.

17. From a poem of Tyutchev's. — Trans.

als and nations but also in the impersonal or pre-personal element. Creation receives its own life as "nature." It is *natura,* i.e., in the process of being actualized but not yet actualized; it finds itself in the struggle between light and darkness, cosmos and chaos.

Nature awaits its humanization, which can arrive through the spirit-bearing man. Even before this humanization, however, while still on the path to it, nature possesses its own spirit-bearing character: "The heavens declare the glory of God; and the firmament sheweth his handiwork" (Ps. 19:1). Since it is spirit-bearing in character, nature is also, in this sense, God-bearing — and it is such not only by its boundless content but also by that ineffable and rationally unfathomable beauty which delights, nourishes, freshens, and fills the soul. Life with nature and the joy of nature are accessible to every human being, even to the unbeliever if the breath of the spirit touches him. This mystery of love for nature and its effect on the soul, the joy of nature, attests, of course, to the spirituality of nature, to the grace of the Holy Spirit that inheres in it.

Nature exists by the sophianic action of the Holy Spirit, and it is normal that the hypostasis of Beauty clothes nature in beauty, which is the *preliminary* image of God's enthronement by the Holy Spirit: "The Lord is enthroned; he is clothed in beauty" (from the Great Vespers). The *beauty of nature* is a self-evident fact — for both believers and unbelievers equally. Nature is beautiful in *all* its forms; and it does not know the formlessness which is ugliness. Even the *tohu vabohu,* the seething and unrestrained element of being, is clothed in the beauty of power, of potential content. It is "without form and void" (Gen. 1:2) not in the sense of the absence of form and forms but only in the sense of their unrevealedness. *Mē on* already sees itself in the idea and, within itself, conceives the latter. Nature is the combination and fullness of actualized forms; any manifestation of idea-form in being is already beauty, which is nothing else but actualized form. In this sense, beauty is the exteriorized sophianicity of creation that "clothes" the latter; it is the reflection of the eternal mystical light of the Divine Sophia. The beauty of nature is *objective.* This means that it can by no means be identified with human emotional or subjective states. The beauty of nature is a *spiritual force* that testifies about itself to the human spirit, although it manifests itself in a nonspiritual, "material" nature, but in a nature that is spirit-bearing. There can be various psychological theories of nature. But none of them is comprehensive, for they investigate different empirical manifestations of the supra-empirical fact of Beauty. All things are beautiful in nature: the elements of water and fire, air and sky, mountains and seas, plants and flowers. All things quicken, nourish, and inspire the human spirit: "soulless" nature manifests itself as spirit-bearing, for it testifies about the Spirit, is His revelation. This beauty of nature has its power and its limits. The power of natural beauty consists in its immediacy, in its pre-conscious elementalness, in its ineluctability.

Since they are nonhuman, or more precisely pre-human, and consequently beyond the *freedom* of the spirit that chooses and that determines itself, nature and the beauty in which it is clothed are revealed beyond good and evil, and consequently amorally. The criterion of morality is inapplicable here, inasmuch as it depends on human freedom and the value judgments of the latter in the sphere of good and evil, as well as in the sphere of sin and temptation. In general, no moral criterion exists for the beauty of nature. Nevertheless, in being revealed to man and possessing him to a certain degree, the beauty of nature participates in the domain of value judgments regarding good and evil. The beauty of nature can — not in and of itself but in and for man — become seductive and tempting, inebriating and bewitching. God Himself planted the garden of paradise, and made all kinds of trees grow in it, including the tree of the knowledge of good and evil, which was beautiful and unseductive for the sinless eyes of man. But Eve looked at this Divine creation with eyes already beclouded by sin, "and . . . the woman saw that the tree was good for food, and that it was pleasant to the eyes, and a tree to be desired to make one wise" (Gen. 3:6). She was seduced by it, and the beauty that clothed creation tempted Eve to sin. From this example alone one can see that "the lust of the flesh, and the lust of the eyes, and the pride of life" (1 John 2:16) attribute God's beauty to the "world" that "lieth in wickedness" (1 John 5:19). It is from creaturely freedom that the beauty of nature acquires the moral coefficient of good and evil. This coefficient refers not to the beauty of nature itself, which, after all, originates from the Holy Spirit and is sophianic in its foundation, but to its application, so to speak. Man can corrupt beauty, but he cannot destroy it.

For man as a spiritual being, an aesthetic criterion of life alone is insufficient. Such a criterion takes him out of the fullness of humanity into a pre-human state, degrades him as a spiritual and free being, who cannot and must not become solely an elemental being. When this elementalness becomes man's free self-determination, it loses its immediacy and spontaneity, and is replaced by imitation, stylization, and pose. And this leads to man's spiritual degeneration; he becomes vulgar and mediocre. When lust, even if aesthetic, is taken as the guiding principle of life, it destroys beauty, for beauty exists not for lust but for spirit, as an action of the Spirit. Art too, to the degree it is inspired by lust, becomes empty and *soulless*.

But besides vulgar, snobbish aestheticism, there is also a tragic aestheticism that is rooted in the disharmony between fallen man and nature. The fact is that the beauty of nature includes the beauty of the human body. Belonging to the natural world with its aspirituality and thus amorality, the human body has a certain degree of power over man. The beauty of the human body affects man and subjugates him like all natural beauty; but it also seduces him precisely as human beauty. Even though all the beauty of nature exists *for* man, it is not human and therefore cannot subjugate man to the degree that human beauty can. Even though it is natural, human beauty subjugates man even in his freedom. In this sense, "beauty is a terrifying thing."[18] Here we get a paradoxical interrelation: beauty, as a manifestation of Spirit in nature, which in itself does not know spirit, acts upon the human spirit by its seductiveness, simultaneously subjugating and inspiring it. Natural beauty alone, however, is *not enough* for man, because spiritual beauty is accessible to him. For him there exists not only the *adornment* by beauty irrespective of what it adorns — Venus or the Madonna, the blooms of paradise or the poisonous "flowers of evil." There is also the spiritual illumination.

Spiritual beauty is not only the outward adornment by beauty but also the illumination by beauty from within; it is a question of incarnate spirit, not soulless body. In its manifestation, however, this kind of beauty transcends the fallen world, in which man has a natural body, not a spiritual one (see 1 Cor. 15:44). To be sure, every human body, as a form, manifests spirit, but it does this incompletely and untransparently in relation to the latter, owing to which an evil spirit can be concealed in a beautiful body and, conversely, a good spirit can be concealed in a grotesque one. Spiritual corporeality is transparent for spirit, and good spirits have beautiful bodies ("then shall the righteous shine forth as the sun" [Matt. 13:43]), whereas evil spirits are deformed (consider the images of angels and those of demons). But as long as this disharmony remains, as long as it remains possible that the same person can be "beautiful like a heavenly angel, but malicious and evil like a demon,"[19] as long as it remains the case that, owing to this opacity of the body for the spirit, individual beauty is to a certain degree a caprice of fate, this beauty can be the cause of the tragedy in which "God battles the devil, and the field of battle is the

18. A phrase from Dostoevsky's *The Brothers Karamazov*. — Trans.
19. Verses from a poem by Lermontov. — Trans.

human heart."[20] In other words, individual beauty can become an instrument of evil, a devil's web (which is why manichean asceticism calls woman a "vessel of Satan").

Of course, the true source of the tragedy is found not in beauty but in sin, in the general corruption due to original sin. An impure, lustful gaze makes the body's nakedness indecent (see Gen. 3:7), whereas for the pure all things are pure and beautiful.[21] For the impure gaze, beauty can act like an evil hypnosis and infernal power, subjecting the human spirit to tragic struggles, whereas the love for beauty is rooted in the primordial depths of the human spirit. This tragedy of beauty is a *symptom* of the illegitimate state of man and thus of all creation as a consequence of original sin.

To be sure, the following question can arise: *How* can beauty, the vestment of Divinity, the ontic aura of the Holy Spirit, become a means to temptation? An answer to this question is given in the narrative of the temptation of Adam and Eve, when the serpent tempted them not only spiritually but also sensually and aesthetically, with the beauty of the fruits and their desirability (Gen. 3:6). The world, created by God with all its abundance and beauty, is not deprived of the power of being by the fact that evil, associated with creaturely freedom, parasitically inhabits it and uses it for its own purposes. *Beauty abides,* and not only in Eden but also in Sodom, although in the latter the experience of beauty is not spiritual but perverted. Beauty is truly beyond good and evil, and consequently it is neutral in relation to the freedom of the spirit, which, nevertheless, is capable of experiencing it in all the fullness of its own self-determination, that is, in the context of all the spiritual values.

Beauty *becomes* good or evil for human freedom, but it does not depend on them for its existence. Thus, besides being proper to the sophianic proto-image of creation, beauty also exists in the fallen world, the world darkened by the fall. Together with other forces, the world also contains beauty. To be sure, this beauty acquires a negative coefficient, so to speak; it is limited and conditional; it cannot be illuminated in the universal spiritual transfiguration of creation, where it will fade. But for the time being it nevertheless remains the flower of creation. Sin and sickness cannot abolish in man the image of God, which constitutes the foundation of his being. But neither can they abolish beauty in nature. And if beauty exists by the divine power that is implanted in creation, this power

20. A phrase from Dostoevsky's *The Brothers Karamazov.* — Trans.
21. See the narrative about St. Nonnus in the *Ladder* of St. John Climacus.

appears to be compatible with the power of evil that has crept into creation. Into the Garden of Eden planted by God there crept the wicked serpent, the instrument of Satan: "the serpent was more subtil than any beast of the field which the Lord God had made" (Gen. 3:1); and without doubt he charmed the woman by the fatal beauty of his green eyes. Neither the radiant beauty of Eden, nor the original innocence of our progenitors, nor even the nearness of God, "walking in the garden in the cool of the day" (3:8), could remove the possibility of the presence of the serpent, which, nevertheless, did not abolish the garden. And this is a symbol of divine tolerance and patience toward evil, whose arena of action is God's creation.

Nature is subject to the force of inertia, and it therefore must be guided and ruled by man. But because man has fallen and has thus become a slave to the elements of the world, all creation is in bondage to "vanity" (Rom. 8:20), "groaneth and travaileth in pain" (8:22), as if in the torments of childbirth, striving to achieve its proper fullness in order to participate in "the glorious liberty of the children of God" (8:21). The force of inertia is increasing; creation has become less sensitive to its own inner calls; and it is subject to intrusions of nonbeing, of "vanity." Furthermore, the forces of nature, which are under the watch of the holy angels, can become a refuge for demons, and the chaos seething under the crust of being is capable of becoming demonic. This chaotic and demonic character of nature can distort her countenance, both by preventing it from being fully revealed and by imparting to it the grimace of the "ancient horror." The inner exorcism of nature was already accomplished by Christ's death on the cross: "the Great Pan died," the demonic possession of nature was abolished, the prince of this world was cast out. Nevertheless, nature remains in an unfinished form and needs to be "transfigured." But this form, sophianic although unfinished, comes from the Holy Spirit.

In this we once again see the *kenosis* of the Holy Spirit. It consists not only in the illumination of creation in general, but also in the acceptance of the *measure* of creation and of the fact that it is not very receptive to the revelation of the Spirit. This poor receptivity and even opposition of creation do not lead the Spirit to abandon it to the fate of its original vanity; rather, He abides in creation and sustains its being. The Lord said about the antediluvian humanity, "My Spirit shall not always be neglected by man" (Gen. 6:3; the King James Version has been modified to conform with the Russian Bible); and He condemned man to be destroyed by the deluge, for the measure of God's long-suffering patience was surpassed. But after the deluge God concluded a new covenant with man, where He said that He would not destroy creation again (Gen. 8:21-22; 9:9-16). And this long-suffering patience of God, by virtue of which the whole cycle of earthly life and all its phenomena "shall not cease" (8:22), is God's kenosis with respect to creation, precisely the kenosis of the Holy Spirit. The power of being and life, which is also the power of beauty, will not cease in the world, despite passive and active resistance, inertia, and outright evil. The creative "let there be" resounds in the world, and the "it was good" shines in it. The Heavenly Father Who is revealed to the world in His Spirit "maketh his sun to rise on the evil and on the good, and sendeth rain on the just and on the unjust" (Matt. 5:45).

Thus, the life of nature has a dual character: beneath the veil of light is concealed the nocturnal darkness. Nature knows its horrors and abysses. That it why it has turned out to be capable of following man in his fall, of being arrested in that imperfect state it found itself in outside of Eden, and even of intensifying this state, of making it more profound. It has become orphaned without man, who has fallen away from it because of his falling away from God; and it has become the habitation of demons, the plaything of its own natural forces ("the elementary spirits"), of the "soul of nature."

But the holy angels who watch over nature have not abandoned it; and ineffaceable is the image of God that is imprinted in nature, which, although not yet reborn, is being reborn. Despite all the cracks of being, the Holy Spirit is its life force, which cannot be defeated by the forces hostile to being. Nature is indestructible and, in this sense, immortal, just as man is immortal, even though death has entered it just as it has entered man.

Nature is *natura,* which means that it is to become itself, that it is in the process of becoming. *Development* is synonymous with life. Blind, disbelieving science calls this "evolution." It understands nature in terms of *random* change, of change not by design, of occasionalism, where out of nothing or out of anything at all it is possible to get everything or anything at all in accordance with absolute randomness. In contrast to the principle of determinism, the principle of *ex nihilo nil fit* [out of nothing comes nothing], there is tacitly proclaimed here the opposite principle: out of nothing comes everything. At least, such must be a consistent theory of evolution out of nothing, if it wishes to be true to itself. But such a consistency would contain an annihilating critique of the theory itself and would expose the contradictory character of its fundamental principle. The adherents of *such* a conception of evolution are, however, never consistent to such an extent, but include in their scheme some teleological principle (e.g., the production of "higher" species), which guarantees a determinate outcome to the evolutionary process and, in general, imparts content and meaning to the whole process. "Development" is interpreted here in a distinctively mythological manner; it is viewed as a certain force that guarantees a favorable outcome to the cosmic process and avoids the formlessness and emptiness that characterize consistent nihilism. And this whole system is based on a blind faith in the creative powers of matter, living or dead, in the creative powers of the evolutionary process itself, in *évolution créatrice,* and so on.

Nevertheless, despite how helpless and unsatisfactory the evolutionary philosophy may be in its different forms, the fundamental intuition of *development* is entirely correct, and the very *fact* of development is indisputable. Untrue and absurd is the opinion that this evolution starts from a place of void. It is only by virtue of inconsistency of thought that the evolutionary doctrine does not lurch into the void, which not only nature but also thought "fears" and cannot tolerate. The truth is that nature is not empty, but full. It is full of logoses, ontic seeds, which pre-contain the *all* of cosmic being. These seeds sprout at different rates and with different energies, but it is precisely *they* that sprout. Therefore, development is not a sentence without a subject and without a predicate, a sentence that contains only a copula of general fluidity, which thought cannot even perceive because of its objectlessness. Development has its *theme;* it has a subject and a predicate, the "what" that develops and the "whereto" or "to what" it develops. In general, evolution acquires a meaning only if it has an inner teleology.

But the teleology of the world is of course given by its ontology. It is established by the action of the Second hypostasis: "All things were made by him; and without him was not any thing made that was made" (John 1:3). Thus, there is a "whereto" or "to what" of development: the latter has both a given element and a proposed element (i.e., the task that it must accomplish) according to the image of the Divine Sophia imprinted in the creaturely Sophia, in those *paradeigmata* [paradigms] or *proorismoi* [prototypes] that determine cosmic being. These "seminal logoses" (according to the excellent expression of the Stoics) are, however, originally implanted in creation only as seeds, which first lie in a dormant state resembling death, in "the earth . . . without form and void" (Gen. 1:2), but are then awakened to life by the creative "let there be" and "let (the waters or the earth) bring forth" — and life *begins.* But this incipient life, which is the action of the Holy Spirit in the world, the presence of His force, undergoes self-actualization, development, becoming, transition from the proposed element to the given element, from potentiality to the dynamic manifestation of entelechic principles. This *dynamism* of life, this fullness and force of life by which "all" things live while actualizing themselves, cannot be explained by any particular laws of "evolution," because life is evolution in itself, absolute evolution. This force of life and development is the force of the Holy Spirit in nature, *the natural grace of life:* "thou takest away thy spirit, they die. . . . Thou sendest forth thy spirit, they are created" (Ps. 104:29-30; the King James Version has been modified to conform with the Russian Bible).

All existing things develop and change; all living things grow. And the mystery of this life and of this growth is the force of the Holy Spirit, which entered into the world at its creation and abides in it by Providence. It is necessary to understand and accept this natural grace of creation in all its inseparability from the natural world without being shocked by an apparent paganism or pantheism which opposes an empty and dead deism that separates the Creator from creation. Where will the natural world get the power to become itself if not from the "let there be" that already exists within its depths? How else will it become that which it already is according to its *meaning?* But in the creation "out of nothing," in this creaturely union of plus and minus, life and development are realized with delays, with destructions, and in general in the struggle with forces hostile to life. This development is accomplished immanently, not by an external mechanical pressure but by an internal life force. Each positive form of being is opposed by an anti-form, as it were, a grimace of being, the phantasms of Achamoth; each effort of life is counteracted by an impotence; each attainment of being corresponds to a particular tension, not only in the spiritual world, but, in its own way, in the natural world as well. In a certain sense, one can say that nature too labors and creatively participates in its self-creation, in conformity with its primordial tasks and meanings. But this effort requires *inspiration* for the victory of day over night, cosmos over chaos, fullness over emptiness and formlessness, and life over non-life, which becomes death.

This inspiration of life is bestowed by the Holy Spirit, is His grace in creation, even in pre-human and as yet nonhuman creation, which is advancing, however, to encounter man, who, in his spirit, is capable of receiving this inspiration by the Spirit. The gifts of the Spirit are diverse, and it is proper to Him to bestow them upon creation. Since creation received the Spirit at its very origin, it possesses the Spirit in its very being. The name of grace-filled creation is Eden, whereas creation without grace is the whole world, in which, besides the general action of natural grace,

there shine the luminous points of ecclesial sanctification: the sanctification of the elements, water, bread, and so on. One can question if the action of the Holy Spirit extends also to "soulless" nature: Can the latter, being alien to the hypostatic spirit, be capable of receiving the Divine Spirit?
Here, however, it is a question not of the hypostatic manifestation of the
Hypostatic Holy Spirit but of His *sophianic* reception. The Divine Sophia
is the foundation of the creaturely Sophia. In the latter, it is not only the
word of creation that is realized but also its life. But what other source of
life can there be besides the Life-giving Spirit?

It should not be forgotten that the bestowal of the gifts of the Holy
Spirit is just as infinitely diverse as their reception. And this *natural* reception is, of course, a particular stage and, in a certain sense, a lower one (insofar as one can distinguish "higher" and "lower" here). In general, the
giving of the Spirit is not a one-sided and mechanical act effected *on* an
object, but a certain interaction. And even natural grace is received or *not*
received by the creaturely element, the "earth," which is capable not only
of cooperating with the action of this grace but also of resisting it. The
important thing is that the world, as the creaturely Sophia, is never abandoned to its proper fate, to the void of creaturely nonbeing, but participates in the fullness of divine being. This "providence" with regard to creation is accomplished by means of the angelic world, which in a certain
sense represents the hypostases of creaturely being, its spirits. One cannot
equate the reception of grace that is bestowed upon spiritual and
hypostatic beings with that which is bestowed upon the natural world,
but both are grace, for gifts are different but the Spirit is the same.

Creation can become spirit-bearing and will be so after the Transfiguration of the world, under a new heaven and on a new earth; and this
calling of creation to spirituality can be recognized in the *sanctification* of
various natural elements. Sanctification, i.e., the communication of the
grace of the Holy Spirit, is possible only by virtue of a general spiritual receptivity, attested by the initial movement of the Holy Spirit upon the face
of the waters; and this sanctification will not end during the further existence of the world. The Holy Spirit is bestowed upon the world in the
creaturely Sophia, through the Divine Sophia. We have here the action of
the Holy Spirit, of His force, but without His hypostatic revelation. The
force of the Holy Spirit acts here *impersonally*, as it were, although similarly to the Logos, Who establishes the *all* of creation. In creation as such,
which belongs to itself and is directed at itself, there exist *logoi*, the logoses
or forms of being, which all proceed from the hypostatic Word, although
the Word Himself in His hypostasis is not revealed in them; and so the

Logos too acts impersonally in the *being* of creation. In her aseity, the creaturely Sophia exists as the word of the world and the soul of the world, as the verbal and living world. With reference to the divine foundation of being, creation is a divine world, whereas in its aseity and self-centeredness it is a natural world, i.e., a world striving to become but not yet having become the full revelation of Sophia. The fall of man, and with him of the whole world, made this becoming more difficult, so that "the whole creation groaneth and travaileth in pain together until now" (Rom. 8:22), "subject to vanity, not willingly, but by reason of him who hath subjected the same" (8:20). But this did not abolish the foundations of the life of the cosmos.

Thus, it is necessary to receive the action of natural grace which is manifested in creation by virtue of the initial creative act, just as it is necessary to receive the creative word that resides in creation; and this word and this grace are nothing else but the sophianicity of creation. It would be incorrect to say that these are the Divine Logos Himself and the hypostatic Holy Spirit; nevertheless, these are the word from the Word and the spirit of God from the Holy Spirit. This constitutes the essential content and life-giving energy proper to creation, the latter's truth and inspiration. Creation possesses its depth and force. One can even say that there is a creaturely soul of the world which includes all things that exist in the world as well as its life and vital self-inspiration. The spirit of God moving upon the face of creation manifests by its force the forms of being concealed in it, just as under the rays of the sun the spring earth gives life to the seeds and plants contained in it. There is a "life force," which even natural science (in vitalism) is discovering today; and this is the spirit of God. And there are the primordial *species,* which are realized in the "development of species," the sophianic logoses of being. Theology (and sophiology in particular) encounters natural science here, whose task is to become the theology of nature.

But nature is impersonal, and sophianic revelations therefore act in it as immanent forces, as if blind potencies of being (although behind and beneath them are hypostatic forces — of the angelic world). This lack of subject in nature, however, is overcome in man, who is the supra-creaturely principle in the world, for he has a spirit that proceeds from God and a hypostasis, which, albeit created, is in the image of God. In this sense, man is the hypostasis of the creaturely Sophia, which is multiple in the hypostases of the human race. As both a created spirit and a spirit who is divine according to his source, man is open both to divine life, in which he participates by virtue of his deification, and to the creaturely

Sophia, whose hypostasis he is. In this sense, he is created as a creaturely god in nature, as a god by grace. His reception of *divine* life is the action of the Image of God in him. Divine life for him is *natural according to creation;* and one should not obscure this naturalness by the unnecessary distinction between *status naturalis* and *gratia supranaturalis* [natural condition and supernatural grace], which appears to surpass the limits of the proper human essence. *Gratia* is, of course, *supranaturalis,* insofar as it enables man to commune with God; but this communion with God corresponds precisely to the natural human essence, which is created to be a receptacle of grace. And in this sense the original Adam was, before his fall, already the king of the world, the high priest and prophet by the power of God acting in him; and in this sense he was a *god-man in the process of becoming.* Adam's fall interrupted the reality of this communion with God, and man was left only with the possibility of the latter as the ontological postulate of his being. This postulate could not be abolished, but neither could it be realized by human powers, without the "descent from heaven" of God the Word Himself. Even man's central position in the world was shaken, insofar as it was connected with the displacement of the ontological center and the subjugation of the king of this world, man, to nature.

The very foundation of the ontological image of man, that is, the image of God, could not be destroyed, however; man remained what he was according to his creation: the hypostatic subject of the creaturely world, which he contains (although only potentially) in his hypostatic being. Man is the logos of the world, and all its particular logoses as well as their mutual relation are accessible to him; and he is also the soul of the world, in which the world lives itself out. In the depths of his thought, man knows the world, and by the force of his life he actively realizes himself in the world, humanizing the latter. This knowledge is not merely a passive mirror reflection of the images of the world in man; it is their creative acquisition. In knowledge, man not only encompasses within himself that which is known, but also proceeds out of himself into the world and is identified with the latter (which is why the word "knowledge" is also applied to the union of man and woman: "Adam knew Eve his wife" [Gen. 4:1]). In this sense, knowledge is the identification of the inner human logos, the eye of the world, with the logos of the world, with both shining in the world from the Divine Logos. But at the same time knowledge is also self-knowledge and knowledge out of oneself, which cannot be realized without self-inspiration. This self-inspiration in the creative act is the stamp of the spirit of God, who pours forth from the Holy Spirit. Creative activity, which does not exist without inspiration, is necessarily proper to the creaturely spirit as bearing the image of God. It is by inspiration that the human depths are revealed (just as in the Holy Trinity the Spirit sounds the depths of God). It is by inspiration that man tests and realizes the possibilities or tasks proper to him, his latent and slumbering word. The faculty of inspiration, like that of active knowledge, belongs to the Image of God in man.

This means that in man there is also a *natural grace of inspiration*, his inspiration by the world and by himself. By means of it, man awakens from his meonic state to life. The objective foundation and content of this inspiration are determined by his communion with the creaturely Sophia. Consequently, it would be incorrect to say that all human inspiration comes *directly* from the Holy Spirit and in this sense is of divine origin. Rather, it would be correct to say that in the creaturely Sophia, in creaturely being itself, the Holy Spirit has implanted the force of life and inspiration as the sophianic foundation of this being. And inspiration is real in man because he has something to reveal and something to be awakened to. In his creative inspiration, the depths and the heights of the world are accessible to man. He feels himself to be one with the world soul; in him is awakened the "cosmic sense" of world unity, and he feels himself to be a natural prophet and a creator (albeit a creaturely one) in this world:

> He touched my eyes,
> And my prophetic eyes opened
> Like those of a frightened eagle.
> He touched my ears
> And they were filled with noise and ringing:
> And I heard the shuddering of the heavens,
> And the flight of the angels in the heights,
> And the movement of the sea beasts under the waters,
> And the sound of the vine growing in the valley. . . .[22]

There is no limit to inspiration, just as there is no limit to the human world which exists in the image of God. Inspiration is natural grace in man, just as life force is the natural grace of the pre-human world. Pa-

---

22. This is a passage from one of the most magnificent poems in the Russian language, Pushkin's "The Prophet." This translation is taken from *The Penguin Book of Russian Verse*, introduced and edited by Dimitri Obolensky (Baltimore: Penguin, 1962), pp. 92-93. — Trans.

ganism knew this force of natural inspiration as the "muse," i.e., as the higher I in man; and it tried to break through to this higher I by means of ecstasy, the going out of oneself, the expansion of oneself, the ascent into higher spheres, which, in this case, are limited to the domain of the world soul, the sophianic unity of the world. Such mystical contacts were perhaps also effected in pythian ecstasy, in the ecstatic experiencing of the mysteries, in the ineffable contemplations of light (Plotinus), in the living sense of cosmic unity in the world soul (in Brahmanism), and so on. Paganism is full of such experiences. In the authenticity of its religious experience, paganism is the religion of the world soul, different aspects of which are known — in the distorting mirror of the spirit of fallen man — in the figure of the "gods." One should not doubt the authenticity of these mystical experiences, although they do not contain a true revelation of God and in this sense are pseudo-revelations. Paganism knows a natural revelation, although one that is distorted and beclouded. The pagan religions are not empty *sophianically*. But being confined within the limits of the natural world and nourished by the inspirations of the natural world alone, they are powerless to know the true Divinity in Its purity and uniqueness. The fall of man, the power of sin in him, affects especially the character of his inspiration, for the latter can be subject to ambiguity and distortion, can be light or dark, good or evil. Inspiration can even become demonic or luciferian, insofar as evil spirits act in the world and are capable of influencing man. This is even manifested in man's religious destiny, in particular in the pagan religions with their perversions. All this is so, but it remains true that the very faculty of inspiration is an imprint in man of his sophianicity, is given to him by the spirit of God, is his natural grace. Without this capacity for natural inspiration, man would have no access to true divine inspiration.

And so, what is this muse in which paganism believed,[23] this muse which we know even today as a special state of inspiration, which comes upon man spontaneously and from outside, as it were? Can one simply place an equals sign between the "muse" (or the "Muse") and the grace-bestowing action of the spirit of God (or the Holy Spirit)? It is not easy to answer this question in any definite sense. It is, of course, impossible to assert that *all* human inspiration is from the Holy Spirit. This can be said only about the prophets of God and their divinely inspired writings. But one must not hastily make such an assertion about inspirations of a com-

---

23. The statement of this problem in Russian theology is associated with the name G. P. Fedotov.

paratively secondary significance, e.g., those in the patristic or liturgical literature. These writings too, however, can contain a degree of anointment by the Holy Spirit that can imply a *greater or lesser* divine inspiration; and thus one cannot limit oneself to a simple "yes" or "no" here.

But what can one say about *sophianic* revelation that is actualized by human inspiration? Does it have a place for the action of the spirit of God, *in spite of* the possibility of contaminations and distortions? In our opinion, it does, insofar as in the revelation of the creaturely Sophia in the world we confess the action of the Holy Spirit. But this inspiration remains only *naturally* spirit-bearing, does not enter into the divine realm, belongs to *natural* grace, which is entrusted to man's possession. Nevertheless, this inspiration comes from the spirit of God: Every soul is quickened by the Holy Spirit, and this is the case not only in the realm of spiritual grace but also in the realm of natural grace. Therefore, one should not diminish but should honor human inspiration and creative activity. For the "muse" or "apollo" is not, of course, the mask or pseudonym of the spirit of God itself, but its *force* acting in creation. It is *spirit*, although it is not the Holy Spirit. Life that is worthy of the name is always inspiration; and conversely, without inspiration, whatever its character may be and whatever its orientation, there is no life. Even the blasphemers against inspiration, who blaspheme against God's world in its naturalness, do so in a particular state of inspiration, although one that is perhaps not radiant. The inspired state and inspiration are so essential for life that, in a certain sense, they can be identified with it, just as conversely, without inspiration we do not have a path to Divinity, and even prayer itself is inspiration.

On the lower rungs of life, this identity of life and inspiration is expressed in elementary spontaneity of movement; on its higher rungs it is expressed in freedom of self-determination, action by oneself and out of oneself, out of one's own individual qualified being. This "out of oneself" is precisely creative self-inspiration.

It follows that the entire creative activity of life, that is, *the whole of human history* to which God had called the human race (with the genealogy of Christ serving as the heart of this history), is accomplished by virtue of this creative inspiration with all its multiform multiplicity. But we know that the paths of history are twisted and intersecting; history is not an idyll but a tragedy. Inspirations in history can be not only diverse but also contradictory, like their fruits. Their differentiation and evaluation can be accomplished only at the *end* of history (however we understand it), at the "last" judgment. However, only the free, creative movements of the soul can be judged, that is, precisely its inspirations. Passive, mechanical acceptance of fate cannot be judged, except, perhaps, for the *absence* of inspiration. "Thou art neither cold nor hot; I would thou wert cold or hot. So then because thou art lukewarm, and neither cold nor hot, I will spue thee out of my mouth" (Rev. 3:15-16), the Spirit tells the angel of the church of the Laodiceans. "Be zealous therefore, and repent" (3:19). But there is no zeal without love and inspiration, which is the flame of life and the motive force of history.

The inspiration that is entrusted to the self-governing creaturely spirit shares the fate of all creation, that is, it finds itself in a state of ambiguity and confusion, and it always has need of exorcism through grace. That is why the unexamined use of the expression "divine inspiration" is totally inappropriate and impermissible here. Nevertheless, inspiration intrinsically comes from spirit, and the capacity for inspiration is implanted in man from the source of all inspiration, the Holy Spirit. And what is especially important is that, being sophianic in its source, the faculty of inspiration can also contain a *sophianic* revelation of God in the world, although this is not a *direct* Revelation of God Himself about Himself. This enables us to understand the possibility of the higher illuminations of humanity, which are bestowed upon the latter in the natural religions, in philosophy, in art, in creative activity in general. Despite the fact that they have a confused character and are troubled by sinful creatureliness, these illuminations are true inspirations, revelations of the spirit living in man and of the sophianicity of the latter. Furthermore, this human inspiration, this manifestation of spirit, does *not* contradict divine inspiration, but rather is its precondition: only in human inspiration is Divine inspiration realized; only in revelation is Revelation given; only in spirit is Spirit bestowed.

Divine inspiration renders golden the summits of natural inspiration; and it is not a mechanical coercion of man, a *deus ex machina,* but a real *meeting* between the human spirit and the Divine Spirit, for the former is porous for the Latter. The creaturely Sophia not only has her foundation in the Divine Sophia but is permeated by her. And this unified sophianicity serves as the foundation of divine inspiration. There is a perfect analogy here with the Divine Incarnation. The foundation of the Divine Incarnation, thanks to the union of the two natures, of the creaturely and the Divine Sophia, of the human nature and the Divine nature, is their common sophianicity. Similarly, the foundation of divine inspiration is the union of the two inspirations, divine and creaturely, in one Divine-human spirit. This union too is accomplished without separation and without confusion, like that of the two natures and of the two wills in the God-Man. The human spirit and the Divine Spirit are (if it is permissible to use this expression) kindred in their sophianicity; and this is why, by analogy with the Divine Incarnation, divine inspiration too is possible, which is the meeting and union of a spirit and the Spirit in a human hypostasis. The spirit of God comes not to an empty place, but encounters the human spirit. We have the prototype for this divine inspiration in the "prophets"; and we have its supreme actualization in *Christ,* the *Anointed* by the Spirit, the Spirit-bearer. The incarnate Son of God, the God-Man, is also Christ, the Spirit-bearer.

Inspiration in general and as the precondition for divine inspiration belongs to the domain of human creative activity and is not acquired without a creative tension, which is the opposite of what Scripture calls the quenching of the spirit (see 1 Thess. 5:19). Creative activity is the effort to transcend the limited element of the given and to enable the unlimited element of the proposed to enter into the element of the given; it is the effort to "outgrow oneself." It is a striving to go out of oneself, beyond oneself, above oneself; and by this striving, creative activity either plumbs its own depths or ascends to meet the spirit descending from above. But even apart from such a meeting, which does not depend upon man, the creative spirit, soaring above itself, can truly ascend and gaze from the heights. This is the sophianic fathoming of one's own sophianicity.

Returning to our initial theme, the theme of the dyadic revelation of the Son and the Holy Spirit, the theme of Their sophianic Dyad, we must say that the *content* of creaturely inspiration, as well as of creaturely life and being itself, is the words of the Word, the ontic *all,* the seeds of being. Word is the *what* of creation and spirit is its *how.* Creaturely inspiration enables creatures to surpass themselves in each of their given states and thereby to grow in themselves. But it is always an inspiration with an object, with a theme; and by itself it is incapable of bringing anything new into that which exists, of enriching being with new themes. This does not mean that it is constrained or limited by a given theme of being, for potentially it contains "all," is so unlimited in this sense that it cannot be a limit. This *all,* which is without measure for creation, is, for all practical purposes, always *new* for creative activity. This novelty is a sign of creative activity, which cannot be a mere repetition of what is already given. The domain of creative activity lies not in the sphere of the given and already attained, but in the sphere of the proposed, with its possibilities. These possibilities, unactualized but being actualized, constitute the source of the *new* in creation, although this novelty is, so to speak, *modal* in character. Creaturely creative activity cannot, of course, produce anything new in theme and being; and thus it cannot enrich God Himself in His creative activity.

But God Himself has left man his share — precisely the human share — of participation in the creation of the world, for He has created the world only in its *potential* fullness. Man is given the power to creatively realize in himself and in creation his own theme and his own given, to realize it as his task, creating himself in a creaturely as well as creative manner, and thus in a new manner for himself. And this novelty, although it is modal in character, forms an *inexhaustible* source for the creative activity of creatures, with its *eternal* novelty. This eternity is not divine eternity, *aeternitas,* in which there is no becoming or time, and no place for novelty, for all things exist there supra-eternally in the fullness of one self-determining act. The *new* can occur only in creation, where, in infinite becoming, eternity is realized, but only a *creaturely* eternity, *aeviternitas.* Concerning creation, God says, in the language of creaturely becoming, "I make all things new" (Rev. 21:5; cf. 2 Cor. 5:17), for creation is always renewed. Insofar as God Himself has included in creation the self-creative activity of creatures, this activity is new even before the face of God Himself as the Creator, although not in His eternity. The ontological bounds of creaturely being with its self-creative activity are preestablished from the beginning. These bounds are given by the sophianic Dyad of Son and Holy Spirit, which, without separation and without confusion, establishes the sophianic foundations of creaturely being as its theme, fate, and supreme goal, never attained but always in the process of being attained. But man is not God and he can never become his own creator or the creator of the world. And if he pretends to be such, he is guilty either of gross self-deception or of metaphysical thievery. Just consider Lucifer, "the prince of this world," thief and liar, and luciferianism in its different forms.

CHAPTER 5

The Revelation of the Holy Spirit

I. The Kenosis of the Holy Spirit in Creation

The kenosis in creation of God Who is in the Holy Trinity signifies His self-diminution with respect to His absoluteness. The absolute God, correlated with nothing but Himself, becomes correlative with something outside Himself.[1] That is, positing relative creaturely being, He enters into a relation with the latter: the Absolute becomes God, and God is a relative concept: God is such for another, for creation; whereas in itself the Absolute is not God. This self-relativization of the Absolute is the sacrifice of God's love for this *other*, which He Himself creates out of nothing. The kenosis of the Father consists in the fact that the Father, Who reveals Himself eternally in the Son and the Spirit in the Divine Sophia, reveals Himself in creation — also through the Dyad of the Son and the Spirit — in the *creaturely* Sophia. But the Father Himself remains, in a certain sense, *outside* of this self-revelation; He is only the *will to* creation, which He transcends. This transcendence of the Father is precisely His kenosis, as if a nonbeing in creation. The kenosis of the Son consists in the fact that He, Who is *all* in creation, diminished Himself to the human form of being in the Divine Incarnation, became the God-Man,[2] entered the world as the lamb of God, sacrificed on Golgotha in the fullness of time.

But what does the kenosis of the Holy Spirit consist in, and in what sense can one speak of it? In the creation of the world this kenosis is expressed in the fact that the Holy Spirit, Who is the fullness and depth of

---

1. See my book *The Unfading Light: On Creation.*
2. See my book *The Lamb of God.*

Divinity, diminished Himself to *becoming* in His revelation in the creaturely Sophia. In the Divine life, the Holy Spirit realizes the fullness adequate to this life and plumbs the depths of God by a unique eternal act. In creaturely being, the Holy Spirit is the force of being and the giver of life, but, according to the very concept of creation, this being and this life exist only as becoming, that is, not in fullness but only in the striving toward fullness. The creaturely eros is the son of Porus and Penia, of abundance and poverty, of fullness and emptiness: the creaturely *all* is formed out of *nothing*. That is why the action of the force of the Holy Spirit is limited in creation in conformity with the condition of the latter, although it is never depleted, for otherwise creation would be abolished, would return to its original nonbeing. The Father, in sending the Spirit in the creative "let there be," restrains the Spirit's force and fullness, as it were — if only by the fact that He manifests them in time, in becoming. This is attested by the "Six Days" with their six (or even eight) instances of "let there be," which constitute the degrees or stages of being and life. This multistage or grad-ual character of being is proper to the life of the world, for the creative "let there be" always resounds in the world in its *different* forms; creation is al-ways the *future* too, not only *nata*, but also *natura*.

This kenosis of the Spirit, the reception of unfullness by Fullness, of becoming by eternity, is completely unfathomable for creation, which knows only unfullness and has only becoming as its vantage point. But it is precisely this kenosis that constitutes the very foundation of the participa-tion of the Spirit in creation, that defines Him as the Creator. The *immeas-urableness* of Fullness is included in the *measure* proper to unfullness, which is inevitable for creation with its "evolution" and growth. In other words, this immeasurableness is contained within the measure of creation.[3]

The form of the kenosis of the Holy Spirit in the creaturely Sophia, or in creation, is the creative "let there be," the force of life and being, nat-ural grace. The path followed by this natural grace is from the movement of the Spirit upon the face of the waters to the transfiguration of creation into a "new heaven and a new earth": "I make all things new" (Rev. 21:1, 5). This natural grace of the Holy Spirit, which constitutes the very founda-tion of the being of creation, exists in the very *flesh* of the world, in the matter of the world. It is the precondition for its sanctification through the reception of the Holy Spirit. The Church knows many different *sancti-fications of matter,* which are included in the majority of the Church sacra-ments and sacramentalia: the sanctification of the waters of the Jordan by

---

3. Particularly pertinent here is John 3:34: "God giveth not the Spirit by measure."

the descent of the Holy Spirit, serving as the basis of all the baptismal and nonbaptismal sanctifications of water; the sanctification of myrrh and oil, of bread and wine, eucharistic and non-eucharistic; and the sanctification of churches, sacred objects, fruits, foods, and in general all manner of *things.*

What, fundamentally, does such sanctification signify? How can things and matter be sanctified? That is, how can they receive and retain the action of the Holy Spirit, i.e., supernatural grace? It is usually thought that only the spiritual can receive the spiritual, whereas, here, things and matter absorb the invisibly descending grace of the Holy Spirit the way the earth absorbs moisture. Matter's receptivity to spirit has as its precondition the creaturely descent of the Spirit, His kenosis in creation. Creation has the Spirit of God from its very origin, and is spirit-bearing in this sense, although this spirit-bearingness knows its *measure.* But this measure is nonetheless such that it already contains the force of the being of creation. And in virtue of this natural or, more precisely, *sophianic* spirit-bearingness, creation is capable of receiving spirit through sanctification. *The similar receives the similar,* and without this similarity, the very concept of sanctification becomes incomprehensible and contradictory. Without it, it would be impossible to refute all those doubts and objections according to which all sanctification, whether sacramental or not, is viewed either as superstition or as natural magic and sorcery, and as such is subject either to rationalistic refutation or occultistic interpretation, which, in essence, are equivalent. The supernatural, i.e., grace, exists neither for rationalism nor for occultism, which knows only a self-enclosed world, although one with different "planes" or "hierarchies." The action of grace is equated here merely with the interaction between a higher plane and a lower one and the influence of the corresponding higher hierarchies.

In sanctification we have a descent of the Holy Spirit and a communication of His force to natural and spirit-bearing creation: the creaturely Sophia is united here with the Divine Sophia, the Holy Spirit with the spirit of God in creation. A mysterious "transmutation" of matter occurs here, not only in the Eucharist, but in all sacramental acts: matter is taken out of this world and borne into the world of grace of the future age, where God will be all in all. There occurs a mysterious, i.e., invisible, transfiguration of creation, in which the latter, while ontologically remaining itself, becomes transparent for the Spirit, receives the faculty of communion with God, is deified. Thus, in this permeability of matter for the Spirit and the resulting "communication of properties" or perichoresis (to use a term of christological theology), we have an inseparable and inconfusible unity of creaturely and divine life. In other words, a *divine-humanity* is being realized here, not in man himself but in the human world and in the world that is in the process of being humanized, a world that has its ontological center in man. This is the deification of creation, under the necessary condition of the conservation of its being.

But this *divine-human* character of grace is fully manifested only in spiritual beings, in man and in angels, that is, in hypostatic spirits who are conscious of themselves. Spirit is known by spirit and looks into the mirror of spirit: spiritual things are compared with spiritual (see 1 Cor. 2:13). If *sanctification* is proper to creaturely matter, then *inspiration* is proper to the human spirit and is a *divine-human* act, a manifestation of eternal divine-humanity in creaturely divine-humanity. This divine-human act, however, is expressed here not in divine incarnation, the union of the *fullness* of the divine nature with the human nature, but in divine inspiration, that is, in the mutual permeation of the human spirit and the Holy Spirit, also without separation and without confusion. In no wise can divine inspiration be understood as the abolition of the human spirit and its replacement or expulsion by the divine Spirit (this is postulated only by theories of literal or direct inspiration). This is a monophysitic conception, analogous to christological monophysitism. This conception implies the fusion or confusion of the two natures with the absorption of the lower by the higher, of the human nature by the divine, as well as the annihilation of man; that is, it introduces a kind of pneumatological docetism where the whole reality of the human creaturely spirit should be retained. Equally unsatisfactory is the "Nestorian" *separation* of the human and the divine spirit in one divine-human act of divine inspiration: the human spirit becomes a *tabula rasa* on which an alien chisel, like a *deus ex machina,* inscribes divine writings — something which is ontologically impossible. The gracious inter-permeation which is divine inspiration presupposes not the passivity of the creative spirit, but its highest tension and the highest degree of creative activity. Grace does not coerce, but comes to man in response to his efforts, just as man cannot surpass his creaturely measure if he is not carried above it by a superhuman, supernatural force. The Spirit of God enables man to fathom the divine depths by probing his own depths. In his creaturely life, man can live by the divine life by becoming transparent for the Divine Spirit.

According to the christological dogma, the union, without separation and without confusion, of the two natures is accomplished in the one life of Christ through the one divine-human hypostasis of the Logos, hypostatically. By contrast, in divine inspiration, a hypostatic union of God with man does *not* occur; rather, the divine nature and the human nature are united in one life. The Holy Spirit does not become hypostatically incarnate, but only "descends" upon man, overshadowing him with His force. The hypostasis of divinely inspired and deified man remains human, but it can allow a place in itself for a life of the two natures. It must not only remain the subject and center of its own creaturely life, but it must also become transparent for the action of the divine nature.

That confused notion which can be glimpsed in the christological doctrines of Nestorianism and adoptionism, *synapheia* and *adoptio,* the union of two heterogeneous hypostases into one "hypostasis of union" by means of their mutual accord, by their becoming mutually transparent — this notion is an impermissible heresy for Christology. But it finds a particular application in pneumatology. Although the hypostasis of the Holy Spirit is not personally revealed in divine inspiration, it does act in it, although in the kenotic form of the gradual revelation of its measure in man, so that he becomes spirit-bearing, not only in his natural but also in his personal being, in his hypostatic consciousness of himself. If in Christ the divine hypostasis of the Logos is the unifying and governing center in the one harmonious life of the two natures, then in divine inspiration, which comes from the Third hypostasis, we get exactly the opposite. The union of the divine nature and the human nature in divine inspiration affects the hypostasis as well and brings it to a certain divine-humanity; in the creaturely, human hypostasis there shines and is revealed the hypostasis of the Spirit, which does not intrinsically belong to the human hypostasis. We have this to the highest degree in the Virgin Mary, Who is not only a spirit-bearing vessel but also the hypostatic image of the Holy Spirit. We also have this, in varying degrees, in the images of spirit-bearing saints. Divine inspiration gives them a hypostatic illumination and suppresses the egotistical centers of their human hypostases, as it were, making them exist not for themselves, but only for the Holy Spirit. This is the gracious death of the personal I for a new life by the Holy Spirit. This also corresponds to the personal character of the Third hypostasis, which does not exist for itself, as it were, and becomes transparent for the other hypostases. The Third hypostasis reveals Christ, the hypostasis of the Son. This is also what the spirit-bearing apostle confirms: "yet not I, but Christ liveth in me" (Gal. 2:20). Thus, in divine inspiration we have a *special form* of divine-humanity, alongside and in connection with the Divine Incarnation.

*　　　*

223

Inspiration must be understood as a *general* property of man, and his capacity to receive divine revelation is only a particular case of this property. Since he is a spirit, although an incarnate one, and since from his creation he bears the imprint of the Holy Spirit, man is spirit-bearing. The human spirit is not closed off; it is permeable and transparent for different inspirations. One can even affirm, as a general axiom of its existence, that the human spirit is *never* solitary and self-enclosed, but is always in contact with other spirits and receives inspiration from them. The human spirit inspires and is inspired. It is such from its very creation; and Leibniz's notion of the nontransparent monad without windows agrees neither with the cosmic character and interconnectedness of the world nor with man's humanness. Above all, man is a *generic* being who is intended to be in spiritual contact with beings similar to him. Every human person is, in this sense, a *place* where all these mutual "influences" intersect. The Divine triune Person is self-enclosed and abides above "influences," for It is trihypostatic and manifests Itself in all Its fullness *within* the trihypostatic intercommunion, which does not abolish but actualizes Its triunity. Humanity, by contrast, is multihypostatic; and therefore its hypostases always enter into contact with one another. Relevant here are all the modes of "influence" of one human being upon another: education, instruction, cooperation, counteraction, and so on. It is impossible to enumerate all these modes of influence, for our life is full of them. To be sure, this state of affairs makes it impossible to distinguish what belongs to a given individual from what belongs to humanity as a whole.

There exists a certain "communism" of spiritual being, the generic man; and only the Divine Eye can distinguish and show every human being (at the Last Judgment) what belongs to him himself and what does not belong to him although it finds a place for itself in him. Of course, these different "influences" form in a human being that unrepeatable mixture of colors that corresponds to his individual and complex personality. In this sense, a concrete human personality — not in its hypostastic consciousness of self, which is simple and singular, but in its life — is always complex and mosaic-like, does not belong to itself to a certain degree. This complexity necessarily presupposes a receptacle for itself, and this receptacle is the personal human spirit with its openness and receptivity to the spiritual. And this complexity refers, of course, not only to content but also to quality: various shades from white to black can participate in the human grayness.

But the complexity is not limited to this. The human spirit is also open to the pre-human and nonhuman world. First of all, there is the animal world, which, without being spiritual, is close to man. Man's relationship with animals is not exhausted by the fact that he commands them; he also loves them, is their friend, and thus receives influences from them. True, these influences are *directly* limited to the psychical domain, which man and the animals have in common, although these impressions, like all of man's life, are also experienced spiritually, so that one can speak of the "influence" of animals upon man. The reverse influence, that of man and thus of the human spirit, upon animals, even though they are deprived of spirit, is obvious: animals *obey* man, can be domesticated and trained, so that a bridge does in fact exist between spirit-bearing man and the animal world, and goes both ways.

Much more important is man's contact with the spiritual, although creaturely, world, with angels and with fallen spirits, "demons." Man can discern human influences, although not always with sufficient precision, but as a general rule he is ignorant of or has only a dim sense of the influences which emanate from the spiritual world and to which he is constantly being subjected. We have the firm teaching of the Church on this subject, but do we know when and how our guardian angels instruct us and save us, or are we able to discern the dark powers that approach us in the form of angels of light? The apostle Paul speaks of the "discerning of spirits" (1 Cor. 12:10) as of a special gift of the Holy Spirit; and the apostle John warns, "try the spirits whether they are of God" (1 John 4:1), and gives advice concerning the discerning of spirits on the basis of their attitude toward the confession of the coming of Christ in the flesh (4:2-3). And consider the Gospel narratives about possession by demons, that is, about violence done by them to the human spirit; these narratives remove the veil, as it were, that conceals the world of fallen spirits. Here one can also mention the temptation of the apostle Peter, which follows his confession and which provokes the Lord to call him: "Satan, thou art an offence unto me" (Matt. 16:23); and let us not forget Judas Iscariot, into whom Satan entered "after the sop" (John 13:27). In general, there is a special gift of the "discerning of spirits," which is acquired at the higher rungs of the spiritual life (but which is so grossly simulated by sanctimoniousness and spiritual ignorance, when false spiritual knowledge covers hardness of heart, darkness of mind, and laziness of thought).

The influence of angels upon man, which can be understood on the basis of their co-humanity,[4] corresponds to their "angelic" ministry: God communicates His grace-filled revelations through the angels. One can in

---

4. See my book *Jacob's Ladder: On the Angels.*

general ask: Is "grace" not the action of the holy angels who do the will of God with regard to man? To be sure, no satisfactory answer to this question can be given, inasmuch as, in the present aeon, the spiritual world remains closed off to man, although such a possibility must be included in a doctrine of grace. One can say that communion with the angels enters into the very humanness of man to the same degree as (although differently from) the generic life of human persons.

It is more difficult to understand the accessibleness of man to the influence of the fallen spirits, although, in the fallen state of man, this influence is quite a habitual fact of our spiritual life: "Put on the whole armour of God, that ye may be able to stand against the wiles of the devil. For we wrestle not against flesh and blood, but against principalities, against powers, against the rulers of the darkness of this world, against spiritual wickedness in high places" (Eph. 6:11-12). The Apostle warns us for good reason; in the field of our soul the wheat is overgrown with weeds, sowed by the enemy of man, and this will be the case until the harvest and the final separation. Aside from its self-creative activity out of its sophianic depths, the human spirit is also an arena of complex and mutually antagonistic influences of the spiritual world, light and dark. In assessing these influences, some go so far as to abolish, in effect, man's personality and humanity, making him a spiritual "robot." They consider "demons" to be the sole reality of human life and history, although under the mask of humanity. This peculiar anthropological docetism, or pandemonism, is not compatible with the Christian faith.

According to revelation, at the last judgment it will be revealed that not demons but Christ is the true reality in man; and it will be the human personality and all humanity, both the entire human race and every individual, that will be judged and held responsible, along with the angels (and, of course, the demons). And this ontological *suum cuique* is, by itself, sufficient testimony against pandemonism, which in effect is a manichean deviation from Christianity (under the pretext of asceticism). It follows that it is possible for the human spirit to receive influences and, to a certain degree, to be influential itself (inasmuch as influence always implies mutuality), while *remaining itself,* preserving its aseity, and not being completely identified with any of these influences. And here, and this is the most noteworthy thing and for us the most significant, man is also capable of receiving direct divine influences, the grace of the Holy Spirit, bestowed in sacraments. The divine enters into creation; the radiant and holy enters into the sinful and darkened. God does not disdain creation, even the fallen kind; and creation, even in its fallen state, retains the capacity to receive divine influences.

But there is another side of this kenosis, which must now be considered. The Holy Spirit is bestowed upon creation not only in gifts of sacrament and divine descent but also in the very being of man according to natural grace. If the power of the Holy Spirit gives life and being to creation, it follows that this power abides in creation *independently*, to a certain degree, of creation's self-determination or fall. The kenosis of the Holy Spirit in creation, which possesses freedom of self-determination, is manifested not only in the fact that He voluntarily limits his power to the measure of creation but also in the fact that His power is compatible with the sinful, illegitimate, and even theomachic self-determination of this creation. Nevertheless, creation's life and being, which exist by virtue of the Holy Spirit, will not be taken away from it, and the power of the Spirit abides even in the enemies of the Spirit. Insofar as they live and have being (and it will not be taken away from them), Satan and his angels ontically remain in contact with this grace of creation, this life-giving power of the Holy Spirit. This power acts even in hell, in hellish satanization, for hell too is a particular form — not of nonbeing and absolute death — but of *life and being*.

II. Divine Inspiration in the Old Testament

Besides the New Testament church, which is the Body of Christ, there is also the "Old Testament church," divine-humanity which is in the process of being realized but which has not yet been realized. The Old Testament, the Old Covenant of God with man, consists in a real relation between God and man, between divine life and human life. The Divine principle enters human life as a supernatural element, which nevertheless unites itself with the natural element. In the Old Testament, humanity turns out to be capable of receiving the divine principle, which bestows itself kenotically, of course, in the form of an adaptive, prefigurative, pedagogical revelation ("the law was our schoolmaster to bring us unto Christ" [Gal. 3:24]). The entire Old Testament is an unending *dialogue* of God with man, as well as the answering dialogue of man with God. If we try to count the number of times the expression "God said [to man]" appears in the Old Testament, we would become convinced that this phrase contains the essential content of the Old Testament. On the other hand, we have here a system of Divine influences and institutions (of cultic, moral, and civil law), which, though human in content, are divine in origin. In the Old Testament divine-humanity we have, without separation and without confusion, two natures and two wills, which, though they are not yet united by one hypostasis, are nevertheless united in a unity of life.

Just as the heavenly Divine-humanity, Sophia in God, is the bi-unity of the dyadic revelation of the hypostasis of the Father in the Son and the Holy Spirit, so the creaturely Divine-humanity in the Old Testament is the bi-une action of these revealing hypostases. In the Old Testament revelation, the Holy Trinity is, in the majority of cases, simply called *God:* God spoke, God appeared, God did. And only by applying to this concealment distinctions drawn from the New Testament can we perceive here the commanding action of the Father through His Word by the Holy Spirit. To be sure, God "speaks" in the Old Testament by His Divine Word, which is "pronounced" as if from lips and which is heard by those who are inspired by the Spirit (the Catholic doctrine of *lumen gloriae* [the light of glory] which is necessary for the seeing of the *gloria* corresponds, in effect, to this inspiration by the Spirit which leads to the knowledge of the Divine, to the hearing of the Word). We therefore arrive at the conclusion that all the words, commands, and actions of the trinitarian God in the Old Testament must be referred to the dyadic bi-unity of the Word and the Spirit: the Word does not "sound" for man without the Spirit and the Spirit is not received without the Word.

Therefore, in both the revelations and the theophanies of the Old Testament, we have not any one hypostasis in isolation (such isolation is in general impossible) but the sophianic bi-unity of Word and Spirit. In the manifestations of the Glory (to Moses and to Ezekiel), Sophia herself, in this bi-unity of hers, becomes accessible to human perception — as the heavenly Divine-humanity manifested to the earthly Divine-humanity.[5] Nevertheless, in these divine-human dyadic revelations, one can distinguish the character of each separate act in the particular directedness toward man of one or another hypostasis. In the Old Testament, God enters into a relation with man primarily as the Word, and He becomes close to man prior to His assumption of the human nature. The Word is *pre*-united with man, *pre*-descends from heaven, becoming in-humanized over the entire long process of the maturation of the Old Testament humanity up to the Divine Incarnation; and the living prefigurations and similitudes are already signs of this Divine Incarnation which is being pre-accomplished. This pre-incarnation of the Logos is being accomplished in man by the Holy Spirit, just as it was by the Holy Spirit that the Logos was made incarnate from the Virgin Mary.

5. See the excursus on Glory in my book *The Burning Bush*.

The Old Testament also knows, however, the preeminent revelation of the Spirit: Divine-humanity as the union of man not only with the Word Who is becoming incarnate but also with the Spirit who is descending upon man. This is the Old Testament Pentecost. A general preliminary question must be asked: *How* is this Old Testament Pentecost possible, and is it really possible? And if it is possible, what is its connection with the New Testament Pentecost? And can this Old Testament Pentecost, even if partial, precede the Divine Incarnation?

This possibility results from the principle of Divine-humanity, the most general foundation of the relations between God and the world; and the Divine Incarnation as well as the Pentecost is the manifestation of this general interrelation. Divine-humanity embraces *all* of the relations between God and the world, necessarily including the in-humanization of the Logos and the descent of the Holy Spirit. Consequently, it extends to the epoch prior to the Divine Incarnation, i.e., to the whole of the Old Testament humanity. Furthermore, the Divine Incarnation is pre-accomplished in the course of the entire existence of humanity: *"Christ is born"*; and the entire process of Old Testament revelation cannot be understood otherwise than as the ongoing Divine Incarnation. But Divine-humanity includes not only the descent from heaven of the Son of God for the in-humanization but also the descent from heaven of the Holy Spirit for divine inspiration. For the in-humanization of the Logos does not exist separately from the participation in it of the Holy Spirit, so that the dyadic interrelation of the Son and the Spirit in the divine revelation remains inviolable. And here the inseparable and inconfusible action of the two dyadic hypostases does not contradict their distinct manifestation in time or the preeminence of the one or the other. In this Dyad, either the one or the other of the hypostases is directed toward man.

The descent of the Holy Spirit upon the Virgin Mary at the Annunciation *precedes* the Divine Incarnation, not, of course, in time (since the two hypostases are inseparable, and the descending Spirit already has within Himself the Son upon Whom He reposes) but according to ontological relation. This descent of the Holy Spirit expands in time to include the whole of the Old Testament history, within the depths of which is born the Virgin Mary, Who is "full of grace." The Holy Spirit "graces" the One Full of Grace already in Her ancestors, "the fathers and prophets," in the entire chosen nation, and, together with them, in all humankind. One can say that the Holy Spirit was the motive force of the entire Old Testament *church*, both in the Temple and outside it. In particular, the "cloud" of glory, i.e., the Holy

Spirit, clearly descends (Exod. 40:34-35; Num. 9:15) into the tabernacle and temple of Solomon at the moment of its sanctification (1 Kings 8:10). And the "ordinances of divine service" (Heb. 9:1) were given by God not only in their power but also in their limitation ("the Holy Spirit this signifying, that the way into the holiest of all was not yet made manifest, while as the first tabernacle was yet standing" [Heb. 9:8]), for all this has only a preliminary and prefigurative character (Heb. 8); it is "a shadow of good things to come, and not the very image of the things" (Heb. 10:1); "He taketh away the first, that he may establish the second" (Heb. 10:9).

It is not only the Divine Incarnation that is anticipated by the power of the Holy Spirit in the Old Testament Divine-humanity, but also the Pentecost itself, which is His descent. The tongues of fire reposed upon the apostles, bestowing upon each of them a *special* gift of the Spirit. The Apostle speaks in general about this distribution of gifts: "Now there are diversities of gifts, but the same Spirit. And there are differences of administrations, but the same Lord. And there are diversities of operations, but it is the same God which worketh all in all. But the manifestation of the Spirit is given to every man to profit withal. For to one is given by the Spirit the word of wisdom; to another the word of knowledge by the same Spirit; to another faith by the same Spirit; to another the gifts of healing by the same Spirit; to another the working of miracles; to another prophecy, to another discerning of spirits; to another divers kinds of tongues; to another the interpretation of tongues: But all these worketh that one and the self-same Spirit, dividing to every man severally as he will" (1 Cor. 12:4-11).

There is no reason to limit the power of these words solely to the New Testament church, if only because the majority of these gifts had already been bestowed in the Old Testament church. (In particular, was it not an Old Testament prophet [Joel 2:28-32] who pronounced the prophecy that was applied by the apostle Peter to the Pentecost?) We have already spoken of the gifts that were bestowed in the Old Testament upon kings, prophets, rulers and military leaders, architects and artists. In order to understand this fact it is important to note that all of these gifts were bestowed in conformity with the personal vocation and particular giftedness of the one chosen. Also playing a role here was purely human inspiration, which encounters divine inspiration, as it were, and becomes — in relation to spirit — divine-human; and this divine-human character of inspiration is the most noteworthy thing here. God's help, the gift of the Holy Spirit, comes in answer to man's creative intensity. The elders and kings, Saul, David, and Solomon, possessed the natural gift of government; the judges, Gideon, Jephthah, and Samson, possessed the military gift; and Bezaleel and his helpers possessed the artistic gift. And this human gift is fructified by the Divine gift: here we have in the *spirit* the divine-human union of two natures, two wills, two energies, without separation and without confusion, in the case of one human hypostasis. And the bestowal of the Spirit is therefore understood in the light of Divine-humanity. This attests the openness of the human spirit to the Divine Spirit and the conformity of the Spirit of God with the human spirit.

A special place is occupied here by the prophetic ministry. It is with reference to the latter that one can most easily succumb to the temptation of the automatic or mechanical interpretation of divine inspiration. The most elementary case of this type is the foreseeing of the future and, in general, the knowledge of mysteries; and it is with reference to this that the prophetic ministry is often interpreted, but this is, of course, an obvious exaggeration or one-sidedness. Nevertheless, one can say that predictions of the future are the work of both human prevision and divine illumination, i.e., a divine-human work. To be sure, it is this divine illumination that makes possible for the prophet a prevision which, in its content, depth, and accuracy, surpasses human intuition (and which in this sense is "miraculous," i.e., a gift of grace). But at the same time this illumination is also a divine answer to human questioning (see, for example, Daniel 10). However marvelous these prophetic illuminations may be, they are capable of entering into the human consciousness and of being expressed in human language. Great prophets are also great men, thinkers, patriots, saints, in general not only men upon whom revelation is bestowed but also men who are worthy of such bestowal, which is why they are considered saints by the Church. The history of different prophets and prophecies can confirm this general idea that the prophets are receptive to the spirit, that they are called to this by fate and by their personal characters. Therefore, upon the prophecies of different prophets lies the stamp of their individual spirit; they are never impersonal, even when they have the character of divine visions or raptures ("I was in the Spirit on the Lord's day" [Rev. 1:10]). Even in their highest illuminations, prophets do not lose themselves but describe their revelations with a precise indication of the circumstances of place and time,[6] thereby confirming the divine-human character of these illuminations.

---

6. How can one not be amazed by the precise dating of Ezekiel's vision of God's Glory: "Now it came to pass in the thirtieth year, in the fourth month, in the fifth day of the month, as I was among the captives by the river of Chebar, that the heavens were opened, and I saw visions of God" (Ezek. 1:1).

The main conclusion that can be drawn from this is that, in the Old Testament too, the Holy Spirit descends from heaven to man in His gifts, and man turns out to be capable of receiving the descending Spirit. This is summed up in the formula of the Nicaeno-Constantinopolitan Creed: "who spake by the prophets" (i.e., primarily the Old Testament ones). To be sure, this prophesying by the Spirit necessarily contains the word which is from the Word, that is, the gift of the Spirit is dyadically accompanied by the revelation of the Word. This prophesying, however, is accomplished precisely by the action of the Holy Spirit, Who awakens the word contained in man. Old Testament man is receptive to the spirit and spirit-bearing not by virtue of the Divine Incarnation, which has not yet been accomplished, but by virtue of his sophianicity, which is the common foundation of both the Divine Incarnation and the reception of the Spirit.

Another question arises in connection with the preceding discussion: The New Testament Pentecost is accomplished in connection with the Divine Incarnation, with the direct participation of the incarnate Word. Christ Himself bestows, through His breath, the Holy Spirit upon His disciples (John 20:22) and promises to "pray the Father" to send the Spirit in His Name (John 14:16, 26), just as He Himself sends the Spirit from the Father (John 15:26). In the sending down of the Holy Spirit in the Old Testament, we do not find such a participation of the incarnate Word. There are a number of relevant texts in the Old Testament concerning the action of the Holy Spirit. Some simply say that "the spirit of God came upon him" (Num. 24:2; cf. Judges 14:19; 15:14; etc.). Others speak of the sending down or bestowal of the Holy Spirit by God: "I have filled him with the spirit of God" (Exod. 31:3; cf. Exod. 35:31). Also: "I will take of the spirit which is upon thee, and will put it upon them" (Num. 11:17; cf. 11:25); "I am full of power by the spirit of the Lord" (Mic. 3:8); "I will pour out my spirit upon all flesh" (Joel 2:28); "where is he that put his holy Spirit within him?" (Isa. 63:11); "I have poured out my spirit upon the house of Israel, saith the Lord God" (Ezek. 39:29). All these texts support the same general idea concerning the descent of the Holy Spirit in the Old Testament, namely, that He is *sent* by God, although, to be sure, without any further definition with regard to one hypostasis or another. On the basis of the further New Testament revelation as well as the dogmatic doctrine of the Holy Trinity as the monarchy of the Father, however, we must conclude that, in the Old Testament as well, the Holy Spirit is sent by the Father.

Israel knew the gifts of the Holy Spirit *prior to* the Divine Incarnation within the limits of God's *providential* government. Israel was God's "vineyard" (Isa. 5), the chosen people. Upon Israel was concentrated the exclusive attention of Providence, so to speak, for it had to produce Mary, the Mother of God. But the fate of Israel does not exhaust the ways of God as far as the economy of salvation is concerned, for the latter includes the fates of all the other nations, the ways of universal history. This is perfectly clear from the historical and prophetic books of the Old Testament and also conforms with the general dogmatic doctrine of the preparation of humanity for the reception of the Savior not only in the Judaic church but also outside it, amongst the Gentiles. And in certain individual cases the interwovenness of the fates of the nations is revealed "pragmatically" in Holy Scripture, although in the majority of cases, it remains hidden. The history of the chosen people is woven into the universal history of humanity, which, for Israel, is immediately manifested in the cultures of Greece, Egypt, and Babylon, in general in the cultures of the surrounding nations. The prophets prophesy about these nations, and the sacred books tell about them. This extra-Judaic history is usually defined by the formal concept of "Gentiles" or paganism. And the divine recognition of this right of the "Gentiles" to exist is expressed at the Pentecost in the overcoming of the Babel confusion of tongues: "every man heard [the apostles] speak in his own language" (Acts 2:6).

A general question must be asked concerning the pre-Christian paganism, this natural old testament: Was it totally deprived not only of the Holy Spirit but even of the *spirit* of God? Was all divine inspiration alien to it? A negative answer to this question is usually considered self-evident. But to what extent is such an answer justified? To what extent does it conform with reality?

To be sure, paganism cannot be considered the equal of the chosen nation, which was God's protected vineyard and possessed a pure, unalloyed truth in the revelation given to it, although it obscured this truth with its sins and pagan contaminations. Such a *purity* of revelation was not given to any other nation. The other nations were destined to follow their own paths, using their own natural powers: "[God] hath made of one blood all nations of men for to dwell on all the face of the earth, and hath determined the times before appointed, and the bounds of their habitation; that they should seek the Lord, if haply they might feel after him; and find him, though he be not far from every one of us: For in him we live, and move, and have our being" (Acts 17:26-28).

This marvelous testimony of the apostle Paul about the common seeking of God on the part of all the brothers by blood of the one human race places before us not only the fact of the divine election of the chosen

233

nation but also the fact of a universal divine vocation: "we are also his off-spring" (Acts 17:28). That is why, for the pagans too, "that which may be known of God is manifest in them; for God hath shewed it unto them. For the invisible things of him from the creation of the world are clearly seen, being understood by the things that are made, even his eternal power and Godhead" (Rom. 1:19-20). And only as a result of sin did it happen that "when they knew God, they glorified him not as God, neither were thankful" (1:21), and thereby fell into a crude paganism, which was a deviation from the norm and an obscuring of the truth that was accessible to them. Continuing this comparison of the Jews and the Gentiles, the Apostle adds: "Tribulation and anguish, upon every soul of man that doeth evil; of the Jew first, and also of the Gentile. . . . For there is no respect of persons with God. . . . For when the Gentiles, which have not the law, do by nature the things contained in the law, these, having not the law, are a law unto themselves: which shew the work of law written in their hearts" (Rom. 2:9, 11, 14-15). Without in the least diminishing the election of the Jews, the Apostle equates here in a certain sense the Jews and the Gentiles as equally needing salvation and equally called to salvation.

This natural equality before God is revealed in the narrative of the calling of the Gentiles, through the intermediary of the apostle Peter, in the person of Cornelius the centurion and his dependents (see Acts 10-11). About Cornelius it is said that he was "a devout man, and one that feared God with all his house, which gave much alms to the people, and prayed to God always" (10:2). He had the vision of an angel of God, who told him, "Thy prayers and thine alms are come up for a memorial before God" (10:4). And Peter himself tells Cornelius, "Of a truth I perceive that God is no respecter of persons: but in every nation he that feareth him, and worketh righteousness, is accepted with him" (10:34-35). This new equating of the Jews and the Gentiles on the paths of righteousness and obedience to God receives here a charismatic confirmation: "While Peter yet spake these words, the Holy Spirit fell on all them which heard the word" (10:44), so that all those present who were circumcised were, together with Peter, astonished "because that on the Gentiles also was poured out the gift of the Holy Spirit" (10:45). And this occurred *before* and independently of baptism,[7] so that Peter could do no more than testify: "Can any man forbid water, that these should not be baptized, which have received the

---

7. With respect to this, Swete says, "A second Pentecost had proclaimed the admissibility of Gentiles to Christian baptism" (*The Holy Spirit in the New Testament* [London: Macmillan, 1910], p. 98).

Holy Spirit as well as we?" (10:47). And he also indicates the same in his account about this event to the apostles and brothers (11:1-8). Also, in his speech at the apostolic council, Peter attests that "God, which knoweth the hearts, bare them witness, giving them the Holy Spirit, even as he did unto us; and put no difference between us and them, purifying their hearts by faith" (15:8-9).

This accessibleness of the Holy Spirit to chosen Gentiles is a fact of the greatest dogmatic importance. Not less important is the general fact of the calling of the Gentiles and the foundation of their church, initiated by God's command to the elder apostle, Peter, and accomplished by the labors of the apostle of the Gentiles, the Jew of Jews, Paul. It is noteworthy that the Acts of the Apostles, which tell about the establishment of the New Testament church by the action of the Holy Spirit, end and are inwardly summed up, as it were, by the definitive abolition of Judaism, which stopped being the Old Testament church. Outwardly, this was manifested in the abolition of circumcision and in a decisive appeal to the Gentiles. Such is the concluding and generalizing accord of this book, which, unless one perceives this inner synthesis, seems to break off unexpectedly in an ellipsis. At first the apostle Paul refers here to that which the Holy Spirit said to our fathers through the intermediary of the prophet Isaiah (6:9-10) on the subject of their embitterment and rejection. And Paul concludes by saying: "Be it known therefore unto you, that the salvation of God is sent unto the Gentiles, and that they will hear it" (Acts 28:28). The Old Testament epoch in the history of the church has ended; and the epoch of the new church of the Gentiles, the epoch of the "wild olive tree" (Rom. 11:17) grafted to the sacred root, has begun. And it will continue until "the natural branches [are] grafted into their own olive tree" (11:24) and the universal Judeo-Gentile church appears in a new fullness.

What does this calling of the Gentiles, of paganism, signify? Is it merely an act of divine arbitrariness and coercion, as it were; or does it have sufficient inner justification, in virtue of which the Gentiles turned out to be receptive to the preaching of Christianity, and even more so than the Jews, except for the chosen? And how should one understand this receptivity if one believes that paganism is a realm of demonic possession? But, as we showed above, such an opinion does not accord with the direct Biblical doctrine; and it contradicts the fact of the conversion of the Gentiles, their reception of the Spirit, the openness of their hearts to Christ. To be sure, demonism and possession were the involuntary lot of natural humanity, and the reception of baptism was therefore inevitably an exorcism (which liturgical symbolism still attests in the rite of baptism, which begins with an "interdiction"). But this possession is not final and does not prevent the reception of grace, natural and supernatural. The pagan religions, which were always subject to error and (under its cover) to demonism, show us, above all, the fatal limits of the natural knowledge of God, owing to which this knowledge was doomed to become subject to religious misunderstandings and errors. It is precisely this idea that the apostle Paul expresses when he speaks about idols: "we know that an idol is nothing in the world" (1 Cor. 8:4), that is, an idol is a religious misunderstanding and error, for "there is none other God but one" (8:4).

In another place, he explains his train of thought as follows: "What say I then? that the idol is any thing, or that which is offered in sacrifice to idols is any thing? But I say, that the things which the Gentiles sacrifice, they sacrifice to devils, and not to God: and I would not that ye should have fellowship with devils. Ye cannot drink the cup of the Lord, and the cup of devils: ye cannot be partakers of the Lord's table, and of the table of devils" (1 Cor. 10:19-21). This means that, in his piety, a Gentile *involuntarily* becomes the victim of a religious illusion which is associated with a demonic deception; but for Christians this is already an apostasy, a partaking at the table of devils.

But the Apostle does not modify here his initial definition, that is, that idols are nothing, a fruit of misunderstanding and error, for he later reduces his interdiction solely to ascetic and pedagogical considerations: "all things are lawful for me, but all things edify not. . . . Whatsoever is sold in the shambles, that eat, asking no question for conscience sake. . . . Conscience, I say, not thine own, but of the other" (1 Cor. 10:23, 25, 29). "But if any man say unto you, This is offered in sacrifice unto idols, eat not for his sake that shewed it, and for conscience sake; for the earth is the Lord's, and the fulness thereof" (10:28). It is evident that those to whom the truth is revealed and to whom true communion is given, cannot, without betraying the truth, partake at the Lord's table with those to whom this is not given. But this is not yet a definitive condemnation of the pagan or, more precisely, the non-Christian religion within its own limits, that is, the ignorance of Christ.

It is necessary to recognize and appreciate the full value of pagan *piety*, expressed in the search for God, in prayer, sacrifice, and good works, for "God is no respecter of persons, but in every nation he that feareth him, and worketh righteousness, is accepted with him" (Acts 10:34-35). In particular, it is remarked about Cornelius that he was "a devout man, and one that feared God with all his house, which gave much alms to the people, and prayed to God always" (10:2); and this made him worthy of seeing the angel of God. We must ask ourselves then: Is it possible that this devout pagan, who continuously prayed to God, actually prayed to nothing or to demons? The Acts of the Apostles affirm the opposite: because of his prayers, he was deemed worthy of seeing the angel of God. And what is said about Cornelius applies to *all* of pagan piety, which despite its inevitable and fatal opacity, bears God's blessing, expressed in the fact that the barren pagan church was called to Christ in the commandment "teach all nations" (Matt. 28:19), in the fact that the apostle Peter's first Christian sermon resounded in *all* languages.

Pagan piety turns out to be possible and even has a positive religious value. This has been established. What conclusion can one draw from this concerning the pagan doctrine? Is it legitimate to see here, at best, nothing more than a religious void, the absence of all presence; or, in the worst case, does the pagan doctrine consist (as is usually thought) of demonism, demonic possession, spiritual delusion, and thus a total absence of the Spirit of God?

Those who accept such a facile conclusion must nonetheless be perplexed by the mysterious fact of Melchizedek, who emerges from the darkness of the nations to bless the very father of the nations, Abraham. This event occurs near Sodom, where, after the defeat of Chedorlaomer and the kings who were with him, Abraham meets first the king of Sodom and then the king of Salem: "And Melchizedek king of Salem brought forth bread and wine: and he was the priest of the most high God. And he blessed him, and said, Blessed be Abram of the most high, possessor of heaven and earth; and blessed be the most high God, which hath delivered thine enemies into thy hand. And he [Abram] gave him tithes of all" (Gen. 14:18-20). This was a meeting of two representatives of the Old Testament, one from the chosen nation and one from the pagan. Our imagination has always been struck by this unknown king and priest, who, evidently, served his local, national cult, but who at the same time also served the most high God. The riddle of this identification is further underscored by the fact that, in response to his blessing, Abraham "gave him tithes of all," clearly as a priest of the most high God. The enigmatic importance of this fact became a focal point of dogmatic interpretation by the New Testament writers. This interpretation reached its pinnacle in the passage in the Epistle to the Hebrews where the image of Melchizedek, who emerged out of the pagan darkness, coincides with that of Christ (see Heb. 5:6, 10). This interpretation of the meeting between Abraham and Melchizedek, "without father, without mother, without descent," is given in Hebrews 7. But even given this New Testament interpretation we must nevertheless recognize the fact of Melchizedek in all its symbolic significance: he represents the spiritual peak of the pagan world and, in a certain sense, he justifies this world in its proper, autonomous existence. Priesthood was bestowed upon the pagan world according to the order of Melchizedek.

One should also note another event in the pagan world, an event just as enigmatic in its own way: the appearance of the prophet Balaam, whom Balak, the king of Moab, called from Pethor on the river (the Euphrates), from "the land of the children of his people" (Num. 22:5), in order to curse Israel. The figure of this prophet is ambiguous and is not without a touch of moral instability, but obedience to the command of God nevertheless triumphs in him: "And God met Balaam [at the altars] . . . and the Lord put a word in Balaam's mouth, and said, Return unto Balak, and this thou shalt speak" (Num. 23:4-5). And in Numbers 24:2, it is said directly, "and the spirit of God came upon him." We find here a direct attestation of the *authenticity* of this prophecy, which does not differ in any way from other true prophecies. Further on, we also find four solemn prophecies, or "oracles," with the blessing of Israel (against Balaam's proper human will). In the last of these prophecies, the spirit of God places upon Balaam's lips a truly messianic text, or at any rate that is how it is understood in the Orthodox interpretation: "I shall see him, but not now: I shall behold him, but not nigh: there shall come a Star out of Jacob, and a Sceptre shall rise out of Israel" (24:17). And as if confirming the truth of this prophecy, he precedes it with the following testimony about himself: "He hath said, which heard the words of God, and knew the knowledge of the most High, which saw the vision of the Almighty" (24:16). Given our general appreciation of the possibilities of paganism and of the results which it achieved, the fact of Balaam must be considered to be as important as the fact of Melchizedek.

And so, the pagan darkness did not, evidently, resist the rays of light from true priesthood and prophecy, that is, from the direct gifts of the Holy Spirit. What is of decisive importance here is not the preestablished purposefulness of these gifts but their very *possibility*. And this idea must be understood and generalized in all its breadth and profundity: the pagan world remains open to waftings of the spirit of God both in its religion and in its culture. It is impossible to examine this question in all its concreteness; indeed, it does not, in essence, lend itself to an exhaustive and precise analysis. Scholarship in "religious history" and "comparative religions" has done much to establish a certain parallelism and convergence between the revealed and unrevealed religions, between Revelation and the monuments of pagan literature. This has been done and is being done partly out of scholarly curiosity, which does not know what to do with the accumulated material or how to interpret it *religiously,* and partly from motives of rationalistic skepticism, which, delighting in these parallels, is attempting to depersonalize and devalue Revelation by erasing its concrete features. Also offering its services is the theosophical "esperanto," which in its syncretism proclaims all religions to be identical for those who know how to find in them a single common content, or which makes out of them an "anthroposophical" stew.

All these affirmations, those of scientific rationalism as well as those of religious syncretism, do contain a positive truth, namely, that revelation exists also outside of Revelation, for the Spirit of God "bloweth where it listeth." In conformity with the spiritual maturity, particular gifts, and historical destinies of paganism, the knowledge of God is realized in it in multiple and manifold ways; and this knowledge is possible only because the Holy Spirit "bloweth" also in the unrevealed (and in *this* sense) "natural" religions. These religions are distinguished by a special mode of knowledge, by their own gift, by a language proper to this natural Pentecost. When we are astonished by and — what is more important — are instructed by this natural revelation of different nations in the great historical religions, we directly experience this breath of the Spirit of God; and we should not shy away from this experience because of an unjustified fear that the uniqueness and truthfulness of our Revelation will be shaken. On the contrary, one should rejoice in the gifts of the Spirit of God bestowed upon these "prophets" as well, who came "from the river" like Balaam, or upon the "wise men from the east," who came to worship Christ. One should rejoice in this inexhaustible love for God and faith in Him, which does not remain unanswered, for "God is no respecter of persons, but in every nation he that feareth him, and worketh righteousness, is accepted with him" (Acts 10:34-35).

And if the pagan world gave to Christianity its philosophy and its art, as well as its logically incisive thought and its science, the gifts of the wise men, this means that this is not foreign to the spirit of God. St. Justin calls Plato and Socrates "Christians before Christ," but one should, of course, also add other names: Heraclitus, Aristotle (the *"Philosophus,"* whom Thomas Aquinas placed alongside the divine sources of faith), and Plotinus, as well as Phidias and other, unknown, masters of Egypt and ancient Greece. The Church places their images in temples, although in the vestibule (as in the Moscow Cathedral of the Annunciation), and this must be understood as direct testimony that they too possessed the spirit of God. There should be no doubt about this, just as it should not be doubted that the founders of the great religions and their books were, to some extent, divinely chosen and even divinely inspired.

It is much more important to establish that this revelation was never unalloyed and pure, that it never possessed the entire and genuine truth, but rather that it was always seen "as through a glass, darkly," always passed through and was refracted in the human prism, which was a prism not only of limitation but also of sin and . . . even of demonism. It is precisely this impression of *fatal complexity* and even of a more fatal confusion and impurity, visible only in the light of Revelation, that we get from *all* the natural religions, as well as from the whole of "paganism," which awaits and needs exorcism. This means that one must, without fear and without temptation, see in paganism an element that belongs to truth and that is thus inspired by the spirit of God, by that *one spirit* of Truth that everywhere guides human beings to all truth. But there is impressed upon us with renewed force the knowledge of how powerless man is to maintain himself on the great height of his divine vocation and to "realize" to the end the gift of the Holy Spirit that is given to him as the fundamental task and theme of his being. The truth of a religious theme is invariably accompanied by an imperfect interpretation of this theme; and, in the present case, it is accompanied by a one-sidedness.

That is why the natural religions form, in their interrelationship, a kind of natural *dialectic* of divine revelation, which is systematically and fully realized in Revelation. Only on the basis of this central synthesis can we understand the particular truths or dialectical moments in the natural religions, both in their truth and in their one-sidedness; and the latter, since it is unexamined, becomes error (or "heresy"). Such errors include the divinization of man in ancient Greece, the negation of the world in Buddhism, the divine all-unity in Brahmanism, and so on. And what is especially important is that we are not given the ability to separate here the light from the darkness, to distinguish the breath of the spirit of God from the sinfully human or even demonically possessed spirit. We recognize the two poles only in their extreme manifestations, in their highest and lowest points, but not in their connectedness and mutual conditionedness. That is why, for those who live in the revealed religion, it is so dangerous to have any contact with one of these "pagan" religions: it is easy to fall into a kind of religious concupiscence and to fall away from the truth.

That is why the prophets of Israel protected God's chosen people from contact with paganism and from being spiritually contaminated by it. But even though the prophets were *pedagogically* right, they remained blind to paganism's authentic and profound content. For the prophets, Egypt, Babylon, and Greece all represented nothing more than the temptation of religious concupiscence, in the same way that, when the apostle Paul was in the Areopagus of Athens (see Acts 17), "his spirit was stirred in him, when he saw the city wholly given to idolatry" (17:16). And this was despite the fact that there shone before his eyes the supreme revelations of the religious art of ancient Greece, which even today inspire us not only with their beauty but also with their religious content. Such pedagogy contains only a certain *relative* truth, which does not give us the right to consider paganism an impenetrable darkness and a demonism (as the apologist Tatian and, in part, all of early Christianity considered it). Even less admissible are paganism's theosophical syncretism and absence of differentiation, for, in the light of the Christian truth, paganism is exposed as a religion that contains falsehood and is infected by demons. Nevertheless, it is possible to have toward paganism a non-pedagogical attitude, which, in the light of the Christian revelation, *distinguishes* its light side from its dark side.

One cannot fail to see that, after the inception of Christianity, paganism unquestionably acquired a negative, demonic coefficient. It became an anti-Christianity. This practical consequence was well understood by the first Christian apologists, who separated themselves from paganism more vigorously than would seem warranted by its essential character. Paganism is justified only as the *past* of a religion which does not yet know Christianity but which is preparing to know it. The naivete of this ignorance exists even today among the pagan nations. But insofar as it opposes Christianity or even arises in opposition to Christianity (the religious syncretism of our own time), this ignorance bears the sinister shadow of anti-Christianity. The fate of the pagan old testament is the same as that of the Jewish Old Testament. Just as Judaism, not recognizing its proper fulfillment in the person of the Messiah, was transformed from a divinely revealed religion into a fierce anti-Christianity, so the natural religions too become anti-Christian in proportion to their conscious rejection of and opposition to Christianity.

It follows that *all* true religions, all religions that contain the experience of Divinity, necessarily have a ray of Divinity, the breath of the Spirit. This truth, as well as the falsehood with which it is mixed and by which it is complicated, can be perceived only on the basis of the fullness of Christianity. In this sense, one can even say that all the true religions form a *pan-Christianity,* that is, that they find or at least can find their truth in Christianity, for the truth is one and comes from the spirit of Truth. Only a positive philosophy of the history of religion, which admits the rays of true revelation in nonrevealed religions as well, is capable of justly appreciating and distinguishing the grain of truth and the admixture of error in non-Christian religions, and of emancipating these religions from syncretistic and fanatical prejudices.

That is why one can also apply to paganism the divine words, "the light shineth in darkness; and the darkness comprehended it not" (John 1:5). The Holy Spirit descends into the darkness that is teeming with phantoms of nonbeing and does not feel aversion to these phantoms, behind which lurk spirits of malice. The Holy Spirit does not contemn this limited capacity to receive Him that is proper to humanity, which is dispersed on the pathways of its history and corrupted in its fallen state. Once again, this is that *kenosis* of the Holy Spirit without which His communion with creatures would be impossible. It is impossible to measure God's love and God's grandeur in God's condescension by measures of human judgment. Both in the natural world and in the sacraments, the Holy Spirit is received worthily or unworthily, but He is bestowed and sent by the Father into the world in order to testify about the Truth. And this kenosis of the Spirit is so profound, this condescension of Divine love is so immense, that we can see the spirit of God, the power of the Holy Spirit (to be sure, apart from His hypostasis), in paganism as well. Otherwise, all of paganism would be condemned, on the pathways of Providence, to inexorable spiritual captivity to the prince of this world; and no light would glimmer in its darkness. Such a fatalism is blasphemous and does not accord with the presence of the *creaturely* grace of the Holy Spirit, which sustains the very being and life of the world.

But this gift of the spirit leads even further: in paganism itself it manifests and presages Christianity. The "pagan church" (an expression used in the liturgical literature) had, at the time of the coming of Christ, reached a maturity that enabled it to receive Him. This was the church of the nations. Paganism was an old testament for Christianity, and will remain so until the end of the epoch of the Gentiles. Not one of the nonrevealed religions is the equal of Christianity (as theosophers of various kinds blaspheme), but all of them have some kinship with Christianity, although they are all surpassed and fulfilled in the latter. And so, the *gifts of the spirit* can be present in paganism too, gifts that are diverse and ascend from measure to measure. And is it not this Christianity, without a manifest knowledge of Christ, that will be attested by the questions and answers at the Last Judgment, when, according to Christ's own testimony, those who served Him during their existence will believe that they did not know Him? (And on the other hand, will He not say "I do not know you" to those who prophesied and worked miracles in His name, but who obviously remained distant from the Spirit of Christ?)

In discussing the problem of ancient paganism and its piety, one cannot avoid touching upon the new atheistic paganism which makes a god out of man and the world. For atheism can take different forms. The atheism of the spirit-deprived "bourgeoisie" (about which it has been said, "they are flesh") is one of the forms of the blasphemy against the Holy Spirit, an abolition of the sacred in man's soul. But however oxymoronic this phrase might sound, there can also be a religious atheism, which we witness in the contemporary humanistic neopaganism: the latter encompasses Christians who do not know Christ but who do the works of love and sacrifice themselves in these works. To be sure, the religious consciousness of these unfortunate pagans is darkened and distorted, but the will of their heart is clearer than their reason. Does the kenosis of the Holy Spirit go so far that these people, who war against religion and reject the Son, can have, in the darkness of their minds and hearts, a ray of the Spirit? One can also pose this question in a more convincing manner: Can the gift of baptism, i.e., the gift of the Holy Spirit, be preserved even in an atheist? The Church's answer to this question is affirmative, for she does not rebaptize atheists who return to the faith. But should this rule not be applied in general to natural man, who possesses the gift of the Spirit from his creation? In any event, anyone who answers "no" to this question wishes to measure the kenosis of the Spirit and His gifts by the measure of the human understanding. A positive hope is given to us by the Lord Himself, when He attests that only the blasphemy against the Holy Spirit cannot be forgiven, whereas the blasphemy against the Son *can* be forgiven. But here he adds, "The Spirit bloweth where it listeth, and thou hearest the sound thereof, but canst not tell whence it cometh, and whither it goeth" (John 3:8; the King James Version has been modified here to conform with the Russian Bible).

All that is creative in human life is accomplished by natural inspiration, which is sophianic by its essence. And all great creators have in their sophianicity this creative force from the Spirit, for the very capacity for inspiration is already a sophianic spirituality, and there is simply no other source of creative life. But this natural and sophianic spirituality is, as we have already seen, the precondition also for the spirituality of grace, where the rays of the Holy Spirit render golden the heart of creation. No one can limit the paths of the Spirit. On the contrary, it must be considered that this spirituality of the "old testament" (in the extended sense of this term) propagates, in unfathomable ways, among the Gentiles wherever worthy men are found. For to the Holy Spirit belongs everything that is great and creative in human life. And if nature is an unwritten Bible, then so are, in a certain sense, the human soul and human history.

III. Divine Inspiration in Christ

Let us note the following feature of divine inspiration in the Old Testament: The Holy Spirit is bestowed and revealed here as a gift or a power, but *not* hypostatically; and this is so to such a degree that this gift is depersonalized, as it were, and viewed merely as a gift of God in general or as the "spirit of God," and not as an express revelation of the Third hypostasis. In general, with regard to the Third hypostasis we *distinguish* its power and action from it itself. This is the case neither with regard to the Father (Who does not reveal Himself except through the Son and the Spirit) nor with regard to the Son. By contrast, the Holy Spirit is known in creation only as a gift, which, however, is, of course, inseparable from the Giver. The relation between the gift and the Giver here is similar to that between the Divine ousia and the Divine energy in the doctrine of St. Gregory Palamas. This doctrine distinguishes the unknowable, one, and simple essence of God from the multiple "energies" of Divinity, from God's actions in revelation. The relation between the ousia and the energy is such that the energy, though distinct from the ousia, is, like the latter, divine, and in this sense is God *(Theos,* not *ho Theos).* Palamas virtually ignores the complex and essential problem of the relation of the energy to the hypostases (if we do not count a number of scattered and imprecise statements). Palamas's theory on this subject can be reduced to the following irreversible proposition: the energy is God, but one cannot say that God is the energy, since He is the ousia that includes many energies.

Likewise, regarding the relation between the hypostatic Holy Spirit and His gifts, the different forms of "spirit" that are bestowed by the Spirit, one can say that the *gifts* of the Holy Spirit *are* the Holy Spirit. This proposition too is irreversible: one cannot say that the Holy Spirit is one gift or another, for He does not limit Himself to any particular gift. Rather, "the Holy Spirit bestows all things" (as the Pentecost sticheron says). That is why this distinction between ousia and energy can be applied with great precision to this relation between an "energy" or gift of the Holy Spirit and His divine hypostasis. Throughout the Old Testament, the Holy Spirit reveals Himself only by His energies, whereas His hypostasis, like His ousia, remains hidden.

To this one must add the following. The Holy Spirit, Who, according to the doctrine of "monarchy," proceeds from the Father, is also "sent" by Him into the world; indeed, there are a number of cases in the Old Testament where it is said that God *sent* or *gave* the gift of His Spirit. This sending of the Spirit in the Old Testament can be attributed solely to the Father, for the Son is not yet revealed and remains hidden, as it were, in the bosom of the Father. The sending down of the Holy Spirit is expressed here in the communication of His diverse gifts, which are His separate rays, as it were. And as the *gift* of the Holy Spirit is the Holy Spirit Himself (although not vice versa), so, in this *pars pro toto* [part taken for the whole], the sending down of a specific gift is also the sending down of the Holy Spirit Himself, a kind of Old Testament Pentecost, which began at the very creation of the world, when "the Spirit of God moved upon the face of the waters" (Gen. 1:2).

But at the same time it is impossible, of course, to separate this sending down of the Holy Spirit from the Son, upon Whom He reposes in the Holy Trinity, although the participation of the Son in this case is not active, but passive, so to speak: It is not the Son Who sends; rather, it is upon Him that the Spirit is sent. It is precisely in the Divine Sophia that the Spirit accomplishes the Word, the revelation of the Son, by Whom "all things were made" (John 1:3) in creation; and it is upon Him in the creaturely Sophia that the Holy Spirit reposes. But, so to speak, *above* this natural and sophianic grace, the gift of the Spirit is bestowed upon man, who in his Image of God already bears the image of the coming Christ. By virtue of this conformity with the Son, of this seal of the Word, man can also receive the seal of the Holy Spirit.

One can therefore say that, here too, the Holy Spirit descends upon the Word Who is in the creaturely Sophia. But the Son Himself does not, prior to His Incarnation, send the Spirit; the Spirit is sent by "God," i.e., by the Father. The Old Testament Pentecost is from the Father upon the Son. Consequently, this Old Testament Pentecost, by virtue of which the Old Testament church exists with all its gifts of grace and institutions, does not follow but precedes and prepares the Incarnation. The order of the action of the hypostases in the world is the reverse of their *taxis:* the action of the Third hypostasis precedes the descent from heaven of the Second, which, in contrast to the Third, does not have a multiplicity of gifts or forms of revelation, but knows only one, integral hypostatic manifestation.[8]

The most salient and important event in this reverse *taxis* is the Annunciation. As "the head of our salvation" (as the Troparion of the Annunciation says), this event is the beginning of the Incarnation; or more precisely, the latter is already being realized in it. But *how* is it being realized? By the Holy Spirit, Who descends upon the Virgin Mary and makes Her the Mother of God. The Holy Spirit, who reposes upon the Son, from Whom He is dyadically inseparable (and with Whom He is inconfusible), brings the Son in and with Himself (the Holy Spirit). And in making the Spirit-bearer Mary His receptacle, the Holy Spirit makes Her womb fruitful, accomplishing "the ineffable triumph of conception without seed" (as it is said in the Great Canon of St. Andrew of Crete). No distinction is made here between *the temporal before and after,* although, *ontologically,* we have precisely this succession. The Pentecost of the Mother of God precedes the Divine Incarnation; the divine conception is accomplished by the divine inhabitation of the Logos through the Holy Spirit, Who in this sense (in the Gospel to the Egyptians) is sometimes called His Mother: by His inhabitation of the Virgin Mary, the Holy Spirit identifies Himself with Her in some sense in Her Divine Maternity. This is possible only if She receives the hypostasis of the Logos in the capacity of the hypostatic Spirit of the conceived Infant; and this in turn is possible only if the Mother of God Herself is filled for this purpose with the Holy Spirit.

With reference to the sending down of the Holy Spirit, the Annunciation was not and could not have been partial, could not have been merely the communication of a particular gift of the Spirit, for it is not a particular gift of the Spirit but the hypostatic Spirit Himself Who inseparably co-abides with the Logos or reposes upon Him. It was only by virtue of this descent of the Holy Spirit that the coming down of the Word could be manifested. As a result, it is in the Annunciation that the heavens open for the first time for the descent of the Holy Spirit, which is also the "coming down from heaven" of the Son. The Son came down not alone but together with the Holy Spirit, Who is inseparable from Him; the *dyad* of the Son and the Spirit in the Incarnation is sent into the world by the Father. Here, the Incarnation and the Pentecost of the Spirit are inseparably and inconfusibly identical: the hypostatic Logos descends together with the hypostatic

8. It is precisely this which is expressed in Hebrews 1:1-2: "God [= the Father], who at sundry times and in divers manners spake in time past unto the fathers by the prophets [= the Holy Spirit], hath in these last days spoken unto us by his Son."

Spirit. This Pentecost of the Annunciation, however, although hypostatic, is partial and limited as far as the domain of its action is concerned: it is entirely focused upon the Virgin Mary. She had a place in the world, since She belongs to this world. But She does not belong to the world in its entirety, for only Mary is the spirit-bearing receptacle unknown to the world, the sealed source, the sacred ark enclosed in the Holy of Holies.

Thus, in relation to the Incarnation, the Annunciation was a complete and therefore hypostatic descent of the Holy Spirit and His inhabitation of the Virgin Mary. But was it such for the Virgin Mary Herself, and precisely what was it for Her? The Holy Spirit's inhabitation of the Virgin Mary was not and could not be a divine incarnation in relation to the Third hypostasis, for, in the first place, divine incarnation is not in general proper to Her, whereas it is proper to the Logos; and second, the Virgin Mary already had Her own human hypostasis. That is why Her inhabitation by the Holy Spirit could only represent His entry into Her life, in the sense not of hypostatic identification but of action by grace, which has its focus in the divine conception and the divine birth, in general in Divine Maternity. This inhabitation was not limited to any one particular gift. The one full of grace received the *fullness* of the Holy Spirit with the indivisible totality of His gifts. But Mary's reception and assimilation of these gifts were also characterized — according to the general law of life in the Spirit — by degrees of growth. Her growth in the Spirit progressed from Her birth and Her presentation in the Temple to the Annunciation; and then from the Annunciation — through Golgotha and the Pentecost — to Her Dormition and Her Assumption, which attests to the fullness of spiritual receptivity and spirituality that She had attained in Her glorification and deification. Without being God or the God-Man, Mary communes with the Divine life in the Holy Trinity in Her perfect spirituality.[9] She follows, like Her Son, the path of kenotic diminution and maternally participates in His salvific passion. To this is added Her apostolic ministry after the Ascension: Her silent and self-sacrificing work for all of Christianity.

And this feat of obedience to the Father's will which consisted in receiving the Divine Spirit and guarding this gift made Her worthy of and ready for glorification, which took place in Her Dormition. To be sure, this glorification was different from that of Her Divine Son and occurred in a different manner: Not only was He glorified by the Father and the Holy Spirit, but He also actively participated in this glorification, inasmuch as His human nature was completely deified. That is why His tri-

9. See my book *The Burning Bush*.

umph over death was both a raising and a resurrection, and His kenosis is completely and definitively overcome in the sitting at the right hand of the Father. It was otherwise for the "Handmaid of the Lord": She tasted natural human death and was *raised* by Her Son (of course, by the power of the Holy Spirit), but was not resurrected; and She was glorified by Her Son in Her Assumption to heaven (which, dogmatically, can be more precisely expressed as a transcending *above the world in its present state*). This creaturely glorification of Hers remains receptive and passive: She does not resist it, but neither does She play an active role in it. In the Mother of God were pre-accomplished that transfiguration of the world and that glorification of creation which are to be fully accomplished by virtue of the Divine-humanity. In Her was accomplished the transfiguration of creation, which in and through Her will be communicated to the entire human race. In this sense, Mary, in Her hypostatic being, is completely transparent for the hypostatic revelation of the Holy Spirit; Her human hypostasis is in union *(synapheia)* with Him. Here we have a duality of natures, Divine and human, as well as a duality of hypostases, of Mary and of the Spirit, which are so mutually transparent that one becomes the manifestation and revelation of the Other.

The descent of the Holy Spirit at the Annunciation was thus not limited to the divine conception and birth; and after the Annunciation was accomplished, Mary's human nature was not left deprived of grace (the notion that She was left deprived of grace constitutes the main heresy of Protestantism with its strange insensitivity to the mystery of the Mother of God). Even after the Birth of Christ, the Virgin Mary abided *in the power of the Annunciation,* i.e., in the presence of the Holy Spirit. She was more than an external instrument in the hands of Providence for the work of salvation; being a human person, She was also a *subject* of the divine conception in conformity with Her participation in it. The Holy Spirit did not abandon Her after the Birth of Christ, but abides with Her forever in all the power of the Annunciation. Consequently, Her Divine Maternity, Her connection with the incarnate Word, also abides forever (which is attested by the icons of Mother and Infant). The human person of Mary the Spirit-bearer attests, together with the God-Man, that it is the combination of the incarnation of the Logos and the Holy Spirit's inhabitation of a human being that constitutes the Divine Incarnation. The Divine Incarnation is not limited to the descent from heaven of the Word, but also includes the descent from heaven of the Holy Spirit; it presupposes not only the hypostatic union of the two natures in Christ but also their bihypostatic interpenetration in the Virgin Mary. Mary is not only the hypostatic humanity of Christ; She is also the hypostatic receptacle of the Holy Spirit. The dyadic character of the interrelation of the Son and the Holy Spirit in the Divine Incarnation is expressed in the fact that the latter comprises two divine hypostatic manifestations of the Son and the Spirit: in Christ and in the Virgin Mary. But this dyadic interrelation is also manifested in the Divine Incarnation itself. The Holy Spirit, Who reposed upon the Virgin Mary at the Annunciation and Who communicated to Her the power of the divine conception, reposes upon the Word of God "come down from heaven" — both in the heavenly abiding of the Word and in His earthly incarnation. In other words, the Divine Incarnation is accompanied by the hypostatic "descent from heaven" not only of the Son but also of the Holy Spirit. Here, the hypostasis of the Son is made incarnate whereas the Holy Spirit incarnates, these two hypostases abiding together without separation and without confusion.

Their abiding together in the Divine Incarnation passes through a number of stages. The eternal, inseparable, and inconfusible reposing of the Spirit upon the Son must be distinguished from His abiding in the human nature of the incarnate Word, an abiding which is realized by the ascent from measure to measure. On the subject of Jesus' childhood it is said only that "the grace of God was upon him" (Luke 2:40; cf. 2:52). This signifies that the Holy Spirit overshadows Jesus' human essence only by His power or "grace." And only in the Baptism does the Holy Spirit descend hypostatically, "like a dove" (Matt. 3:16), thus accomplishing the adoption by the Father of the *entire* God-Man, not only in the Divine but also in the human essence. This is a new and as if second descent of the Holy Spirit from heaven (iconography likens the first descent, at the Annunciation, to the second, representing the Holy Spirit on icons of the Annunciation in the form of a dove). To be sure, here one must distinguish not *two* descents, but two different *modes* of descent or manifestation of the power of the Spirit: the first mode, the Annunciation, refers to the humanity of the Most Holy Mother of God, whereas the second, the Baptism, refers to the humanity of Christ and is in this sense Christ's Pentecost. Jesus becomes *Christ*, i.e., the Anointed by the Spirit, the Spirit-bearer; and in His coming the world has not only the incarnation of the Logos but also the Spirit reposing upon Him. About this Spirit Who reposes upon Him and Who lives in Him, Christ Himself speaks (in Luke 4:18) with the words of Isaiah: "the Spirit of the Lord God is upon me" (Isa. 61:1).[10] And Jesus Himself attests

---

10. Cf. Acts 10:38: "God anointed Jesus of Nazareth with the Holy Spirit and with power . . . God was with him."

that, by the Spirit of God, He casts out demons (Matt. 12:28), which is why the failure to believe this is a blasphemy against the Holy Spirit. But this idea must, of course, be understood in a broader sense: it signifies that Jesus is Christ, the Spirit-bearer, in His entire ministry; and He accomplishes this ministry as one filled by the Spirit.

This inspiration of Christ by the Holy Spirit is attested by a number of particular events. For example, when the seventy returned and told how the spirits were subject to them, "in that hour Jesus rejoiced in the Holy Spirit, and said, I thank thee, O Father, Lord of heaven and earth" (Luke 10:21; the King James Version has been modified here to conform with the Russian Bible). This text clearly shows that Jesus was Christ, anointed and inspired by the Spirit.[11] This "rejoicing" is accompanied (see Luke 10:21 and further; Matt. 11:25-30) by Christ's solemn revelation about Himself. The Holy Spirit leads Christ into the desert; and when the spirit of evil approaches Him, it is opposed by the Holy Spirit. And then the Spirit leads Christ out of the desert in order that He undertake a public ministry, which inevitably culminates in Golgotha, where "through the eternal Spirit, [He] offered himself without spot to God" (Heb. 9:14). In other words, with the coming of Christ on the earth, by virtue of His anointment in His personal Pentecost which is His baptism, the anointment becomes accessible in Him to the entire world, although as yet in a particular and limited manifestation.

The next act of this Pentecost of Christ is the Transfiguration. The presence of the Holy Spirit upon Christ the Anointed has been uninterrupted, but now it becomes palpable for His disciples as well,[12] as "the kingdom of God come with power" (Mark 9:1). The Holy Spirit is precisely this kingdom of God. This manifestation of the Holy Spirit as Glory is accompanied by the overshadowing of Christ by a bright cloud (Matt. 17:5),

---

11. Swete remarks justly, "In the personal life of the Lord as it is revealed in His Ministry, the Holy Spirit is seen to inspire every movement of thought and will" (*The Holy Spirit in the New Testament*, p. 59).

12. By way of analogy it is permissible to cite the example of St. Seraphim of Sarov, who, being a spirit-bearer, manifested, as it were, his transfiguration in the Holy Spirit to Motovilov, *showed* the Holy Spirit to Motovilov. [This is the most famous incident in the life of St. Seraphim, possibly the greatest Russian saint. N. A. Motovilov was a young landowner who in the winter of 1831 was visiting Seraphim at the hermitage of Sarov. Seraphim was explaining to him that the entire goal of Christian activity lies in the acquisition of the Holy Spirit. But Motovilov did not understand how one can be certain of being in the Holy Spirit. At this point, he was told to look at Seraphim's face, and he saw that a great light was streaming from it, that it was brighter than the sun. — Trans.]

which in other cases too is a form of the palpable manifestation of the Holy Spirit. It is also accompanied by a voice out of the cloud, which says, "this is my beloved Son" (17:5). The Father thereby attests that Jesus is adopted by the Holy Spirit, an adoption that was also announced during the descent of the Holy Spirit at the Baptism.[13] The manifestation of Christ in the glory of the Transfiguration is therefore as much a christophany as it is a pneumatophany. It is a dyadic act, and it is therefore one of the most powerful testimonies that, in Christ, the incarnate hypostasis of the Logos is *dyadically* united with the hypostasis of the Holy Spirit, without separation and without confusion.

At the threshold of His salvific passion, Christ speaks, in His Last Discourse, of this same glorification which corresponds to the Transfiguration and which anticipates events that are already inwardly imminent: "Now is the Son of man glorified" (John 13:31). In the suffering unto death at Golgotha, the God-Man in His human nature is "forsaken by God," that is, the constant reposing upon Him of the Holy Spirit becomes impalpable, in contrast to the Holy Spirit's palpable presence in the Transfiguration. This reposing is potentialized, as it were. Once again there is manifested that kenosis of the Holy Spirit which, in the Incarnation, is constant and parallel to Christ's kenosis. The initial reposing of the Holy Spirit upon Jesus the Divine Infant and Divine Youth, a reposing which is proportional to the measure of human growth and limited by this measure, is already the kenosis of the Spirit. And the reposing of the Holy Spirit upon Jesus after His hypostatic descent upon Jesus' human essence on the Jordan, is also manifested not yet fully, but only by gifts, as Christ Himself attests with the words of Isaiah: "The Spirit of the Lord . . . hath anointed me to preach the gospel to the poor; he hath sent me to heal the brokenhearted, to preach deliverance to the captives, and recovering of sight to the blind . . . to preach the acceptable year of the Lord" (Luke 4:18-19). This passage enumerates the different ministries and thus the different gifts of the Holy Spirit, among which Christ Himself included the casting out of demons and all kinds of healing. But this is not yet that fullness of life in the Holy Spirit which is eternally proper to the Logos outside of His kenosis. This kenotic measure is abolished, as it were, in the Transfiguration, where, in the light of the coming events of the glorification, i.e., Gethsemane and Golgotha, the disciples see the *fullness* of the Holy Spirit reposing upon Christ, in His appearance in Glory.

13. In the Liturgy of St. Basil the Great, the Holy Spirit is called "the gift of adoption."

But the kenosis of the Spirit is then reestablished, and reaches its peak of intensity in the Passion when Christ is overcome with the sense of being forsaken by God. This forsakenness does not come suddenly and instantaneously; we can measure its growth, as it were. *Before* Gethsemane, at the end of the Last Discourse, Christ can still say, "Behold, the hour cometh, yea, is now come, that ye shall be scattered . . . and shall leave me alone: and yet I am not alone, because the Father is with me" (John 16:32). This passage, like many others in the Last Discourse, contains an encrypted message concerning the Holy Spirit, for the Father Who is in Heaven abides with the Son (Who has descended to earth) in the Holy Spirit, Who has been sent by the Father to repose upon the Son; and the Holy Spirit is this union of the Father and the Son, this "with," this *met' emou*, which unites the two of them.[14] And then in Gethsemane the kenosis of the Son, which proceeds in parallel with the kenosis of the Spirit, Who limits the power of His presence, reaches such an extreme that Jesus is overcome with the sense of His imminent death: "My soul is exceeding sorrowful, even unto death" (Matt. 26:38; cf. Mark 14:34). He still addresses the Father with a prayer, however: "Abba Father." In the Golgotha suffering unto death, He addresses not the Father but God: "My God, my God, why hast thou forsaken me?" (Matt 27:46; cf. Mark 15:34). This sense of being forsaken by God, so different from the earlier "the Father is with me" (John 16:32), is the extreme kenosis of the Holy Spirit, who "forsakes" Him. But He is also forsaken by the Father; and the Suffering One cries out, like Job, to the most high, most remote, and inaccessible God (and in this we find the most perfect conformity between the Old Testament prefiguration and the Prototype).

This "forsakenness" should, of course, be understood in the sense that the palpable action of the Holy Spirit is diminished to a completely potential state, although it is not abolished; for reposing from all eternity upon the Son in His divine essence, the Holy Spirit, once He has descended, also abides permanently upon the Son's human essence. Thus, it is a question precisely of the kenosis of the Spirit as far as His activity is concerned. That the Spirit of adoption does not completely forsake the God-Man is attested by His cry before death: "Father, into thy hands I commend my spirit" (Luke 23:46). His union with the Father in the Holy

14. In this sense this passage is completely similar to the cryptogram about the Holy Spirit in Matt. 18:20: "where two or three are gathered together in my name, there am I in the midst of them." Here, "in the midst of" *(en mesōi)* undoubtedly refers to the Holy Spirit, Who is the uniting power of the Church.

Spirit is not abolished even by death, although the power of life from the Life-giving Spirit is diminished in Him; the bond of life uniting the soul and the body is broken. The death of Christ is therefore not only the extreme limit of the kenosis of the Son but also the extreme limit of the kenosis of the Holy Spirit reposing upon Him. One can express this idea by a paradox: in this common Passion of the Son and of the Spirit, hypostatic Love, loving and for the sake of love, abstains from love, refrains from manifesting its power and effectiveness.

The reposing of the Holy Spirit upon the Son is not interrupted even by the death of Christ, but remains in a kenotically depotentialized form, in which it approaches inactivity, without, of course, ever becoming totally inactive. The Divine Logos retains His Divinity even in the death of Christ; and in this sense He abides "on the throne with the Father and the Spirit" (a phrase from the liturgies of St. John Chrysostom and St. Basil the Great). With His soul, Christ descends into hell in order to preach; and this form of His activity is, of course, inspired, as in the days of His earthly ministry, by the Holy Spirit reposing upon Him: "The Spirit of the Lord is upon me" (Luke 4:18). And finally, the body of Christ in the grave, which does not know corruption, is preserved from the latter by the Holy Spirit reposing upon Him (and it is the Holy Spirit Who makes the relics of saints "incorruptible" in a special sense). According to the Church teaching, Christ, Who "was in the grave by His flesh" (also a phrase from the liturgies of St. John Chrysostom and St. Basil the Great), never lost the connection of His spirit with His body, and this *connection* is precisely the action of the Holy Spirit reposing upon Christ. Thus, the Holy Spirit shared, as it were, the beyond-the-grave destiny of the incarnate Logos, not abandoning Him even in death.

This raises a more general question: Is the afterlife state of human beings accessible to the action of the Holy Spirit? Can His grace penetrate death's stronghold?[15] We do not have a *direct* answer to this question in the Church teaching, but we do have an indirect one, based on a comparison of certain facts. We must give an *affirmative* answer to this question on the basis of the fact that the Holy Spirit indisputably descended into hell together with Christ, because the Two are without separation and without confusion. Here, we must consider the preaching in hell not as a unique event of Christ's three-day abiding in the grave, but as an event continuing in its power, so that Christ's preaching in hell

---

15. There is a fuller discussion of this in the third volume of this trilogy, *The Bride of the Lamb* [available in Boris Jakim's English translation, published by Eerdmans, 2002].

continues for those who did not know Him on earth. Likewise, the action of the Holy Spirit (which is received, to be sure, not by the entire human being but only by his soul and his spirit) continues as well. It continues in the action of the prayers of the Church for the deceased and, in particular, in the action of the Divine Eucharist. It also continues by virtue of the presence of the spirit-bearing saints in the afterlife world, of these saints who are conductors, as it were, of God's grace in the infernal darkness (here one can add the holy angels); and in general it continues by the power of prayerful love both here and there. But is also clear that this abiding of the Holy Spirit in the afterlife world is accompanied by a special kenosis of His Revelation, for He, the Giver of Life, acts here in the kingdom of death.

But He and His power prepare the path to universal resurrection. Christ's resurrection too is accomplished by the *Holy Spirit* according to the will of the Father, but also by Christ's own power. The fact (directly attested by Holy Scripture) that Christ was raised by the Holy Spirit confirms the connection between His being raised by the Father and His resurrection by His own power. The power of life, the triumphant power of the resurrection, is one: the *Holy Spirit*. But the action of the Spirit in the *complex* dual nature of the God-Man is accomplished in a dual manner: On the one hand, the resurrection is a new creative act of the Father. It consists in the victory over death and is accomplished by the Holy Spirit, by His life-giving power, which, as a new principle, enters the world that is damaged by sin. But on the other hand, inasmuch as, by virtue of His kenotic feat, the God-Man becomes worthy of resurrection, He raises Himself; and in the same measure this resurrection is thus accomplished by the Holy Spirit reposing upon Him. We can establish an analogy here, which, however, is no more than an analogy: Christ is raised by the power of the same Spirit by Whom He raised the dead during His earthly ministry. But that raising was not a complete but only a partial victory over death, since those who were raised died again when the time came. By contrast, Christ's resurrection was a complete and definitive creative act of the Father by the action of the Holy Spirit.

And so, in Christ's resurrection we have two aspects of the participation of the Spirit: in one aspect, He participates as God, accomplishing the creative act of the Father upon the God-Man; in the other aspect, the Holy Spirit is in a common kenosis with the Son, inspiring Him as the God-Man. These two aspects of the action of the Holy Spirit, which merge in the one act of raising-resurrection, have a parallel in the two natures of the God-Man, and also correspond to the fact that, having descended upon earth in the Son and reposing upon Him, the Holy Spirit at the same time does not leave heaven, i.e., His divine being.

This *kenosis of action* of the Holy Spirit differs from the kenosis of the Son, which is a *kenosis of hypostasis* and in this sense is a "coming down from heaven," with the abandonment of the latter, as it were. This is not the case as far as the Holy Spirit is concerned: His descent at the Pentecost *unites* heaven with earth, erects a ladder between them. Christ's resurrection is also His glorification, although not His definitive glorification. His glorification is always accomplished by the Holy Spirit. But since the Holy Spirit has already reposed upon Him and consequently there could be no new descent upon Christ, it can only be a question here (as in the case of the Transfiguration) of a new *manifestation* of the Spirit in His power. This increase of the action of the Holy Spirit in power corresponds to a diminution of His kenosis: In raising Christ, the Holy Spirit manifests Himself as *Glory* in the glorification of the God-Man; the kenosis of the Holy Spirit's *action* in Christ approaches its end, as does the kenosis of the Son. The High-priestly prayer concerning the cessation of the kenosis now approaches its fulfillment: "And now, O Father, glorify thou me with thine own self with the glory which I had with thee before the world was" (John 17:5). Glory is the Holy Spirit in His supramundane reposing upon the Son as well as in His glorification on earth, in the raised body of Christ, which is the *spiritual* body (see 1 Cor. 15:44-49), i.e., a body totally obedient to and transparent for the Spirit, the glorified body. We have direct testimony in the Gospel about the relation between the glorification and the power to send the Holy Spirit: "In the last day, that great day of the feast, Jesus stood and cried, saying, if any man thirst, let him come unto me, and drink. He that believeth on me, as the scripture hath said, out of his belly shall flow rivers of living water. (But this spake he of the Spirit, which they that believe on him should receive: for the Holy Spirit was not yet given; because that Jesus was not yet glorified.)" (John 7:37-39).

The superabundant grace of the Holy Spirit is now bestowed by Christ as such: Christ not only performs works by the Holy Spirit, but He Himself *sends* the Spirit. Here we have in mind John 20:21-23: "as my Father hath sent me, even so send I you. And when he had said this, he breathed on them, and saith unto them, Receive ye the Holy Spirit: Whose soever sins ye remit, they are remitted unto them; and whose soever sins ye retain, they are retained." The Father sends the Son by the Holy Spirit, by Whom the Incarnation is accomplished. Similarly, the Son now sends the apostles by the Holy Spirit, and bestows Him upon them by a breath in this anticipation of the Pentecost. This signifies that the Son is already in possession of the Holy Spirit, and consequently the kenosis of the Spirit in Him is approaching its end, for the glorification has been accomplished. But it has not been accomplished fully and definitively, since the *ascent* is still continuing: "I am not yet ascended to my Father. . . . I ascend unto my Father, and your Father; and to my God, and your God" (John 20:17). With reference to the Holy Spirit this ascent can signify only the increasing reception of the Spirit by Christ, while the kenosis of the Spirit continues to diminish and approaches its end. This "ascent" is realized in the Ascension, which is also a work of the Father by the Holy Spirit; the elevation to heaven signifies the going out of the kenosis into the fullness of the life of the Holy Trinity, that is, it signifies a glorification that is not only earthly but also heavenly. Henceforth the Holy Spirit reposes upon the God-man, just as He eternally reposes upon the Logos ("before the foundation of the world," i.e., in supramundane eternity). A perfect conformity is established between the life of the Son and that of the Spirit, which is expressed by the image of the "sitting at the right hand of the Father." This is the accomplished deification of the God-Man in His human nature, which is no longer an obstacle to His abiding in the bosom of the Holy Trinity. The *personal kenosis* of the Son is exhausted, as is the kenosis of *action* of the Holy Spirit, Who, according to the Forerunner's expression, is now given to the Son *without measure* (see John 3:34).

As we have already seen in the first volume of this trilogy, *The Lamb of God,* however, the Son's high-priestly ministry is completed in heaven, precisely in the ten-day interval before the sending down of the Holy Spirit, which sending down is, in some sense, the work of the Son: "It is expedient for you that I go away: for if I go not away, the Comforter will not come unto you; but if I depart, I will send him unto you" (John 16:7; cf. 15:26). And this work of the Son is defined in the following terms: "I will pray the Father, and he shall give you another Comforter, that he may abide with you for ever" (John 14:16). What can be the significance of these mysterious words: "I will pray the Father"? First of all, this prayer must be distinguished from the general high-priestly intercession by virtue of which Christ is "the mediator of the new testament" (Heb. 9:15), "wherefore he is able to save them to the uttermost that come unto God by him, seeing he ever liveth to make intercession for them" (7:25). This is the redemptive work of Christ, Who "because he continueth ever, hath an unchangeable priesthood" (7:24). In this prayer to the Father that He send down the Holy Spirit, we have an act not of eternal but of temporal ministry (however paradoxical it may be to speak of the temporal in heaven, we are compelled to this by the direct testimony of Revelation), that is, the accomplishment of the work of the Incarnation. For the Son Himself, this prayer, which gives Him the possibility of sending down the Holy Spirit into the world, is also the completion of His redemptive ministry, and therefore the overcoming of His kenosis: the Son is filled by the Spirit to such a degree that He now sends the Spirit *in His Own Name.*

But how does the Holy Spirit Himself participate in this prayer, and does He participate in it at all? We must postulate this participation a priori, for the Incarnation, just like the whole of Christ's work, is accomplished with the continuous participation and action of the Holy Spirit. We find sufficient, though indirect, evidence for this participation of the Holy Spirit in the prayer for His being sent down; and by no means can His sending down be understood as a purely passive obedience, without any relation to His volition. First of all, in the Last Discourse the Holy Spirit is called "another Comforter [*allon paraklēton*]" (John 14:16). The word *"paraklētos"* has a double meaning here: it means not only Comforter but also Advocate or Intercessor. And it is precisely in this latter sense that the Holy Spirit is "another," *allos,* in relation to Christ (cf. 1 John 2:1, where Christ is called the Paraclete in the sense of Advocate). It is in this sense that it is said about the Holy Spirit that he "maketh intercession [*huperentunchanei*] for us with groanings which cannot be uttered. . . . He maketh intercession for the saints according to the will of God" (Rom. 8:26-27). In this same chapter of Romans (8:34), the same thing is said about Christ: "[He] is at the right hand of God . . . [and] maketh intercession [*entunchanei*] for us." Consequently, Both "maketh intercession" — the Spirit and the Son.

And we must now ask: If, in the ten-day interval, Christ "prays" to the Father that He send down the Spirit, does this not mean that the Holy Spirit prays for the same thing or, more precisely, that Christ prays by the Holy Spirit, Who intercedes for us with "groanings which cannot be uttered"? If the Holy Spirit abides with Christ during the whole of the Latter's ministry, can it be that He parts company with Him when Their works become identical? This identity of works is revealed in the promise that there will come "another" Comforter, in and through Whom "ye [will] see me" (John 14:19), for "he shall receive of mine, and shall shew it unto you" (16:14).

We thus arrive at the conclusion that the Holy Spirit prays together with the Son or in the Son, or that the Son prays together with the Holy Spirit and by the Holy Spirit, that the Spirit be sent down into the world, or more precisely, that the Son *could* send Him from the Father. For the Son this means the complete cessation of His kenosis and the reestablishment of the fullness of His possession of the Holy Spirit Who reposes upon Him and Who cannot be sent by Him without this condition. For the Holy Spirit this means the cessation of His kenosis in relation to the Son, to such a degree that He can be sent into the world by the Son. The initial divine equilibrium is restored. In heaven, in the sitting at the right hand of the Father, change can no longer take place in Christ, the God-Man, Who abides as the supra-eternal God in His glory.[16]

Thus, the Son *sends the Holy Spirit,* Who, being sent, descends into the world. We now confront in all its acuteness a problem that has been the subject of so much disputation in the history of dogma: What does this *sending* of the Holy Spirit by the Son and the Father mean — with reference to the supra-eternal procession and with reference to the Incarnation, the "economy" of our salvation?

The problem of the sending of the Holy Spirit by the Father and the Son (or through the Son) has been much debated in the polemic between West and East on the subject of the doctrine of the procession of the Holy Spirit; and because of this context the problem has been falsely posed. In the Filioque camp, the sending of the Holy Spirit by the Son was seen as an extra argument in support of the notion that, once the Spirit is sent by the Son, He consequently proceeds (= is produced) from the Son as well. By contrast, the Eastern camp went to the extreme of denying all connection between the supra-eternal relations in the Holy Trinity and the sending of the Holy Spirit by the Son, seeing in this a gift received by the Son as a reward for His obedience in His earthly ministry. Both sides are wrong, because they confuse two different problems; but both are also right, each in its own way. It is true that the sending of the Holy Spirit is grounded upon the immanent being of the Holy Trinity, but it is also true that, in the economy, there is established a particular domain of interrelations. These new interrelations depend on the immanent relations, but they also complicate the latter.

In conformity with the monarchy of the Father, His hypostasis, the Principle that is revealed in the two revealing hypostases, the Son and the Spirit, defines Them and is defined in relation to Them — through generation in relation to the Son and through procession in relation to the Holy Spirit. And in relation to Both of Them, in relation to the dyad of Son and Spirit, the hypostasis of the Father is defined through Their mu-

---

16. "But he [Stephen], being full of the Holy Spirit, looked up stedfastly into heaven, and saw the glory of God, and Jesus standing on the right hand of God" (Acts 7:55).

tual union, without separation and without confusion, in the Divine Sophia. In relation to the world, this dyad is the foundation of its creation by the Father, through the Word and the Holy Spirit; and then the Father sends the Son and the Holy Spirit into the world, in a definite order and interrelation. This sending of the Two, being dyadic in nature, establishes a special interrelation between Them. It establishes the *order* of Their sending into the world; and one can distinguish two epochs here: before the Incarnation and after it.

In the first epoch, the Father *first* sends the Holy Spirit, and this sending of the Spirit entrains the sending of the Son (which is spoken of in Isaiah 48:16: "and now the Lord God, and his Spirit, hath sent me"). The sending of the Holy Spirit by the Father *before* the sending of the Son is attested in the Old Testament, where God "at sundry times and in divers manner spake . . . by the prophets" (Heb. 1:1) and "put his holy Spirit within him [Moses]" (Isa. 63:11). We then find it in the Divine Incarnation: the Virgin Mary becomes the Mother of God as a result of this descent of the Holy Spirit. Therefore, about the Divine Incarnation itself one can say that the Son is sent into the world by the Father through the Holy Spirit (or by the Father *and* the Holy Spirit). And during the Son's entire earthly ministry, up to and including His glorification in the Resurrection and the Ascension, He is Christ, i.e., the anointed of the Holy Spirit, Who is sent upon Him and Who, in turn, sends Him and guides Him, as it were.[17] The dyad of the two revealing hypostases, sent into the world by the Father in the Divine Incarnation, is mutually defined in such a manner that the sending hypostasis (to be sure, by virtue of the initial sending down from the Father) is the Third, while the sent hypostasis is the Second. But at the same time this sending of the Holy Spirit into the world is not His manifestation as such, but remains conditioned by the Incarnation of the Son, is in a certain sense instrumental with respect to the Incarnation. Divine-humanity, which is realized in creation by the Incarnation, is directed toward the world by the hypostasis of the Logos; whereas the manifesta-

---

17. It is significant that, in Acts 1:2, about the resurrected Christ, and even about the day of the Ascension, it is said: "Until the day in which he was taken up, after that he through the Holy Spirit had given commandments unto the apostles whom he had chosen." In other words, this final work of His ministry (in this case, both high-priestly and prophetic) He also accomplished by the Holy Spirit reposing upon Him, i.e., as Christ, the Anointed by the Spirit. This thought is summed up in Peter's speech addressed to Cornelius: "God anointed Jesus of Nazareth with the Holy Spirit and with power; [and He] went about doing good, and healing all that were oppressed of the devil; for God was with him" (Acts 10:38).

tion of the Holy Spirit merges with or is eclipsed by the Logos, as it were. The Holy Spirit manifests the Divine-humanity of the Son, not Himself. But this epoch, as we have said, concludes with the glorification of Christ in the ascent to heaven and even earlier in the Resurrection. Together with Christ, the Holy Spirit also departs from the world and ascends to heaven, the Holy Spirit Who reposes upon Christ and does not have an independent existence in the world apart from Christ (except the express communication of His gifts). By the will of the Father, the Holy Spirit is sent into the world together with the Son and departs the world together with Him in the Ascension of the Son to heaven. And in the course of His earthly ministry before the Resurrection, the Son does *not* send the Holy Spirit upon the apostles or upon others, although He Himself does the works of love by the Holy Spirit, like the spirit-bearing righteous men in the Old Testament.

The situation changes after the Ascension, which inaugurates a new epoch in the sending down of the Holy Spirit. In the Divine Incarnation, Christ united Himself with the world, in a certain sense making it His own body and men His brothers. At the same time, His dyadic union with the Holy Spirit changes in character. In relation to the Holy Spirit, Christ's glorification signifies that the kenosis has been overcome; and by virtue of this, He is dyadically united with the Holy Spirit in the same way that They are eternally united in the Holy Trinity. But as a result of the Incarnation, He is united with the world in such a manner that He has the power to send the Holy Spirit; the words "all power is given unto me in heaven and in earth" (Matt. 28:18) can be applied here. For the Holy Spirit, Christ is now the *path* (and not vice versa, as it was before the Incarnation and in the Incarnation, from the Annunciation to the Ascension). He now sends the Holy Spirit into the world from Himself and upon Himself, as it were, for He Himself is the essence and content of the revelation of the Holy Spirit in the world, inasmuch as the Spirit reveals not Himself but Christ. Whence the identification of the revelations of Christ and of the "other Comforter" in the Last Discourse: the Holy Spirit "shall teach you all things, and bring all things to your remembrance, whatsoever I have said unto you" (John 14:26), "for he shall not speak of himself; but whatsoever he shall hear, that shall he speak . . . for he shall receive of mine, and shall shew it unto you" (16:13-14); "he shall testify of me" (15:26). In other words, if previously the Holy Spirit was sent into the world by the Father upon the Son *in order to* accomplish the Incarnation, He is now sent into the world by the Son *in virtue of* the accomplished Incarnation. And sent by the Son, the Holy Spirit is now directed toward the world in His own hypostasis; He *Himself* descends into the world, rather than being sent into it only for the sake of or on the occasion of the sending down of the Son. After the Incarnation, the Son became the unique path into the world, for the Holy Spirit cannot be sent down into the world apart from and independently of the Incarnation. On the contrary, He can be sent down only in the context of the Incarnation; and His sending is its continuation or completion, the actualized *Divine-humanity,* which is Christ with the Holy Spirit reposing upon Him.

A mysterious break in continuity thus occurs between these two epochs, which can be called the Old Testament church and the New Testament church (if the latter is considered to start not with the Annunciation but with the Pentecost). This mysterious discontinuity corresponds to the ten-day interval between the Ascension and the sending down of the Holy Spirit, and it is accomplished in heaven by means of what is expressed in the words of the Lord: "I will pray the Father, and he shall give you another Comforter, that he may abide with you for ever" (John 14:16). This "I will pray" is still a kenotic mode in which the God-man addresses the Father from out of the depths of His Divine-humanity; but in it the kenosis is being overcome and the Divine-humanity is being completed, for this prayer already has the power of *being heard:* "All power is given unto me in heaven and in earth." This prayer is a new self-definition and the final self-definition of the God-Man, by which He becomes God, the Son of God in His humanity.

The prayer to the Father that He send down the Spirit is a prayer for the definitive glorification of the God-Man, by virtue of which there is established for Him no longer a kenotic but a divine interrelation with the Spirit reposing upon Him. And in this interrelation, by virtue of the accomplished Incarnation and the establishment through the latter of a *connection* with the world and with man, it is not the Spirit Who sends or Who institutes the divine-human work, but the Son, Who ascends to heaven not to abolish but to definitively consolidate this connection by the sending down of the Spirit: "It is expedient for you that I go away: for if I go not away, the Comforter will not come unto you; but if I depart, I will send him unto you" (John 16:7).

Why does this prayer occur in heaven? Because, in its content, it presupposes that the work of the Incarnation has already been accomplished; indeed, this prayer is the final and concluding act of the Incarnation. How does this prayer in heaven to the Father, at His right hand, differ from all the known prayers to Him on earth? Man has no answer to this question, at least in his earthly existence, for this prayer is accomplished beyond the limits of the latter. It is sufficient for us to understand the *place* of this divine mystery in the general economy of our salvation. With this final prayer and by virtue of it, Christ's earthly ministry is accomplished and He abides in heaven as God, and also as the God-Man. He no longer prays to the Father with a human prayer, as He prayed kenotically during His earthly life, although He does *intercede* as the God-Man, having ascended to heaven with His blood, "to appear in the presence of God for us" (Heb. 9:24), just as the Holy Spirit intercedes for us with "groanings which cannot be uttered" (Rom. 8:26). But this intercession on the basis of "the sacrifice of himself" (Heb. 9:26) is not a prayer; rather, it is the abiding *power* of the redemptive sacrifice, into which enter those who are saved by the faith in the Lord Jesus Christ (even as the "intercession" of the Holy Spirit is the wings and inspiration of the prayer of those who are accomplishing their salvation).

Inasmuch as the Son's prayer to the Father, which, to be sure, the Father could not have failed to hear, inasmuch as this prayer concluded the work of the Incarnation and the Son's kenosis, it established an utterly *new* relation in the dyad of the Son and the Holy Spirit, not in their eternal being, of course, but in their "economic" directedness at creation: the Son acquires a new power — the power to send the Holy Spirit into the world. What does this new fact change and what does it leave unchanged? It changes the *order* of the dyadic revelation: The Holy Spirit no longer comes first, followed by the Son, Who is made incarnate in, with, and through Him. The incarnate Son of God, the God-Man, is now first; and He is followed by the Holy Spirit, Who is with, in, and through Him. The Holy Spirit is now the "Spirit of Christ" (Rom. 8:9), the "Spirit of . . . [the] Son" (Gal. 4:6), in the sense of His being sent into the world: This is an interrelation not in the Trinity but in the Dyad of the Son and the Holy Spirit.

But the fundamental interrelation in the Holy Trinity which is defined as the monarchy of the Father remains unchanged: the Father is the revealed hypostasis, the Principle, whereas the Son and the Spirit in their dyad are the revealing hypostases. In relation to the world this significance of the Father as the Principle of the self-revelation of the Holy Trinity, in relation to which the Second and Third hypostases are only His *images*, is expressed in the fact that the Father *sends* into the world, whereas the two revealing hypostases *are sent*. This relation of sending and being sent is not identical with the one that unites the Father as engendering the Son and the Son as being engendered by the Father, on the one hand; or with the one that unites the Father as originating the Holy Spirit and the Holy Spirit as proceeding from the Father, on the other. Nevertheless, it is connected with these relations, inasmuch as generation and procession are *concrete modes* of the self-revelation of the Father in the two revealing hypostases, which determines the further interrelations of these hypostases.

Thus, the general relation consisting in the fact that the Father sends, whereas the Son and the Holy Spirit are sent by the Father, remains invariable for *all* interrelations within the sent dyad of the Son and the Holy Spirit, in which only different *modes* of this sending are distinguished. This question must therefore be liberated from any *direct* identification or connection with the theory of "origination" (or "production"), which equally taints, though in different ways, the thought of both Orthodox and Catholic theologians. Not only is there no such origination in the Holy Trinity, but this interrelation presupposes a certain kenotic accomplishment and the resulting mutual determination of the hypostases. This interrelation begins with the primacy of the Holy Spirit, continues with the primacy of the Son, and is completed in the future age with Their complete equality, when there will be neither sender nor sent, but God will be all in all, in the fullness of the accomplished self-revelation of the Father in the Holy Trinity in creation.

Thus, the Father sends the Holy Spirit into the world, and the Son sends Him too;[18] but these two sendings refer, so to speak, to different planes or interrelations, and we should not confuse them, as the Catholics do, who eagerly take this occasion to repeat once more that the Holy Spirit is sent by the Father *and* the Son (for He proceeds from the Father *and* the Son, *filioque*). This "and" is inappropriate here because it unites two different principles on an equal basis and reduces sending directly to procession. "Through" *(dia)* would be more adequate, not in the sense of origination, of course, but in the sense of instrumentality, "by means of" (to be sure, with the preservation of the autonomy of each of the hypostases). It thus turns out that the Father initially sends the Son into the world by means of the Holy Spirit; and then He sends the Holy Spirit through the Son. Consequently, the Father, in general, *sends into the world;* that is His power as the Principle. But within the limits of the sent Dyad,

---

18. This dogmatic idea is well expressed in the following magnification on the feast of the Trinity: "We magnify You, Christ giver of life, and we honor Your Holy Spirit, Whom You have sent from the Father to Your divine disciples." It is interesting that this imparts to the feast of the Pentecost a christological accent, an accent of the day "of the Lord."

this sending is realized in such a manner that the direct *accomplisher* of this sending, the sending hypostasis, is either the Son or the Holy Spirit, in relation to the Divine-humanity being accomplished through the Incarnation. The sender is the Father, whereas the direct accomplisher of the sending is first the Holy Spirit, and then the Son.

Thus, there are *two* sendings: the initial or original one and the direct or instrumental one. The Father's sending of the hypostases is directed not only at the sent hypostasis but at the entire sent *dyad*, revealing the Father, of the Son and the Holy Spirit in Their union without separation and without confusion: the sending down into the world of one of these two hypostases is *never* realized without the participation of the other. Therefore, in a certain sense, there is always sent precisely the dyad that is directed toward the world by one or the other of its hypostases; and then within the limits now of a dyadic interrelation, one or the other hypostasis is the sending one, depending on the character of the sending. Thus, generally speaking, there are *two* sendings, which must always be distinguished, especially since the same term "sending" is used for each of them: (1) *sending in the proper sense*, which is proper to the Father alone, as the Principle; and (2) *dyadic sending*, within the limits of the dyad of the Son and the Holy Spirit, which is the realization of the first sending.

Now that we are equipped with these radical distinctions, we can navigate without difficulty around the pertinent expressions in the Last Discourse. Let us consider six of them.

First of all: "I will pray the Father, and he shall give you another Comforter, that he may abide with you for ever" (John 14:16). This refers to the completion of the Son's kenosis, by virtue of which the fullness of His divine glory is restored and, as the God-Man, He receives the power to send the Holy Spirit into the world. This prayer signifies a change in the interrelation of the dyadic hypostases: the sent hypostasis becomes the sending one, and vice versa.

Second: "But the Comforter, which is the Holy Spirit, whom the Father will send in my name, he shall teach you all things" (14:26). The Father sends down the Holy Spirit *through* the Son as the direct accomplisher of this sending — "in my name."

Third: "When the Comforter is come, whom I will send unto you from the Father, even the Spirit of truth, which proceedeth from the Father, he shall testify of me" (15:26). This passage combines two ideas: (1) the eternal procession of the Holy Spirit from the Father, which is nothing other than an extended definition of the Third hypostasis, i.e., the Spirit Who proceeds from the Father (which is parallel to the definition: the Son Who is engendered from the Father), this definition conforming with the particular solemnity of this speech; and (2) the idea that the Father's sending of the Holy Spirit is accomplished *through* the Son, which idea is expressed with lapidary succinctness: "I will send unto you from the Father." The Father is the Principle from which this sending as well as the procession of the Holy Spirit proceeds; and the Son is the one who directly accomplishes this sending.

Fourth: "If I go not away, the Comforter will not come unto you; but if I depart, I will send him unto you" (16:7). This refers to the connection that exists between the completion of the kenosis in the Ascension and the change in the dyadic interrelation of the Son and the Holy Spirit that occurs given Their respective sending: it is no longer the Spirit Who sends; rather, it is the Son Who sends by virtue of His definitive glorification. Nothing is said here about the initial sending of the Holy Spirit by the Father; after what has been said, this sending is self-evident. It is a question only of the "economic" sending within the limits of the dyad of the Son and the Holy Spirit, with the sending one now being the Son.[19]

Fifth: "When he, the Spirit of truth, is come, he will guide you into all truth" (16:13). Here we have the final phase of the revelation concerning the sending of the Spirit: This is not a passive sending and not merely a communication of the *gifts* of the Holy Spirit or an action by His *power,* which was proper to the Son during His earthly ministry when He was guided (or "sent") by the Holy Spirit. It is rather the active and hypostatic coming of the Holy Spirit. For a *sending* always includes a harmonious self-determination of the sent one and the sender: the latter determines, while the former is determined, not in passive obedience but by virtue of a harmonious union. The kenosis of the Holy Spirit is just as voluntary as that of the Son. The Father sends through the Son; the Holy Spirit goes, but He goes by His own will: the Comforter "is come."

Sixth: There remains one final text, the words of the resurrected Lord when He appeared to His disciples: "Peace be unto you: as my Father hath sent me, even so send I you. And when he had said this, he breathed on them, and saith unto them, Receive ye the Holy Spirit: Whose soever sins ye remit, they are remitted unto them; and whose soever sins ye retain, they are retained" (John 20:21-23). Is this not *already* the Pentecost?

---

19. This idea of the sending down of the Spirit from the Father through the Son is summed up in the apostle Peter's discourse on the day of the Pentecost: "Therefore being by the right hand of God exalted, and having received of the Father the promise of the Holy Spirit, he hath shed forth this, which ye now see and hear" (Acts 2:33).

Or what is the relation of this event to the Pentecost? It differs, at any rate, from the Pentecost in that it has a limited character: the Holy Spirit is sent by Christ only upon the apostles, not upon "all" human beings and not upon the whole world, as in the Pentecost. Further, this sending down is limited here to one particular gift, the gift to "bind" and to "loose," which initially was promised to Peter alone (Matt. 16:19), but then was promised to all the apostles (18:18), in anticipation of the Passion. This express gift bestowed upon the apostles corresponds, as it were, to a hierarchical laying on of hands by the Supreme High-Priest Himself.

But this sacrament, first promised to and then fulfilled upon the apostles, is still only an anticipation of the Pentecost, similar to the anticipation that we have in the Last Supper, accomplished by Christ *before* His crucifixion, before the breaking of His body and the shedding of His blood. Time with its bounds is ontologically overcome here, as it were, and that which had been pre-accomplished inwardly is now pre-accomplished outwardly. But one should also note that the "breaking of bread," instituted by Christ in anticipation of the Passion and of the glorification, is no longer accomplished by Him Himself — even *after* the Resurrection. Nor is it accomplished by His disciples *before* the Pentecost. It is accomplished by them only *after* the Pentecost and, of course, by virtue of the latter. We have the relevant testimony of the sacred historian: "And they continued stedfastly in the apostles' doctrine and fellowship, and in breaking of bread, and in prayers" (Acts 2:42; cf. 2:46). Similarly, having received the Holy Spirit from Christ, the apostles are nonetheless told by Christ Himself that the Pentecost still awaits them: "the promise of the Father, which . . . ye have heard of me" (Acts 1:4); "ye shall be baptized with the Holy Spirit" (1:5); "ye shall receive power, after that the Holy Spirit is come upon you" (1:8). And accordingly, the apostles together with others (1:13-14) awaited this event in the upper room in Jerusalem and there received the Holy Spirit. This is the fulfillment of that which was announced to them by Christ when He gave them the Holy Spirit.

Thus, in John 20:21-23, we have a confirmation of the general idea that, "economically," in the dyadic interrelation of the Second and Third hypostases, it is precisely Christ Who sends the Holy Spirit upon the disciples; and this sending, which must yet be fully accomplished in His definitive glorification, is attested here in advance as a pre-accomplishment, for all its conditions are present and have been fulfilled. We have, together with the Pentecost itself, its pre-celebration, as it were, in the course of the entire Pentecost of the Church, starting with Easter.

IV. The Pentecost

What happened at the Pentecost? What is the line of demarcation that divides the life of the world before the Pentecost and after it? We know that the gifts and actions of the spirit of God had been bestowed upon the world from its very foundation, that, in particular, they were bestowed in the epoch of the Old Testament as well as in the epoch of the Incarnation. The utterly new thing that occurred in the Pentecost was not the descent into the world of the "spirit of God" in the capacity of His gifts, but the descent of the hypostatic Holy Spirit Himself. And the descent now was not within definite limits, not on Christ and the Mother of God alone, but also on the apostles, as well as on all who were with them. This reception was then extended to all human beings and even to the whole world (which is expressed by a symbolic representation of the cosmos in the icon of the descent of the Holy Spirit). This is the *hypostatic* descent of the Holy Spirit into the world, which is completely analogous to the descent from heaven of the Logos for the purpose of His Incarnation.

But what evidence is there that *this* is the significance of this event? In the New Testament there is no Gospel devoted specifically to the Holy Spirit. If we attentively read the second chapter of the Acts of the Apostles and, in connection with it, the chapters that immediately follow it, we will not find here any *direct* indication of the *hypostatic* descent of the Holy Spirit; and one can even understand this event by analogy with Old Testament examples of the *action* of the Holy Spirit upon kings and prophets. To be sure, we read that "all were filled with the Holy Spirit [*pneumatos hagiou*]" (2:4) (this time even without an article!), and "began to speak with other tongues, as the Spirit [*to pneuma*] gave them utterance." And in the prophecy of Joel, cited here, it is said, "I will pour out of my Spirit [*apo tou pneumatos mou*] upon all flesh" (2:17).

Further, in the course of the entire book of the Acts of the Apostles, we read about the Holy Spirit or the gift of the Holy Spirit, "whom God hath given to them that obey him" (5:32); or even: "it seemed good to the Holy Spirit, and to us" (15:28). The Holy Spirit is bestowed, speaks, sends; in general, the entire book of the Acts of the Apostles is a narrative about the manifest actions of the Holy Spirit in the primitive church. But *none* of these testimonies can serve as indisputable proof that what is meant here is the hypostatic Holy Spirit Himself Who acts in the Church, and not the spirit of God in general, sent from God. In addition, there is no direct testimony about His *hypostatic* revelation. Only His gifts are spoken of.

And if one were to limit oneself to these texts (which are similar to numerous other texts of the New Testament), it would be impossible to affirm that the Pentecost represents precisely the descent of the Holy Spirit Himself, and not just a superabundant sending down — never repeated, it must be confessed, in the life of the Church — of *His gifts*. And the prophecy of Joel, applied to this event by the apostle Peter, says, "I will pour out of my Spirit [*apo tou pneumatos mou*]" (Acts 2:17), rather than "I will pour out my Spirit [*to pneuma mou*]." One can say that, even as in the Old Testament the gifts of the Holy Spirit were sent down but He Himself did not descend hypostatically, so here too the express superabundance of gifts and even the sign of the tongues of fire do not yet, in themselves, attest to the hypostatic manifestation of the Holy Spirit (just as the Old Testament manifestation, for example, of the "Burning Bush," burning but not being consumed, was not such an attestation).

In general, the "tongues of fire" were only a *vision:* "And there appeared unto them cloven tongues like as of fire [*hōsei puros*]" (2:3). The expression *"hōsei"* ("like" or "as") is also applied to the manifestation of the Holy Spirit at the Baptism in the form of a dove, *hōsei peristeran* (Matt. 3:16; *hōs* in Mark 1:10, Luke 3:22, John 1:32). But at the Baptism too the Holy Spirit descended not *in* a dove, as if inhabiting it, but *like* a dove, which was His visible emblem, as it were. Likewise, the tongues of fire were only an emblematic vision, not the hypostatic indwelling of the Holy Spirit in the fire. One can say the same thing about the entire external manifestation of this *spiritual* event, the descent of the Holy Spirit.[20] "And suddenly there came a sound from heaven as of [*hōsei*, which once again indicates that what we have here is a subjective expression in external sensations of an objective spiritual event] a rushing mighty wind, and it filled all the house where they were sitting. And there appeared unto them cloven tongues like as of fire, and it sat upon each of them" (2:2-3). And then the event itself is attested: "And they were all filled with the Holy Spirit" (2:4).

We receive textual confirmation that the narrative of the Pentecost attests to the descent into the world of precisely the hypostatic Holy Spirit Himself only if we read it in context with the Savior's direct promise in the Last Discourse: this promise is the prophecy and the Pentecost is the fulfillment. The Last Discourse speaks of the Comforter or, more expressively, of "another" Comforter, Who is equi-hypostatic in relation to

20. "The whole was a vision, as St. Luke is careful to explain, but a vision which corresponds to a great spiritual fact which at the same moment accomplished itself in the experience of all who were present" (Swete, *The Holy Spirit in the New Testament*, p. 71).

the hypostatic Logos. And with reference to the Comforter, the Discourse uses the third-person *personal* pronoun (as we have indicated, the Holy Spirit almost never speaks in Scripture in the first person): "But the Comforter, which is the Holy Spirit . . . he shall teach you all things, and bring all things to your remembrance" (John 14:26); "another Comforter, that he may abide with you for ever" (14:16); "he shall testify of me" (15:26); "I will send him unto you" (16:7); "he will guide you into all truth: for he shall not speak of himself. . . . He shall glorify me: for he shall receive of mine, and shall shew it unto you" (16:13-14). We can understand all this only if we take it as spoken with reference to a Person and, moreover, to a Person Who is perfectly similar to the Person of the "other Comforter," Christ. And it is in the light of this personal coefficient, as the fulfillment of *this* prophecy, that we consider the event of the Pentecost to be the descent of the Third hypostasis Himself into the world: not of spirit but of the Spirit, not of the gifts only, but of their Source, the Paraclete.

The *personal* character of the descent of the Holy Spirit is also confirmed by the following New Testament texts: "but all these worketh that one and the self-same Spirit, dividing to every man severally as he will" (1 Cor. 12:11); "the things of God knoweth no man, but the Spirit of God" (2:11); "the Spirit searcheth all things, yea, the deep things of God" (2:10). Also: "the Spirit also helpeth our infirmities . . . the Spirit . . . maketh intercession for us with groanings that cannot be uttered" (Rom. 8:26). And finally, to a certain extent: "And grieve not the Holy Spirit of God, whereby ye are sealed unto the day of redemption" (Eph. 4:30). But that appears to be all.[21] This constitutes the fundamental difference between the Old Testament outpourings of the Holy Spirit in His separate gifts and the Pentecost: The outpourings in the gifts were sent, so to speak, from heaven, transcendentally; the outpourings in the Pentecost are sent by the hypostatic Holy Spirit Himself, descending from heaven into the world. That is, the outpourings in the Pentecost are immanent to the world. In the Pentecost, not only are gifts bestowed, but the very hypostasis descends.[22] True, the hypostasis remains invisible and is con-

21. Cf. L. S. Thornton, *The Incarnate Lord* (London: Longmans, Green, 1928), pp. 325-26.

22. "That this advocate will be invisible and purely spiritual does not make against His personality; it is in that which is most spiritual in ourselves that we find evidence of our own personal life. That He fulfills the whole of our Lord's personal functions towards the Church, that He belongs to the category of Paraclete — Teacher, Director, Protector, Counsellor — this invests Him with all the essential attributes of that which we understand by personality" (Swete, *The Holy Spirit in the New Testament*, p. 292).

cealed (not revealed) by the vision of the "tongues like as of fire"; and the descent of the hypostasis is manifested only in gifts. The hypostasis cannot be seen and worshipped, as the shepherds and magi could worship the Logos come down from heaven, the Divine Infant Jesus lying in the manger. The invisible presence of the hypostasis of the Holy Spirit is manifested only in a particular abundance of gifts, but of gifts that were known also outside the Pentecost. What does this descent of the hypostasis of the Holy Spirit signify?

This question once again raises us to the peaks of theology and places us before the most fundamental doctrine of Divine-humanity. The descent into the world of the Third hypostasis, after and in connection with the descent of the Second hypostasis, places us before the fact that this descent of the Third hypostasis is necessary for the paths of Divine-humanity. It is not enough to have a mere communication, external and transcendental, of the gifts of the Holy Spirit; such communication was typical for the Old Testament. On the contrary, the *inner connection* between the accomplished Incarnation of the Son and the descent of the Holy Spirit is defined by Christ with such power and authority in the Last Discourse that it must serve as our direct dogmatic guide here. There is the fact that the Father sends from heaven into the world *not one hypostasis but two*, not only the Son but also the Holy Spirit; but the descent from heaven of the Son is accomplished in the Incarnation, whereas the descent of the Holy Spirit is *not* expressed in such a manner. We confront here the mystery of the Divine economy.

Nevertheless, the reason of the Incarnation is revealed to us (to the extent our human understanding can fathom it), as is the descent of the Holy Spirit. Both are defined by the dyadic interrelation between the Second hypostasis and the Third hypostasis in the self-revelation of the Holy Trinity, or in the Divine Sophia. The Divine Sophia is the ideal word of the Word, clothed in Beauty and realized by the Holy Spirit. She is the bi-unitary revelation of the Two hypostases. The creaturely Sophia has her foundation in the Divine Sophia by the act of creation, in which nonbeing is called to being through the submergence of its sophianic principles in becoming. In the being of the creaturely world, the logoses of being, revealed from the Divine Word, acquire their living reality, proceeding from the Holy Spirit.

Thus, in the ground of its being, the creaturely world is dyadic — verbal and spirit-bearing. These two principles of being, content and reality, are inseparable: idea-words cannot have the power of being if they are not actualized in reality, just as the being of this reality cannot remain in the darkness of wordlessness and nondifferentiation. Thus, in the creaturely Sophia the revelation of the trinitarian God is accomplished in the Word by the Holy Spirit; and therefore, just as for the descent of the Word, an ontological place is reserved in creation for the Holy Spirit, for His descent into the world.

The Divine-humanity that is being accomplished in creation presupposes the union, without separation and without confusion, of the divine and human natures, or of the Divine and creaturely Sophia, in the one hypostasis of the Logos; but this union itself, which is precisely the Divine Incarnation, is accomplished by the Holy Spirit. Furthermore, *the Holy Spirit Himself is this union*, the connecting hypostasis, which *incarnates* the Word in descending upon the Virgin Mary and then upon the God-Man Himself, Jesus. The fullness of the Divine Incarnation, or its reality, is precisely the Holy Spirit. Thus it transpires within the limits of Christ's earthly abiding and, of course, thus it remains in eternity, in heaven "at the right hand of the Father," where the Holy Spirit *reposes* upon the Son. The Divine-humanity that is accomplished within the limits of Christ's earthly life is confined to the God-Man Himself, and does not go beyond this. But the God-Man's human nature contains the fullness of the Adam and is destined to actualize this fullness in humanity through the Church as the body of Christ, to manifest the power of Christ on the pathways of the completion of His salvific kenosis and the glorification of His human nature.

But Christ's departure from the world in the Ascension does not signify His disincarnation and the cessation of His connection with humanity. This connection is to be actualized and confirmed, as it were, as the life of Christ in humanity and the life of humanity in Christ. And the actualization of this connection, as if a new manifestation or a renewal of Christ's incarnation, is precisely the descent of the Holy Spirit, sent by the Father in the Name of the Son, or (which is the same thing) by the Son from the Father. Christ's Divine-humanity, raised by Him into heaven but preserving its power in the world, is accomplished once again, as if in a kind of repetition of the Annunciation, through the descent of the Holy Spirit, Who is united, without separation and without confusion, with the Son, with Christ the God-Man, and reposes upon Him. And so, the Holy Spirit, in descending from heaven in His own Person, thus brings once again, as it were, the incarnate Christ.

It is in this sense that one must understand the identification, as it were, that Christ makes between His own coming and the coming of the Spirit: "another Comforter, that he may abide with you for ever . . . he dwelleth with you, and shall be in you" (John 14:16-17). Likewise: "I will not leave you comfortless: I will come to you. Yet a little while, and the world seeth me no more; but ye shall see me: because I live, ye shall live also" (14:18-19). What we have here is a revelation of the mystery of *the abiding of Christ in the world by the Holy Spirit or in the Holy Spirit,* of Their dyadic co-existence, which is confirmed by the following, not less mysterious, passage: "At that day[23] ye shall know that I am in my Father [i.e., by the Holy Spirit, Who unites the Father and the Son; this "in" signifies the Holy Spirit], and ye in me, and I in you [also by the Holy Spirit or in the Holy Spirit]" (14:20). Thus, this passage indicates, on the one hand, the dual aspect of Christ's presence in His Divine-humanity: the appearance of Christ in the days of His earthly ministry and then in the parousia. On the other hand, it indicates the inseparable presence of the Holy Spirit, reposing upon Him.

This expresses the fundamental fact that *Christ is never separated from the Holy Spirit.* Both the Incarnation and the Divine-humanity are therefore the work not of one hypostasis, but of two, the Son and the Holy Spirit in Their dyadic union. *Such is the dyadic axiom* — both with regard to the Divine and creaturely Sophia, or Divine-humanity, and with regard to the theophany of the Logos in the world.[24] Thus, the descent of the Holy Spirit is a new act in the Divine Incarnation: the return of Christ in the Holy Spirit, Who is "another Comforter," *allos,* not *heteros* (as commentators have justly observed), i.e., not second and in this sense other or new, but the same, only manifested in a new manner. Christ's words concerning the Paraclete ("that he may abide with you for ever" [John 14:16]) can therefore refer both to the Holy Spirit and to Christ Himself, as if despite the Ascension: "I am with you alway, even unto the end of the world" (Matt. 28:20). This is one Comforter, but a *bi-unitary* one: Christ, anointed by the Holy Spirit reposing upon Him without separation; or the Holy

23. *"En ekeinē tēi hēmerai,"* that is, on the very day of the Pentecost, which, however, includes the continuing Pentecost and thus is ontologically identified with the "last day." We owe a debt of gratitude to Fr. Kassian (Bezobrazov) for pointing out the significance of this expression.

24. This idea finds liturgical expression in the fact that the day of the Baptism of the Lord is also called the day of the Epiphany; and what is meant is the manifestation of the entire Holy Trinity in Its three hypostases: "The adoration due the Holy Trinity was manifested, Lord, when You were baptized in the Jordan; for the voice of the Father bore witness about You when He called You the Only Begotten Son, and the Holy Spirit in the form of a dove announced the confirmation of this word" (Apolytikion, first tone, of the Epiphany). Likewise, the day of the Pentecost is called the day of the Holy Trinity.

Spirit, reposing without separation and without confusion upon Christ, and therefore manifesting Him. These are two aspects of *one Divine-humanity*. This fundamental dyadic axiom serves as the foundation of the connection, approaching identity, that is established between the Ascension and the Pentecost. This leads to further dogmatic conclusions of major importance.

First of all, it becomes perfectly obvious that, for the accomplishment that is intended here, the Old Testament *gifts* of the Holy Spirit are insufficient, however great they may be. What is necessary is the descent from heaven of the hypostatic Holy Spirit Himself, the Third hypostasis. For it is not by gifts alone but hypostatically that the Holy Spirit reposes in eternity upon the Word of God, and it is also hypostatically that He reposes upon Christ, the Incarnate Son of God. And only His hypostatic descent into the world is sufficient to bring into the world the life and power of the incarnate Christ and His abiding in the Holy Spirit. Not the gifts of grace, but the Grace-giver Himself, the true Holy Spirit, has the power to continue and complete the work of Christ's Divine-humanity. It goes without saying that the *hypostatic* descent of the Holy Spirit is accompanied by the fullness of His gifts, which was not and could not be possessed by the Old Testament humanity, which did not know this hypostatic descent. (But this does not mean that this fullness is communicated all at once and immediately to humanity, for it cannot be attained until the long path of the kenosis of the Holy Spirit on earth is completed.)

A second dogmatic consequence, not less obvious or important, is that, although the descent from heaven of the Son of God for the Incarnation and the descent from heaven of the Holy Spirit for the Pentecost are two particular moments of accomplishment in the Divine Incarnation, they are, in their *content*, not different stages of revelation (unlike the Old and New Testaments). On the contrary, their content is *identical*:[25] The Holy Spirit reveals Christ, and Christ acts and is revealed by the Holy Spirit. This is a bi-unitary revelation. In conformity with the distinctly personal character of the two hypostases, however, each of them is defined in His own manner in this mutual revelation: Christ, the incarnate Word, provides, so to speak, the *content* of this revelation; He is the Truth. On the other hand, the Third hypostasis is the Spirit of Truth, the guide

---

25. L. S. Thornton (in *The Incarnate Lord,* p. 349) says the following: "The content of the Paraclete's message is the Son, whom He will glorify by continuously taking of the Son's revelation and declaring its meaning to the disciples. . . . The Spirit is thus an *alter ego* of the Son."

to all truth (John 16:13), or, according to the old patristic comparison, the breath of God's lips. The Holy Spirit is, as it were, the transparent medium in and through which the Logos is seen. This corresponds to the hypostatic character of the Holy Spirit as hypostatic love. For love has itself in another, exists only in self-identification with another; it does not exist, as it were, in and for itself, but this non-existence manifests the whole power of its existence, for it is by love that the other exists, that life in the other is realized.

The hypostatic life of the Holy Spirit therefore consists in manifesting Christ, Christ's power, Christ's life. It is by virtue of the Holy Spirit that the apostle could say about himself, "not I, but Christ liveth in me" (Gal. 2:20). This dyadic identification between the revelation of Christ in the Holy Spirit and the revelation of the Holy Spirit in Christ is attested by Christ Himself in the Last Discourse when He says, "the Comforter, which is the Holy Spirit, whom the Father will send in my name, he shall teach you all things, and bring all things to your remembrance, whatsoever I have said unto you" (John 14:26); "when the Comforter is come, whom I will send unto you from the Father, even the Spirit of truth, which proceedeth from the Father, he shall testify of me" (15:26); and especially in the summation: "when he, the Spirit of truth, is come, he will guide you into all truth: for he shall not speak of himself; but whatsoever he shall hear, that shall he speak: and he will shew you things to come. . . . All things that the Father hath are mine: therefore said I, that he shall take of mine, and shall shew it unto you" (16:13, 15). This text, which was the subject of so much disputation in connection with the problem of the Filioque (a problem with which it actually has no connection), discloses the fundamental interrelation between the Father, as the revealed hypostasis, and the Son together with the Spirit, as the revealing hypostases, with this revelation proceeding through the Word in the Spirit.

In accordance with this, the subject of the apostle Peter's preaching on the day of the Pentecost is *not the Spirit Himself*, but exclusively *Christ*, Who, "being by the right hand of God exalted, and having received of the Father the promise of the Holy Spirit, he hath shed forth this, which ye now see and hear" (Acts 2:33), with those who are baptized "in the name of Jesus Christ" (2:38) being given the promise of the gift of the Holy Spirit. And the apostles themselves considered themselves to be witnesses of Christ by virtue of the Holy Spirit: "we are his witnesses of these things: and so is also the Holy Spirit, whom God hath given to them that obey him" (5:32). And the baptism "in the name of the Lord Jesus Christ" is invariably accompanied by the descent of the Holy Spirit, but not vice versa (except in the case of Cornelius, which has a special significance); and in certain individual cases, this connection is expressly underscored.

This identification of the revelation of the Christ and that of the Holy Spirit is repeatedly attested in the New Testament. The connection between the prophecies of the Old Testament, "by the spirit of Christ," and of the New Testament, "by the Holy Spirit," is represented in the following manner by the apostle Peter: "Of which salvation the prophets have enquired and searched diligently, who prophesied of the grace that should come unto you: searching what or what manner of time the Spirit of Christ which was in them did signify, when it testified beforehand the sufferings of Christ, and the glory that should follow . . . which are now reported unto you by them that have preached the gospel unto you with the Holy Spirit sent down from heaven" (1 Pet. 1:10-12). Also: "if any man not have the Spirit of Christ, he is none of his" (Rom. 8:9); "that the God of our Lord Jesus Christ, the Father of glory, may give unto you the spirit of wisdom and revelation in the knowledge of him" (Eph. 1:17); "I know that this shall turn to my salvation through your prayer, and the supply of the spirit of Jesus Christ" (Phil. 1:19); "God hath sent forth the Spirit of his Son into your hearts" (Gal. 4:6).

Finally, the third dogmatic conclusion is that, although a hypostatic descent of the Holy Spirit in the entire fullness of His gifts occurred in the Pentecost, this was not a *hypostatic* manifestation; His hypostasis remains invisible and unknown to the world. This constitutes the limit of the Pentecost for us: in this sense, it is a grace-bestowing manifestation of the Spirit, but not yet a hypostatic one. We find here a certain lack of conformity between the hypostatic descent from heaven and the nonhypostatic manifestation: the former is not yet accompanied by the latter, and thus can be separated from it, at least in temporal revelation. Furthermore, with regard to the gifts of the Holy Spirit, which always pour forth upon the Church, the Pentecost is an event that, although it has an abiding power by its consequences, is, in itself, *not* complete. On the contrary, this event had a beginning, but it does not have an end. The Comforter is sent "that he may abide with you for ever" (John 14:16); and this eternal abiding is the *continuing* Pentecost, never exhausting itself, and, in this sense, it is *eternal life*.

Here one must rigorously establish the essential difference between the descent from heaven of the Word in His incarnation and the descent of the Holy Spirit. The former has as its content the manifestation of the incarnate Logos in Jesus Christ, the hypostatic Divine Incarnation in a particular historical Person, in a particular place and at a particular time of a definite duration, in the entire *concreteness* of the mode of His theophany. But such a concreteness is *absent* in the descent of the Holy Spirit. The Holy Spirit is historically or empirically invisible; His presence is mysterious. If in certain cases, at least in the primitive church, His descent was palpable, it was His gifts that were clearly and powerfully palpable, but His hypostatic being remained and remains unknown. His presence is recognized according to a certain *state* of life, of inspiration, not according to a personal apprehension of Him Himself; and the subject or content of the inspiration is Christ.

In conformity with this absence of concrete form, the action of the Holy Spirit, even though He descends into the world and overshadows humanity united in the Church, does not know any limits. Here it is once again confirmed that the Spirit "bloweth where it listeth" (John 3:8). He does not have any concrete human or even natural form, and is therefore not constrained by place or time. He is supra-temporal, although precisely because of this He acts in time. He is supra-spatial, although, once again because of this, He acts in space, everywhere and nowhere, always and never. "Existing always," He is called to "come" and "dwell in us" (as the acathistus to the Holy Spirit says), i.e., in particular persons in a particular place and at a particular time. "The Spirit of God dwells in you" (Rom. 8:9; the King James Version has been slightly modified to conform with the Russian Bible) according to the Apostle, but the Spirit of God dwells nowhere, and He must be worshipped not just in Jerusalem or on Gerizim but everywhere. He does not have a human countenance, although every human countenance that is made radiant by the grace of the Spirit, especially and preeminently that of the Mother of God Who is Full of Grace, manifests Him.

The presence of the Holy Spirit is invisible and mysterious; it is like the breath of the wind, about which one cannot tell "whence it cometh, and whither it goeth." His presence cannot be held on to, just as it cannot be attracted by the mere force of one's will. Sometimes His presence flees us, but sometimes it is the most intimate, gentle, personal, and genuine thing in our lives. It is as if gentle transparent fingers touch our hardened heart, burning and melting it, so that it is "illuminated with sacred mystery" (as it is said in the Matins service). If you try to deny this supreme, supernatural reality, because you cannot see it with your eyes and perceive it with your senses, if you try to persuade yourself that there is no Spirit, but instead only a psychological emotion — you will see yourself and your life in a cold, deathly, satanical light; you will taste spiritual dying before death, for "the Holy Spirit quickens every soul" (also from the Matins service). But the Holy Spirit comes, and you become other than yourself. You feel fullness in partiality, abundance in meagerness, eternal joy in the pain of semi-being, catharsis in tragedy, the triumph of eternal life in dying, resurrection in death. "And thou hearest the sound thereof, but canst not tell whence it cometh, and whither it goeth:²⁶ so is every one that is born of the Spirit" (John 3:8). And nothing prevents us from understanding this "birth" not only in the strict sense (baptism) but also in the broadest sense of all contact with the Spirit.

The descent into the world of the Holy Spirit, that He may abide with us forever, is His *final* descent; it knows neither a return ascent to heaven nor any interruptions. But by descending He does not leave the Holy Trinity, in which He abides from all eternity, uniting the Father with the Son and reposing upon the Son. In this sense, is the Holy Spirit not that "right hand of the Father," at which, according to the figurative expression, sits the Ascended Christ in the Father's Glory and Love, which precisely corresponds to the "right hand"? And in general, in virtue of the supra-temporality and supra-spatiality of the Holy Spirit, there are no obstacles to His abiding both in Heaven and on earth. The *descent from heaven* into the world signifies here only that union of God with the world by the deification of man which was accomplished in the very heart of creation by Christ and becomes, in the Holy Spirit, the irrevocable possession of the creature. This descent can therefore know different measures — not one, unique, absolute measure such as that of the incarnation of the Second hypostasis, but the limitless possibility of ascent from measure to measure (here we have yet another meaning of the Gospel text that is full of meanings: "God giveth not the Spirit by measure" [John 3:34]). In each particular case of the bestowal of the Spirit there also occurs His hypostatic descent, for the Holy Spirit *Himself* bestows His gift. This gift, in this sense, is the Holy Spirit; but the Holy Spirit is not this gift, for He is not exhausted by it.

Having assumed the human nature in His Incarnation, Christ was forever united with it; and in his ontological essence, the Old Adam, i.e.,

26. The subject of this text, *to pneuma,* is understood both with reference to the breath of the wind (as in the King James Version) and with reference to the Spirit Himself. But nothing prevents us from keeping both meanings: the wind is a natural simile for the Spirit. The Lord's declaration therefore indicates both the image and the Proto-image; otherwise, the very thought here would not be accessible.

the natural, creaturely, fallen man, became the New Adam in Christ. Humanity came to belong to Christ. But it was not only necessary that Christ, by virtue of his Divine-human freedom, in His two wills and energies, assume humanity as His own. It was also necessary that humanity itself, in its depths already united with Christ by virtue of the Divine Incarnation, receive Christ into its own life, become Christ's — "the body of Christ." This is what is accomplished by the Holy Spirit by His descent, by means of which He bestows upon humanity the life of Christ in its fullness, inspiring humanity with this life. The descent of the Spirit therefore signifies the fulfillment of the work of Divine Incarnation in the world and in humanity; and at the Pentecost the Holy Spirit descends not upon the Virgin Mary, as at the Annunciation, and not upon Jesus, as at the Epiphany, but upon all of humanity and all of nature (the "cosmos" of the icons of the Pentecost).

The deification of all creation occurs. The Incarnation of Christ and the descent of the Holy Spirit are two aspects of one and the same act: the act of Divine-humanity. Heavenly Divine-humanity, Sophia, uniting itself here with creaturely Divine-humanity and being ontologically joined with the latter in the God-man, reveals itself as the supreme meaning and goal of creation. The Incarnation, which has universal force because it is accomplished in the person of Christ, does not exhaust the work of Divine-humanity. This work continues *beyond* the Divine Incarnation, in the descent of the Holy Spirit upon *all* humanity, upon *all* creation. Here, this work has an extensive, not an intensive, universality. And *after* the descent from heaven of the Son there necessarily *follows* the descent of the Holy Spirit, "another Comforter," in Whom Christ Himself abides on earth, but now not by a personal abiding, but as *the power of Christ* bestowed by the Spirit; He abides not visibly, but mysteriously. Although, for the "kingdom of grace," in the aeon of the "militant church," the two hypostases of the Divine-humanity, the Son and the Holy Spirit, have, through Their descent from heaven, united Their life forever with creation, They do not appear to creation in Their hypostatic being: Christ acts only as Christ's power, or is bestowed as His mysterious Body and Blood, but not as a Person; and the Holy Spirit is known only by His gifts. This is, of course, not the final and definitive self-revelation of the Dyad of the Son and the Holy Spirit.

The Pentecost is directed toward *eschatological* culminations, as is the Ascension, whose promise consists in the fact that the One Who ascended to heaven will come again by descending from heaven. One must remember that the prophecy of Joel that is applied by the apostle Peter to the

Pentecost has a specifically eschatological character.[27] It takes at its point of departure "the last days" ("and it shall come to pass in the last days, saith God, I will pour out of my Spirit upon all flesh" [Acts 2:17]), which are, in general, equated with the whole New Testament epoch; and its end point is the coming of the "great and notable day of the Lord" (2:20), i.e., the end of the world or, more precisely, of this aeon. In this eschatological aspect, the Pentecost has not yet come; more precisely, it has not been accomplished, for its accomplishment is only at its beginning. And without question, it was at its beginning when Peter pronounced his speech, applying the text of Joel's prophecy. But the beginning, especially in the language of prophecies, already contains the final accomplishment.

In the parousia, Christ will come not only in His power, but also in His Person. But will the Holy Spirit come in His Person, or will the world always know Him only as the coming and going breath of Divine inspiration? Here we confront an as yet unfathomed mystery — the manifestation of the Countenance of the Third hypostasis. Our feelings are similar to those that could have been experienced by the Old Testament humanity, which awaited the Redeemer with hope and longing. The Old Testament humanity was powerless to know what was unmanifested, even though it sometimes approached it in its presentiments, even though it sometimes almost glimpsed Him (in the Messianic prophecies). But today we who resemble those Old Testament men in our relation to the hypostatic manifestation of the Holy Spirit, we do not have even such a presentiment. Indeed, we do not have any presentiment at all, for all the images purported to be true (in Montanism or Gnosticism) have been found to be false and blasphemous. We do not have an image. . . . And even that image which is unquestionably true is, in reality, unknown and inaccessible to us: the image of the Most Pure and Most Blessed Mother of God in Her state of heavenly glorification. But Her earthly image, which we did not see but which we know (and which has inspired Her icons), has already stung our heart. . . . This image of infinite meekness, humility, love, and tenderness, of "spiritual beauty," *the beauty of holiness,* is

---

27. The entire context of Acts 1:6-8 is worth noting. The disciples ask Christ prior to His Ascension, "wilt thou at this time restore again the kingdom to Israel?" (In their language and for them this signifies the final eschatological culmination.) And the Lord, deflecting the direct question ("it is not for you to know the times or the seasons, which the Father hath put in his own power"), nevertheless indicates to them the form of this culmination. He gives them not a direct but an indirect answer to their question: "ye shall receive power . . . [of] . . . the Holy Spirit . . . come upon you." This power is precisely the eschatological culmination, which has not yet been revealed.

invincible. Before this image, if it appears to the world and becomes accessible to it, no human heart will persevere in its hardness, but will melt and will be transfigured by the fiery tongue of love. "Beauty will save the world" (Dostoevsky, *The Idiot*) — but this will be the beauty of Holiness.[28]

But the paths of Beauty-Holiness are unsearchable, for they are not subject to logical understanding. Beauty-Holiness is a true Miracle, the only one deserving of this name, for it is Transfiguration. But before it is actualized, Beauty-Holiness is a mystery. However, not knowing this mystery and refraining from futile attempts to comprehend it with our human powers, we nevertheless already know it, i.e., we know that *it is* and that it is *for us*. In relation to this mystery, we feel ourselves not in an empty world but as if in the Old Testament. The same thing holds, relative to the *hypostatic* revelation of the Holy Spirit, for the event that represents the completion of the New Testament and, in this sense, the foundation of the New Testament Church: the Pentecost.

Like the descent of the Son of God, which was His kenosis, *the descent of the Holy Spirit* is the kenosis of the Third hypostasis. The very "descent" into the world, the participation in creaturely life on the part of divine life, is already a kenotic act. But the kenosis of the Holy Spirit must be understood differently from the kenosis of the Son. The latter is the removal

28. Beauty will also save the world from the enchantments of illusory beauty, pseudo-beauty, which is alienated from and even hostile to Holiness. It will save it from the pseudo-beauty of the "whore," whose image can be found in the Old Testament (the Proverbs) as well as in the New (Revelation), in opposition to the true Beauty of Christ's Bride (The Song of Songs and Revelation). Beauty, as beautiful appearance, which has preserved the outward radiance of the Holy Spirit but has separated itself from His power, which has become an instrument of sin and temptation, the lie of Sodom — this beauty is a whited sepulcher, inwardly full of a corpse's decomposition. It is sufficient for this pseudo-beauty to lose its opacity, its external character, and it will disappear like a mirage, exposed and condemned in its own ugliness. In the *preliminary and external* manifestation of beauty as the power of the Spirit, however, it is irresistible and defeats spiritual beauty, which is invisible, inward, true, unmanifested. Furthermore, this pseudo-beauty *competes* with the beauty of holiness, and this constitutes the tragedy of beauty, the most intimate tragedy of the life of fallen man in the fallen world, the tragedy of the fallen Sophia. This tragedy of the coexistence of two principles in connection with the beauty of the world, the principle of Sodom and "the ideal of the Madonna," was felt with a special acuteness by the Russian genius (Gogol, Dostoevsky), which requires a special sense of beauty as the all-conquering power, as the action of the Holy Spirit. But Beauty will defeat beauties in their soulless beautifulness; only spiritual beauty will become real, and true spirituality will arm itself with the power of beauty and become invincible and irresistible.

of divine glory, the self-diminution of divine life in the God-Man, which is restored through the feat of His earthly life. By contrast, in the kenosis of His descent from heaven, the Holy Spirit is not diminished in His divine life and does not lose His Glory, for He Himself is this Glory in His hypostatic being. In exact conformity with this, in descending from heaven, the Holy Spirit does not leave the latter but abides in all His divine magnificence. His kenosis is expressed in His directedness toward the world, in His *connection* with the world, which connection is signified, strictly speaking, by His descent from heaven; and this connection is a *new* one, different from that which had existed since the very creation of the world, when the Spirit of God moved upon the face of the waters. And in the course of the entire Old Testament the Spirit of God precisely moves *upon* the face of creation, where He is sent by an express act of the Father, as if from outside, for the Spirit of God did not have His own place in the world. But after the Incarnation such a place came into existence: this is precisely Christ's humanity, which, although it ascended to heaven for glorification in the personal body of Christ, abides in the world *by virtue of the Divine Incarnation,* precisely as the work of Christ that is being accomplished by the Holy Spirit. It is by virtue of Christ's Incarnation that the Holy Spirit abides in the world.

But the *power* of this abiding is limited and does not correspond to the *fullness* of the gifts of the Holy Spirit. This limitedness depends on the receptivity of the world and of humanity. If the fullness of the Divine life in Christ is determined by the measure of the human nature, then here the measure of the reception of the Holy Spirit is determined by the degree of this reception, where the determining principle is human freedom. Grace does not coerce freedom; it convinces it. A kind of *duel* occurs between freedom and grace, between creaturely humanity and the gifts of the Holy Spirit. There is no doubt as to the final outcome of this duel, if only because the Holy Spirit wields the invincible power of Beauty. But this duel has duration and spatial extent. And in general the apostle Paul calls the Church a growing body or organism, while the Gospel calls it a tree growing from a seed and knowing its times and seasons. And the kenosis of the Holy Spirit in His gifts extends to all these times, although, ontologically, these are already the "last times" in relation to the fullness of divine culmination. His gifts are not received in the full measure of their bestowal, and therefore they are not bestowed in their full measure.

The kenosis of the Holy Spirit consists precisely in His voluntary self-limitation in the face of creaturely freedom and inertia. If love is patience united with humility, then the hypostasis of Love, the Holy Spirit, manifests Himself here as Patience and Humility: having come into the world, grace, by its essence being *indeclinabilis et insuperabilis* [stubborn and unconquerable], stops expectantly at the door of every heart. "Behold, I stand at the door, and knock: if any man hear my voice, and open the door, I will come in to him, and will sup with him, and he with me" (Rev. 3:20). (It is implied that, "if he does not open the door, I will not come in.") This is said not only about Christ, but also about the Holy Spirit, Who by His inspirations of grace knocks on the heart of man, calling him to acquire the Christ Who lives in him, according to the dyadic principle: "if any man have not the Spirit of Christ, he is none of his" (Rom. 8:9). This image expresses that interrelation of grace and creaturely freedom which in general is characteristic for the action of the Third hypostasis in the world in His kenosis.

The Divine Incarnation, received by creaturely freedom in the person of the Virgin Mary, was accomplished without hindrance in a single act and was realized — through the Savior's earthly life — in the course of a definite, limited, and even relatively brief period of time. Creaturely freedom could no longer hinder or resist this divine act of descent from heaven and the assumption by God of the human essence. But such was not the case with regard to the accomplishment of the *work* of Divine Incarnation in the world, which consists in receiving God and which belongs to the domain of creaturely freedom. The descent of the Holy Spirit was accomplished at the "third hour," also at a definite moment of time, just as the descent from heaven of the Word and His Incarnation by conception was accomplished at a definite moment of time. But in contrast to the Divine Incarnation, which finds a definite place for itself in the world in the person of the God-Man, the descent of the Holy Spirit has a domain of action that is spatially indeterminate and temporally unlimited — the whole world in its freedom.[29] Therefore, if the kenosis of the Word refers to the state of the Divine Incarnation *before* glorification, the kenosis of the Holy Spirit refers to His very descent into the world. Being pre-accomplished, as it were, in the Pentecost, this descent is further accomplished in the course of our entire aeon — in the "last times." Thus, the kenosis of the Holy Spirit is not His self-diminution through the abandonment of the Divine Glory in the fullness of His Divine being (as in the kenosis of the Word), but consists in condescension or adaptation, as it were, to creaturely inertia, infirmity, and opposition to His entry into the world. Having descended from heaven, the Holy Spirit encounters, as

---

29. Here we find revealed yet another meaning of John 3:34, this text which has many meanings: "God giveth not the Spirit by measure."

it were, interference or limitation upon His entry into the world; and therefore He remains as yet *above* the world, as it were, seeking to become attached to it, to deify it, to become united with it. This kenosis of the Holy Spirit continues in the course of our entire aeon.

And this kenosis of the Spirit is united with the relative ineffectiveness, as it were, of the Incarnation in the world. Having received from the Father, as the fruit of His ministry, "all power .. in heaven and in earth" (Matt. 28:18), Christ does not yet possess this power in actuality, inasmuch as the Holy Spirit has not yet taken possession of the world and transfigured it. In the language of christology, this can be expressed by saying that, of Christ's three ministries, two have been fulfilled, whereas the third, the royal ministry, is still continuing. Christ is the King, but His enthronement has not yet been accomplished. It is being accomplished by the action of the Holy Spirit, by the power of the Pentecost. The Holy Spirit has descended into the world; however, He has not yet made His abode in us (which is why, in the prayer to the Holy Spirit, we pray, "come and make Your abode in us"), but is only in the process of doing so. That is why Christ is the King but He does not reign; on the contrary, in "the form of a servant" (Phil. 2:7), He suffers together with His humanity, even though He abides in His heavenly Glory.

Thus, the *different* modes of the kenosis of the Son and the Holy Spirit are interwoven and united in a single accomplishment — the coming of the Kingdom of God (which is "at hand"[30] now that the Incarnation has occurred). And the basic text concerning Christ's enthronement ("for he must reign, till he hath put all enemies under his feet" [1 Cor. 15:25]) refers precisely to the action of the Holy Spirit in the world, to the power of the Pentecost. This resolves the apparent contradiction between the glorified state of Christ in heaven and the continuing kenosis of His royal ministry in the world. This kenosis is also the kenosis of the Holy Spirit, Who is bestowed only to the extent He can be received by creation; His kenosis merges in this sense with the kenosis of Christ's royal ministry. This ministry will be completed when the kenosis of the Holy Spirit, as well as that of Christ, is totally overcome, "when God will be all in all,"

---

30. This phrase, which opens the preaching of both the Forerunner and Christ, has as its first object the Incarnation, but it also attests to the descent of the Holy Spirit as the "kingdom of God," immediately in the Baptism of Christ, and then in the world Pentecost. This is indicated by the Forerunner, who with particular insistence attests that among people there is One Who will baptize by water and the Spirit, i.e., Who will again send the Holy Spirit upon the waters of creation on the day of the Pentecost.

when the Kingdom of God is established in all creation. Until then, although He is glorified, Christ continues to be crucified in the world in His humanity and the Lamb continues to be slaughtered in the Eucharistic sacrifice of this continuing Golgotha. *Christ is in the process of being enthroned in the world by the Holy Spirit,* and the kenosis of the Spirit is therefore also the earthly kenosis of the glorified Christ. For static rationalistic thought, this antinomy appears to be a contradiction, but this apparent contradiction is *dynamically* overcome in the living stream of the Divine-human deification of creation.

An essential fact clearly follows from this: The Pentecost is continuing in the world; it has begun but it has not been completed.[31] The gifts of grace of the Holy Spirit, now not in the vision of the tongues of fire but invisibly, continue to pour forth into the world, invisibly transfiguring it. The Holy Spirit inspires humanity, thereby taking part in its history. The kenosis of the Spirit, one and indivisible, makes His revelation continue "multifariously and manifoldly" in *history* — the history of the Church, of humanity, of the entire world. The kenosis of the Spirit includes His particular inspirations, His different gifts, in human creative activity, making Him the all-penetrating principle of life.[32] If one can speak of a kind of pan-Christism in the sense of the essential victory of Christ over the world, won in the very heart of the latter, then in another sense one can also speak of the all-penetrating action of the Holy Spirit in the world, striving to possess and transfigure the world completely. One can see how this pan-pneumatism, this doctrine of the inhabitation of the world by the Holy Spirit ("every soul is quickened by the Holy Spirit"), could have been accused of pantheism, an ambiguous and not always consistent notion, replete with illusory terror.

But, to be sure, this *continuing* Pentecost of our aeon is not a bad infinity, which has neither completion nor fullness. On the contrary, it strives to accomplish itself *to the end,* to the point where "God will be all in all." And in this sense the Pentecost leads to the eschatological culmination and to a new aeon; it merges with the parousia. At the same time, the life of grace in the Holy Spirit leads us beyond the limits of earthly, empir-

---

31. Swete (*The Holy Spirit in the New Testament,* p. 83) writes the following: "The day of the Pentecost was the beginning of a Divine economy, which is to continue to the end of the present age."

32. H. W. Robinson (*The Christian Experience of the Holy Spirit* [London, 1928], p. 87) writes: "The cardinal principle [of the revelation of the Spirit] . . . is the principle of 'kenosis', i.e., the selfemptying and humiliation of spirit when it expresses itself, as it always must, in 'degrees of reality' lower than itself."

ical life, insofar as it unites us with the world on the other side, with the kingdom of saints and angels, with the glorified church.

The fact of the *continuing* Pentecost is also connected with the absence in it of a *hypostatic* revelation of the Holy Spirit, Who manifests Himself only in His gifts. In contrast to the Second hypostasis, Who in His descent manifests Himself all at once, although He conceals His Divinity in His kenosis even from Himself, as it were — in contrast to the Second hypostasis, the Third hypostasis manifests His Divinity but conceals Himself. The *hypostatic* manifestation of the Holy Spirit belongs to the future age in the capacity of the crowning of His entire revelation in His Divinity. That is why, even on the feast of the Pentecost, the aspect of the Holy Spirit considered is not so much His hypostasic descent as His being sent *in His gifts* by the Son from the Father. He is considered not as a subject but as an object (if one can use such an expression), not as the Giver but as the Gift. The Son is essentially the active person here, which is why, liturgically, this feast basically has a christological character. What is celebrated here is more Christ's completion of His ministry than the action of the Third hypostasis Who descends into the world. In a negative manner this is confirmed liturgically, by the *silent* celebration (as if one is immersed in deep shadow) of the day of the Holy Spirit; it is as if we celebrate a mystery of the future age, for which the present age does not have any words. To this corresponds the poverty of the theological interpretation of the Pentecost, which considers it to be only a means to salvation, not a new and independent fact of the descent of the Third hypostasis into the world. All questions related to the *theology* of the Pentecost are reduced to the following ill-posed and thus false question: What conclusions relative to the procession of the Holy Spirit, understood in the sense of origination, can be drawn from the fact of the sending down of the Holy Spirit from the Father by Christ? In other words, can this be interpreted for or against the Filioque? Scholastic phantoms of the imaginary dogma have veiled from the eyes of theologians the great power of this event, whose only equal is the Birth of Christ.

V. The Gifts of the Pentecost

1. The Descent of the Holy Spirit

The descent of the Holy Spirit gave knowledge of Divine-humanity to "the disciples and apostles" and, through them, to the entire Church. The content of the apostolic preaching concerns the crucified Christ (Acts 2:23). The entire book of the Acts of the Apostles is a triumphant hymn about the Resurrection,[33] and it is permeated with triumphant joy in the Holy Spirit (which is why this book is read on the radiant days of the Pentecost). A new sense of the Church as life in Christ by the Holy Spirit, of unity in the love of the Church, was born in the world. This was the *catholic*[34] sense of church unity, in fulfillment of Christ's mysterious commandment: "A new commandment I give unto you, That ye love one another" (John 13:34). And we immediately have before us the fact of this new life in the sobornost[35] of the body of the Church, which is born simultaneously with the apostolic preaching, as the first and fundamental gift of the Holy Spirit — an organic, ontological multi-unity. Those baptized under the influence of Peter's first preaching (about three thousand souls) "continued stedfastly in the apostles' doctrine and fellowship, and in breaking of bread, and in prayers" (Acts 2:42), "and all that believed were together, and had all things common" (2:44). "And the multitude of them that believed were of one heart and of one soul: neither said any of them that ought of the things which he possessed was his own; but they had all things common . . . and great grace was upon them all. Neither was there any among them that lacked" (4:32-34). (Therefore, the attempt to conceal part of the money gained from the selling of the possession by Ananias and Sapphira is considered by the apostle Peter to be a "lie to the Holy Spirit" [5:3].)

This catholicity, which corresponds to Christ's commandment, "Go ye therefore, and teach all nations" (Matt. 28:19), is attested by the symbolic miracle (however one interprets it) of the preaching intelligible in all languages, in contrast to the Babel confusion of languages, which represents the destruction of catholicity: "And they were filled with the Holy Spirit, and began to speak with other tongues, as the Spirit gave them utterance" (Acts 2:4). This catholic communion is accompanied by the

---

33. This explains the custom in the Orthodox Church of reading The Acts of the Apostles before the Plashchanitsa (the icon depicting Christ in the tomb) during the Easter service, on the night of Christ's Radiant Resurrection.

34. The term "catholic" here refers not to Roman Catholicism but to the universality of the Church, to its sobornost (see n. 35 below). — Trans.

35. Sobornost is the Russian term for the "catholicity" of the Church; the adjective form is *sobornyi* (catholic). Sobornost (derived from *sobirat'*, to gather, and related to *sobor*, council) is the unity of the Church as a divinely inspired fellowship. It is community in love, communion in the spirit, the free union of the faithful in the pure heart of the Church. — Trans.

Eucharistic communion, the "breaking of bread." The Eucharist was possible only by virtue of the Pentecost. The being filled with the Holy Spirit changes the very personalities of the apostles. They become different people, as it were: "Thou hast made wise men out of illiterate ones; Thou hast made theologians out of fishermen" (as it is said at the Pentecost vespers). Timid men become bold: "Now when they saw the boldness of Peter and John, and perceived that they were unlearned and ignorant men, they marveled" (Acts 4:13).

But this spiritual regeneration does not abolish individualities, does not make individuals resemble one another. As before, we see Peter, Paul, John, and the others, with their marked personalities; and the sending down of the Spirit thus signifies not a mediumistic possession, but a state of personal inspiration, in which the individual tension of the human spirit receives the Divine Spirit. The apostles become strong in word and spirit, and receive the power to work miracles. The most remarkable thing in the life of the apostles, as well as in the life of the other sons of the "apostolic age," is that the coming of the Holy Spirit is, for them, something unquestionable and indisputably palpable; and this is the case not only for those upon whom He descends but also for those who are bystanders. The inspiration of the Holy Spirit loses its mysterious character, as it were; it becomes explicit and indubitable. The Holy Spirit descends with the laying on of the apostles' hands; He fills — at a certain moment — the apostles themselves and the apostolic fathers, as the Acts of the Apostles repeatedly attest. And so it becomes completely clear and verifiable whether or not certain persons have received the descent of the Spirit. Those who have received it testify by the Holy Spirit: "we are his witnesses of these things; and so is also the Holy Spirit" (5:32); "it seemed good to the Holy Spirit, and to us" (15:28) (in the course of time, this phrase became an official formula, often vacuous and pretentious).

This presence of the Holy Spirit Himself, independently of the particular gifts bestowed by Him, is the most remarkable aspect of the apostolic church and imparts a particular concreteness to its life. This is not merely divine inspiration from above, but precisely the grace-bestowing presence of the Holy Spirit Himself. Particularly significant in this respect are the numerous cases of direct guidance by the Holy Spirit.[36] These cases clearly demonstrate that, in the Pentecost, not only are the gifts of the Spirit bestowed, but the Holy Spirit Himself has descended hypostatically, and it is He Himself Who acts through His gifts: the Giver

36. See Acts 10:19; 11:12; 13:2-4; 16:6-7; 20:22; 21:4; 21:11.

is recognized in the gifts. "The Acts of the Apostles" are the works of the Holy Spirit that are accomplished through the apostles. These "Acts" are the works of His guidance of the Church, which guidance became ontologically possible only through His descent. But one must distinguish cases of such direct *guidance* from the communication of the *gifts* of the Holy Spirit: these gifts are a direct action of the Holy Spirit, but they do not contain His personal revelation.

Both the Acts of the Apostles and the apostolic epistles speak of the different gifts of the Holy Spirit or of "being filled" by Him, but this is *not* accompanied by that sense of His *personal* guidance which is spoken of in certain particular cases. In other words, there can be a reception of the gifts of the Holy Spirit without His *personal* revelation (in particular, all sacraments have this character). That which is described in the Acts of the Apostles is therefore not the general norm which can be applied to any and all receptions of the Holy Spirit. On the contrary, this was an exclusive event in the life of the Church, which has not been repeated (to be sure, we cannot say that it will never be repeated, for the Holy Spirit can repeat it whenever it pleases Him). Likewise, life in Christ, or His personal presence (and not merely a general sense of His power and life), is bestowed, if He wills it, in certain special and extraordinary cases: to the apostle Paul, to the first martyr Stephen, to certain saints. Similarly, the power of the Holy Spirit is communicated in sacraments and gifts, whereas His presence (His manifestation, as it were) is felt only in certain extraordinary cases, if He wills it. In the overwhelming majority of cases, His presence is replaced by inspiration or, more precisely, by a divinely inspired state.[37]

That is why it is completely erroneous to make that which is reported in the Acts of the Apostles the norm for all men and for all times, and to seek on this basis not only general inspiration but also concrete guidance in all the decisions of life. Such an understanding, characteristic of certain religious movements, replaces the fullness of the Divine-human life in the Church with magical suggestiveness or a mechanical *deus ex ma-*

---

37. Perhaps, to this distinction between the personal revelation of the Holy Spirit and His grace-bestowing action, it is possible to apply (with certain modifications) the distinction between ousia and energy which lies at the basis of St. Gregory Palamas's theology. The personal revelation of the Holy Spirit corresponds to ousia (which Palamas considers to be totally transcendent), whereas the grace of the Holy Spirit corresponds to energy. Palamas's theology is so undeveloped and unfinished, however, that we still need a special study of the true meaning of the doctrine and of the real significance of its basic concepts.

china. The Holy Spirit bestows His inspirations and instructions in response to human efforts and seekings, joining the one and the other in a unified act of human inspiration illuminated from above by grace, that is, in an act of Divine-human inspiration (which, in an abbreviated manner and therefore imprecisely and even ambiguously, is usually called divine inspiration). The element of human seeking and creativity cannot be abolished or replaced by some chiromancy or magical suggestiveness, in which man is transformed into a *tabula rasa* for the recording of outside influences. To be sure, the Holy Spirit guides those who seek Him and bestows upon them His power and wisdom, but this wisdom is also human wisdom, inspired by the Holy Spirit. That is why, except for cases of supreme saintliness, which also is not always infallible, even the most inspired thoughts and decisions are humanly limited; and in this sense, they are not infallible. They are only relatively, not absolutely, true. Even with reference to the life of the Church, one must speak of the *infallibilitas* of the Church only in the sense of its *indefectibilitas,* of the *sufficiency* of each of its answers given in the framework of relativity.

Thus, even for the apostles and for their epoch, direct guidance by the Spirit of God was something exceptional, a special and express act of the Spirit of God. Such guidance was not continuous and constant. The divinely inspired state, which was transformed into a particular state of ecstasy ("he was filled with the Holy Spirit") at times of personal creative intensity, was sufficient even for this epoch in which the Spirit was superabundant.

In other words, such guidance is a special gift, *one of the gifts* of the Holy Spirit, alongside others; but it is not an action of the Holy Spirit as such, which would exclude human creative self-determination, capable of receiving divine inspiration. The apostolic ministry consisted not only in acting under guidance, but also in accomplishing feats of personal creative activity, which necessarily involved audaciously exposing oneself to spiritual *risk*. Such was the apostle Paul's decision to preach to the Gentiles (first in Antioch: see Acts 13), for which he did not have the kind of direct "guidance" that the apostle Peter had from the Spirit (Acts 11:12).

2. *The Gift of Prophecy*

One should mention in particular the gift of prophecy and the appearance of prophets in the primitive church. After the cessation of the Old Testament prophecy with its special vocation and ministry, there appears the New Testament prophetic ministry. It does not yet have a highly distinctive character, but it nevertheless differs from the Old Testament prophetic ministry in that it comes *after* the Incarnation and is a gift of the continuing Pentecost.[38]

The gift of prophecy was not a general gift bestowed by the apostolic laying on of hands (except in a few exceptional cases, as in Ephesus [see Acts 19:6]). Rather, it was a special gift, proper only to certain persons. This agrees with the place occupied by the gift of prophecy in the apostle Paul's enumeration of the gifts of the Holy Spirit; he places prophets right after apostles: "first apostles, secondarily prophets, thirdly teachers" (I Cor. 12:28). Generally speaking, prophecy is a normal ministry, as it were, in the primitive church, and is considered as such in Paul's enumeration of the gifts of the Spirit (I Cor. 12:10). To this we may append the following exhortations of the apostle Paul: "Quench not the Spirit. Despise not prophesyings" (I Thess. 5:19-20); and "desire spiritual gifts . . . that ye may prophesy" (I Cor. 14:1; cf. 14:39). In Paul's epistles, there is no precise definition of prophet and prophecy. First of all, prophecy is compared with teaching. Such is the interpretation of the gift of prophecy given in I Corinthians 14 and developed primarily in opposition to unintelligible glossolalia: "he that prophesieth speaketh unto men to edification, and exhortation, and comfort [*paraklēsin*]" (14:3). The power of prophecy is further described in such terms: "But if all prophesy, and there come in one that believeth not, or one unlearned, he is convinced of all, he is judged of all: and thus are the secrets of his heart made manifest; and so falling down on his face he will worship God, and report that God is in you of a truth" (14:24-25).

In the primitive church the gift of prophecy was considered universal and self-evident, as it were, as a manifestation of the action of the Holy Spirit: "Let the prophets speak two or three, and let the other judge. If any thing be revealed to another that sitteth by, let the first hold his peace. For ye may all prophesy one by one, that all may learn, and all may be comforted. And the spirits of the prophets are subject to the prophets" (14:29-32). Here, prophesying represents a kind of liturgical rite, like the modern sermon, whose origin can be traced back to ancient prophecy. But the preaching of sermons or prophesying can also be done outside the liturgy and even by persons who are not ordained. There is no indication by the

---

38. Swete (*The Holy Spirit in the New Testament*, p. 108) writes: "The coming of the Spirit had restored to the Church the gift of prophecy, and the prophets . . . took rank in the Church above the local bishops and deacons."

apostle Paul that prophets were members of the clergy in any sense at all, and this would scarcely conform with the indeterminacy of the hierarchical order existing then. It is sufficient to recognize that prophets were charismatics in the general sense of this word.

But in other cases, prophecy differs from teaching. In particular, in the Acts of the Apostles, prophecy refers primarily to the foreseeing of the future. And we have a grandiose example of New Testament prophecy concerning the future in the Revelation of the apostle, evangelist, and prophet John the Theologian. The gift of prophecy is, in general, included in the gift of apostleship, inasmuch as, in particular, some of the apostles were writers of divinely inspired sacred books (2 Pet. 1:20).

One cannot fail to see examples of prophetic ministry in certain decisive events of apostolic preaching. Such is the apostle Peter's preaching to the centurion Cornelius. Although it was prepared by a special vision and a direct command from the Spirit (as was the case with the ancient prophets), the fulfillment of this command required prophetic sacrifice and audacity. This is even more evident in the example of the apostle Paul, who, even without any particular external signs and obeying only his inner voice, began to preach to the Gentiles. This took place in Antioch: Having failed amongst the Jews, "Paul and Barnabas waxed bold, and said, It was necessary that the word of God should first have been spoken to you: but seeing ye put it from you, and judge yourselves unworthy of everlasting life, lo, we turn to the Gentiles" (Acts 13:46). And only because of this prophetic audacity is Paul sent to Jerusalem to the "apostolic" council for the examination of this decision (Acts 15).

We have a prophecy of similar power in the apostle Paul's discourse about the fate of Israel (Rom. 9-11). Here we have, so to speak, a whole range of prophecy: first, an immense sorrow of the soul, an affliction which recalls that of the prophet Daniel (Rom. 10), perplexity, a question addressed to God: "I have great heaviness and continual sorrow in my heart. For I could wish that myself were accursed from Christ for my brethren, my kinsmen according to the flesh: who are Israelites" (Rom. 9:2-4); and the *prophetic answer*, the revelation of the "mystery" (11:25) that "all Israel shall be saved" (11:26). Prophecy will not end in the Church even in the last times, when God will "give power . . . unto two witnesses . . . [who] shall prophesy a thousand two hundred and threescore days" (Rev. 11:3), or to "two prophets [who] tormented them that dwelt on the earth" (11:10). In Revelation, the very "testimony of Jesus" (19:10), i.e., the active and creative profession of faith in Him, is explained as "the spirit of prophecy" (19:10). Thus, New Testament prophecy is expanded and generalized here to the ultimate degree, for the prophetic spirit comes to include the entire power of "the testimony of Jesus."

Precisely such an interpretation of the power of the Pentecost as universal prophecy is furnished by its authentic exegesis in Acts 2:16-21; this exegesis is given by Peter himself in his first discourse inspired by the Holy Spirit, immediately after His descent. Peter uses the prophecy of Joel (Joel 2:28-32) to explain what has occurred ("this is that which was spoken by the prophet Joel"). What do we find in this prophecy? One must first point out that it is placed in a general eschatological framework: "it shall come to pass in the last days" (2:17), which are described in images of Judaic apocalyptic eschatology. "And I will shew wonders in heaven above, and signs in the earth beneath; blood, and fire, and vapour of smoke: the sun shall be turned into darkness, and the moon into blood, before that great and notable day of the Lord to come" (2:19-20).

The event of the Pentecost thereby receives an eschatological interpretation: it is understood to include this entire aeon until the very end of the world. This necessarily leads to the conclusion that the Pentecost has a duration equal to this entire aeon (and of course beyond it) and that, consequently, it is by no means exhausted by its initial moment, i.e., by the events that occurred that day in Jerusalem. Indeed, this is self-evident, for however important in the life of the Church may be the apostle Peter's first discourse and the resulting establishment of the first Christian community (about three thousand persons), this is simply incommensurate with the immensity of the event as it is explicated by Peter himself in the light of the prophecy of Joel. This is directly attested in Peter's words: "For the promise is unto you, and to your children, and to all that are afar off, even as many as the Lord God shall call" (Acts 2:39).

The very event of the Pentecost thus acquires a prophetic character, is directed toward the future, toward that *Future* which, according to Christ's promise, will be shown by the Holy Spirit (John 16:13); and this prophecy is included in the very power of the event of the Pentecost as its spiritual wings. And it is remarkable: When we turn to the content of Joel's text, included in this eschatological framework, we do not find in it anything except a prophecy about universal prophesying: "And it shall come to pass in the last days, saith God, I will pour out of my Spirit upon all flesh: and your sons and your daughters shall prophesy, and your young men shall see visions, and your old men shall dream dreams: and on my servants and on my handmaidens I will pour out in those days of my Spirit; and they shall prophesy" (Acts 2:17-18). (The Old Testament analogue of this text is Moses' speech, which is read on the feast of the Pentecost: "would God that all the Lord's people were prophets, and that the Lord would put his spirit upon them!" [Num. 11:29].) This prophecy has a universal character, but its authentic exegesis indicates that the prophetic gift includes the very *power* of the Pentecost. Clearly, it is a question here not of the particular gift of prophetic ministry among other gifts and ministries (as in 1 Cor. 12:4-5), but of the general and fundamental gift of the Pentecost.

What then is the nature of this gift and what does its power consist in (besides the express gift of teaching, which is, of course, a particular gift, not a general one)? In the Old Testament we already see the gift of prophecy expressed in a particular ecstatic state, which, being visible to bystanders, was thought to be essential for prophecy. There existed particular prophetic schools: "the sons of the prophets" (2 Kings 2:15); there is undeniably an analogy here with certain ecstatic movements in paganism. The impression made by the apostles upon bystanders after the descent of the Holy Spirit was, "these men are full of new wine" (Acts 2:13), that is, they were in a certain state of madness or possession. Likewise, the descent of the Holy Spirit upon those being baptized was accompanied by manifestations visible to all (cf. the story of Simon the sorcerer [8:17-19]). But such ecstasy was only an external (and, of course, scarcely necessary) manifestation of the same spiritual possession which accompanied the gift of prophecy (and which sometimes provoked the Old Testament prophets to behave like "holy fools," to perform strange and incomprehensible acts that appeared crazy to men of "common sense").

The gift of prophecy makes a man *other* than himself; it makes him live a life not his own but which he assimilates as his own. In prophecy, we go out of ourselves ("ecstasy") and a new principle of life enters into us. Prophecy is the *meeting* and union of the human spirit with another principle. It is an extremely *active* state of the spirit, in which the latter strives to meet the higher principle, in order to become fructified by and identified with it. In this sense, prophecy is an extremely *creative* state of the human spirit, in which the latter strives to receive creative conception and to accomplish spiritual birth (it does not create out of itself, out of the void of its creaturely nothing, becoming frozen in an impotent theomachic pose). Prophecy is also what we call inspiration; moreover, it is identical with inspiration, being the joy and rapture of the latter.

On the human side, prophecy is *the eros of the spirit*. This aspect of prophecy is examined by Plato in his *Symposium* (a work which is the pinnacle of natural inspiration) with a profundity that almost surpasses the measure of human inspiration. Eros, as is man, is a son of Porus and

Penia, of the creaturely and noncreaturely principles.[39] The winged god gives man the power to ascend into the world above in order to be inspired by this world and to give birth in beauty, to create. In his pagan limitedness, Plato did not know where Eros comes from or who he is, but he was able to provide a useful mythologeme for the theologeme of prophecy.

Of course, there can be diverse inspirations, just as there can be diverse spirits, but there is only one true inspiration and only one true eros: the prophesying about which the prophet Joel speaks. What its object or theme is does not have decisive significance for prophesying; that is a question of fact. What is essential is to live in a creative and inspired manner, to realize life's possibilities and inner tasks, to consider life not only as something given but also as a task to be accomplished. What is essential for prophesying is Christian activity, to consider history as a creative act and task. The gift of prophecy, as a general gift of the Pentecost, signifies that, henceforth, Christian man makes history in an inspired and prophetic manner and is responsible for it.

According to this authentic interpretation, the Pentecost is a *universal consecration in prophecy,* for which every individual receives his particular gift (in the sacrament of confirmation: "the seal of the gift of the Holy Spirit"); and in this sense no member of the Church is deprived of his proper gift. These gifts can be diverse, but the prophetic spirit remains unchanged in them, for prophecy is not a special gift or profession, but rather a particular *qualitative character* of all the possible gifts. And it is in this qualitative sense that the following words of the Apostle should be interpreted: "there are diversities of gifts, but the same Spirit. And there are differences of administration, but the same Lord. And there are diversities of operations, but it is the same God which worketh all in all" (1 Cor. 12:4-6). And only by way of clarification of this general idea does Paul append an enumeration of these diverse gifts: "the manifestation of the Spirit is given to every man to profit withal. For to one is given by the Spirit the word of wisdom; to another the word of knowledge by the same Spirit; to another faith by the same Spirit; to another the gifts of healing by the same Spirit; to another the working of miracles; to another prophecy; to another discerning of spirits; to another divers kinds of tongues; to another the interpretation of tongues: But all these worketh that one and the self-same Spirit, dividing to every man severally as he will" (1 Cor. 12:7-11). This enumeration, evidently, is not exhaustive, as is confirmed by the concluding "as he will."

39. See the pertinent chapters about the male and female principles, and about genius and talent in the human spirit, in my book *The Unfading Light.*

This emphasizes the diversity of the gifts of the one Spirit, as well as the presence of the Spirit Himself in each of these gifts, *pars pro toto* [a part representing the whole] or *totum in parte* [the whole in a part].[40] This diversity of the gifts of the Spirit corresponds to their *fullness,* as symbolized by the *number* of fullness — the *seven* gifts of the Holy Spirit. There is also an analogy with the seven sacraments, as well as with the Old Testament symbolism of the candlestick with seven candles (Exod. 25:32; 37:20-23), which in the New Testament vision of John, the Seer of Mysteries, corresponds to "the seven golden candlesticks" around the Son of Man, holding "seven stars in his right hand" (Rev. 2:1) — which attests that the Holy Spirit reposes upon Him. These seven stars are also interpreted as the Angels of the seven churches, while the seven candlesticks are interpreted as the seven churches, but this ecclesiological interpretation does not change, of course, the basic meaning of the number seven as *fullness.*

The diversity of gifts signifies a multiplicity of forms of prophetic inspiration, among which one can specially note the prophetic ministry in the strict sense, which is creative directedness toward the Future, the search for paths. Prophecy therefore signifies the universal *spirit-bearingness* of Christian humanity after the Pentecost, which humanity, in its creaturely, human inspiration, is capable of receiving and being inspired by the gift of the Holy Spirit. Human inspiration becomes *divine-human* here and prophetic in this sense. This is an inner deification of the human spirit, a union of creaturely and noncreaturely essences in the human spirit, a new *divine-humanity of the human spirit,* which is united with the divine-humanity of the *human nature,* assumed into the unity of the divine life in Christ.

To be sure, this idea can in no wise be understood to mean that, after the Pentecost, it became a self-evident given that *all* human inspiration is prophetic and of divine origin. It is quite the opposite. This is not a given, but a supreme task that must be accomplished, a task that is inwardly proposed in the Pentecost. In the latter, the Holy Spirit truly descended upon men, but without depriving them of their proper human freedom and proper human inspiration. There is no special sacrament of divine inspiration (although Roman Catholics wish to see such a sacrament in the *charisma infallibilitatis* of the Pope when he speaks *ex cathedra*). Prophecy, or inspiration from above in answer to human striving, is a free gift, which is bestowed directly by the Holy Spirit; it is the direct sac-

---

40. This text of the apostle Paul begs to be compared with the definition of the Spirit of Wisdom in the Wisdom of Solomon, 7:22-23.

rament of the Pentecost, which sacrament is, of course, not interrupted or abolished in the Church by the presence of the official sacraments. "The Spirit bloweth where it listeth," and "as he will." But God's call is irrevocable. And prophesying is, in general, *creative activity* ignited by inspiration and given wings by audacity; it is creative eros in the Church, in spirit-bearing humanity. Prophesying, as creative activity and inspiration, is directed toward the Future, not above but through the present, which is pregnant with the future.

Such too was Old Testament prophecy, which in this sense was always essentially *historical,* i.e., it was rooted in a living sense of contemporaneity, in a sense of the needs or "problems" of the latter. It is legitimate that, in this case, the subject or content of prophecy is determined by its "problem."[41] It is only by a profound inner "living out" of contemporaneity and its problems that one comes to understand it prophetically as a task that unites today with tomorrow and yesterday. The true subject of prophecy is therefore *history,* understood in its inner content as *apocalypse,* as well as that which lies beyond and above history, i.e., the end of this aeon, eschatology: The complex concept of "the last times" encompasses the idea of history, understood as apocalypse and included in eschatology. This concept contains the Kantian antinomy of time, insofar as the latter, on the one hand, presupposes *flow* and excludes the "last" times, while, on the other hand, postulating for itself a limit or end (as well as a beginning). "The last times" are an apocalyptic, coherent, content-full, organized time, which is included in supra-time, in eschatology: this is not the negative time of quality-less flow, but the positive time of becoming. In any case, the "last times" must not only "flow by"; they must also be creatively actualized.

The gift of prophecy in the Pentecost is thus directed toward temporality or history. But this is only one aspect of the Pentecost, corresponding to the *dynamics* in the life in the Church; the latter also has its *statics.* And for this statics there does not exist any time or history; this is the kingdom of eternity and eternal life in God — in Christ by the Holy Spirit. The life of the Church, gracious and sacramental, bears the imprint of immobile eternity, of divine givenness, which must be protected and cannot be increased owing to its exhaustive character.

---

41. In this sense, prophets with their living sense of history and its acute problems differ from apocalyptics with their bad, overrefined reveries, who strive to reveal the future *beyond* history, outside of any connection with the present, for which this future is a *deus ex machina.*

The Church, as the Divine Incarnation and the Descent of the Holy Spirit, thus has two aspects: eternal life and temporal or historical life. This bi-unity corresponds to the union of the two natures in Christ: Divine and human, noncreaturely and creaturely, eternal and subject to time. And it also corresponds to the bi-unity of the Divine nature and the human nature in the sacrament of the Pentecost, in the deification of man through the descent of the Holy Spirit. To this eternal aspect of the life of the Church corresponds not prophecy, which is characterized by temporal development and creative activity, but priesthood, which stands guard over the fixed institutions of the Church.

It is necessary to distinguish these two aspects, which characterize the one life of the Church, in the aeon of the "last times." This aeon has its limits, and beyond its time there will follow another supra-time or other supra-times. This explains why the apostle Paul put a lower value on the gift of prophecy than on the royal gift of love. Axiologically, without charity or love this gift loses its spirit-bearing significance and becomes humanly impotent and empty, "as sounding brass, or a tinkling cymbal" (1 Cor. 13:1). "And though I have the gift of prophecy, and understand all mysteries, and all knowledge; and though I have all faith, so that I could remove mountains, and have not charity, I am nothing" (13:2). This also corresponds to the general eschatological assessment of prophecy in its connection with historical time and thus its limited nature, once again in comparison with the eternal power of charity or love: "Charity never faileth: but whether there be prophecies, they shall fail; whether there be tongues, they shall cease; whether there be knowledge, it shall vanish away. For we know in part, and we prophesy in part. But when that which is perfect is come, then that which is in part shall be done away" (13:8-10). This is not a belittlement of prophecy (or of knowledge), but its more precise definition: being directed toward time, it is always "in part," and this partial and relative character of prophecy vanishes in the light of the absolute, of Love and Eternity, when, in a certain sense, the time of this aeon ceases to be.

This cessation of time, occurring in time, has a twofold meaning: First, with reference to time, aeonically, it signifies a change in the mode of temporality, the appearance of a certain supra-time (and in this sense, there can be an indeterminate number of times, as well as states of life, besides our present one). Second, with reference to eternity, it signifies a participation in the latter, in the capacity of the depths of time; it signifies "eternal life," as a special mode of the experiencing or "living" of time. In this sense, eternal life is already revealed to us here, in time, to which it is not subject; and it affirms itself outside or above time, as it were. Revealed herein is the nature of man as a created-uncreated, creaturely and divine spirit, a temporal-eternal being.

3. Spiritual Life

The Lord describes the reception of the Spirit as a new birth: "That which is born of the flesh is flesh; and that which is born of the Spirit is spirit" (John 3:6). This new life appears in the old man, whence arises the antithesis and opposition of these two principles of life: according to the spirit and according to the flesh, the spiritual man and the natural man (Rom. 8: 1, 5, 9; Gal. 5:16-17, 25; 1 Pet. 4:6). This new life is our life in Christ by the Holy Spirit. In the Pentecost, Christ's humanity becomes a reality by the Holy Spirit. The Dyad of the Son and the Spirit, in Their inseparability and inconfusibility, determine the life of the Church. Therefore, this life is simultaneously life in Christ ("yet not I, but Christ liveth in me" [Gal. 2:20]) and life in the Holy Spirit ("ye are the temple of God, and . . . the Spirit of God dwelleth in you" [1 Cor. 3:16]). There is neither separation nor opposition here: the reality of life in Christ is the body of Christ, animated by the Holy Spirit dwelling in it. This makes understandable the convergence, approaching identification, of the life in Christ and the life in the Holy Spirit, as can be seen in the following comparisons from the apostolic epistles: We are "justified by Christ" (Gal. 2:17) and "by the Spirit of our God" (1 Cor. 6:11); we are "sealed" (Eph. 1:13; 4:30) and "circumcised" (Col. 2:11) in both; we have joy (Phil 3:1; cf. Rom. 14:17), faith (Gal. 3:26; 1 Cor. 1:9), love (Rom. 8:39; Col. 1:8), and fellowship (1 Cor. 1:9; 2 Cor. 13:14) in both.[42] Likewise, sanctification is sometimes attributed to Christ (1 Cor. 1:30; Eph. 5:26; Heb. 2:11; 10:29; 13:12) and sometimes to the Holy Spirit (Rom. 15:16; 1 Cor. 6:11; 2 Thess. 2:13; 1 Pet. 1:2); this indicates the unity of this act which is accomplished dyadically by the Second and Third hypostases.

The being clothed in Christ, which is accomplished by the Holy Spirit, is at the same time adoption by God. The God-Man Himself in His human nature was adopted by the Father in the descent of the Holy Spirit, as was attested by the Father's voice calling from heaven: "This is my beloved Son" (Matt. 3:17). Consequently, for the God-Man too the

---

42. *Essays on the Trinity and the Incarnation*, by members of the Anglican Communion, ed. A. E. J. Rawlinson (London: Longmans, Green, 1928).

Holy Spirit was the Spirit of adoption. And for us too He is the Spirit of adoption, by virtue of our union with Christ: "ye have received the Spirit of adoption, whereby we cry, Abba, Father. The Spirit itself beareth witness with our spirit, that we are the children of God: and if children, then heirs; heirs of God, and joint-heirs with Christ" (Rom. 8:15-17). "And because ye are sons, God hath sent forth the Spirit of his Son into your hearts, crying, Abba, Father. Wherefore thou art no more a servant, but a son; and if a son, then an heir of God through Christ" (Gal. 4:6-7). "Ourselves . . . which have the firstfruits of the Spirit, even we ourselves groan within ourselves, waiting for the adoption, to wit, the redemption of our body. . . . Likewise the Spirit also helpeth our infirmities: for we know not what we should pray for as we ought: but the Spirit itself maketh intercession for us with groanings that cannot be uttered" (Rom. 8:23, 26). "Now he which stablisheth us with you in Christ, and hath anointed us, is God; Who hath also sealed us, and given the earnest of the Spirit in our hearts" (2 Cor. 1:21-22). "[We] have been all made to drink into one Spirit" (1 Cor. 12:13); "ye were sealed with that holy Spirit of promise" (Eph. 1:13). "That the God our Lord Jesus Christ, the Father of glory, may give unto you the spirit of wisdom and revelation in the knowledge of him: the eyes of your understanding being enlightened" (Eph. 1:17-18). "Ye are . . . the epistle of Christ . . . written . . with the Spirit of the living God" (2 Cor. 3:3). The *fruits* of the spiritual life are produced by virtue of this grace-bestowing action: "ye have your fruit unto holiness, and the end everlasting life" (Rom. 6:22). Galatians 5:17-23 set the fruits of the flesh (desiring that which is contrary to the spirit) in opposition to the fruits of the spirit (desiring that which is contrary to the flesh): "the fruit of the Spirit is love, joy, peace, longsuffering, gentleness, goodness, faith, meekness, temperance" (17:22-23; cf. Eph. 5:9). The doers of the works of the flesh shall not inherit the kingdom of God (1 Cor. 6:10), as opposed to those who are "washed . . . sanctified . . . justified in the name of the Lord Jesus, and by the Spirit of our God" (6:11), for the kingdom of God is "righteousness, and peace, and joy in the Holy Spirit" (Rom. 14:17).

The general idea expressed in this series of New Testament texts, which is far from exhaustive,[43] is that the Holy Spirit, being communicated to man through the Church, produces in him a new, spiritual life, or, in the language of theology, bestows *grace* upon him. "Grace" is a theological term, not a Biblical one; it serves to generalize various manifesta-

---

43. See Swete (*The Holy Spirit in the New Testament*, especially pp. 169-279) for a complete list of such texts, with commentary.

tions of the spiritual life (in the Bible, the word "grace" is used in the most diverse senses). The doctrine of grace occupies an important place in contemporary theology (of the different confessions).[44]

Through the descent of the Holy Spirit, so-called *spiritual life* arises in the members of the Church. This is a wholly new fact, which depends entirely on the Pentecost and is impossible prior to it or outside it. This fact is described in its various aspects in Scripture and in the ascetic literature. However diverse its manifestations or aspects, spiritual life contains a constant element: man receives something higher than himself, a supernatural principle. But this principle is assimilated by him, enters into his proper life, which thereby becomes natural and supernatural at the same time.

What are the preconditions of spiritual life? First of all, it is inaccessible to entities or forms of being that do not possess the spiritual principle, entities for which the spirit is alien: this includes the whole animal world and the pre-animal world, plants and minerals. Second, spiritual life cannot be produced by human activity, however elevated the latter may be, but presupposes the participation of divine power, which descends upon man. Despite their high spiritual level, Socrates and Plato, Buddha and Lao Tzu, as well as other righteous men and leaders of pre-Christian and non-Christian humanity, do not know the life of *grace* in the Holy Spirit. There is a qualitative difference here, analogous to the difference established by Christ between the greatest of those born of women, John the Baptist, and the least in the Kingdom of God (i.e., one who, in this case, possesses the grace of the Holy Spirit), who is nonetheless greater than John (Matt. 11:11). This does not diminish the fact that there is a naturally spiritual life in man, which possesses the sophianic principle and can be called a life of *natural grace*. It differs from and is inferior to the life of spiritual grace in that the latter contains a divine power. Grace is a supernatural gift, which can be given or not given; but nothing human can complement or replace it. This was clearly manifested in the primitive church in the laying on of hands by the apostles, to whom this grace was communicated.

Man is an incarnate spirit. On the one hand, he has a natural life, a psycho-corporeal existence. On the other hand, he is a spirit and has his proper spiritual nature. Since it is a spark of Divinity that has received the personal principle and become a person, his spirit has the potential

---

44. See *The Doctrine of Grace*, a collection of articles by different authors. Published by the Theological Committee of the Lausanne Conference, 1932.

for divine life, which can become a reality by the power and action of the grace of the Holy Spirit. In this action, divine life becomes, as it were, the proper nature of the human spirit; and man lives this life in parallel with that of his natural essence. He lives bi-naturally, but unihypostatically. The kinship between the human and angelic spirits is manifested here. Angels do not have their own natural world and, being creaturely, they participate in the nature of Divinity and in divine life, while at the same time participating, in their own manner, in human life.[45] Similarly, the co-angelic essence of the human spirit participates in divine life, while preserving its autonomy.

By its nature, the human spirit is neither closed nor impenetrable. It is created in the image of the Divine spirit, which, being one and trihypostatic, is thus "communal" and mutually transparent. The Father lives in the Son and in the Spirit; the Son lives by the life of the Father and of the Spirit; and the Spirit lives by the life of the Father and of the Son. Creaturely beings, too, are open to communal being, as race (human) or assembly (angelic). This mutual transparence of creaturely spirits, this capacity to receive "influences," is expressed not only in a certain commonality of life within the limits of the creaturely essence (which is a self-evident fact), but also in the capacity to receive divine life, to be deified. Having in itself the image of God, i.e., an essential conformity with Divinity, the human spirit has the capacity to receive the Divine Spirit and to be livingly united with the latter (*humanum divini capax est* [the human is capable of receiving the divine]), while preserving its proper natural life, although transforming it in conformity with the new powers entering into it.

But in order to be actualized such a possibility presupposes a certain state of readiness of the human spirit for communion with God; but this possibility is paralyzed by the fact that the spirit has been made heavy and worldly as a result of original sin. This possibility is restored by the Incarnation, by which Christ realized the norm of the relations between the spirit and nature in man, the equilibrium of the two principles. The principle of spiritual life thus appeared in the human race through its participation in the New Adam, Christ. This possibility is actualized by the Holy Spirit, Who makes man a participant in Christ's life. But this life in Christ is the communion with the Holy Spirit; and according to the form of this life, "Christians" become "spirit-bearing." This is accomplished as a new, spiritual birth in man, through baptism by water and the Spirit. This is a new fact of life: the doors of the inner cell of the human spirit are opened

---

45. See my book *Jacob's Ladder: On the Angels.*

for the entry of the Holy Spirit. This is an action of God in man, which is accomplished by God's will ("the Spirit bloweth where it listeth"), although, by God's will, it is connected, in the life of the Church, with sacrament, specifically with baptism. In the life of the God-Man as well, baptism signified the descent of the Holy Spirit, and that is what it signifies in every human life.

In the living assimilation of the divine gift, man preserves his natural essence with its freedom; but this essence, the Old Adam, remains burdened by the bad heritage of original sin as well as by personal sinful habits. Therefore, spiritual life becomes, first of all, the arena of the struggle and antagonism of the spiritual man and the natural man, of the spirit and the flesh, of righteousness and sin. The very existence of this antagonism of life, the sinner's consciousness of sin, is already a fact of incipient spiritual life; and every step on this path, every small victory, is assisted by grace. Spiritual life is therefore necessarily an *ascetic* path and even a tragic one; and only at certain chosen points of this path does grace illuminate the pilgrim, who is exhausted by the vanity of his efforts. Moreover, this path is without end, for the struggle between the Old Adam and the New Adam is irreconcilable. But the farther a human being advances in this spiritual struggle, the more real his own spirit and his spiritual life become for him, and the more indubitable become the gifts of grace, the fruits of the spirit.

Efforts of the spiritual life whose goal is "the acquisition of the Holy Spirit" (the divinely inspired phrase of St. Seraphim of Sarov) have a predominantly *negative* character — the character of struggle with oneself, ascesis. Not power but infirmity is experienced by individuals on the spiritual path. "Repent ye, for the kingdom of heaven [i.e., in this case, spiritual life] is at hand" (Matt. 3:2); and the path to the kingdom of heaven is unceasing repentance, *metanoia,* the desire to *change,* to become a new man. Self-renunciation and the bearing of the cross, patience which saves our souls, spiritual poverty which is the path to the Kingdom of Heaven, and humility as the quality that sums up this entire way of the cross — that is what constitutes the Christian spiritual life. The gifts of the Spirit are given, not taken; they are awaited, but one has no claim upon them. And grace from above illuminates the bowed heads of penitents. Humility in spiritual life consists not only in the consciousness of one's sin, but also in knowledge of one's creatureliness and of the fundamental metaphysical nothingness that characterizes the latter: *All* things are given to creation by the Creator; and before the face of the Creator, creation knows and must know its original nullity. Humility thus has two aspects: ascetic and ontological. In humility, the human spirit strives to become a *tabula rasa* for the Spirit of God; it strives to lose its proper life, which is sin and nothingness. To die according to nature in order to come to life according to the spirit, *stirb und werde*, that is the wisdom of humility: "Except a corn of wheat fall into the ground and die, it abideth alone: but if it die, it bringeth forth much fruit" (John 12:24).

Examined in this aspect, spiritual life in the natural man presupposes a receptivity to the Spirit, an *active passivity* (if one can use this expression), which is characterized by a certain spiritual limpidity. The *gift* of the Holy Spirit is received here as a certain *given* which comes down from heaven to earth, is a kind of eternally continuing descent of the tongues of fire. Only in this way can one receive such a gift descending from heaven; and in the dialectic of the Christian life, the grace-bestowing illumination of the Spirit can be realized only in connection with this passivity of reception, this humility of the self-renouncing man, who falls to his knees. This passivity of the human essence, which does not resist the entry of the Divine Spirit, is a new spiritual creation or, according to the Gospel expression, a new birth of man.

This new life in the Spirit is, of course, indescribable and inexhaustible: "the things of God knoweth no man, but the Spirit of God" (1 Cor. 2:11); and we can find only a few indications of this life in the apostolic epistles. The life of grace in the Holy Spirit, uniting our life with Christ, is bestowed in the Church in specific ways such as sacraments, sacramentalia, and prayers, as well as by direct illumination. One should not consider these two paths to be opposed, however, for there is one active Spirit and the grace bestowed in the sacraments continues to operate beyond the limits of their immediate celebration. In the descent of the Holy Spirit were given not only the cloven tongues, reposing upon each of the apostles, but also their *unity*, or the fullness of the Church, which is the abiding Pentecost. In this sense, the Church is simultaneously the organization and the organism of spiritual life.

The churchly character of spiritual life leads to further questions concerning its reception. The direct subject of spiritual life is the individual human person. That is why when one speaks of salvation, i.e., the attainment of a life full of grace, one usually means *personal* salvation, inasmuch as the feat of ascesis, as well as the acquisition of humanity, can be accomplished only by separate individuals. If we go no further than this personal aspect of salvation, however, we risk considering the Church as a mere series of separate atoms. This will abolish the very concept of the Church as a unity, whereas the Church exists precisely as a *multi-unity*, akin to the natural multi-unity of the human race. But we know that the "catholic" nature (or sobornost) of the personal consciousness is disclosed precisely in churchly love; and the gift of love, which is from the Holy Spirit, makes this sobornost of churchly life as a body composed of multiple members a self-evident reality. Likewise, the sacraments are bestowed from the entire Church and for the entire Church, although they are received by individual persons. The sacraments are essentially churchly, and they thus liberate man from the condition of his isolation. That is why the spiritual life of individual persons in the Church takes on a universal character in its power and significance. This connection cannot be fully understood at the present time, but isolation in salvation and in the spiritual life is impossible: "And whether one member suffer, all the members suffer with it; or one member be honoured, all the members rejoice with it" (1 Cor. 12:26). The catholicity or integrity of life realized in each member is the fundamental quality of spiritual life.

The motive force of Christian asceticism is therefore not the religious egoism of personal salvation, isolating an individual person from the whole and separating a member from the body. Its motive force is love: "For this is the love of God, that we keep his commandments" (1 John 5:3). Love for God is the first commandment, but it is indissolubly linked with the second and equal commandment: "Thou shalt love thy neighbour as thyself." "He that hath my commandments, and keepeth them, he it is that loveth me . . . if a man love me, he will keep my words: and my Father will love him, and we will come unto him, and make our abode with him" (John 14:21, 23). This abode is the Holy Spirit, Who by His coming makes us an abode of the Son and, with Him, of the Father. That is, He makes us an abode of the Holy Trinity. The identification of love for God and love for one's neighbor, i.e., the rejection of all egoism, reaches its pinnacle in the following passage from the apostle of love: "We love him, because he first loved us. If a man say, I love God, and hateth his brother, he is a liar: for he that loveth not his brother whom he hath seen, how can he love God whom he hath not seen? And this commandment have we from him, That he who loveth God love his brother also" (1 John 4:19-21). This commandment of love for God becomes the ascetic commandment not to love the world, for the latter is the kingdom of sin: "Love not the world, neither the things that are in the world. If any man love the world, the love of the Father is not in him. For all that is in the world, the lust of the flesh, and the lust of the eyes, and the pride of life, is not of the Father, but is of the world" (2:15-16). Therefore, Christian asceticism is catholic or universal in nature, for it is the path of love for God as well as for one's neighbor, "the burning of the pitying heart," according to Isaac the Syrian.[46] In contrast to Buddhistic asceticism, Christian asceticism is, in this sense, not self-mortification, not the path to nirvana, but the affirmation of life in love.

It is necessary to note another feature of this Christian asceticism. It is not an acosmism (and certainly not an anti-cosmism), not an absence of love for the world as God's creation, in which man is given a central and dominant place. That world which the apostle John instructs us not to love is actually the sinful sickness of the world, connected with man's sinful relation to it. It is not the world as God's creation, which God so loved that He did not spare His own Son for the sake of its salvation. For this world, as God's creation, man must have love, for he is connected with it forever *according to creation,* and his salvation includes the salvation of the world, its healing — the healing of the whole world (see Rom. 8:19-22).

Christian asceticism consists in following Christ, in bearing His cross, in following the path of Christ's obedience to the will of the Father, in accomplishing not one's own will but that of the Father, in bearing an easy yoke and a light burden in meekness and humility of the heart. Christ traced the path of humility by love for the Father and obedience to His will; and He was thereby glorified, being glorified from the Father by the Holy Spirit. Christian asceticism is the bearing of the image of Christ in one's heart, as the apostle says: "I bear in my body the marks of the Lord Jesus" (Gal. 6:17); "[we always bear] in the body the dying of the Lord Jesus" (2 Cor. 4:10). Christian asceticism is a cross in the image of Christ's cross, and only upon this cross does the Holy Spirit descend. And the very love for the cross that flames up in man is a gift of the Holy Spirit. And just as the God-Man's earthly life can in a certain sense be called the acquisition of the Holy Spirit, since it proceeds from humiliation to glorification, so each Christian, in following Christ and acquiring his life in Him, thereby becomes worthy of being an abode of the Holy Spirit, Who exists in the world and bestows Himself upon human beings: "Come and make Your abode in us," O Comforter![47]

But the truth about the cross consists not only in the fact that it is

46. From *Ascetic Orations* 48.

47. Here we again have the antinomy of the kenosis of the Holy Spirit in His descent into the world: The Holy Spirit, having come into the world, "is everywhere and fills everything." He refrains, however, from imposing Himself upon human freedom. He awaits its call, "come and make Your abode in us," before coming and filling the heart of creation with His power and life.

necessary to receive it and to carry it, but also in the fact that it is necessary to *take up one's own cross,* to choose it. There is an indissoluble connection between its passive carrying and its active taking. In some cases, these two elements can merge to the point of indistinguishability, when, for example, a person accepts as if by free choice the events that occur in his life, the external fate to which his life is subject. But these two elements can also diverge. This dialectic of the cross, in which activity and passivity, receiving and taking, intersect and are united at a single point — this dialectic has its source in the fundamental antinomy of the Christian path, which we must now examine.

One way to acquire the Holy Spirit is to renounce the world, to live a life of spiritual passivity in humility and spiritual poverty.[48] This is the normal and necessary way to overcome sin in oneself; without it, there can be no reception of the Holy Spirit, no deification, for the latter cannot be reconciled with the world. Is this, however, the sole path of Christian life, which exhausts all the possibilities and, therefore, all the obligations of the latter? A careful examination of this question compels us to answer that it is not the sole path: The path of the Christian cannot and should not remain solely the path of passive humility; he must inevitably allow a place in himself for creative activity, for the taking of responsibility, for self-determination and the audacity that is inevitably connected (and even in a certain sense identical) with the latter. The Spirit that lives in us demands this of us, calls us to this.

The cross is not only passive reception; it is also active taking, creative self-determination and audacity. The Apostle speaks of the diverse ministries and diverse gifts of the one Spirit living in the Church. But these diverse gifts are also different vocations; they are not proclaimed to man from outside and are not imposed on him from above (as an "obedience"), but are acquired by him in answer to an inner call, are chosen by him. Of man it is demanded that he rise and go where the spirit is calling and leading him. To be sure, errors and failures are possible in this election, as in all human works and decisions, but the very decision and election, the determination of one's path, is accomplished by human freedom and creative self-determination.

---

48. This path can therefore so easily become one of outward *obedience* to one person or another, to an elder (the "starets" of Orthodoxy), to the Pope in Catholicism, the "elder of elders" (to use the expression of the Russian philosopher Konstantin Leontiev). Inner passivity seeks to arrange itself also as external passivity, and the Judaic law which is absent in Christianity is replaced by a living law in the person of an elder.

Even the most ascetic paths, where responsible self-determination appears to be abolished and replaced by obedience, are chosen freely and audaciously. In going into the wilderness or abandoning the world for a sanctuary, in surrendering oneself entirely to the direction of an elder, an ascetic performs an act of creative election and responsible self-determination. And even Christ Himself, when he said to the apostles, "Follow me," did not command them, but asked them, as it were, appealing to their self-determination; and in response, they "left their nets, and followed him" (Matt. 4:18-20). In its most decisive forms, asceticism presupposes in its *initial* decisions the most intense activity and self-determination, both in hearing one's inner call and in following it.

This is not only a psychological necessity, in virtue of which it is impossible for man to abolish his will, for to "renounce" one's will requires the maximal intensity of will. This is a *spiritual* necessity, which is commanded by the spirit that lives in us. For the spiritual principle in us is not only a principle that opposes the inertia of flesh and sin, but also a creative, life-giving principle. If we examine the Lord's earthly life from this point of view, we will without difficulty distinguish in it two aspects. The first aspect consists in suffering all the sorrows and hardships that are inevitable in the life of the sinful world (the so-called *oboedientia passiva* of the Protestants). The second aspect consists in making a certain decision that makes inevitable the collision with the Jewish leaders and the death on the cross; this is in general the voluntary election of the way of the cross, the *oboedientia activa*. Christ Himself formed His life according to a specific decision, in conformity with the will of the Father, which He — creatively — discovered in the depths of His divine-human consciousness. He did not just accept the cross as fate or necessity; He *went to meet* it. Christ was sent into the world to become the redemptive sacrifice; that was His life's vocation and His gift, proper only to Him; and He accomplished this *ministry* as a free creative activity of His life, and this activity, as such, included the extreme of audacity and responsibility. The taking up of the cross in obedience to the Father's will was therefore united in Him with the consciousness of freedom: "Therefore doth my Father love me, because I lay down my life, that I might take it again. No man taketh it from me, but I lay it down of myself" (John 10:17-18).

The descent of the Holy Spirit necessarily presupposes in us not only the presence of repentance ("purify us of all foulness," as the prayer says), but also a prophetic spirit, that is, creative inspiration bestowed from "the treasure-house of goods and the Giver of life." This constitutes the fundamental dogmatic difference between the Christian worldview and the anti-cosmic worldview of Buddhism: death or at least nirvana wafts from the latter, whereas the former is inspired by the Giver of Life. By the breath of the Spirit, the Christian is not taken out of the world and history, but, on the contrary, is included in them creatively, in a new manner. Those natural capacities and the corresponding vocation that are proper to man are introduced by the Spirit into the Christian ministries, in conformity with His special *gifts*. In his enumeration of the gifts of the Holy Spirit, the apostle Paul mentions even such gifts as "the word of wisdom" and "the word of knowledge" (1 Cor. 12:8), that is, those capacities which are natural to man but which the coming of the Holy Spirit makes Christianly (i.e., divinely) inspired. All the human activity that is realized in history and culture in various manifestations of the latter can become capable of receiving the Spirit, the inspirations of the Pentecost. Furthermore, this activity, as a "ministry," is included in the path of salvation. (The Church recognizes this notion by canonizing certain saints because they are charged with particular ministries related to cultural and historical activity: equi-apostolic emperors and princes, icon painters, ecumenical teachers, physicians, etc. To be sure, any such list cannot be exhaustive, for the continuing life of the Church presents new forms of saintliness. Moreover, there are unrecognized saints with as yet unrecognized ministries.)

What is especially important is that the two paths — ascetic humility and creative audacity, obedience and the acceptance of responsibility — are antinomically harmonized in spiritual life. Moreover, the two must be in a certain state of mutual equilibrium; the absence or impoverishment of the one cripples the other. If it is oriented toward humility and obedience alone, Christian life takes on traits of buddhistic world-renunciation, spiritual slavery, or Old Testament legalism (which is outwardly expressed in the illegitimate predominance of institutionalism, ritualism, hierarchism; in general, in the predominance of the external organization of the visible church to the detriment of spiritual and creative life). By contrast, a one-sided orientation toward personal audacity and prophecy destroys churchliness, provoking sectarian fragmentedness (this is how it was in the early Church, and this is how it currently is in Protestantism, which is guilty of abusing the notion of anti-hierarchical "prophetism," at least in its verbal self-definition). Antinomy is not contradiction, and antinomism is even inevitable and fruitful in the spiritual life. Both aspects, humility and prophetic audacity, belong equally to *spiritual life*, to the concrete unity of the self-definition of the spirit, opening up to receive divine life.

The fact is that man, the bearer of the image of God, is a creature, and a fallen one to boot: having been redeemed by Christ and having received the grace of the Holy Spirit, he can stand in the presence of God only in repentance and humility, which makes him open to divine life. But man is also a creaturely god by nature, who becomes such by grace. He feels himself called to live in the human race with its history, in this world, where the Kingdom of God is being realized. He feels himself to be a worker and creator, "a king, high priest, and prophet"; and it is to this vocation of man that the Gospel parable about the talents refers (not to mention the questions and answers at the Last Judgment), where man is held responsible for the multiplication of the talents given him and their legitimate use. The idea of the "militant Church," which is called to preach the Gospel to all nations, teaching them to accomplish all that is commanded by Jesus, this idea presupposes an active, responsible, creative attitude toward life. And the correct relation between humility and audacity is one in which the former nourishes the latter, while the latter actualizes the former. Torn away from humility, audacity is vulnerable to the temptation of demonism, of self-assertion, which seeks its own and therefore does not know Christian love, is not moderated by this love. One can say that, if humility is our love for God, then audacity and responsibility are our love for the world and for man. Audacity represents the second commandment, equal to the first. These are the two wings on which the human spirit soars upward.

Some may say that the ascetic feat of humility must precede audacity, that a man must prepare himself for audacity by purifying himself by repentance. But this assertion is false, for the paths of repentance and humility cannot end within the limits of this present life, and thus we have here only a pious evasion. There must be audacity in humility and humility in audacity, which is inseparable from the acceptance of responsibility, for these two paths are not opposed and therefore can be combined. The opposite of humility is pride, and the opposite of audacity is slavery and legalism; these truly are incompatible.

Those who practice only humility are guilty of a concealed legalism, which is overcome and rejected by Christianity (this is the theme of the apostle Paul's Epistle to the Galatians). Those who desire to reduce Christianity to obedience alone, i.e., solely to the external law, angered the apostle Paul. He called them "false brethren unawares brought in, who came in privily to spy out our liberty which we have in Christ Jesus, that they might bring us into bondage" (Gal. 2:4). They distort Christianity, which knows the commandments but does not know a law above it; Christianity is freedom and, consequently, creative activity. "Stand fast therefore in the liberty wherewith Christ hath made us free" (5:1), "for, brethren, ye have been called unto liberty" (5:13). The Apostle links freedom with justification by faith in Christ, not by works of the law: "ye are all the children of God by faith in Christ Jesus" (3:26) who have received "the Spirit of his Son" (4:6), "wherefore thou art no more a servant, but a son; and if a son, then an heir of God through Christ" (4:7). In other words, humility and the resulting obedience are an expression of the fear of God, which is the beginning of wisdom (Prov. 1:7), as the sense of creaturely reverence before the Holy and as man's first and inextinguishable consciousness of himself before God ("Depart from me; for I am a sinful man, O Lord" [Luke 5:8]). At the same time, the apostle of love attests: "There is no fear in love; but perfect love casteth out fear. . . . He that feareth is not made perfect in love" (1 John 4:18). Love includes both freedom and the audacity of the sons of God.

There, finally, is yet another parallel to the relation of humility and audacity: the relation of *faith* and *works*. If we reject the Roman Catholic idea of *meritum*, which also had a strong influence on Orthodox theology, the relation between faith, even the most vital and effective *(efficax)* but nonetheless passive, and works, in which man must manifest his activity and responsibility — this relation is perfectly analogous to that between humility and audacity. Protestantism seeks a way out of the indeterminate opposition between faith and works in quietism, in the exclusive primacy of faith, whereas Catholicism seeks it in the idea of merit and the corresponding recompense. In essence, faith and works constitute the fullness of the life of the spirit; they are similar to breathing in and breathing out, and cannot be isolated or separated. Salvation by faith is humility, whereas salvation by works and responsibility is audacity.

We see this fundamental relationship in the life of the Christian in different manifestations of the life of the Church. Being united with Christ by the Incarnation, a Christian becomes a son of God, born of God; and receiving the Holy Spirit by the Pentecost, he lives a divine life in his creaturely essence. This adoption or deification is realized as the reception of grace, where one is purified of sin. Man is redeemed by Christ and reconciled with God in the essence of the old Adam, which does not die even in the new birth in Christ by the Holy Spirit. In this sense, man is the living antinomy of the old Adam and the New Adam. In the former, he is all repentance and humility; in the latter, he is the audacity of the love of the sons of God.

We may be asked the following question: Why is the "spiritual life" usually understood as the ascetic path and only as this path? Such an understanding is an Old Testament reaction with the restoration of nomism, salvation by the law; in practical religious terms, it is a one-sidedness and even an impoverishment of the Christian spirit. It is instructive to compare the ascetically stylized form of monasticism with the apostle Paul's teaching in the epistles to the Galatians or to the Romans, or even simply to verify in the light of the Gospel the accepted and apparently self-evident axioms of "obedience" and the "renunciation of the will." Here, one must keep in mind that the ascetic rules and examples that arose in the heroic periods of monastic asceticism as acts of *creative* audacity have been transformed in the course of time into a law whose observance or non-observance permits or prevents the acquisition of the Spirit. Nevertheless, one cannot fail to see that, when actualized, heroic asceticism as it is practiced in hermitage, monasticism, or inspired obedience has the character of creative *audacity:* It is often accompanied by struggle and characterized by the breaking of fleshly and spiritual connections. In general, it is a completely free and even willful act.[49]

Even more important is the fact that certain individuals follow the creative and therefore audacious and responsible path of heroic asceticism not because of meagerness and passivity but because of an abundance of strength and creative intensity. Therefore, it is by no means correct to oppose monasticism with its asceticism to the audacity of creative activity. True monasticism is full of audacity, for it is a form of personal creative activity, *alongside* all the other forms of such activity. Indeed, when an ideological and practical sign of equality is placed between Christianity and pseudo-monastic obedience, it is necessary to reject such an identification as a misunderstanding.

"Obedience" can be (and often must be) a *method* or means of spiritual life (in particular, in the monastic life, it is as much a spiritual necessity as a disciplinary and technical one), but it should never be considered a goal in itself, or even a means in itself, justified in itself. On the contrary, obedience is valuable only insofar as it is an act and a function of *freedom*. It is freely accepted and inwardly determined by freedom; and freedom, as the possibility of disobeying, always stands guard over true obedience. The value judgments of freedom[50] must govern obedience, which by no means

---

49. Typical in this respect is the life of St. Alexis, "man of God," who ascetically violated fundamental human relationships: he abandoned his bride on their wedding night and caused much suffering for his parents, who did not even know how he died.

50. We have an example of this in the relation of St. Symeon the New Theologian to his elder, Symeon the Pious: after the latter's death, St. Symeon would light a lamp before his image, thus canonizing him.

should become an enslavement to the grand and small inquisitors, who pretend to infallibility and assert spiritual despotism under the pretext of monastic "eldership." Otherwise, obedience becomes idolatry,[51] against which the New Testament apostle of love warns us not without reason: "Little children, keep yourselves from idols" (1 John 5:21), while another apostle attests, "where the Spirit of the Lord is, there is liberty" (2 Cor. 3:17).

One cannot fail to recognize that, with regard to the ascetic path, there exists a valuable *tradition:* treasures of spiritual experience have been accumulated, which not only must not be neglected, but which must be carefully preserved and used, as is in fact being done (although, in this domain too, nothing should be absolutized; in particular, the "Philokalia"[52] should not be transformed into a kind of Gospel, but should be used only after "reflection"). There is no such tradition concerning the creative paths of Christian audacity (if we do not count that *false* tradition which merely legitimizes the status quo established for a given period and which the conservative and even reactionary spirit, the spirit of cowardice and inertia, pronounces to be the guiding principle of Christian "sociology"). This discrepancy is explained by the different directions and intensities of these two currents of spiritual life. Inasmuch as the spiritual life consists in warring against sin and obeying the commandments on the paths of Christian humility and repentance, it has certain common and typical features. In its struggle against sin, every human soul follows the same path, which has been best studied and measured by the specially gifted elect of this path, the Christian ascetics. In its spiritual ascent, the human soul is the same among different individuals and in different epochs; it becomes extrahistorical, as it were, and loses its historical flesh. The depths of the soul with the pathology of passions can be an object of a "spiritual science" (just as great artists like Shakespeare could penetrate the various historical veils that conceal its depths). Here, we have a uniformity, a repeatability, even a certain lawlike regularity. Therefore, there is a legitimate place here for spiritual instruction and guidance.

But there is nothing like this in the case of creative activity and audacity: there is no tradition and no repetition; everything is unique and

---

51. One can paradoxically define this antinomic nature of the monastic spirit in the following manner: *obedience* in freedom, *humility-audacity* in their inseparability as different aspects of intense spiritual effort.

52. A collection of ascetical and mystical writings (in Greek) dating from the fourth to the fifteenth centuries, compiled mainly by Nicodemus of the Holy Mountain (1782). It has had an immense influence on Eastern Orthodox spirituality. — Trans.

individual, new and original. To be sure, one should not caricature this idea: in the domain of human relationships, individuality too has its typical and uniform manifestations. But the creative and individual element consists precisely in that which distinguishes it from the typical relations, however small this difference may be; and that is why one can even say that there are no cases that are similar to the point of being identical. Creative self-determination is always new, individual, and original; and, in this sense, it is atypical and does not conform to any law. (To be sure, we observe this more clearly in more or less outstanding personalities, those who "make history," than in the "crowd," although, in essence, this relationship always remains the same.) If one would like to have a spiritual map of this path, it is universal history, which is not repeated and, most importantly, does not end with and is not exhausted by any one epoch. That is why, in its creative self-determination, human personality has its autonomy, accepts responsibility for itself, is creatively audacious; and *there is no other way for it to exist.* Moreover, one cannot evade this self-determination, by encapsulating oneself in obedience.

We thus affirm *the fact of history,* with its new and constantly changing aspects, with its creative diversity, which is inexhaustible. Insofar as creative inspiration represents a manifestation of the prophetic spirit, the absence of rules and the newness of the path correspond to the very spirit of prophecy, which is directed toward the new and the unknown. There cannot be a "Philokalia" for creative activity, for the latter is outside of law and regularity. But at the same time there is no Christian creative activity that does not, in its heart, contain infinite humility and repentance before God for the sins of its creaturely and fallen being. The same Spirit bestows upon the Christian both the power of repentance and the energy of creative activity.

4. The Gift of Love

"The love of God is shed abroad in our hearts by the Holy Spirit which is given to us" (Rom. 5:5). The action of the Holy Spirit is manifested in the flaming up of love, for the Holy Spirit is the hypostatic Love itself of the Holy Trinity, which is revealed in the world as grace-bestowing, supranatural, divine love. Therefore, "he that loveth not his brother" "is not of God" (1 John 3:10); "if we love one another, God dwelleth in us, and his love is perfected in us" (4:12); "he that loveth not knoweth not God, for God is love" (4:8).

This definition has an *ontological* significance; it indicates not only that love is a *quality* of God but also that the very *being* of God is love. This definition can be understood in the light of the dogma of the Holy Trinity, according to which the absolute divine personality is triune with all the power of sacred trinitarity, as three distinctly personal subjects, while at the same time having one substance and even one life. This identification of trinity in unity is precisely trinitarian love. Hypostatic love, completing the trinity in unity, is the Holy Spirit. This is what makes possible the identification of God and love, be it the "love of God" (1 John 2:5; Rom. 5:5), or the love of the individual hypostases: the love of the Father (1 John 2:15; 2 Cor. 13:14), the love of Christ (2 Cor. 5:14; Eph. 3:19; Phil 1:8; 1 Tim. 1:14), or the love of the Spirit (Rom. 15:30).

The capacity for love is the seal of God's image in man: "Behold, what manner of love the Father hath bestowed upon us, that we should be called the sons of God" (1 John 3:1). The objective possibility of love (which is absent in the monohypostatic subject, for whom only egocentrism is possible) is connected with the *multi-unity* of the human race (as well as of the angelic assembly), according to the image of the triunity (which thus is also a multi-unity) of the Holy Trinity. The multiple centers of individual being are connected by the unity of life or unisubstantiality, which is given in the *genus,* but which is only *proposed as a task* in individual being, and which thus is an object to be attained (or not attained) in the free multi-unity of love, in the sobornost of life.

The capacity for love, or the vocation of love, in which the fullness of life is realized, is a feature of the image of God in man and thus is above all a gift of *natural* grace as the *postulate* of love. Love is accessible to man, not only to original man uncorrupted by sin (thus, Adam recognizes and loves his wife, in her consubstantiality with him [see Gen. 2:23-24], and recognizes his future children in her), but even to fallen man, although here love struggles against self-love and unlove. Love as "altruism," as the capacity to transfer to some extent one's personal center into another being, is one of man's indisputable *natural* virtues and knows different manifestations: family love, friendship, and love of country (in general all the different ways in which egotism is overcome), as well as spiritual love for God. Love has multiple levels: it is found in the entire trinitarian composition of man — spirit, soul, and body.

One can see embryonic traces of love even in the animal world: the principles of corporeal and psychical consubstantiality are implanted in the *generic* character of the life of animals, making them resemble man (see Gen. 1:21, 25). This generic essence of all creatures is the foundation of lower, animal love, in the form of herd instinct, or even maternal (and sometimes paternal) instinct; and here we sometimes find examples of true self-renunciation in love. The animal world is included in man; and so the love that exists in the animal world is included in human love. The mutual attachment of animals and man refers to this domain. For man, this is a lower form of love, especially if he considers it a higher and unique form of love, and thus descends to the level of animals. The relationship between man and the animal world, man's lordship over the latter, includes the norm of their mutual love; and here, in accordance with his dominant position in nature, man's task is to educate the animals and, by humanizing them, to raise them, to the extent this is possible for them, to the higher love for God through man. But, to be sure, since they are deprived of spirit, in animals this love never goes beyond the *psychical* domain.

But one should not forget that the psychical element, the element of the soul, is a necessary element in the makeup of man and thus participates in human love. The latter can never be solely spiritual in character, but must also have a psychical character in a certain sense. Psychical love is, in turn, an expression of the corporeality of the animal and human nature. Love that is *solely* spiritual would disincarnate the human spirit, and that is unnatural and impossible. It is a question here of complex interrelationships and spiritual proportions. Animal love, which by its psychical character is also proper to man, not only is not the sole form of love as far as he is concerned, but is included in spiritual love. But in the animal world, love remains limited: it is not accompanied by the higher vocations that are proper to man's spiritual essence. The fullness of human love is revealed when all the aspects of man's being participate in it, under the governing influence of the spirit. Man is called to encompass both psychical (more precisely, psycho-corporeal) and spiritual love, but he is also capable of limiting himself to the inferior love associated with the psycho-corporeal, animal side. But one can ask: Are these psycho-corporeal impulses in man, these emotions and passions, worthy of bearing the elevated name *love*? The wise genius of language says "yes," and this is justified by the fact that, in their generic character, even these inferior forms of human love manifest consubstantiality and altruism, although in highly limited and distorted forms.

The capacity of man not only for psychical but also for spiritual love makes the higher forms of love accessible for him — from spirit to spirit: Such is the love for God, which is the foundation of all religions, and such is the love for one's neighbor, which is altruistic in the exact sense, i.e., in the sense of love that is like that for oneself. There is no reason to limit the capacity for such love in the pre-Christian world to the Old Testament church alone, while denying it to all of paganism. Can one assert that the most pious representatives of paganism — Cornelius, Socrates, Plato, Plotinus, and others — lacked the capacity of love for God? Can one assert that all the heroes of antiquity lacked the capacity of love for one's neighbor, and that the pagan vices were nothing more than "beautiful vices"? To assert this would be to deny the inextinguishability of the image of God in man, which image is primarily manifested in the capacity of love for God and love for one's neighbor, in other words, in the capacity for religion and morality. But natural man has these capacities solely as natural capacities, that is, as capacities that are limited by his corruption due to original sin and by his powerlessness to realize the fullness of love without the help of divine grace.

Even natural man is capable of nurturing the gift of love that he receives by natural grace, however, and therefore of knowing the value of love. Therefore, the commandment of love can be known — with certain qualifications — even beyond the limits of Revelation or of the Old Testament church. The Old Testament humanity did know the law of love for God and for one's neighbor as a commandment of God, on which "hang all the law and the prophets" (Matt. 22:40), according to the testimony of the Lord Himself. Nevertheless, this was not yet the "*new* commandment" (John 13:34) about love that the Lord gave to His disciples in the Last Discourse. It must nonetheless be affirmed that even this Old Testament commandment of love, despite the fact that it is difficult and even impossible to fulfill by man's natural powers alone, was addressed precisely to natural man. This means that this commandment corresponds to a *natural postulate* of his consciousness. By its very existence, this commandment attests that, although he is fallen, natural man is capable of loving God and his neighbor, and that, consequently, appropriate efforts for its fulfillment are demanded of him, namely, the labor and ascesis of love. The presence of this postulate in natural man serves as the natural basis for receiving the gift of love, this *gift of grace,* which, as in all things, is bestowed not by a mechanical act of coercion *(deus ex machina),* but by a *synergistic* union of the gift of the Holy Spirit and man's efforts directed at receiving this gift.

Thus, there can be an *asceticism* of love, that is, a method and discipline of love. This discipline and path of love are revealed in a divinely inspired manner by the apostle Paul in 1 Corinthians 13. The doctrine of love expounded there can be understood as an unfolding of the *immanent* con-

316

tent of love, of those properties which participate in and are presupposed by the power of love; and it can also be understood as the teaching of the *path* of love and of its constituent elements or virtues, whose acquisition permits one to attain love itself. It is noteworthy that the majority of the apostle Paul's definitions of love here have not a positive but a negative character; they indicate not what love does and what it is, but what it does *not* do and what it is *not*. Furthermore, not one of these achievements is, in itself, equal to love, but is only an "excellent way" (1 Cor. 12:31) to it. "Love suffereth long, and is kind: love envieth not; love vaunteth not itself, is not puffed up, doth not behave itself unseemly, seeketh not her own, is not easily provoked, thinketh no evil; rejoiceth not in iniquity, but rejoiceth in the truth; beareth all things, believeth all things, hopeth all things, endureth all things" (1 Cor. 13:4-7).[53] It should be noted that all of these virtues, which form as it were the white-light spectrum of love, are also accessible to the natural man, at least as a path, an ascesis, a human effort, in response to which comes God's grace. One can say that this passage describes *natural* love as it is expressed in the work of man on himself. But at the same time, in its integral of grace, this love is superior to all particular gifts, even the highest ones (those mentioned in 1 Cor. 13:1-3: the speaking with the tongues of men and of angels, the understanding of mysteries, faith, prophecy, the working of miracles, "altruism" in the capacity of love), for the gift of love, this gift of grace, is the Holy Spirit Himself and only it has eternally abiding significance: "love never faileth" (13:8).

The apostle Paul's doctrine of love distinguishes two aspects of love as a unified divinely inspired or Divine-human act: (1) the natural and human aspect of love, which is associated with human effort; and (2) love as a gift of grace from the Holy Spirit. To be sure, the latter cannot be acquired by human powers; and inasmuch as it is the true power of love, it is inaccessible to the natural man, who has only the *will* to love, who can only seek love. In this sense, one must acknowledge that true love exists only in the Church as the gift of the Pentecost. It cannot be attained beyond the limits of the Church, and it could not be attained even by the Old Testament Church, even though the latter knew the commandment of love. But at the same time this love is given only in response to the *seeking* of it. And such seeking must be proper to the members of the Church, who have the gift of love not automatically, not for free, but gain it only by fulfilling the commandments. We are struck by the fact that, in the Last

53. The King James Version has been modified here to conform with the Russian Bible. Specifically, "charity" has been replaced with "love." — Trans.

Discourse, the Lord says repeatedly, "A new commandment I give unto you, That ye love one another; as I have loved you, that ye also love another" (John 13:34; cf. 15:12, 17). Why is this a *new* commandment? Do not the law and the prophets depend on the commandment of love (see Matt. 22:40)? The only answer to this natural question is that what the Lord means here is precisely the acquisition of love as a gift of grace from the Holy Spirit — and do not forget that the main subject of the Last Discourse is the promise that the Holy Spirit will come (see above). But the Lord gives this promise precisely as a *commandment,* which is clearly directed at human will. Consequently, human effort is required in order to acquire the love by which Christ loves us. And this is the love in the Holy Spirit, as is made fully clear by the final words of the High-priestly prayer: "that the love wherewith thou hast loved me may be in them, and I in them" (John 17:26). This Love is the Holy Spirit Himself, and these words clearly refer to the gift of love in the Pentecost.

Let us now examine different aspects of this love in the Holy Spirit as *churchly love,* which poured forth in the world in the Pentecost. The primary and fundamental gift of this love is churchliness or ecclesiality itself. The Church is not only a society, but also a real, living consubstantiality or multi-unity, the "Body of Christ." The descent of the Holy Spirit, actualizing for us Christ's Divine-humanity and our participation in the latter, makes for us the Church of Christ as the unity of the Divine and creaturely Sophia that *reality* which is recognized by the action of the Holy Spirit, by the "new," churchly love. This love not only links people psychologically and empirically; it unites them spiritually by bringing them into the supraempirical, sophianic unity of the Church as a supernatural given.

This love is the ontic power of participation in the higher reality of the body of the Church. (The apostle Paul develops this general idea in different forms in 1 Corinthians 12, in the Epistle to the Ephesians, and elsewhere.) The Church is not created by love, for she exists in "the fellowship of the mystery, which from the beginning of the world had been hid in God" (Eph. 3:9); but *for us* she is actualized by our love, by the action of the Holy Spirit qualified as churchly love: "That we . . . speaking the truth in love, may grow up into him in all things, which is the head, even Christ: from whom the whole body" (4:14-16). Psychology becomes ontology; the society of men becomes churchliness. On the wings of grace, the Holy Spirit transports man from his natural state into one of grace, transforming him from the old Adam into the New Adam.

This operation of the Spirit has its special name, *koinōnia:* "The grace of the Lord Jesus Christ, and the love of God, and the communion [*koinōnia*] of the Holy Spirit, be with you all" (2 Cor. 13:13). The gift of communion, *koinōnia,* is the *first* gift of the Pentecost as the manifestation of the Church; and it is also the *supreme goal* established by Christ Himself for all humanity in the Church: "that they may be one, even as we are one: I in them, and thou in me, that they may be made perfect in one" (John 17:22-23); by the way, this "in" *(en, eis)* is the Holy Spirit, churchly love. This love receives a sacramental expression in the "breaking of bread," in the communion with the one Body of Christ, as it is characterized in the first testimony of the Acts of the Apostles (2:42) about the life of the Church: "they continued stedfastly in the apostles' doctrine and fellowship [*tēi koinōniai*], and in breaking of bread, and in prayers." It is manifested in a particular sense of churchliness, a sense of dissolving in the whole, of living multi-unity, in which the personal is not abolished but integrated into a unity of sobornost. The *koinōnia* of the Holy Spirit is churchly sobornost as the supreme reality of the Church, but it is also the goal that is to be attained and therefore the regulative norm.

Churchly love, in the image of the Holy Trinity, overcomes the isolation of egocentrism by the power of the *whole,* which enters into the soul as a higher reality: "whosoever will lose his life for my sake shall find it" (Matt. 16:25). Here, one first has to deny oneself (16:24), to abandon one's self-assertion, and then, in response, the soul is filled by the life of the whole through love. The individual gains for himself a center higher than his own; and instead of being eccentric and egocentric, he becomes concentric with respect to the whole. Such overcoming of egocentrism *already* occurs in a certain sense in manifestations of natural love for one's family, one's country, one's group, for humanity in general. But this is a psychological fact, not an ontological fact, and it cannot go beyond the limits of empirical reality. These limits can be transcended only in the Church through the Holy Spirit. These natural-grace movements of the human soul are the natural substratum for the Holy Spirit's koinonic gift of communion in love. These movements can have the significance of works of love, of self-discipline, of the path to love as *koinōnia,* about which the apostle Paul speaks in 1 Corinthians 13.

Does this concentrism of churchly love signify an abstraction from all personal connections, the dissolving of the latter in the unity of the whole? Or does the whole remain here a *concrete multi-unity,* which it already is in natural being? Does churchly love become abstract and impersonal; or does it preserve its personal character in the union of the whole? It is sufficient to pose these questions to understand that love as a gift of grace does not destroy anything (except sin), but rather raises everything worthy of it to a higher concreteness of multi-diversity in multi-unity. This idea is confirmed by the repeated comparison of the Church with the body, which has many and diverse members: "fitly joined together and compacted by that which every joint supplieth, according to the effectual working in the measure of every part" (Eph. 4:16). In other words, individual links of love exist in churchly, supra-individual love. Although the personal principle is revealed and realized in these links of love, this love is illuminated by the Spirit and included in the communion of churchly love. There are different forms of such love: friendship, the love between relatives, relations between the sexes (above all, marriage), and then, correlatively, monasticism. Let us begin with friendship.[54]

Friendship is a *personal* relation in love, rooted in the life of the Church. One loses one's soul for Christ's sake with reference to a particular person to whom one is linked by friendship; and this communion of pair-syzygy determines life in churchly love. Even though the relations of friendship have a pairwise character in each particular case, they can be repeated, since one and the same person can enter into different alliances of friendship; and a natural hierarchy is established among these alliances such that one true Friendship is realized among many friendships and friends. Exclusivity does not necessarily characterize friendship, although it can exist in particular cases.

The foundation of churchly friendship is Christ's Friendship with us. He tells His disciples: "Ye are my friends [*philoi*]. . . . I have called you my friends; for all things that I have heard of my Father I have made known unto you" (John 15:14-15). With these words the Lord establishes, in churchly love, a *personal* relation toward Himself, a certain reciprocity of love, alongside or in fulfillment of the love for all or for the multi-unity of the whole. The Greek language distinguishes different kinds of love, in particular *agapē* and *philia*.[55] Agapic love is love in general, which includes

---

54. The chapter on friendship in Pavel Florensky's *Pillar and Ground of the Truth* represents a true theological revelation, because for the first time friendship as an ecclesial relation has been incorporated in the theological doctrine of the Church, and is seen as having a legitimate place in the life of the Church. [*The Pillar and Ground of the Truth* is available in Boris Jakim's translation (Princeton, N.J.: Princeton University Press, 1997). — Trans.]

55. This has been noted by Pavel Florensky in *The Pillar and Ground of the Truth*. Cf. Anders Nygren, *Agape and Eros: A Study of the Christian Idea of Love* (London: SPCK, 1932). In the Synoptic Gospels the noun *agapē* is encountered only in Matthew 24:12 and Luke 11:42, without any particular significance; the verb is encountered more frequently, but it can refer to love for God, to love for one's neighbor, or to the natural feeling of love, as in

various forms and nuances of love, whereas philic love is qualified, individualized, personal love, love as friendship.[56]

A third Greek word for love, *erōs,* is not used in the New Testament Greek (or in the Septuagint), although it is encountered in the patristic literature.[57] Above we interpreted *erōs* to mean inspiration, the transcendence of oneself, ecstatic love. Friendship, as a certain spiritual pair-syzygy, also includes traits of erotic love in this sense, for it is accompanied by or even consists of a particular *mutual* inspiration, an overcoming of personal self-enclosedness through the life together of two persons, but "with one soul." To be sure, the erotic character of this inspiring love lacks the intensity that characterizes love between man and woman. But the concept of "erotic" love should, in this sense, be emancipated from all traces of sexuality. Popular word-usage associates erotic love with sexuality, but already in Plato such an association is absent (see Alcibiades' discourse concerning Socrates in the *Symposium*). In its most general sense, "friendship" can exist between man and woman, and in this case, it assumes the inspiring character of spiritual eros.

In general, the concept of friendship as personal love and the spiritual eros that accompanies it must be extended to include *different* forms of this love; and the difference between the sexes does not by any means play the central role here, although its existence obviously qualifies or conditions love itself. This includes different forms of family love: love for father and mother, brothers and sisters, etc. In general, personal love is diverse and does not admit any single definition. What is important is to establish that these forms of natural love can also become forms of churchly love, precisely by receiving the gracious gift of this love by the ac-

---

Luke 6:32 (Nygren, p. 83). "The introduction of the word *agapē* as a technical term seems to be due to Paul" (Nygren, p. 83). Of course, the most frequent use of both *agapē* and *agapan* can be found in the Fourth Gospel.

56. In the Gospel, the Lord's relations with His personal friend Lazarus and with Lazarus' sisters Mary and Martha are expressed not only by the general *agapē* but also by the concrete *phileis, philos, ephilei.* Toward His "beloved disciple," the Lord mainly uses *agapan,* but He also uses *ephilei* (John 20:2). In the threefold interrogation of Peter, which is conducted with mounting intensity, in the first two cases it is a question of love in general, *agapē,* whereas in the final case it is a question of personal, philic love: *phileis me.*

57. The Greek title of Symeon the New Theologian's *Hymns of Love (Amores)* is *Erōtes,* evidently with reference to the Holy Spirit. Gregory Palamas uses this word in the same sense: "The Spirit of the supreme Word is as if a certain ineffable Eros [*tis Erōs estin aporrētos*] of the Engenderer toward the ineffably engendered Word" (*Capita physica, theologica,* etc.; *PG* 150, col. 1145).

tion of the Holy Spirit, even though there is no special sacrament that establishes and sanctifies these forms of love.[58] This is done by virtue of life in common in the Church, by a certain illumination of the spirit, which is analogous to prophetic illumination.

In the dual character of churchly love as agape and as eros, there is manifested the antinomic duality of the Christian path as ascesis and creative activity, of repentant humility and creative inspiration. Self-renunciation is realized in agape: an individual dies in his egoism in order to live in and by the whole. In eros, an individual, experiencing inspiration to the point of self-transcendence, ascends to creative self-revelation. Agape can be realized even by a solitary individual; it even presupposes a certain spiritual isolation, with withdrawal into the inner cell of the heart. By contrast, eros is the going out of oneself, a certain opening of the heart by the power of inspiration, which is given by the eros of love. In syzygial connectedness, an individual begins to see himself in and through another. He acquires in the other a spiritual mirror of himself, not for narcissistic self-love (which is possible only in a condition of temptation and corruption, irrespective of whether it is a question of agape or eros) but for the self-affirmation of himself through the other. Here, the self-affirmation that is necessary for the creative act loses the poison of self-love (although, in the condition of temptation and corruption, a potentiated self-love can arise, a spiritual delusion *à deux*, a bad *hen dia duoin*, inasmuch as anything that is human can become ambiguous and sinful).

Friendship as spiritual "syzygy" (to use the gnostic expression employed by Vladimir Solovyov) is the most general expression of love as eros, without regard to distinction of sex. But the primary domain of eros is the interrelation of the male and female principles in man, inasmuch as, in his fullness, man consists of the union ("and") of these two principles: "So God created man in his own image, in the image of God created he him; male *and* female created he them" (Gen. 1:27). Inwardly, in the spirit, man is defined by the polarity of the male and female principles;[59]

---

58. There once existed the ancient rite of adelphopoiesis ("brother-making"), which sanctified personal friendship. About this rite, see Fr. K. Nikol'sky, *On Offices in the Russian Church Which Were Found in Early Printed Liturgical Books* (St. Petersburg, 1885): The Rite of Adelphopoiesis, with appendices, pp. 371-89. This rite characterizes the love of brothers as "love in Christ," as "spiritual love." These characterizations, of course, have a capital dogmatic significance for understanding the religious value of personal eros between friends. This idea can also be applied to relations between men and women which do not have the character of conjugal love but rather the character of friendship.

59. See my book *The Unfading Light*, the chapter on man.

and even in his external being, man is not only male or female, but precisely male *and* female. He is this ontological *and,* which expresses the fullness of Divine-humanity, of the image of God in man. It corresponds not to just one of the hypostases, not to the male or female principle taken separately, but to their dyadic union. This is the basis for a particular form of love in man, predominantly syzygial and expressly inspiring in character, insofar as there is a distinction here between spiritual gifts and their mutual fulfillment. Love-friendship between the male and female principles in man is expressly ecstatic, creative, inspiring; it is eros.

This relation would be simple and clear if it remained solely spiritual. And it is such in individual cases recorded by history. Here we have an anticipation of life "as the angels of God in heaven" (Matt. 22:30). But in fallen humanity this relation is complicated by sex and the function of reproduction, which presupposes not only spiritual but also psycho-corporeal differences between the bearers of the male and female principles. Spiritual eros turns out to be included in the life of sex, and ascesis is given the capacity to overcome this complexity on the way of the cross of eros, or to ascetically abolish eros itself. The male and female principles were introduced in the composition of the animal world at the creation. God did not create all living things in their fullness all at once; instead, He implanted in them the power to multiply, saying, "Be fruitful, and multiply" (Gen. 1:22). This multiplication initially presupposed a sexual difference, as we can conclude not only from the general definition concerning creation "after his kind," but also from the narrative of the presentation of the animals to man (Gen. 2:19); moreover, "for Adam there was not found an help meet for him" (2:20). What is meant here is a woman, as is clear from the narrative that follows. At their creation, God said to man as male and female the same thing that He said to the animal world: "Be fruitful, and multiply" (1:28).

Sex and sexual reproduction, as the axis of animal being, therefore bear the imprint of God's direct will: they are included in life by God's creative power. Consequently, within the limits of the animal world, sex and sexual reproduction are not tainted by sinful or shameful desire, since one cannot speak of sin in the animal world. The latter finds itself below sin and becomes accessible to its influence only through man. That is why animals do not know sexual shame, even as man did not know sexual shame *before* the fall: "And they were both naked, the man and his wife, and were not ashamed" (Gen. 2:25). The fire of life which is present in sex as the principle of reproduction, this fire burned, shedding light, but it did not consume, as it consumes the fallen nature. Perhaps it had already consumed the fallen essence of the fleshless spirit who, perverting his own fleshless nature, enflamed himself with animal sexual lust and was able to infect our progenitors with this lust. At the very least, the serpent's temptation contains an allegorical indication of his sexual character, as is evident in the fact that the fallen progenitors realized that they were naked: "Who told thee that thou wast naked?" (3:11), God asks Adam. At first, naming the animals and seeing their sexual pairedness, Adam was not tempted by the nakedness, for he had not yet "found an help meet" (2:20). This temptation by the animality of sex came to him not from the animal world, but from his "help meet," his own wife.

In the first man, the animal function of reproduction was united with the spiritual principle of syzygy as the spiritual eros of the male and female principles. This was *friendship* in the proper sense of the word, as the acquisition of an "other," an alter ego, "an help meet."[60] But at the same time this "help meet" or friend was a fleshly "other," formed out of Adam's flesh, out of his "rib," as he slept (Gen. 2:21), that is, when he was beyond the conscious control of the spirit. It was only in a state of prophetic vision that Adam recognized this fleshly bi-unity, when he said about the woman brought to him by God, "This is now bone of my bones, and flesh of my flesh: she shall be called Woman, because she was taken out of Man" (2:23). And "they shall be one flesh" (2:24). Thus, from the very beginning, spiritual love for the "help meet" is joined with fleshly union in fulfillment of the commandment to multiply. This joining of spiritual and fleshly union results from the spiritual-corporeal nature of man as an incarnate spirit. A connection is preserved here with the animal world, which at the same time is *transcended* by the presence of the spiritual principle in man and by its harmonizing, spiritualizing power. But this harmonization of sex and spirit, so essential for man, turned out to be the most difficult of tasks, and the relation between sex and spirit turned out to be unstable, as demonstrated by the fact of the fall. The latter exerted an influence on man's entire life and, through him, on the entire world; but its most intimate effect was on the relationship between the male and female principles in man.

This change can be expressed as follows: in man, *sex was awakened* as a rebellious, autonomous element, an element of desire and passion which not only was not subject to the spirit but which subjected the spirit to itself: "and thy desire shall be to thy husband" (Gen. 3:16); and such also

60. This sentence contains an untranslatable wordplay involving the Russian words *druzhba* (friendship), *drug* (friend), and *drugoi* (an "other" or alter ego). — Trans.

became the desire of the husband for the wife. Sexual life in man lost its initial harmony and took on a tragic character. In man, sex is an incarnate antinomy: it makes him an animal, but at the same time he cannot totally become an animal except in the lowest depths of his fall, in a kind of de-humanization, about which the Bible speaks with reference to the antediluvian corruption: "he also is flesh" (Gen. 6:3). In the animal aspect of sex, man tragically finds himself both above and below the animal world, for the latter, not having spirit, remains innocent in the sexual life, whereas, in man, sexual life is experienced as a loss of "innocence." But at the same time this differentiation between male and female qualifies in a very essential way the *spirit* of man, who is in no wise an "androgyne" (although every man is, to a certain degree, androgynous in his spirit), but is male *or* female. Their desire for each other and their friendship can also exist in a purely spiritual form, free of the flesh and of passion, but at the same time it is defenseless against the infection of passion. In no wise does sex exhaust the difference between the male and female principles. Rather, sex is the chain fettering the spiritual love of male and female. Eros is enslaved and oppressed by sex to such an extent that the latter has appropriated and thus distorted in the eyes of many the very name *erōs,* which is usually understood only sexually, although it is not really such. At the same time, man's very being, that is, his reproduction, is twisted into the fatal knot of eros and sex: "I was shapen in iniquity, and in sin did my mother conceive me" (Ps. 51:5). Man is conceived in sin and shame.[61]

The antinomy of eros and sex, which exists for every human being (any exceptions have a pathological character), seeks ascetic resolution in various forms of their struggle against each on paths of their possible harmonization. The simplest path, the pseudo-ascetic one, consists simply in the mortification of both eros and sex. The goal here is to desexualize man through sexual ascesis, which in general occupies such an important place in the ascetic practice. This desexualization, like natural asexuality, is sometimes thought to be equivalent to the purity of innocence, although it is not really such. It seeks, in general, to abolish the male and female principles in man, transforming man not even into an "androgyne," but into a neutered being. It thus tries to modify God's will concerning the creation of man, to correct God's plan. Except for cases of natural defectiveness, which are more common than one thinks and are often taken for genuine ascetic desexualization, this goal remains unrealizable and

---

61. It is in this context that one should understand the purifying prayers pronounced over the mother, recited immediately after birth and forty days later.

false. In essence, sex is not rejected even in monasticism, which distinguishes, at the very least, between monks and nuns. Consequently, even
the assumption of the "angelic image" of monasticism does not disqualify
an individual from belonging to the male or female gender. The mortification not only of the "flesh," i.e., sex, but also of eros in man would be —
if it were not impossible — spiritual suicide. But by no means should
Christian asceticism be suicide. The intensity of eros as the spiritual energy of inspiring love is the fiery element which seeks to be overshadowed
by the Holy Spirit and which receives Him, inasmuch as the following
principle is valid with regard to the gifts of the Holy Spirit: "Ask, and it
shall be given you; seek, and ye shall find" (Matt. 7:7). In order to understand and accept this truth, one must fully restore the significance attributed to the power of love as spiritual eros, given the presumed presence of
the male and female principles in Revelation itself.

The Church, as well as its foundation, churchly love, is represented
in Revelation not only by images of agapic and philic love, but also by images of spiritual eros, of inspiring and inspired love, of a certain divine ecstasy. In this connection we must first try to decipher the sacred mystery
of *The Song of Songs*, this most New-Testamental book in the Old Testament, and perhaps in the entire Bible. The inclusion of this book in the
canon, an inclusion so repugnant and incomprehensible for people of an
anti-erotic spirit, is a true miracle, worked by the Holy Spirit. Compared
to the other canonical books, it is the "Holy of Holies" of the Bible, as
both Christian and Jewish exegetes call it. Rationalistic exegesis sees in it
merely an example of love poetry, although a sublime and unsurpassable
one; but we must affirm that it is nothing other than an apotheosis of
love. As an epithalamium, a nuptial song, it portrays a bridegroom and
his bride in their search for each other. But they are not the true protago-
nists of this sacred drama (unique of its kind in the Old Testament, as
well as in the New).

The true subject of *The Song of Songs* is not the bridegroom and his
bride and their human love, but *Love* itself. This theme is expressed in the
concluding chapter in words in which the entire power of *The Song of Songs*
is concentrated and for the sake of which it was perhaps written. Here are
these words: "Set me as a seal upon thine heart, as a seal upon thine arm:
for love is strong as death; jealousy is cruel as the grave: the coals thereof
are coals of fire, which hath a most vehement flame" (8:6). But the end of
this passage has a significant variant: not "vehement flame" but "flame of
God" (and this is the only direct mention of the Name of God in this
book). Thus, this book is written about the Holy Spirit, the flame of God,

Love. It expresses the special character of the love that exists between Christ and the Church, which is the Holy Spirit. One can say that Christ loves the Church by the Holy Spirit, and that the Church loves Him in the Holy Spirit, Who abides in the Church. In the New Testament this idea is expressed in Ephesians 5, where the mystery of marriage is elucidated with reference to Christ and the Church. To this one should add other Old Testament and New Testament figures of the marriage feast borrowed from the domain of the mutual love of husband and wife, bridegroom and bride.

These figures are summed up, as it were, in the final chapter of Revelation: "And the Spirit and the bride say, Come. And let him that heareth say, Come" (Rev. 22:17). What is meant here, of course, is the Church in Her relation to Christ; and here the love of the Church, which is the "Spirit," is represented as the love of the "bride" for the Bridegroom. Elsewhere we find: "the marriage of the Lamb is come, and his wife hath made herself ready" (19:7); "the wife and bride of the Lamb" (21:9;[62] the "and" here is equivalent to "i.e.," indicating the special form of the love between the Church and Christ). There is an analogous relation in mariology,[63] where the Mother and Daughter of God is the "Unwedded Bride." In all these figures, the Male principle corresponds to the Logos, whereas the Female principle corresponds to the Spirit. As for Christ and the Church, this is an unfathomable mystery whose revelation will come only in the future age with the hypostatic revelation of the Holy Spirit, a revelation that this age does not know. But what is important for us is that this figure of love is, if not unique, at least typological in churchly love; in particular, it indicates the relation between the bridegroom and the bride. Let us examine this question in more detail.

Insofar as this form of love, together with agapic love, belongs to the Church through the action of the Holy Spirit, it must considered as a form of love that is given to man and included in the range of churchly love, of love as a gift of grace. But in order to understand all the power of this gift of grace, we must first consider the natural gift that corresponds to it, for the natural gifts are the substratum, as it were, for the action of grace; they are the creaturely call and questioning. It is indisputable that the inspiring power of eros is also given in the natural relationships between people, as friendship or the syzygial union of life. There are absolutely no grounds to assert that this power, in its very *existence*, is connected with the fall of man.

---

62. This phrase is translated from the Russian Bible. — Trans.
63. See my book *The Burning Bush*.

On the contrary, like other spiritual powers, it is a gift of natural grace, which has its source (like all things in creation) in the life-giving power of the Holy Spirit. And the image of eros in the pagan old testament, e.g., in Plato's *Symposium*, tends not to refute but to confirm this conclusion. The creative power of love, the fiery force of inspiration, is embodied in Plato's work in images that are so convincing that they seem self-evident. The Platonic eros is *not* connected with relations between the sexes; it has a general character. But it also includes the love of the male and female principles, which is based on their spiritual difference, as well as on their unity in the human essence. The male and female principles are united without separation and without confusion in human sophianicity, which exists in the image of union in the Divine Sophia, of the revelation of the Second and Third hypostases, of Their bi-unity. This bi-unity exists in the eternal Proto-image, the Divine-humanity, and it receives its seal in the creation of man "in the image of God" as man and woman, the bearers of the two principles, which exist without separation in separate being and without confusion in joint being.[64]

This dual qualification of the creaturely spirit must be extended to the world and to the fleshless spirits, inasmuch as they all bear the image of God, which is fully disclosed for creation in the separate being of the two principles. But in man this spiritual difference is complicated by the existence of the psycho-corporeal element: the male and female principles of the spirit are realized here as man and woman. They are meant not only to experience a spiritual love (where the woman is the "help meet," i.e., the friend, and the husband is the head, i.e., also a friend, but manifesting his friendship in a different manner) but also to "be one flesh" (Gen. 2:24): the spiritual union here is accompanied by a bodily union, whose task is reproduction, commanded by God to man (Gen. 1:28) and to the entire animal world. This fullness of conjugal love, being included in the fullness of the image of God in man, was, of course, harmonized in such a way that the union of husband and wife in one flesh should not have a *fleshly* character, but should be subject to the spirit and entirely spiritualized. The fall of man, which found its most intimate expression in the life of sex, destroyed this harmony and replaced it with a tragic disharmony, which is experienced in different ways in the life of love in its entirety and in its different aspects.

64. See Vladimir Solovyov's work *The Meaning of Love*, which is unforgettable despite being somewhat marred by a one-sidedness as regards the question of sex and marriage.

As a consequence of the fall, *sex* appeared, this fiery element of man's being, an element that received autonomous existence in the capacity of the power of life in fallen man. But at the same time, by virtue of the unity of life in man, this element is connected with his spirit, constituting both the wings and the chains of the latter. Having lost its transparence for the spirit and now clothed in the "coats of skins" (Gen. 3:21) of the flesh, the body of man became three things: a revelation of man's spirit, his "spiritual body"; a veil impenetrable for the spirit, his "natural body"; and finally, the flesh. And spiritual or "syzygial" love (to borrow the expression used by Vladimir Solovyov in *The Meaning of Love*) united itself and (which is much worse) became mixed with fleshly love. This is expressed, for example, in the fatal ambiguity of the term *erōs*, which can mean both spiritual love and sensual "eroticism." For this reason some think that a merciless war should be declared against eros, that it should be annihilated because of this ambiguity. But that would be to annihilate man himself, which is something directly opposed to God's will. It would be to annihilate him in all senses: first, physically, since his very existence depends on sexual love; and then spiritually, since his inspiration and creative activity are connected with the fiery element of eros, which — alas! — is spiritual-corporeal in nature. There remains the path of the "sublimation"[65] or transfiguration of eros, the path of its emancipation, if not from its connection with the body (which would mean the disintegration of man's spiritual-corporeal makeup, his disincarnation, which is impossible), then from the fetters of the flesh, from enslavement to the body.

There can be various paths of the "transfiguration of eros," of the battle for eros, for its higher, spiritual embodiments and against its lower, fleshly embodiments; and in a certain sense the path of the salvation of eros coincides here with the path of spiritual life. One must first note the possible forms of spiritual love or friendship between representatives of the two principles, in whom the fleshly principle is overcome (if not absolutely, then within the limits accessible to man) ascetically or by love itself. Not because of repugnance for the flesh (which repugnance is condemned by the Church) but for spiritual and ascetic reasons, this spiritual love must never — with regard to its very purpose — become a fleshly love, even a conjugal love; nevertheless in its spiritual power it exists and has the right to exist, insofar as it is a creative energy of the spirit. In virtue of

---

65. The question of sublimation receives a comprehensive examination in B. P. Vysheslavtsev's book: *The Ethics of Transfigured Eros,* Paris, 1931.

the unbreakable connection between the fleshly and spiritual principles in man, the ascetic path in this battle of the spirit for the spirit appears to be especially difficult and even dangerous. But this cannot justify the killing of love itself as a creative power of the spirit, especially since in the domain of the spirit there are no guarantees that any path is true and safe, since the life of the spirit is always connected with creative activity and freedom, initiative, the audacious acceptance of responsibility.

If the very power of love in man represents not a sinful contamination resulting from his corruption because of the fall, but his original, though sin-tainted, vocation, it is necessary to recognize that love — not in its lower aspects but in its highest aspirations and conquests — is a gift of natural grace, which seeks and finds its sanctification by the Holy Spirit in the Church. True, in this case this sanctification is not communicated through a special sacrament but is accomplished in the general process of the life of grace in the Church. But the absence of a special sacrament does not mean that this side of the life of the spirit is deprived of grace. This is true also of other aspects of human life that are not sanctified by any special sacrament. Spiritual birth in baptism, the gift of the Holy Spirit in confirmation, and communion with Christ in the Eucharist imply the sanctification and benediction of *all* human life, and in particular of the power of spiritual love, which manifests itself in human relationships insofar as they are not corrupted by the fall. The natural powers are nourished by the grace of the Holy Spirit in conformity with the general power of churchly life. And if personal love is one of the forms of churchly love, then, as such, it is sanctified from within and its inspirations proceed from the inspirations of the Spirit.

The ascetic overcoming of sex in the relations between the male and female natures, that is, spiritual love and friendship, occupies a legitimate place in the general structure of churchly love as the *personal* principle of eros. But spiritual love does not exhaust all the possibilities of love, which, in conformity with man's makeup, is spiritual-corporeal in character. Man is not only a spiritual and personal but also a corporeal and generic being; and sexual life is connected not only with sinful lust in man but also with the generic function of reproduction and family. Therefore, the relations between the sexes can also be directed along the channel of generic, family love, which is accompanied by the fulfillment of God's commandment concerning reproduction.

Marriage unites two forms of love: personal love and generic (family) love. On the one hand, the sacrament of marriage sanctifies the personal love of the bridegroom and the bride, which love is (or at least can and even must be) a spiritual love, friendship; and it crowns man (which corresponds to the rite of crowning in the Orthodox marriage ceremony). On the other hand, the sacrament of marriage sanctifies sexual life and the reproduction that depends on it. The sinful principle of lust that is associated with the life of sex is neutralized here, as it were. Grace pacifies and takes the sorrow out of the life of sex, which is justified by reproduction. The antinomy that exists between the spirit and the flesh, between spiritual love and fleshly union, an antinomy that is expressed both in passionate sexual desire and in the aspiration to transcend sex in spiritual communion, this antinomy is not abolished here, but it is pacified by the grace of the sacrament of marriage as the sacrificial path of communion and reproduction.

In the whole Old Testament, as well as outside the Christian Church, marriage is considered to be a natural sacrament. Consequently, the Church too considers the personal love of the bridegroom and the bride, as well as their communion based on a mutual vow, to be an example of sanctification by natural grace. In the Old Testament, no particular need arose for an express sanctification of the marriage union, perhaps partly because the generic function of marriage, reproduction, which contained the future Sacred Seed of the Divine Incarnation, eclipsed the personal love and friendship between bridegroom and bride, relegating this personal love to a secondary place in the consciousness. This weakening of the *personal* character of marriage was also expressed in the permitting of polygamy and in the levirate, which underscored the *generic* character of marriage. The antinomy between fleshly and spiritual love, which in paganism found resolution in orgiastic and phallic cults and in sacred prostitution, becomes exceptionally acute in Christianity thanks to the emancipation of the life of the spirit that it produces. And this naturally leads to the postulate that sexual life can receive the help of grace through the sacrament of marriage.

Sexual life is ascetically regulated by this sacrament, first of all because in conjugal love it does not need to be a mere servant of lust, and also because it receives a sacrificial justification for itself in reproduction. Furthermore, the sacrament of marriage is a benediction of personal love as spiritual friendship. Inasmuch as the gift of this love is bestowed by the Holy Spirit, Who is the eternal Glory in the Holy Trinity and the Glory of the God-Man in the Incarnation, the sanctification of marriage, with the symbolic placing of crowns upon the head, is a "crowning with glory and honor."

At the same time, sexual life is *ascetically* permitted. This ascesis of sexual life places definite limits on its freedom, however: it is not only per-

mitted and sanctified, but it is also bound and limited *spiritually*, in particular by being subordinated to spiritual love. That is why, in virtue of this
ascetically limiting tendency of the Church with reference to sexual life,
Christianity permits only monogamy, and forbids divorce and fornica-
tion. This does not mean that spiritual love or friendship is conceived as
being possible only once; on the contrary, it can occur many times and in
different ways. It means, rather, that the love that is united with fleshy
communion, with sexual life, must be unique. The exceptions (second and
third marriage, and divorce), despite all the abuses connected with them,
only confirm the general rule. The sacrament of marriage in the Church
must therefore be understood with reference to original sin and the resulting tragic upheaval of human life, which became burdened by *sex*, i.e.,
by passion and lust, in the mutual relations of man and woman. By blessing spiritual love, this sacrament moderates and ascetically regulates the
life of the flesh by its grace.

Insofar as the sacrament of marriage is intended to liberate the personal eros in man from the burden of sex, it is the path to conjugal chastity, the gift of which is requested in the rite of this sacrament.[66] However,
this is, of course, not a straight path, but a round-about one, and one connected with the acceptance of the commandment to be fruitful and multiply. But there is another path of chastity, the straight one, but one that,
to be sure, involves the renunciation of this commandment. This is the
path of active chastity, of sanctified virginity, of the voluntary "eunuchs
for the kingdom of heaven's sake," in contrast to the eunuchs who "were
so born from their mother's womb" (Matt. 19:12), and who, even in the
monastic state, do not know the ascetic victory over sex. This state, not of
de facto celibacy, which can be merely a result of personal fate and which
can be experienced as involuntary misfortune, but of virginity accepted as
a feat of ascesis — this state is a different path of the overcoming of sex in
man, consisting in the direct battle against sex, assisted by God's grace.
This state consists, first of all, in the desire to restore that image of the
original man which he had before his fall and before he was clothed in the
"coats of skins" of sensuous flesh; and second, it consists in assuming
"the angelic image" in the sense of renouncing for oneself the commandment of reproduction, which is alien to the angels, for the latter constitute a "congregation" or a "choir," not a genus.[67] It should be noted that,

---

66. "Accord to these Your servants a peaceful life, prosperity, chastity, and mutual
love in a union of peace, a much perpetuated progeny, the grace of childbearing."

67. See my book *Jacob's Ladder: On the Angels*.

just as angels do not lack a concrete qualifiedness or specificity of the spirit, so those who assume "the angelic image" do not cease being male or female, although they aspire to liberate themselves from gender. They do not become neuter beings, which would be a crime against man's onto-logical *essence.*

The virginity path to chastity is more sanctified than the marriage path, which is a kind of a compromise with sex. Thus, we read in the Book of Revelation (14:1-5) about the "one hundred forty and four thousand" who "were redeemed from among men." They have the "Father's name written in their foreheads" and sing "a new song before the throne." "These are they which were not defiled with women; for they are virgins. These are they which follow the Lamb whithersoever he goeth. These were redeemed from among men, being the firstfruits unto God and to the Lamb." The "order" of chastity is, of course, headed by the Virgin Mary with the "beloved disciple" John, adopted by her, and with John the Fore-runner. In the Church, active chastity and virginity exist in the institution of monasticism.

Virginity and marriage, as two paths to chastity and the victory over sex, i.e., the path of the disciplined renunciation of sexual life and the path of conjugal ascesis and reproduction,[68] not only coexist in the Church but must be understood and accepted in their antinomic conjugacy. By virtue of this conjugacy, these paths, even though they are opposed, nevertheless presuppose and posit each other. That is why the sacrament of marriage in the Church must be understood and accepted *in connection with* the sacrament of monastic tonsure, which includes the re-nunciation of marriage. When either of these principles is asserted to be the only valid one, it becomes not merely one-sided but even heretical: *Pace* Rozanov,[69] marriage should not be viewed as a condition that is supe-rior to virginity, for God Himself has attested that the latter is the su-preme path for man. Nor should monasticism be understood as an aver-sion to marriage, for such a view is condemned by the Church. The two paths presuppose and imply one another, so the Lord's words in Matthew

---

68. The Apostle says, "Adam was not deceived, but the woman being deceived was in the transgression. Notwithstanding she shall be saved in childbearing, if they con-tinue in faith and charity and holiness with chastity" (1 Tim. 2:15; the King James Version has been modified here to conform with the Russian Bible). From this it is clear that childbearing is not opposed, in a certain sense, to chastity.

69. Vasily Rozanov (1856-1919) was a Russian writer who developed a striking and original philosophy of the primacy of sex in human life. — Trans.

19:12 can be applied to both of them taken together and to each separately: "He that is able to receive it, let him receive it."[70]

At the present time, monasticism is understood as a "renunciation of the world." But in order to understand this idea correctly, one should ask oneself: Does this mean that the Christians who are not monks are free of all "renunciation of the world"? Orthodoxy does not know that distinction between Gospel "commandments" and "precepts" on the basis of which Catholicism distinguishes between "first-class" and "second-class" Christians. All of Christ's commandments are addressed to all Christians: "thy commandment is exceeding broad" (Ps. 119:96) and "He that is able to receive it, let him receive it." Christ addresses to all Christians without distinction the universal and perfect commandment: "Be ye therefore perfect, even as your Father which is in heaven is perfect" (Matt. 5:48); and all "precepts" and all "commandments" with their distinctions are dissolved in the depths of this commandment. And it is to all Christians that the apostle of love addresses his exhortation, "Love not the world, neither the things that are in the world" (1 John 2:15). And it is to the whole multitude of the people, to those who follow the monastic path and to those who follow the family path, that the Lord addresses His exhortation, "If any man come to me, and hate not his father, and mother, and wife, and children, and brethren, and sisters, yea, and his own life also, he cannot be my disciple" (Luke 14:26). What can be added to the maximalism of these words by any monastic or nonmonastic renunciation of the world, since this is a general requirement addressed to all Christians?

But does this mean that monasticism abolishes the Old Testament commandment to respect one's parents, or God's commandment concerning family love, sanctified by the sacrament of marriage, or the Old and New Testament commandment to love one's neighbor as oneself, or the Lord's "new" commandment to love one another, or, in general, love for God's creation? Understood in this sense, Christ's words would lead to hatred and hostility toward the world, to a manichean, not Christian, attitude toward life. His words do not authorize us to dispense with the com-

---

70. Virginity in the Church is more primary and essential than monasticism; the latter is only the historical form, established by the Church, for the former. As such, the monasticism of today does not fully coincide with virginity, despite the fact that the vow of virginity is the most central of the monastic vows, and even the only essential vow. Persons are now admitted into the monastic order who have lived a long conjugal life or who have naturally, because of age, lost sexual desire.

mandment to love and to work at love; and they do not abolish the connection of every individual person with the whole human race and with the world. What they do is establish a hierarchy of love, so to speak. It is love for God which is the first commandment; and love for one's neighbor is only the second commandment, although it is equal to the first. And a Christian must love Christ more than he loves any of his neighbors and loved ones, so that he would be capable of sacrificing his love for them for the sake of his love for Christ. There is a hierarchy here, and a place for ascetic labor and self-control, but there can be and should be no place here for a manichean rejection of God's creation. Ascesis must be practiced by all human beings, and only the paths of this ascesis differ. For those who follow the monastic path, this ascesis can, in its own way, be (but does not have to be) more rigorous and severe than the ascesis of those who do not follow the monastic path; but there cannot be any renunciation of the world here in the sense of true hatred of it. We do not find such hatred in the Gospels. Indeed, it should not exist in Christianity.

This brings us back to the fundamental problem of the paths and forms of love. They differ, of course, in marriage and virginity, a particular case of which is monasticism: the latter excludes that which is the norm for marriage. But the concrete forms of love are, in general, not repeated in their individual distinctiveness. We must pose an essential question: As far as virginity and monasticism are concerned, are the forms of *personal love* as spiritual eros preserved, or are they rejected as inferior? The history of monasticism with its heroic feats of asceticism appears to indicate that they are not preserved. Hermitage, solitude, reclusion are forms of monastic life in which the individual is completely isolated from the rest of humanity in his presence before God, and appears to concentrate solely on the first commandment, that of love for God. The second commandment, equal to the first, is observed only in the general sense of churchly catholicity before the presence of God. Is this the sole norm of the monastic state, however, and is the monk truly a *monos* for whom people do not and must not exist as subjects of a *personal* relationship, of personal love (just as in prison there are no human beings, but only numbers)? But we know from the history of monasticism that such isolation is only a temporary state, which is replaced by a return to people, to human communion. Even if we recognize the existence of such solitary monasticism in all its inflexibility as the feat of repentance and prayer, we must also recognize the fact of the existence of monastic communities, the life of monks in the world with people and for people, as a form of virginal life in the service of people. We see before us the figures of the Forerunner, the preacher of repentance, and of John the Theologian, the apostle of love, as well as of great saints, such as St. Sergius, St. Seraphim of Sarov, and the Russian elders, who were centers of love and attracted great multitudes of people. While recognizing the first form of love, that of the hermits, we must also recognize and understand the second form of love, whose prototype, John the Forerunner, says of himself, "I am the *friend* of the Bridegroom" (cf. John 3:29). And by saying this, he personifies this love as friendship, which is united with his ministry as Forerunner.

In general, the distinctive spiritual "solipsism" of monastic isolation or hermitage cannot be *generalized;* it cannot be considered the sole norm of the "angelic image," obligatory for all. On the contrary, isolation should be practiced only in the general context of the spiritual life, as one of the dialectical moments of the latter. Here too, the *catholicity* of churchly being qualifies this "dwelling in the wilderness," which thus does not become a true solipsism but remains within the bounds of the agapic union of churchly love, realized by prayer. The absence of direct relations with people is possible and bearable only if there is an *inspired* intensity of love for God. The model for this love is *The Song of Songs,* spiritual marriage in the image of Christ and the Church. The passive condition of negative asceticism does not suffice here; what is needed is active ascent, ecstasy, crowned by the grace of the Spirit. That is why the great ascetic saints are not only masters of asceticism but also bearers of charismatic inspiration in the union with Christ and the Holy Spirit.[71] The celestial echoes of this solitary spiritual eros are conveyed to us by the *Erōtes* of Symeon the New Theologian and by the conversations of St. Macarius of Egypt, St. Seraphim of Sarov, and other saints. In addition, in the troparion to female martyrs, the Church speaks about the ecstasy of the "spiritual marriage" with Christ: "I love Thee, my Bridegroom." In general, one can say that, in isolation from people, when the external possibilities of love are removed and there remains only a general catholicity of consciousness (since desert hermits too pray *"our* Father," not *"my* Father"), ecstatic spiritual eros is the pre-established form of love for God. In its active intensity, the state of hermitage resembles prophetic inspiration.

As far as communal monasticism or monasticism in the world is concerned, it knows love in *both* of its aspects, impersonal or universal (agape) and personal (philia and eros); but it knows it in a different (though similar) manner from those who live outside monasticism. The

---

71. But that is also why ascents to the high peaks which are *not* accompanied by spiritual gifts can cause spiritual insanity.

difference consists, of course, in the absence here of conjugal and family love: the latter is associated with sexual life, which in monasticism must be combated by ascetic struggle. But the possibilities of personal, philic love and the inspirations that accompany them, i.e., of spiritual eros, are by no means rejected in monasticism. The monastic state should not be inhuman; on the contrary, it finds its proper domain in virtue of the "sublimation" of accumulated and unused spiritual energies.[72] It is not cold eunuchs, "so born from their mother's womb," who enter the kingdom of heaven, but those who have "loved much," even prostitutes. There are no grounds to assert that only personal spiritual isolation is appropriate for monasticism and that communal living in monasticism is only an external, topographic cohabitation of inwardly unconnected and solitary souls, and not a spiritual family or union of friends. Even apart from the fact that such a condition cannot be realized in practice in certain monastic situations in the world (the exercise of hierarchical ministries, various forms of active monasticism), even ideologically this can be justified only by replacing Christianity with manicheism or Buddhism. In general, one should not exaggerate the significance of the monastic state in the Church, making it a sort of Christianity *kat' exochēn,* a Christianity par excellence. What is valid for the whole of Christianity is also valid for monasticism, which is only a particular case of Christianity, *one of the states* of the latter. And what is crucial for this path, at least as far as love is concerned, is not institutional monasticism with all the encrustations that have covered it over the course of its history, but virginity, which runs parallel to marriage, the two being different forms and paths of love. Thus, the particular character of monasticism does not change anything in the general nature of love.

The Holy Spirit does not abolish the different forms of natural love. They are clothed in natural grace and are thus receptacles for the love that is bestowed by the Holy Spirit as a gift of grace. By the breath of the Holy Spirit these forms of natural love are elevated to a higher state, to a state suffused with grace. The love that is a gift of the Holy Spirit is diverse and manifold, for it is said about the gifts of the Spirit that both the gifts and the ministries are diverse. God is love, and where love is, there is God. There is the love of creatures for the Creator, of angels and men for God. The fulfillment of this love is a gift of the Holy

---

72. We are of course speaking of pure, nonfamilial monasticism. The monasticism of persons who have a family from a previous marriage represents a clear duality and in this sense resembles ascetic widowhood.

Spirit in man, to whom it is given to seek God and, with this seeking, to love Him by a natural love. The Holy Spirit bestows love for Christ and, in Him, for the Father. The fulfillment of love in creation is a gift of the Holy Spirit, bestowed upon man in response to his natural seeking of this love, in fulfillment of the natural gift of this love, proper to man. There is universal love, uniting the multi-unity in the Church in the image of the Holy Trinity, in which hypostatic love is the Holy Spirit. Man, created in the image of God, fully realizes this image only in the multi-unity, when he becomes a universal person.[73] There is also universal love for the world, for all of God's creation, not for the concupiscent world that has fallen away from God, but for the world whose head is man. This love for the world is proper to natural man as a natural gift of grace which he has according to his creation, but it is sanctified by the Holy Spirit Who inspires man to serve creation and to rule it while serving it. There is, finally, the personal love of human being for human being, in the image of the mutual love of the equi-personal hypostases in the Holy Trinity, for the Father loves the Son and the Holy Spirit *in His own way,* the Son loves the Father and the Holy Spirit *in His own way,* and the Holy Spirit loves the Father and the Son *in His own way.* Personally qualified love is proper to the natural man as the supreme gift of natural grace. And in response to this gift, which seeks divine inspiration, the gracious gift of personal love is bestowed in its different forms, including the possibilities of personal inspiration.

Finally, there is love for love itself, the flame of the heart and the fire of the spirit, which human language calls inspiration and which descends upon those who seek it. This is not love for all people, and not love for particular persons. Rather, it is love for oneself, or, more precisely, for what is *one's own* in its *supreme,* divine state. In this state of love, a man is his own "neighbor," about whom it is said, "Thou shalt love thy neighbour as thyself." Inspiration, having its source in inner eros, desires to become filled with the spirit, to possess itself, to go out of itself or surpass itself. In its limited natural state, it is inspired only by man's proper spirit, which contains the gift of natural grace bestowed upon him at his creation, a gift that is obscured and diminished but not destroyed by sin. From the grace of the Holy Spirit it receives a supernatural, divine source of inspiration, becomes divinely inspired, receives Life. "The Holy Spirit quickens every soul"; and this power of life is love, and its fruit is *inspira-*

---

73. The Russian word that is translated by "universal" here is *sobornyi,* the adjectival form of sobornost. See n. 35 above. — Trans.

tion. And when it is illuminated, the blind natural eros becomes capable of receiving the Divine grace of the Holy Spirit.[74]

Let us, in conclusion, examine once more the *generic* principle in love. The generic principle, or the sentiment of family or kinship, qualifies love in a particular manner: as paternal, maternal, filial, fraternal, etc. As a personal-generic, hypostatic-natural being, man at the same time needs personal eros and agapic love as well as generic, natural love. Here, in the relation between the personal and generic principles in man, there exists a kind of antinomy, insofar as personality, separating itself from the genus, strives to affirm itself in its selfhood, while the generic principle lulls personality to sleep. In conformity with God's creative determination, the human genus is a family, a multi-unity multiple according to hypostasis and unitary according to nature, in the image of the Holy Trinity. On the one hand there is luciferian individualism, which in its extreme rebellion strives to separate itself from genus and forebears; and on the other hand there is the sleepy and depersonalizing conservatism of the genus; and both of them oppose, in their one-sidedness, the image of God in man, in which the day of personal consciousness is indissolubly united with the night of the maternal womb. This generic principle resembles the general muscular sensation of one's own body, about which it is said, "no man ever yet hateth his own flesh; but nourisheth and cherisheth it, even as the Lord the church" (Eph. 5:29). This principle represents love for one's own flesh, not only personal but also generic. The generic principle qualifies the personal principle, is the predicate of the latter, so to speak; it is the very life of personality in its primordial sources. One should not forget the exclusive

---

74. In the present study we are examining only the general question of the autonomous nature of love, in its different forms. The erotic domain has never been an object of independent study (either dogmatic or pastoral) in Christian theology, and the latter cannot offer anything that is parallel to Plato's *Symposium* or even certain pages of Aristotle. A special study of this question has been written by Anders Nygren: *Agape and Eros: A Study of the Christian Idea of Love,* part I. The main achievement of this book is its theme. But the author's treatment of his theme, which leads him to the opposition and mutual exclusion of agape and eros, is unsatisfactory owing to its abstractness. Foreign to the author is the entire sophiological problematic of Divine-humanity, and moreover he considers the question outside of any connection with triadology, and in particular outside of any connection with the revelation and action of the Holy Spirit. In general this book suffers from all the poverty of Protestant dogmatics, although it contains some subtle comments and observations. In general, Nygren denigrates eros as a non-Christian or pre-Christian principle, opposing erotic love to agapic love as "egocentric and theocentric outlooks" (p. 162).

significance that is ascribed to genus and genealogy both in the Old Testament (which is, after all, nothing else but a religion of genus, specifically of the chosen nation, whose God is "the God of Abraham, Isaac, and Jacob") and in the New Testament.[75]

The sentiment of family and genus, rooted in blood relation, belongs also to spiritual love. The principle of genus and nation is not only a psychical and fleshly but also a spiritual principle, as a creating and creative energy. Family and race constitute a spiritual reality, which is known not only in life but also in death, and perhaps more in the latter than in the former. In its authenticity, this principle contains the essential and natural grace of the Holy Spirit, reposing upon all proto-reality. When it passes into the spiritual consciousness and is spiritually transfigured, this principle receives the gift of gracious love from the Holy Spirit. The imprint of this gift clearly marks the love that the spiritual leaders and prophets of Israel have for the chosen nation (cf. the song of the Mother of God: "He hath holpen his servant Israel, in remembrance of his mercy; as he spake to our fathers, to Abraham, and to his seed for ever" [Luke 1:54-55]). But the duty to love one's nation in spirit and grace is obligatory for all men. Or can we deny that the love of Sergius of Radonezh, the great Russian saint, for his parents and his nation had a spiritual quality? And, we dare to ask further, is our own grateful remembrance of and love for our dear departed ones, our fathers and brothers, completely deprived of the grace of the Holy Spirit? And maternal love, is it without grace? It is sufficient to ask these questions to become convinced that this love for one's ancestors and race ("laws"), as it was personified in the consciousness of the pious pagans Socrates and Plato (see his *Phaedo*), receives or rather is worthy of receiving the gift of love from the Holy Spirit.

But this form of love differs both from personal and erotic love and from universal and agapic love, these forms of love in which the loving one goes out of himself, transfers his own center into the loved one or loved ones. Here, love is concentrated in the loving one himself, though not on his hypostasis but on his nature in the capacity of the genus. It is concentrated not on his proper being but in and through others. In the concreteness of his being, every man has his proper nature, possesses humanity *not* in indifferent abstraction or in fullness but in a specific form

---

75. Here one must first of all mention that the Gospel (of Matthew) opens with "the book of the generation of Jesus Christ, the son of David, the son of Abraham." The Lord is called the son of David a number of times and accepts this name, not to mention the fact that He Himself calls Himself the Son of Man.

or part, joined to the whole the way a branch is joined to the tree or the way a member is joined to the body. Here, a part is dynamically equal to the whole. Love for genus, like God's love for His nature, Sophia, is personal in the loving one, but not personal in the loved one, i.e., the genus. But this genus represents for the loving one not only a being or nature, but also the totality of persons qualified by this nature; and generic love is thus a principle that is both personal and natural. Generic love is the site of the feeling for *humanity* and then for Divine-humanity in the human personality. In a certain sense, the generic consciousness in man is even more profound and more essential than his personal consciousness.

5. The Limits of the Pentecost

Does the power of the Pentecost have *limits?* It is sufficient to ask this question for the answer to become clear: there are no limits and can be no limits to the Pentecost. In the Pentecost, the Holy Spirit descended into the world not for a temporary stay, where He would accomplish a definite and limited task and then depart (if only temporarily), just as Christ departed the world in His ascension. No! The Holy Spirit descended into the world to abide in it, but He did this while remaining in heaven and uniting heaven with earth. In the Pentecost, all things in the life of this world that have been called to being by God have received the Holy Spirit and His power; and they have been deified by this power, in fulfillment of the previously received power of the Incarnation. This sounds like a paradox, since the action of the Pentecost is invisible and inaccessible for experience.

However, we must not forget about the general character of the manifestation of this power, that is, about the *kenosis* of the Holy Spirit, in virtue of which His action is revealed only in conformity with the preparedness of creation for this action, in conformity with creation's receptivity. The kenotic precondition of the Pentecost is the patience of the Spirit, Who, in descending into the world, accepts the *temporality* of its being. This temporality and the relativity that accompanies it limit for each given moment the capacity of the world to receive the Holy Spirit. But, in accumulating power, this temporality leads to a certain integral of time where the kenosis of the Spirit will cease and God will be all in all. The ongoing Pentecost of the world is the *mystery* of the world's being, the ontology, history, and eschatology of the world.

In the creation, the Holy Spirit bestows being ("let there be"), reality, the power of life, and beauty upon creatures. At the end of time, the world will not be created anew; it will be transfigured. To be sure, a number of prophetic texts speak of a *new* creation: "I create new heavens and a new earth" (Isa. 65:17); "we . . . look for new heavens and a new earth" (2 Pet. 3:13); "I saw a new heaven and a new earth: for the first heaven and the first earth were passed away; and there was no more sea" (Rev. 21:1); "behold, I make all things new" (Rev. 21:5). But these texts actually refer to a *renewal* of the old creation, not to a new creation in place of the old (cf. God's covenant with Noah: Gen. 9:8-17), or to an abolition of the old creation. They therefore refer precisely to the transfiguration of the world.

This transfiguration is accomplished by the Holy Spirit — by a fire that melts the universe. Even as, at the creation, the ontic and life-giving power of the Spirit operated in the world that was being created, so this power will accomplish the transformation of the world for *new* being. This transfiguring power of the Holy Spirit should be understood on the basis of His creative power in the world. The descent of the Holy Spirit at the Pentecost was accomplished *in the world,* and although He reposed with visible tongues of fire upon the apostles, He descended into the whole natural world with His invisible fire; for His action was, of course, not confined by the walls of that room in Jerusalem. This general idea is iconographically expressed by the representation of the "Cosmos" on icons of the Pentecost, while liturgically it is symbolized in the decoration of churches on the feast of the Pentecost by plants and flowers, which, in addition, the faithful hold in their hands, as if placing them, along with themselves, beneath the freshening rain of the heavenly fire.

The transfiguration of the world was *pre*-accomplished in the Pentecost, for the transfiguring power had already descended into the world, just as the deification of man was pre-accomplished in the Incarnation, whereas, in the Resurrection, death is trampled by death. The world is not only death's graveyard, but also God's field, in which the natural body is sown in order to be "raised a spiritual body" (1 Cor. 15:44). The world is covered by a rough crust with deformities and fissures, but beneath it a royal purple is concealed.[76] Inwardly, the world is already glorified, be-

---

76. This is a reference to the prologue of Vladimir Solovyov's sophiological poem "Three Meetings" (available in the translation by Boris Jakim and Laury Magnus in *Vladimir Solovyov's Poems of Sophia* [New Haven: Variable Press, 1996], p. 23):

I, not believing the deceitful world,
Beneath rough matter's crust, have yet had
Tangible proof of the incorruptible royal
Purple, have recognized the radiance of divinity . . . — Trans.

cause Christ was glorified on the mount of the Transfiguration, when heaven and earth, the mountain, the vestments, and, in them, the entire world saw and received the light of Tabor; and also because He was glorified in His glorious resurrection, in which the body of the Glory was manifested. Just as Christ does not need to be glorified and resurrected again in order to come into the world in glory, so the Holy Spirit too does not need to descend again from heaven in order to transfigure the world at the hour of Christ's Second Coming.

The action of the Holy Spirit in the world is manifested, first of all, in the sanctification or spiritualization of the cosmic matter. Just as, at the creation of the world, "the Spirit of God moved upon the face of the waters" (Gen. 1:2), with the waters clearly signifying here the proto-matter of the world, its *hulē* or *mē on,* the primordial chaos of "the earth . . . without form and void" and covered with darkness — so at the baptism of Christ[77] the Holy Spirit, Who had descended upon Him, sanctified the waters of the Jordan and, by this descent into the world, laid the foundation for the *new* matter of the world. One should not diminish the importance of the fact that, in the sacraments, the Church sanctifies matter, the material elements of the sacrament — bread and wine, water, oil, chrism, as well as the human body (not to mention various other sanctifications of matter outside the sacraments). This sanctified matter is not only employed as the material elements of the sacrament, but in general it exists in the world and remains in the latter (and sometimes, as on the great feast of the blessing of the waters, it is the watery substance in general, the primordial element of the world, that is sanctified).

This "religious materialism," which unconditionally unites matter with spirit and identifies the two, as it were, by spiritualizing matter through sanctification, usually provokes perplexity and misunderstanding: it is often thought to depend on some sort of magic or sorcery. There is a widespread belief that "dead nature" cannot receive spirit and that spirit and nature are heterogeneous. But dead nature does not exist in the world, just as in general there does not exist anything which is absolutely dead and which could not live and be quickened with and in man, and thus bear its own life within itself; for if the proto-matter, the original material of the world, is truly the substratum of the whole of cosmic life and thus of human life as well, then it possesses this proto-energy of life. On the other hand, spirit and matter should not simply be opposed; rather, they should

---

77. In the troparion recited before the Feast of the Epiphany it is said directly, "Christ came to the Jordan to sanctify the waters," of course by the Holy Spirit.

be juxtaposed and coordinated in one manner or another, since man, in his ontological makeup, is an incarnate spirit, that is, in him the spiritual principle is inseparably though mysteriously united with matter to such a degree that the one cannot exist without the other. Therefore, one must affirm that there does not exist any abstract matter, any matter which is enclosed in its empty and immobile being. The concept of *mēden* (nothing and something), used by Plato to define the cosmic matter, remains valid in its extended and all-encompassing definition: *mēden* is nothing and all, for it is not empty, "dead" matter. Rather, it is the being of the all, which is always being filled up. It is *something* which is always arising.

The proto-matter is not alien to the spirit; it is not that which is most remote from the spirit.[78] Rather, it has a direct and intimate connection with the Holy Spirit, Who gives it reality, ontic force, and in this sense creates the "matter" of being, its *res esse*. The initial qualitylessness of the proto-matter (which is erroneously equated with deadness) is precisely this reality as such, considered apart, as it were, from its mode of being, its proper logos. If the *all* of cosmic being, in its qualifiedness as its different modes, ideas, or logoses, belongs to the Logos ("All things were made by him; and without him was not any thing made that was made" [John 1:3]), then this pre-qualitative or extra-qualitative reality as such, "without form and void" (Gen. 1:2) and in this sense equally proper to all the forms of being, belongs to the life-giving Spirit. As alogical and silent about itself, this reality is known, according to Plato, by a certain "illegitimate judgment"; in other words, it is not subject to *logical* knowing. But logical knowing, in and of itself, does not yet touch reality, because beyond or beneath the ideas of being there is this "difficult genus" of Plato, this *nothing* which is also *all*. This nothing is mute but it exists; it does not have a name, but it receives all names. In other words, it is reality itself as the power of being, the power of life, matter, substance. Philosophy and science have defined it in different ways, using the auxiliary concepts of particular scientific theories (atoms, electrons, quanta, etc.). But these qualifications always form, so to speak, a second plane of being, behind which is the first: this is the receptacle, the *ekmageion*, according to the unsurpassable definition that Plato has given to this "difficult genus."[79]

78. See my book *Die Tragödie der Philosophie* (Darmstadt, 1928).

79. By virtue of their inner development, the contemporary natural sciences are coming to understand matter as force or energy, i.e., they are coming to a "let there be" conception of being, and on this path they are encountering the theology of the Holy Spirit. Cf. L. Garland, *The Idea of the Supernatural* (London, 1934).

Matter, understood simply as reality or ontic force, is precisely the direct action of the Holy Spirit in creation, in the *initial* Pentecost before the first day of creation. Not only does spirit not oppose matter, but it is identified with the latter as energy. It is the *power* of matter. To be sure, spirit is not exhausted by being or by this proto-matter of reality; it is not "the unconscious," i.e., the impersonal principle of Schopenhauer and Hartmann. On the contrary, it is, above all, consciousness and precisely consciousness of self. But this consciousness of self needs a reality, from which it would not only be repelled or reflected as from the *not*-I, but which, as its nature, would also serve as the foundation of its self-revelation, for the spirit is an I which has a nature and lives in it. In this sense, the proto-matter belongs to spirit, is connected and coordinated with it, and to this extent it is spiritual. In this sense, one can speak of absolute spiritual reality, the spiritual "proto-matter" of the Divine Sophia, who is not only the pan-organism of ideal forms, the idea of ideas of the *all* in the Logos, but also the realization and the being of the all in the Holy Spirit. And by analogy with this reality of the spiritual proto-matter in the Divine Sophia, creation too has its creaturely proto-matter, its reality of matter capable of being spiritualized.

This spiritual quality of creaturely matter, which is determined by the positive relation of the latter to the spirit, can have different modes or degrees, ranging from the extreme alienation of "dead" matter (or rather, of matter that is deadened, that has fallen into a state of "unconsciousness") to its complete transparence for the spirit, which is the state of spiritualized matter. The original "earth" or "waters," the proper substratum of the creaturely Sophia in her altero-being in relation to the Divine Sophia, presupposes the maximal materialization of the proto-matter, the element of the world's autonomous being. Spirituality is depotentialized here into matter, although, even in this state, matter does not lose its potential spirituality, its connection with and receptivity to the spirit. This is expressed in the Biblical testimony that "the Spirit of God moved upon the face of the waters" (Gen. 1:2), calling to life that which was contained within them. This already laid the foundation for the *spiritualization* of matter, through its vivification, which occurred during the course of the six days of creation and ended with the creation of man's body (into which God Himself breathed of life) out of the earth (Gen. 2:7), i.e., out of the proto-matter.

Consequently, the initial "not I," the "dead" matter, is already included in man's spiritual life, is raised to the spirit, becomes "sensation." Sensation is by no means alien to the spirit. On the contrary, it belongs to the spirit as one of the forms of its life, although one that does not exhaust this life. To deprive the spirit of sensation would be to disincarnate it, that is, to abolish man's very essence. One can distinguish different forms of sensation in man, sinful or holy, but one cannot separate sensation from the spirit. The spirit is not opposed to man's psychical and corporeal life; rather, it lives in the psychical and the corporeal, determining them and being determined by them. Matter melts, as it were, losing its inertia and impenetrability; it becomes transparent for the spirit and spirit-bearing. It stops being unconscious and becomes conscious. It is brought into the life of the spirit, which "conquers" nature. Thus, the life of the spirit slumbers in matter, and it must be awakened.[80]

This character of matter explains its ability to become the "matter of sacrament," to be a conductor of spiritual gifts for the incarnate spirit intergrown with matter, i.e., for man. Spiritualized, sanctified matter, which in sacrament becomes the substratum for divine life, for the Holy Spirit, this matter, when it is received by man, is integrated into the fullness of his essence, into his spiritual and corporeal being. The matter of sacrament is the spiritualized matter of the future age, just as the waters of the Jordan are already the "water of life .. proceeding out of the throne of God and of the Lamb" (Rev. 22:1) in the New Jerusalem.

The matter of the world had already experienced a change when it became the flesh of Christ. Being truly human and as such belonging to this world, the flesh of Christ was at first distinguished from the common human matter by its sinlessness and thus its primordial transparence for the spirit, although it still preserved a touch of rebelliousness as a result of the general weakening caused by original sin ("the spirit .. is willing, but the flesh is weak" [Matt. 26:41]). To be sure, the descent of the Holy Spirit upon Jesus in the Baptism strengthened His human nature and thereby helped to bring Him to the state of higher spirituality, which was to be confirmed and crowned by His personal feat. Rendered obedient to the spirit, the flesh of the God-Man was glorified, that is, it fully received the transfiguring action of the Holy Spirit. This glorification is accomplished in a preliminary manner on the mount of the Transfiguration, and then in its definitive fullness in the Resurrection and in the heavenly glorification of Christ.

The fact that Christ was not only resurrected by His own power but was also raised by the Holy Spirit signifies that the Holy Spirit spiritual-

---

80. Technology and man's technological conquest of nature represent an initial form of this awakening.

ized the matter of Christ's flesh, which spiritualization corresponds to the victory over death and to the state of the *spiritual* body in its glorification. But this spiritualization and glorification of the body of Christ was limited to the body of Jesus. However, the *entire* human essence in its ontological kernel was assumed and saved by Christ, and was destined to receive the salvific fruit of His death and resurrection, for He is "the saviour of the body" (Eph. 5:23). And together with man, the entire world, all of creation, which is subject to vanity, yearns to be delivered from the children of man.

This extension of the power of Christ's resurrection to the entire human race (but with the preservation of personal freedom) and to the entire world was accomplished in the Pentecost by the Holy Spirit. The Holy Spirit thereby realized the work of Christ, the victory over death. The latter had entered the life of the *entire* world, not only the life of man but also the life of all being; and that is why the substance of the world had become *matter*. Matter is the condition of *fallen* substance. The Holy Spirit, Who had poured forth into the world in the Pentecost and abides in the world, bestowed upon the world the power to be transfigured and resurrected. The Holy Spirit's *approach* to the world was through Christ: "Repent ye: for the kingdom of heaven [i.e., the kingdom of the Spirit] is at hand" — that is the first preaching of John the Forerunner and of Christ Himself. But now it is at hand not externally, as was the case when the Holy Spirit moved upon the face of the waters and in the course of the whole Old Testament. It is now at hand inwardly, for the Incarnation has prepared a place for it in the world. Sacraments, in which this power of the Holy Spirit is manifested (to be sure, only in a hidden, mysterious manner) in matter, attest to this abiding power of the Spirit.

One can say that *the fate of the world has already been decided* — in the sense of its final salvation and transfiguration. A supramundane force is already present in the world, sufficient to save and transfigure it. The presence of this force is not only mysterious in the sense that a sacrament is mysterious, while being accessible to the spirit. It is a true *mystery*, which is accomplished in the world and in history, but not without tragic opposition, for in the world "the mystery of iniquity doth already work" (2 Thess. 2:7): the "mystery, Babylon the Great, the mother of harlots and abominations of the earth" (Rev. 17:5). The world remains in its fallen, sinful state, into which it has been brought by the fall of man; and it yearns to be "delivered from the bondage of corruption" (Rom. 8:21). As before, death reigns in the world, and the mystery of sin and of the flesh is being enacted there. In the course of this aeon, the action of the power of the

Holy Spirit, which is present in the natural world, is not manifested there as visible and palpable change that corresponds to an inner, metaphysical change. We can only postulate this universal transparence of the world for the spirit, this spiritualization of the creature and of matter, which is represented by different symbols in the prophetic books (in particular, by the descent from heaven of the New Jerusalem in Revelation 21–22).

But it would be useless to attempt to go further than this ontological postulate, whose realization is included in the overall mystery of the revelation of the Spirit in the future age. We can do no more than mention a few landmarks indicated by Revelation. Thus, the transfiguration of the world is connected, first of all, with the coming of Christ in glory, accompanied by the universal transfiguration and renewal of heaven and earth, by the raising of the dead and a transformation of the living (1 Cor. 15:52-53). Revelation directly connects this resurrection with the action of the Holy Spirit: "if the Spirit of him that raised up Jesus from the dead dwell in you, he that raised up Christ from the dead shall also quicken your mortal bodies by the Holy Spirit" (Rom. 8:11; the King James Version has been modified here to conform with the Russian Bible). The raising from the dead is to be accomplished by virtue of Christ's resurrection ("if there is no resurrection of the dead, then is Christ not risen" [1 Cor. 15:13]; "as in Adam all die, even so in Christ shall all be made alive" [15:22]), effected by the Holy Spirit. The transfiguration of the world must be included in the universal resurrection, for it is clear that resurrected humanity cannot live in an untransfigured world, which is why the two events are connected in Revelation.

Thus, the power of the Pentecost in the natural world, as well as in the human world, transcends the limits of this age and passes into the life of the future age, for all has already been accomplished for this transition. Nevertheless, the power of the Holy Spirit is knowable for us only in supernatural life, in the "kingdom of grace," i.e., in the Church and in the sacraments, which remain mysteries for natural life and do not exist for the latter, so to speak. The special character of "the last times," or of the New Testament, consists in this lack of conformity between the *fullness* of the accomplishment in the heart of creation, on the one hand, and the *absence* of this accomplishment in the world or, more precisely, the failure of the world to perceive it and receive it, on the other.

What can this apparent inaction or powerlessness of the Spirit in the world with its material inertia and impenetrability signify? The answer to this question was already given above: this inaction or powerlessness signifies the *kenosis* of the Holy Spirit in His descent into the world.

The Spirit Himself is present in the creation and overshadows it with His touch, His "grace," bestowed in the Church; but He does not reveal the fullness that He has. There is an analogy here with the kenosis of the Son, Who came into the world in a state of humiliation, in "the form of a servant" (Phil. 2:7), although beneath the veil of flesh "in him dwelleth all the fullness of the Godhead bodily" (Col. 2:9), and "of his fullness have all we received, and grace for grace" (John 1:16). But His Glory will be manifested only in His second and dread coming. And the kenosis of the Lord in His earthly condition continues in the world and in humanity, although He Himself with His human essence ascended in Glory to heaven. The world is following the path that leads to the assimilation of Christ's gift, but it has not yet come to the end of this path.

That is why the descent of the Holy Spirit, which was to actualize this gift for the world, also occurred kenotically; otherwise, it would have been a direct transfiguration of the world, coinciding with Christ's second coming. But this descent had first to prepare the world for this transfiguration, for the world was not yet ready to receive Christ. The world could not have withstood the active *power* of the Holy Spirit's coming, which would have been for it destructive and consuming, not transfiguring, just as the world could not have survived the appearance of the Son of God in His Glory. The kenosis of Divinity is equally necessary for the world whether it is the Second hypostasis or the Third hypostasis that descends into it. And therefore the Pentecost is the kenosis of the Spirit, taken upon Himself when He descended into the world. This descent and therefore this kenosis were prepared by the kenosis of Christ, by His Incarnation. The Holy Spirit could descend into the world and find a place in it for Himself only by virtue of the Incarnation.

Here we must distinguish the two aspects in the very essence of Christ which correspond to the Old Adam and to the New Adam, to His two centers. Christ glorified *in Himself* the human essence by His Resurrection, Ascension, and Sitting at the right hand of the Father; He created for the human essence a new center of attraction in Himself, which ontologically is now the unique and true center. This center, however, has not yet been actualized for humanity; or more precisely, humanity has not yet assimilated it: "He came unto his own, and his own received him not" (John 1:11). The Holy Spirit descended in order to actualize this center, to manifest Christ to His humanity through the Church, the Body of Christ. He descended to make humanity Christ's, *to actualize the salvation of the world,* brought by the Savior. But this task is essentially a kenotic one also for the hypostasis of the Holy Spirit. Let us recall here the supra-eternal hypostatic kenosis of the Holy Spirit in the Holy Trinity, where, as hypostatic Love, He makes Himself transparent and empties Himself in showing the Son to the Father and the Father to the Son, while concealing Himself. Consequently, the Holy Spirit actualizes His personal being only by showing the Others'. In the Pentecost, this hypostatic kenosis is applied to showing to the world the Son Who has come into it, to actualizing Him for the world. But in conformity with this general kenosis of the Holy Spirit, there is also the special kenosis of His self-revelation in the world — not in His Divine fullness, but to the extent that the world can receive Him in its creaturely and sinful infirmity. The inability of the world to receive the Spirit fully, the world's unpreparedness for this reception, evokes Divine condescension, the kenosis of the Spirit. Fullness becomes less than full; immeasurableness is subordinated to measure. Present in the world, the Holy Spirit refrains from acting upon it directly; He spares it in its altero-being, in which God is not yet all in all.

This kenosis of the Holy Spirit corresponds to His hypostatic character. Although the kenosis of the Spirit is connected with the kenosis of the Son, it nevertheless differs from the latter. First of all, the metaphysical contours, so to speak, are different: the Son of God descends from heaven as if abandoning it. This does not mean that He loses His Divinity and His place in the Holy Trinity; but, personally, for Himself, He depotentializes this Divinity to such an extent that He "becomes flesh" and includes creaturely being in His life. Divine Glory is returned to Him in the glorification, just as He Himself returns to heaven in the Ascension. The kenosis of the Son is therefore a determinate event in His relation to the world; it is limited in time, with a beginning and an end (although the end is not a complete one in all respects). The kenosis of the Son continues in a particular sense in the kenosis of the Holy Spirit.

Here we must recognize the full significance of the fundamental fact that the Holy Spirit is *sent* by the Father into the world, and that this sending, like the sending of the Son, already presupposes the necessity of *kenosis*. This sending is a kenotic act, although it is accomplished in different ways for the Son and for the Holy Spirit. This kenosis of the Spirit is revealed to us by Revelation, although not as fully as that of the Son; but it follows with necessity from the very fact of the sending *into the world*, for this descent into the world cannot be realized by Divinity without self-limitation and voluntary self-diminution. Divinity in its power and glory cannot enter the world without destroying or ontologically melting it, as it were. The world must be brought to a state where it can receive the coming of the God-Man in glory and where God will be all in all. Until then, the deification of the world which is the descent of the Holy Spirit can only be "in part." It is, so to speak, a kenotic adaptation on the pathways of the salvation of the world through deification. And the accomplishment of this salvation is governed by the will of the Father, Who sends the Son and the Holy Spirit into the world in a determinate and pre-specified manner, with the kenosis of the Son being inwardly related to the kenosis of the Holy Spirit as ground to consequent, as goal to accomplishment. And precisely this relation expresses the participation of the Son in the accomplishment of His own kenotic work through the kenotic work of the Holy Spirit. The sending down of the Holy Spirit is therefore represented as a work of the Father with the participation of the Son: "I will pray the Father, and he shall give you another Comforter" (John 14:16); "the Holy Spirit, whom the Father will send in my name" (14:26); "the Comforter . . . whom I will send unto you from the Father" (15:26); "if I depart, I will send him unto you" (16:7). The sending has its own kenotic plan, determined by its goals of ministry.

In contrast to the kenosis of the Son, the Holy Spirit, in descending into the world, does *not* abandon heaven and does *not* empty Himself of Divinity. The task of the Holy Spirit is not the in-humanization of God as in the Incarnation, but the deification of man by allowing him to participate in divine life. The kenosis of the Holy Spirit consists not in His self-emptying through the removal of Divinity, but in His voluntary self-limitation, in the subordination of the Immeasurable to measure. This is, of course, a kenosis of love, of divine condescension, where the Divine absoluteness enters into a connection with creaturely relativity. Such condescension of absolute Divinity to relative being was accomplished by God in the creation of the world, where the latter was posited as an altero-being, alongside God. Here, the condescension is continued with regard to the salvation of the world. God adapts Himself, as it were, not only to the fact of the altero-being of the world, but also to its alienation from Him. The world is not only outside God but is also in opposition to its Creator because of the prince of this world. In other words, it is not the world that strives to meet God; rather, it is God Who descends from His heights and adapts Himself to man. This *adaptation* of Divine love and condescension are precisely the kenosis of the Spirit, which limits and diminishes the power of His action in the world. His action in the world is not without measure, but from measure to measure.

How is it possible for God to limit His own power? That is the critical question regarding the kenosis of the Holy Spirit, and it is also the mystery of Divine life and of the Divine love for the world. We can affirm the existence of this mystery on the basis of revelation, but we cannot fathom it, inasmuch as it belongs to the interior life of Divinity, which is inaccessible to creatures. In essence, this is the mystery of God's creation of the world out of nothing: How does the Absolute, without losing its absoluteness, give a place alongside itself to the relative, and even have a relation with the latter? In other words, how does the Absolute become God for the relative? And how does Divinity act in the creaturely world not with all its power but as a function of the capacity of the world to receive it? Divinity goes beyond its own limits, as it were; it comes into contact with the creaturely nothing, as a principle of limitation. Thought collides with an extreme antinomy here, which attests to an unfathomable Divine mystery. But this mystery exists not to be hidden in a cloud of unknowing, but to be revealed; and its real revelation is given in the life of the world.

Although in and of itself the kenosis of God is a divine mystery, man can gain some knowledge of it. At the very least, he knows that kenosis is kenosis, i.e., a voluntary self-limitation by virtue of divine love. Love lives by sacrifice; and the kenosis of the Holy Spirit is a sacrifice of love, brought by the very hypostasis of Love. If in our limited, human experience of love we know how painful it is to limit our love, to hide it, to fail to express it fully, we can draw a certain conclusion about Divine Love, which yearns to pour forth but cannot, for it is stopped by the limited receptivity of creation. Divine Love is limited here by *un-love*, by the power of "the prince of this world," by the world itself — not only because of its creatureliness, but also because it has become petrified in its fallen state. This restraint of love is enacted in the name of love, of that love which desires to preserve intact the being of the world and of man, even with its distortions and limitations, but in its proper nature and in its ontological freedom. Love would prefer its revelation to be incomplete rather than destroy with its overwhelming force the proper form of created being by disrupting its inner rhythm and freedom. This respect for creaturely freedom, which is connected with creaturely limitedness, is the Creator's love for His creation. The sacrifice of this love consists in the fact that God must suffer the world with its imperfection,[81] without destroying its proper self-determination. He must suffer and . . . wait. And this restraint, this moderation, this kenosis of the Holy Spirit, is Love's self-sacrificing love.

---

81. Christ says, "O faithless and perverse generation, how long shall I be with you? how long shall I suffer you?" (Matt. 17:17).

Thus, in the life of the world, the Holy Spirit, Who descended in the Pentecost, has no limit except His own kenotic self-limitation, by which He enters the world process, the world's history. This means that the action of the Holy Spirit takes part in God's government or guidance of the world, which in theology is called Divine Providence. Without considering this problem in all its scope, let us note the participation of the Holy Spirit in Divine Providence, which, according to the generally accepted doctrine, is accomplished by the entire Holy Trinity, as well as by its individual hypostases, in conformity with the personal character of each of them. The Father acts, in general, in the world through the Hypostases that reveal Him: the Son and the Holy Spirit. Christ is the foundation and the goal of the entire cosmic and historical process, which is actualized by the Holy Spirit. The Holy Spirit actualizes Christ in the history of humanity, which, inwardly, is the history of the Church. The Holy Spirit is the inspiring and guiding power by which the world and humanity become Christ's. And insofar as this represents the "enthronement" of Christ in the world, the Kingdom of God is realized by the Holy Spirit.

In general, it must be considered a christological and pneumatological axiom that all of Christ's works are actualized by the Holy Spirit. And conversely, the Holy Spirit does not actualize anything in the world which is not a work of Christ's. In this sense, it is appropriate to speak of the Pentecost in history, as well as beyond the limits of the latter, in eschatology. Here, one can only briefly establish this general connection between the Pentecost and the end of the world, which has already been pre-accomplished in the Pentecost, and which is why the "last times" have already begun. If Revelation attests that Christ's resurrection was actualized by the Holy Spirit, then the future universal resurrection will also be actualized by Him, as well as the end of the world and its transfiguration. All this is inwardly and mysteriously connected with the future event which Revelation designates as Christ's Second Coming, or His new appearance in the world.

This event ends the present aeon. This appearance of Christ, similar to the sending down of the Son and the Holy Spirit into the world, is a *new* event in the relations between God and the world. The source of this event is the will of the Father, Who determines it by His power. It thus lies beyond our spiritual horizon and is inaccessible to this aeon. Even within the limits of this age, however, it is clear that nothing that has already occurred in the world can be excluded from this event, and the descent of the Holy Spirit, Who abides in the world, retains its full power. His descent prepares in the world and in history the Second Coming ("And the

Spirit and the bride say, Come" [Rev. 22:17]), and there is no question that it plays an important role in the accomplishment of the Second Coming. There can be no argument about the power of the Holy Spirit at the Last Judgment, or about His action "after" or beyond the Judgment, in "heaven" or in "hell." This is a further unfolding of the action of the Pentecost, and all this can be understood as the ongoing Pentecost.

This general idea must be complemented by another: In His descent from heaven in the Pentecost, the Holy Spirit penetrates, by His action, beyond the limits of this earthly world and enters the world of the after-life. One can also inquire into the participation of the Holy Spirit in Christ's descent into hell. If the Lord was separated from His Spirit neither during His ministry nor in His death,[82] if on earth He preached and worked miracles by the Holy Spirit, being anointed by Him as the "Christ," this anointment by the Holy Spirit did not leave Him, of course, even when He descended into hell. Christ's descent into hell accomplished the spiritual resurrection of the souls worthy of and capable of receiving resurrection. And this resurrection of souls ("the first resurrection") was accomplished, of course, not without the participation of the Holy Spirit, the giver of life and the resurrector.

Further, one can ask: Was the Pentecost accomplished only for the earth, or was it also accomplished for the realms under the earth, on the other side of the gates of hell and death? Were these gates impenetrable for the Spirit? And if they were not impenetrable for the Spirit (just as they were not for Christ) — and there can be no other answer to this question — then we must postulate the action of the Pentecost and of the gifts of the Spirit in the world of the afterlife. In particular, is the gift of the remission of the sins of the deceased by the prayers of the Church (in which remission we are taught to believe by the Church herself) not an operation of the Holy Spirit and an afterlife sacrament, as it were? For the reception of this remission is not analogous to a judicial amnesty with the punishment waived; rather, it is a kind of *healing*, where the capacity to live a new life, to be born into this life, is acquired.

This whole eschatological and afterlife aspect of the Pentecost remains unrevealed to us, although it is postulated with some degree of certainty. It must be affirmed, however, that the Pentecost does not have any

---

82. "My God, my God, why hast thou forsaken me?" (Mark 15:34). This cry signifies that, in His dying, Christ was abandoned by the Holy Spirit, the Giver of Life, but this abandonment was immediately overcome in the Father's embrace: "Father, into thy hands I commend my Spirit" (Luke 23:46).

limits — either in the dimension of depth or in the dimension of breadth.[83] It is just as universal as the Incarnation of Christ. To limit the Pentecost to the confines of history would be to limit the Church in the same way. And if such limits cannot be conceived for the Church, then neither can they be conceived for the Pentecost. Where Christ is, there also is the Holy Spirit; and all things that are accomplished by Christ are accomplished by Him through the Holy Spirit, the "other Comforter," given by the Father, "that he may abide with you for ever" (John 14:16).

6. Divine-humanity

The Pentecost is the realized and perfect *Divine-humanity*. The Divine-humanity is the appearance on earth of the God-Man, who has united in His Person the heavenly and the earthly Adam. It is the Divine Incarnation, but it is equally the descent into the world of the Holy Spirit, Who abides with us forever (cf. John 14:16), although He was not made incarnate. As far as the Divine-humanity is concerned, this eternal abiding with us of the Holy Spirit corresponds to the Incarnation of the Son. The two things are inseparably linked not only in fact but also in essence: "It is expedient for you that I go away: for if I go not away, the Comforter will not come unto you; but if I depart, I will send him unto you" (John 16:7), "another Comforter" (14:16), Who "shall glorify me: for he shall receive of mine, and shall shew it unto you. All things that the Father hath are mine: therefore said I, that he shall take of mine, and shall shew it unto you. A little while, and ye shall not see me: and again, a little while, and ye shall see me, because I go to the Father" (16:14-16). This *identity*, as it were, of the revelations of the Second and Third hypostases is precisely the Divine-humanity, heavenly and earthly, the Divine Sophia and the creaturely Sophia. The self-revelation of the Holy Trinity, as the revelation of the Father in the revealing hypostases, the Son and the Holy Spirit, is the Divine Life, the Divine World, the Eternal Sophia. The creaturely world is created in the image of this Divine Sophia, on the basis of the Divine Sophia, in such a way that the divine proto-images of being have received extra-

---

83. In this connection there arises the question: Is the realm of hell and of "eternal" torments shut off from the action of the Holy Spirit, and what does this action consist in here? This question concerns eschatology and is examined in volume three of this trilogy [*The Bride of the Lamb*, available in Boris Jakim's translation, published by Eerdmans, 2002].

divine being by being submerged in the creaturely nothing, in becoming, thereby acquiring an autonomous existence in the creaturely world. In its creaturely sophianicity, the world has become a *mirror* of the Divine world; its images are not illusory, however, but really exist. This mirror has become clouded and distorted because of the world's sinful falling away from its proper image, but it has nevertheless preserved its mirror quality: even though it is fallen, the creaturely world is the creaturely *Sophia,* although the image of her being has been divided into sophianicity and anti-sophianicity (for there does not exist anything that is extra-sophianic or nonsophianic; sophianicity is synonymous with being itself).

This division is *not* insuperable. Its overcoming in the Divine plane includes the overcoming of the duality of the forms of the Divine Sophia, eternal and creaturely. In this way, creation is deified: divine life is communicated to it; and it is raised from the creaturely Sophia into the creaturely-Divine Sophia. So great is God's love for creation that, in calling the latter to being, He gives it *His Own,* the Divine Sophia, as the foundation of its being, in order, further, to give it Himself as well, uniting it with His own Divine life. This is precisely the foundation of the Divine-human process. Humanity, the center and cryptogram of the world, is the image of the Divine Humanity. It is thus called to approach the Proto-image, and this convergence can go so far as to become a living identification with the Proto-image. This is the task and goal of creation. God creates future "gods by grace" for inclusion in the multihypostatic multiunity of the Holy Trinity and in the unity of Divine life. This is the final foundation of the creative act. The creaturely Sophia must be united in one life with the Divine Sophia on the basis of the unity of hypostasis living in the two natures: The idea of the Chalcedonian dogma, of the unihypostatic bi-unity of the two natures, Divine and human, of the Divine and the creaturely Sophia, must receive not only a christological but also an anthropological and cosmological significance.

This union of the Divine and creaturely Sophia, of Divinity and nature, apart from the ontological unity between them, which they have by virtue of the sophianicity of creation, could have been accomplished by virtue of the "in-hypostatization" of the creaturely Sophia in the divine hypostases of the Son and the Spirit. This hypostatic union of the Divine and creaturely Sophia is accomplished first in the Incarnation of the Logos, in the appearance of the God-Man, Who, given the unity of the Divine-human hypostasis, has one life in the bi-unity of the Divine and creaturely Sophia, of the Divine and human natures. In Christ there was accomplished not only the redemption of sin and thus the correction of the division and distortion of creaturely being that were a consequence of man's fall, but also the deification of creation through its union with the divine nature, the Divine Sophia. Divine-humanity, which in heaven is the eternal foundation of the world, was accomplished in the latter through the appearance of Christ, the God-Man, in Whom dwells the entire fullness of Divinity and of humanity.

But Divine-humanity did not find completion even in the Divine Incarnation. It could have found this completion if Sophia were only the revelation of the Logos and thus identical to the latter. But Sophia/Divine-humanity is the revelation of the Logos by the Holy Spirit, Their inseparable bi-unity. For the eternal Divine-humanity, or the Divine Sophia, both of her hypostatic sources, the Word and the Holy Spirit, are equally essential; and she is correlative with both of these hypostases. That is why the reunification of the Divine and creaturely Sophia, or the deification of creation, must be accomplished in both personal centers, in both hypostases, in the Logos and in the Holy Spirit, in Their concrete interrelation.

The Divine Incarnation of the Second Person of the Holy Trinity alone is therefore insufficient for Divine-humanity; it must be accompanied by the *personal* descent into the world of the Third hypostasis. This descent is not merely an instrumental gift and in this sense an excess and superfluous one, which did not have to be bestowed, or one which is only auxiliary with regard to the Divine Incarnation. No! The descent of the Holy Spirit is just as necessary and essential for the sophianization of the world or the accomplishment of the Divine-humanity as the Incarnation itself. In the *one* Divine-humanity, in the one deification or sophianization of the world through man, there is not one but two personal centers, two Kings, two Intercessor-Comforters (although only one salvation): the Word and the Holy Spirit. The Pentecost, or the descent of the Holy Spirit, is therefore an event that is entirely parallel to and inseparably united with the birth of Christ. In each of these two acts of the Divine-humanity, the operations of the two hypostases are united: the birth of Christ is accomplished by the power of the Holy Spirit, sent by the Father, whereas the descent of the Holy Spirit is accomplished by the power of Christ, Who sends Him from the Father. The difference pertaining to the *hypostatic* character of the theophany remains, however. The Son becomes incarnate and is in-humanized, while the Holy Spirit descends and makes His abode in men. The Holy Spirit manifests to the world Christ Who has come, while the Son fills the world with His Spirit. This difference between the hypostatic acts corresponds to that between Their hypostatic properties; and without this difference these acts would be repetitive instead of complementary in the work of the salvation of the world through the sophianization of man. The descent of the Holy Spirit is the *fulfillment* in man of the Image of God, which is manifested in the world in Christ. His descent therefore clothes man in Christ, in the Divine-humanity.

This leads directly into the fundamental *ontological* theme of the doctrine of the Pentecost. This doctrine is usually confined to soteriology, i.e., to the doctrine of salvation or grace. But the Pentecost has a much more fundamental and essential significance, precisely with reference to Divine-humanity. The Dyad of Son and Spirit determines the Divine-humanity in God. By the will of the initial hypostasis, the Father, this Dyad predetermines the Divine-humanity in the created world, the creaturely Sophia, at the very creation of the world; and this Dyad realizes the Divine-humanity in the world through hypostatic unification with the latter in the Incarnation and the descent of the Holy Spirit. The Incarnation and the descent of the Holy Spirit are, in effect, in a relation of temporal succession: the Incarnation precedes the descent; the Incarnation is the ground, the descent is the consequent. But this relation of succession is a complex one. In essence, there is no succession here; *ontologically,* there is no first and no second, no antecedent and no derivative. The two are equally important, for they are only different aspects of the actualization of the one self-revelation of Divinity. The two are equally divine, despite the order in the "taxis" of the Second and Third persons of the Holy Trinity. The Divine-humanity includes on an equal footing the Incarnation of the Logos and the descent into the world of the Holy Spirit. But the Pentecost, as the second event in the succession, is precisely the accomplishment of the Divine-humanity.

The Father[1]

The Father . . . Is it possible to say anything about Him, who is Silence, Mystery, the Transcendent even in the Holy Trinity? He is revealed, but only in the other hypostases. He Himself remains transcendent and inaccessible — "in heaven." He remains unknown and hidden. Is not the only path to Him *docta ignorantia* (according to the expression of Nicholas of Cusa), learned ignorance, the path of *apophatic* theology,[2] which does not affirm anything, but negates everything, so that negation, NOT, is the sole affirmation? Is the Father not the Absolute, which is hidden from us in the obscurity of absoluteness and which is separated from us by the glaciers of transcendence? Is the Father not in fact that "it," that unconscious or preconscious *Urgottheit*, out of which the very gods are born, in which they arise together with being itself? Is the Father not the terrifying solitude of the eternal night in and from which light shines only as a secondary act? Is not even this "Not," this "it," too explicit a definition of the indefinable airless cold of the interstellar spaces in which all would freeze if it actually existed? Is it not, furthermore, the logical shadow of an abstraction which attempts to remove from the object of thought all its attributes and is left with the emptiness of *nothing*, an emptiness that is impossible to conceive? Is it not a pure zero, incapable of being grasped by the pincers of abstraction? But how can thought make this leap into emp-

---

1. In the original Russian edition, Bulgakov indicates that this section can also serve as the "prologue" to the first and second volumes of his trilogy on Divine-humanity, i.e., *The Lamb of God* and *The Comforter.* — Trans.

2. On the relationship between apophatics and kataphatics, see my book *The Unfading Light,* ch. I.

tiness? How can it think the unthinkable and nonexistent? Can thought here do anything except lay down its weapons and die in the face of this icy *néant*?

But the Absolute is never thought, never known, never exists in its *abstract* absoluteness, solely as the icy night of nonbeing. Such an Absolute is truly a *non-sens* of abstraction. Even abstracting thought must have something from which it might be reflected and thus acquire content; and the Transcendent never remains only in its transcendence, but has a *trans,* which not only conceals but also defines it. In other words, the Absolute itself is *relative* in its absoluteness, just as the Transcendent is *immanent* in its transcendence if it truly exists and has significance *(gilt),* if it does not turn into a zero for thought and being, into a void for both the one and the other. Even the NO of apophatic theology is necessarily connected with a certain kataphatic YES; the former is a dialectical moment of the latter and signifies a mystical perception of reality.[3] The absoluteness of the Absolute in relation to the relative, just as the transcendence of the Transcendent in relation to the immanent, signifies only that between them there does not exist any equality or adequacy. The Absolute and Transcendent is more profound and full of content than the relative and immanent, and it is therefore the source of the latter.

The Absolute and Transcendent is a Mystery, for which the relative and immanent is a *revelation,* while in relation to the Absolute itself the relative is a *self-revelation.* The category of mystery and revelation has a much more general and fundamental significance than the category of cause and effect. The category of cause and effect is often applied not only where it is appropriate, in the empirical domain, where *causa aequat effectum,* but also where this adequacy does not exist, i.e., in relations between the noumenal and the phenomenal. Kant's *Ding an sich,* mute in the capacity of a "limit concept" *(Grenzbegriff),* does not remain concealed behind phenomena in the capacity of the unknowable, but is revealed in them, although not adequately; and it is only for this reason that it becomes knowable. Therefore, the empirical is the *revelation* of the noumenal, which in this context corresponds to the Absolute or Transcendent (characteristically, the category of revelation is absent in Kant's "cubistic" philosophy). Revelation of the noumenon in phenomena presupposes a subject, a predicate, and the copula between them. It presupposes that which is revealed, that which reveals, and a certain unity or identity of the two: a mystery and its revelation.

3. See my book *Die Tragödie der Philosophie.*

Mystery is correlative with revelation and does not exist apart from it, just as the Absolute and Transcendent does not exist apart from the relative and immanent. Moreover, this is a relation of identity: the Absolute and Transcendent is a Mystery in its revelation, which is its *life*. Only abuse of abstraction can permit one to understand the Absolute as something thing-like and lifeless. This clearly contradicts the fullness of being, which is considered here as dead immobility. Being is life; and no being except living being (although in different states of life) is given. The concept of *life* as creative self-revelation must therefore be included among the fundamental philosophical categories in which the Absolute and Transcendent is conceived. All being is this self-revelation and revelation, but, of course, to different degrees.

God, in the Holy Trinity, is the Absolute and Transcendent in relation to the world. But, in His own being, is not God Himself in some sense relative and immanent with regard to what is *beyond* God? But is He Himself in this sense the revelation of this true Absolute and Transcendent? Such a second "level" of the Absolute is usually postulated by the doctrine of theological impersonalism. The latter, considering impersonal being to be more primordial than and therefore metaphysically superior to personal being, postulates a certain proto-Divinity *(Urgottheit)* in which God arises and in which, in particular, persons, personal centers, as well as the whole Christian Trinity, come into being. This conception, characterizing Neoplatonism and the Christian mysticism of Eckhart and Boehme, is erroneous both religiously and metaphysically, inasmuch as it places the impersonal above the personal, the preconscious above the conscious, and, consequently, the soulless above the spirit. This conception is totally incompatible with the *personalism* of Christian philosophy.

For Christian philosophy, the supreme and therefore initial form of the Absolute is *personal* being, which is actualized in an absolute manner in the congregate personality of the Divine triunity, of the trihypostatic hypostasis. Christian philosophy proceeds from this being and does not seek any further foundation for itself. This philosophy takes as its basis here not only the divine revelation itself but also the insights of reason; and it cannot recognize any other character of the Absolute. God is the Absolute, the Transcendent, the personal and trihypostatic entity that is revealed in the relative and immanent being of the world as the divine principle of the latter and as the Personality which has this principle for Itself and which lives in it by Its own life. This revelation of the Absolute in the *world,* however, is such that it presupposes the self-revelation of the Absolute in itself, which in turn is included in the revelation of the Absolute to the world. The being of the Transcendent is an *absolute relation* in the Absolute itself, or the Holy Trinity. The relation between God and the world, between the Creator and creation, is in turn characterized by two opposite features: the revelation of the Creator in creation is *inadequate,* for creatures cannot fully know their God and Creator, but know Him only "in part" (1 Cor. 13:9);[4] but at the same time, creatures *conform* to the Creator, for they are sophianic in nature, and bear His seal and image. This conformity, however, particularly in the fallen world, which has lost its proper proto-image, remains as "through a glass, darkly" (13:12).

It is erroneous to say that God is unknowable for and in creation, for such alienation of the world from God would signify a blasphemy against the Creator. But it is also erroneous to say that He is known by the world. He remains unknown in knowledge and known in unknowability as a living Revelation, a Mystery in the process of being revealed. Between the Creator and creation lies this frontier of the inadequacy of knowledge, which is expressed in the necessary connection and interrelation of apophatic and kataphatic (negative and positive) theology. These two theologies cannot exist separately from one another without the result being error. Without its kataphatic counterpart, apophatic theology is *empty* and ultimately leads to practical atheism, of the sort we have in agnosticism. It receives its legitimate place, however, as a *limit* that indicates the inevitable inadequacy of kataphatic theology, although the latter is true knowledge of God, for it contains a revelation of Divinity. Apophatic theology thus acquires the significance of an epistemological barrier and corrective to all positive theology; it protects us against the constant threat of anthropomorphism, which is nothing other than the assertion that the human knowledge of God is perfectly adequate. This anthropomorphism differs essentially from true anthropologism, which is based on a recognition of man's *conformity* to God and the resulting *relative* adequacy of the knowledge of God, with the recognition that this knowledge is inexhaustible. One can say that in this sense anthropologism is a *critical* anthropomorphism. Apophatics introduces in theology the *via eminentiae* and the *via negationis,* the way of transcending and the way of negation, as correc-

---

4. It is true that, in 1 Corinthians 13:12, Paul adds, "now I know in part; but then shall I know even as also I am known." That is, he admits — in the framework of eschatology, when "God will be all in all" — *adequate* knowledge, "even as also I am known," by God. Even this state of deification, however, does not exclude a difference between the Creator and creation, as the One who is revealed and that which receives the revelation; and the apostle's words refer, in our opinion, only to the measure of this revelation.

tives to the human knowledge of God in view of creaturely limitedness. Apophatics attests to the limitlessness of the revelation, to the inexhaustibility of the Divine ocean for creaturely knowledge. This is the living sense of Mystery and of its revelation, which at the same time is the consciousness that man has of his creatureliness. Apophatics has an equivalent in the mystical path of communion with God, which differs from the path of knowledge in that, in it, the distinction between the knower and the known is obliterated, as it were, and is replaced by their unity and identity.

This path of union in the empirical knowledge of God, which we find not only in Christian but also in non-Christian mysticism, in Brahmanism, in Neoplatonism, as well as in the nonreligious mysticism of the "cosmic feeling," this path of union is capable of receiving different religious coefficients, since the night of consciousness contains different possibilities. The knowledge of God can be totally alien to this mystical feeling, which can signify a dissolution of the I in the cosmos, a cosmotheism, a mystical paganism.[5]

The true mystical revelation of God occurs not in the night of extinguished consciousness, but in the midday light of consciousness. The path here is not discursive, however, but intuitive, not the path of the Logos, but that of the Holy Spirit.[6] Cognition and intuition are two paths of revelation, two wings carrying man into a domain that is unknown, to be sure, but that reveals itself to knowledge. And this revelation exists in the image of the self-revelation that occurs in divine life, in the depths of the Holy Trinity, which, in itself, is eternal self-revelation, not immobile, lifeless

---

5. We have this in the methodology of theosophical or anthroposophical occultism, where the path of spiritual life, which is equated here with knowledge of God, leads to the self-identification of the I with different cosmic essences, and thereby to self-abolition. The microcosm, which contains the image of God, dissolves in the macrocosm, whereas the reverse relation is the true one: the macrocosm must be taken into the microcosm. Thus, what occurs here is not the humanization of the world, but the dehumanization of man. The personal spirit, the subject who is the image of eternity in man, is abolished.

6. In this respect we are guided by the account of a mystical experience where the ineffability of the revelation is accompanied by personal consciousness: "I knew a man in Christ above fourteen years ago, (whether in the body, I cannot tell; or whether out of the body, I cannot tell: God knoweth;) such an one caught up to the third heaven. And I knew such a man, (whether in the body, or out of the body, I cannot tell: God knoweth;) how that he was caught up into paradise, and heard unspeakable words, which it is not lawful for a man to utter" (2 Cor. 12:2-4).

knowledge, but hypostatic and living self-positing. Here, a distinction is thus made between that which is revealed and that which reveals, between the Subject of the Revelation and the Revelation itself, with all this, of course, taking place in hypostatic being. The hypostasis that is revealed, the *Principle,* from which the Son is born and the Holy Spirit proceeds, is the Father, whereas the hypostases that reveal the Father in divine life and wisdom, in the Divine Sophia, are the Son and the Holy Spirit.

This divine knowledge of God in self-revelation, in contrast to the creaturely knowledge of God, is absolutely *adequate.* There is no separation between apophatic and kataphatic knowledge here, except in the sense that on the one hand there is the hypostasis of the Father, the hypostasis that is revealed, the hypostatic Divine Depth and Mystery, the Divine Subject of self-revelation; and on the other hand there are the Revealing or kataphatic, so to speak, hypostases of the Word and the Spirit, the hypostatic self-revelation that trihypostatically realizes the fullness of divine self-consciousness, the triunely hypostatic I.

In the depths of the Holy Trinity, in God and for God, there is therefore no place for any *mystery* in the sense of the inadequacy of the Father's self-revelation. "God is light, and in him is no darkness at all" (1 John 1:5). In His Word the Father speaks Himself. He is, as it were, pre-verbal or nonverbal Thought thinking itself, Thought about Thought, *noēsis tēs noēseōs,* according to Aristotle's brilliant expression. But this Thought engenders itself in the Word, in which nothing remains unthought and unexpressed, unmanifested verbally. There is a perfect identity between the Father's proper, inner Word, restrained in silence, and the hypostatic Word, which is engendered from the Father and which is His own uttered Word. The Son has and knows nothing that the Father does not have; and the Father does not possess anything that is not manifested in the Son. This is attested by the Word of the Father about Himself and about the Father; some of these testimonies concern His divine-human, kenotic ministry, while others have a more general character.[7]

The chief pertinent text from the Synoptics is from Matthew 11:27: "no man knoweth the Son, but the Father; neither knoweth any man the Father, save the Son" (cf. Luke 10:22). In John 10:15, we find: "as the Father knoweth me, even so know I the Father" (cf. 6:46). Also: "he that hath seen me hath seen the Father. . . . I am in the Father, and the Father in me" (14:9, 11); "I have known thee" (17:25). Also pertinent are all of Christ's testimonies in which He identifies Himself with the Father in life, will, and

---

7. Cf. the comparison of texts in my book *The Lamb of God,* p. 311.

works: "The Father loveth the Son, and hath given all things into his hand" (John 3:35); "the Father . . . sheweth him all things that himself doeth" (5:20; cf. 5:19); "I seek not mine own will, but the will of the Father which hath sent me" (5:30; cf. 6:38); "as my Father hath taught me, I speak these things" (8:28); "I do always those things that please him" (8:29); "I have not spoken of myself; but the Father which sent me, he gave me a commandment, what I should say, and what I should speak" (12:49); "the word which ye hear is not mine, but the Father's which sent me" (14:24); "I speak that which I have seen with my Father" (8:38; cf. 12:50); "that I have heard of my Father" (15:15). And all this is summed up in the identification: "I and my Father are one" (10:30; cf. 10:38); "if ye had known me, ye should have known my Father also" (8:19); "he that hateth me hateth my Father also" (15:23); "I am in the Father, and the Father in me" (14:11; cf. 14:20); "thou, Father, art in me, and I in thee" (17:21; cf. 17:23); "we will come unto him, and make our abode with him" (14:23).

The perfect adequacy of the revelation of the Father in the Son is attested by Scripture so undeniably and irrefutably that one does not need to insist on it. Indeed, this adequacy follows from the very relation of spiritual fatherhood and sonhood, where the Son is the hypostatic image of the Father ("the brightness of his glory and the express image of his person" [Heb. 1:3]), while the Father shows Himself in the Son. One can say that here the Divine Predicate, the Word, is absolutely adequate to the Divine Subject; but this identity is realized in two different hypostases, about which it can nevertheless be affirmed: "I and my Father are one," that is, Their separateness is affirmed at the same time as Their identity in mutual love.

But the Father is revealed not only in the Son but also in the Holy Spirit. As a result, this self-revelation is characterized by the same features as in the case of the Son, by adequacy and identity. But now these features refer not only to the Father, but to the Father and the Son, or to the Father through the Son; in a word, the relation is not immediate, but mediated. On the one hand, the Apostle directly attests the adequacy of God's revelation in the Holy Spirit: "we speak the wisdom of God in a mystery, even the hidden mystery, which God ordained before the world unto our glory. . . . God hath revealed [these things] unto us by his Spirit: for the Spirit searcheth all things, yea, the deep things of God . . . the things of God knoweth no man, but the Spirit of God" (1 Cor. 2:7, 10-11). On the other hand, we have the Son's testimony about the adequacy of the Holy Spirit to the Son Himself and, through Him, to the Father: "Howbeit when he, the Spirit of truth, is come, he will guide you into all truth: for he shall not speak of himself: but whatsoever he shall hear, that shall he speak. . . . He shall glorify me; for he shall receive of mine, and shall shew it unto you. All things that the Father hath are mine: therefore said I, that he shall take of mine, and shall shew it unto you" (John 16:13-15). The following series of equalities is affirmed here: The Third hypostasis, "another Comforter," in His revelation "takes" from the Second hypostasis; according to His hypostatic character, the Third hypostasis does not speak His Word, but confirms and actualizes the already spoken Word, but this Word, the Son, is also the Word of the Father. Therefore, the Third hypostasis, like the Second, reveals the Father — but He does so not directly, but only through the Son. And so we have one Revealed hypostasis, that of the Father; and two revealing hypostases, those of the Son and the Holy Spirit.

This one bihypostatic and dyadic revelation of the Father is, as we already know, the Divine Sophia, the image of the Holy Trinity in its proper depths, the Divine world, Divine-humanity. This is the self-revelation accomplished in the Holy Trinity, in the two Revealing hypostases, by which the Divine Sophia is directly hypostatized. It is for this reason that we speak of the Divine Sophia in a certain specific sense: the Logos is Sophia (but not vice versa); the Holy Spirit is Sophia (but not vice versa); and finally the dyadic union of the Logos and the Holy Spirit is Sophia (but not vice versa). These particular equalities express the relations of hypostatization: of the hypostases and hypostatizedness. But now we arrive at a new equality: *the Father is Sophia* (but, of course, not vice versa). This equality expresses the idea that, insofar as Sophia is objective, divine self-revelation, she reveals and expresses the hidden essence of the Father; she is His genuine predicate, whose true Subject He is. Sophia, as Divine-humanity, *belongs* to the Father; she is *His* revelation. In this sense, the Father is Divine-humanity; however, He is the Divine-humanity which is not manifested, which is hidden and mysterious, but which is becoming manifested in divine self-revelation. The Divine-humanity is the manifested countenance of the Father. It is the Mystery of the Father, hidden in Him, but manifested by the Revealing hypostases.

The same idea can be expressed in a new series of equalities: *In the order of* self-revelation the Father is equal to the Son: "I and my Father are one" (John 10:30), although not vice versa: "my Father is greater than I" (John 14:28). And the Father is equal to the Holy Spirit, although not vice versa. And the Father is equal to the Son *and* the Holy Spirit, although, of course, also not vice versa. The image of the Father shines fully in the Son and the Holy Spirit. The interpenetration and mutual transparence of the hypostases correspond here to trinitarian life. For creaturely being, where a hypostasis is self-enclosed being and is repelled and reflected from the other, such mutual transparence is absent (except in love as a gift of grace). Here, this doubling of the self-revelation of God as the Father in the Son and the Spirit appears to be unnecessary and even impossible. "I and my Father are one" — what can this mean except that the distinctly personal beings of the Father and of the Son are livingly identical, are "consubstantial" by virtue of interhypostatic love? And it is of course the same with regard to the Holy Spirit. It is for this reason that one can say that Sophia, being the revelation of the hypostases of the Son and of the Holy Spirit, is at the same time the revelation of the Father, in all the power of divine Fatherhood. One must remember that the Revealed hypostasis is the Father, for Whom it is proper to engender and originate by procession, while giving Himself. Fatherhood is synonymous with self-renunciation, with self-revelation in others.

Let us now consider the self-revelation of the Father in creation. The Apostle says, "I bow my knees unto the Father of our Lord Jesus Christ, of whom the whole fatherhood [*patria*] in heaven and earth is named" (Eph. 3:14-15; the King James Version has been modified to conform with the Russian Bible). This establishes the identity of fatherhood in heaven, in the Holy Trinity, and in creation, on earth. And if the Father in heaven, the Father of the Lord Jesus Christ, is also "our Father," this must be understood in the sense of that very same Fatherhood in self-revelation and love. The creaturely Sophia, as the creaturely Divine-humanity, exists in the image of the heavenly Sophia or the heavenly Divine-humanity, i.e., as the revelation of the Father's self-revelation. Man is created *in the image of God,* but this image is the Divine-humanity as the image of the Father. The image of the Father is the Son, Who manifested Himself in the God-Man, and the Holy Spirit, Who manifested Himself in the Mother of God. Man is created in the image of God, as male and female, according to the two images of the revelation of fatherhood, as sonhood and as mother-daughterhood. The image of the son of man corresponds to the image of the Son of God; and the two are identified in the God-Man. The image of the mother of man, but also of the daughter of God, is manifested in Eve, who after the fall ceded her place to the New Eve, Mary. Man is created for Godsonhood and Goddaughterhood; that is the Creator's supreme gift to His creation: "as many as received him, to them gave he power to become the sons of God . . . which were born, not . . . of the will of the flesh . . . but of God" (John 1:12-13).

This gift of the adoption of men in the Son of God, the God-Man, is bestowed by the Holy Spirit, the Spirit of adoption, Who gives birth to them "maternally" as children of God and clothes them in Christ. This is attested by apostolic texts and especially, of course, by the Lord's Prayer, where human lips utter the words, "Our Father which art in heaven." But this gift is the supreme love and condescension of the Creator for creation, in relation to which the Creator and God becomes also the Father. This gift must have an ontological correlative in order for it not to be an ontological impossibility. And this possibility consists, of course, in the *conformity* of God to man; it consists in Divine-humanity, in which the Heavenly Sophia is the foundation of the creaturely Sophia, the two being united and identified in the God-Man by the Holy Spirit. Therefore, to the idea that the Divine Sophia, the Heavenly Divine-humanity, is the image of the Father, we must add that the creaturely Sophia too, the earthly divine-humanity, exists in the image of the Father, although she is manifested in the images of the God-Man and the Mother of God, Jesus and Mary. The Creator is God, but it is precisely the Father Who is the Creator par excellence. The world is created by the Holy Trinity, by the trihypostatic God; and each hypostasis has manifested itself in creation in conformity with its hypostatic property. But the origin of creation proceeds from the Principle in the Holy Trinity, "from God the Father Almighty, Creator of heaven and earth." He is the Primary Will to creation as the creaturely image of self-revelation. Creation is another image of *His* self-revelation by the Son and the Holy Spirit, of the Divine Sophia in the creaturely Sophia. The interrelation in self-revelation that exists in the depths of the Holy Trinity is also manifested in the creation of the world.

And this relation is manifested not only in the creation of the world, but also in the Providence for the world, as well as in its salvation, in its economy. One cannot fail to see that God the Provider is the Father Who watches over His creation. Here, as well as in the creation of the world, He possesses primary will, power, care for the world. True, this Providence is realized through the action of the two other hypostases, but they are *sent* by the Father. This sending signifies the revelation of God's love in the Providence, which is completely analogous to the self-revelation of the Father in the Son and in the Spirit in the depths of the Holy Trinity, and then in creation. It is sufficient to attentively examine Christ's words uttered in the Sermon on the Mount and in other cases to become convinced that He attributes Providence to God the Father. And of course the most incontestable testimony here is the Lord's Prayer.

The Father's will not only directs the life of the world but is decisive in its final destiny, in particular with reference to the end of the world: "of that day and that hour knoweth no man, no, not the angels which are in heaven, neither the Son, but the Father" (Mark 13:32; cf. Matt. 24:36); "come, ye blessed of my Father, inherit the kingdom prepared for you from the foundation of the world" (Matt. 25:34); "to sit on my right hand, and on my left, is not mine to give, but it shall be given to them for whom it is prepared of my Father" (Matt. 20:23); "in my Father's house are many mansions" (John 14:2); "wait for the promise of the Father . . . it is not for you to know the times or the seasons, which the Father hath put in his own power" (Acts 1:4, 7); God "hath appointed a day, in the which he will judge the world in righteousness by that man whom he hath ordained" (Acts 17:31).

Accomplishing power is attributed to the Father, Who, in visions of the Apocalypse, sits on a throne (Rev. 4:2) and is called God the Almighty, "which is, and which was, and which is to come" (1:8). Thus, in the vision recorded in the fourth chapter of Revelation, the twenty-four elders fall down before the one who sits on the throne and say, "Thou art worthy, O Lord, to receive glory and honour and power: for thou hast created all things, and for thy pleasure they are and were created" (4:11). Further, the book held in the right hand of the one who sits on the throne is opened by the Lamb, as the Redeemer Who "hast made us unto our God kings and priests" (5:10). The completion of history is represented as the work of the Father through the Lamb: the kingdom of the world becomes the kingdom of "our Lord and of His Christ" (11:15; cf. 12:10), "for the Lord God omnipotent reigneth . . . for the marriage of the Lamb is come" (19:6-7). And at the end of the world the heavenly city descends "from God" (21:10), and "the Lord God Almighty and the Lamb are the temple of it" (21:22), and His servants "shall see his face; and his name shall be in their foreheads" (22:4). In a word, that fullness of accomplishment is approaching in which God will be all in all. And the coming of this fullness is represented in the Apocalypse as the *work* of the Father. The idea that the Synoptic Gospels and the Acts of the Apostles only hint at with lapidary conciseness ("the times or the seasons, which the Father hath put in his own power" [Acts 1:7]) is developed here in its fullness: the Father is the God of history, and the Lamb is its doer.

It is evident from these passages that the Holy Trinity, *as God,* is directed toward the world by *the hypostasis of the Father.* To this one must add that, conversely, when the texts refer simply to God, they mean precisely the Father, so that the two expressions are synonymous for all intents and purposes. To be sure, this observation is valid only for the New Testament usage, since the Old Testament does not contain any direct revelations concerning hypostatic distinctions in God. One can establish as a general fact that when a New Testament passage refers simply to God in connection with Jesus Christ and the Holy Spirit, it is the Father Who is clearly meant. This implies a certain verbal nuance of *distinction* between God the Father and the other hypostases with reference to Their divinity. These texts are so numerous that it is difficult to cite all of them.[8]

The general character of these numerous texts is such that they distinguish and in a certain sense oppose God the Father and the Lord Jesus Christ, the Son. And this contradistinction is intensified by the fact that Christ, invariably called the Lord and the Son of God, is *never* called God. This usage is retained in the Nicaeno-Constantinopolitan Creed: "I believe in one God the Father Almighty . . . and in one Lord Jesus Christ, the . . . Son of God [although there was added against the Arians, 'very God of very God'] . . . and in the Holy Spirit, the Lord. . . ."

In the Old Testament, God is usually designated by the word "Lord," and we often find the combination "Lord God" (the mystical tetragrammaton: Yahweh-Adonai). The word "Lord" is also used in this combination in the New Testament, but exclusively with reference to the Father, so that the *Lord God* becomes, as it were, the proper name of the Father. It is never used with reference to Christ, Who is called simply Lord; or with reference to the Holy Spirit, Who is called the Spirit of God, the Holy Spirit, the Spirit of the Lord, the Spirit of Christ. (He is never even called "Lord," which appellation is applied to Him only in the Nicaeno-Constantinopolitan Creed.) Nevertheless, the consubstantiality of the Holy Trinity is irrefutably attested, most clearly in the *comma Johanneum:* "there are three that bear record in heaven, the Father, the Word, and the Holy Spirit: and these three are one" (1 John 5:7).

To be sure, the nuance expressed in this usage should by no means be understood in the unitarian sense that only the Father is the true God, that only He has divinity, whereas the Son and the Spirit do not have it. That would shake the trinitarian dogma — and may God keep us from this! But we cannot neglect this fact; it implies a special notion which must be included in the doctrine of the Holy Trinity. Moreover, as we have

8. See Acts 2:36; 3:13; 4:24-30; 10:38; Rom. 1:7; 8:3; 8:32; 15:6; 15:16; 1 Cor. 1:3; 2 Cor. 1:2; 13:14; Gal. 1:1; 1:4; Eph. 1:2; Phil. 1:2; 1:11; 2:11; 4:6; Col. 1:3; 1 Thess. 1:1; 2 Thess. 1:2; 1 Tim. 1:2; 2 Tim. 1:2; Titus 1:4; Philemon 3; James 1:27; 1 Pet. 1:3; 2:4-5; 3:18; 3:22; 4:11; 2 Pet. 1:1; 1:2; 1:17; 2 John 3; Rev. 1:4-6, 8; 3:12; 5:13; 6:16; 7:10; 11:15-17; 12:5, 10; 19:6-7; 19:10; 21:3-7, 22; 22:1, 3. [Bulgakov quotes the passages themselves, but here I indicate only chapter and verse. — Trans.]

seen, in certain texts the Father is directly called not only the Father but also the Lord and God of Jesus Christ. Observing this fact during the Lord's earthly ministry, when He called the Father His God and Father, we might be able to limit its significance by linking it with the kenosis of the Lord. Having emptied Himself of His divinity, He could to a certain degree look out at the Father from His humanity, as at God, but a kenotic interpretation of this fact is clearly insufficient. Such an interpretation can explain the cry on the Cross, "My God, my God, why hast thou forsaken me?" (Matt. 27:46), this extreme kenosis, in which the very consciousness of sonhood is obscured; but it cannot explain the words of the Savior to Mary Magdalene *after* the resurrection: "to my Father" and "to my God" (John 20:17).

We arrive at the conclusion that, in a certain sense, the Father is *God* even for the Son — not only in His kenotic humiliation but also in His glorified state in heaven. Consequently, He is such for the Son in the eternal life of the Holy Trinity, not only in the economic but also in the immanent Trinity. Holy Scripture directly attests to this. One cannot directly confirm the same thing as far as the Holy Spirit is concerned, inasmuch as Scripture never speaks of the Person of the Holy Spirit. But this can be *indirectly* established *a fortiori* on the basis of the general interrelation of the Son and the Holy Spirit, Who is sent by the Son and reveals Him.

There is another fact we must consider, a fact that is also established on the basis of Scripture, although not as clearly as the previous fact. The relations between the Father on the one hand and the Son and the Holy Spirit on the other are defined not only by Their birth and procession, respectively, from the Father and by His sending Them, but also (in a sense that cannot be more clearly defined for man) by Their *prayer* to the Father as God. We have in mind here not only the prayer of the God-Man, the Son of God, in the state of kenosis; we already know that Christ prayed without ceasing and that this was true prayer, not one that was performed just to set an example.[9] In this feat of prayer the God-Man showed God all the accomplishments of His ministry, from the first temptation in the desert to the second and final temptation at Gethsemane and on Golgotha (the earlier years of His life being shrouded in silence). To Whom did He pray and to Whom did He instruct His disciples and followers to pray? He prayed to His Father and to His God, Whom he saw in the person of the Father. The interrelation between God and the Son of God, the Lord Jesus Christ, that is attested in the apostolic texts cited

9. See *The Lamb of God,* pp. 283-84, 309-10.

above, is realized by works in His life of prayer within the limits of His earthly ministry.

We must also ask the following: If the prayer of the Lord "in the days of his flesh" (Heb. 5:7) was, in its *content*, determined by His kenotic ministry ("when he had offered up prayers and supplications with strong crying and tears unto him that was able to save him from death" [Heb. 5:7]), can *the very fact* of the prayer, or its *possibility*, be sufficiently explained by the kenosis alone? After all, a prayer, irrespective of its content, is a *personal act* of the one praying, an act which expresses his personality. The Personality of the God-Man, even in the state of kenosis and when it assumed the creaturely human essence, remained the same as in eternity, that is, it remained that of the Son of God in His unchanging and eternal relation to His Father in the Holy Trinity. The kenosis refers to the *life* of the God-Man's Personality, to its state, but it does not refer to His Personality itself; on the contrary, according to the Chalcedonian dogma, the entire power of the Incarnation consists in the unchanging nature of the God-Man's Personality.

Thus, we must necessarily conclude that, in Christ, the God-Man, it is the Logos Himself, the Son of God, Who prayed to the Father; and this possibility of a life of prayer must receive a sufficient foundation in His hypostatic being. If we understand the general possibility of the Incarnation on the basis of the *correspondence* of the Divine and human natures and even their primordial identity in Sophia, Heavenly and creaturely, then, with regard to personality, the Son of God is *kindred* with the sons of God by grace, who have their God in the Heavenly Father and pray to the Father as God and to God the Father: *Our Father!* They pray together with the God-Man, Who pronounces: "My Father! Thy will be done!" Even the Lord's Prayer itself, *Our Father,* is given to us in the name of our common divine-human Godsonhood. The sons of God *by adoption* are sufficiently audacious to utter this prayer by virtue of their union with the Son of God *according to essence:* they can pray in this way because He Himself taught them "as John also taught his disciples" (Luke 11:1).

This prayer of Godsonhood already contains that self-evident identity of the names of the Father and God which is attested by Scripture; and the expression of Godsonhood is precisely the prayer to God as the Father and to the Father as God. In other words, the possibility of the prayer of the God-Man cannot be explained simply as a consequence of the Divine Incarnation; rather, it is included in the Son's eternal hypostatic being, in His relation to the Father as the Father and God. The Son's relation of prayer to the Father as His God is not temporary, but eternal. Otherwise, this relation would be impossible for the God-Man. To consider His life of prayer as merely a temporary state, which has its beginning in the Incarnation and its end in the Ascension, is contradictory since this would introduce a change in the very personality of the Son of God, which is identical to itself both in the Incarnation and outside of it.

Furthermore, and this is the most important thing here, it is erroneous to think that Christ's life of prayer ceased even after the Ascension, for the latter is by no means a disincarnation, by no means the abolition of the Divine-humanity and of the union of the two natures in Christ. On the contrary, it is the eternalization of the Divine-humanity. The glorified Christ is the God-Man or, according to the New Testament expression, "the man Christ Jesus" (1 Tim. 2:5). Even after the Ascension, during the "Ten Days," Christ prays the Father (John 14:16) to send the Holy Spirit into the world. Consequently, the Son's relation of prayer to the Father does not cease even when He takes His place at the right hand of the Father. And if not then, when could it cease? *After* the Pentecost? But here we have yet another fact whose dogmatic significance must be examined with reference to the question that concerns us: Christ's high-priestly ministry, expressed in His advocatory offering of His own blood: "we have an advocate [*paraklēton*] with the Father, Jesus Christ the righteous. And he is the propitiation for our sins: and not for ours only, but also for the sins of the whole world" (1 John 2:1-2). This High Priest is "the mediator [*mesitēs*] of a better covenant" (Heb. 8:6); "this man, because he continueth ever, hath an unchangeable priesthood. Wherefore he is able also to save them to the uttermost that come unto God by him, seeing he ever liveth to make intercession for them" (7:24-25), as "the mediator of the new testament" (9:15), who has entered "into heaven itself, now to appear in the presence of God for us" (9:24), as a "high priest over the house of God" (10:21). The work of the High Priest is prayer with the offering of sacrifice. Although Christ, "after he had offered one sacrifice for sins for ever, sat down on the right hand of God" (10:12), this single offering of sacrifice, which the Apostle contrasts with the repeated sacrifices in the Old Testament, is not a one-time act but has eternal validity and, if one can use this expression, eternal duration. The sitting of the Son at the right hand of the Father, which crowns His ministry with glory, does not abolish His high-priestly advocacy, His intercession for the world in prayer by virtue of His sacrifice, even as the one-time character of this sacrifice does not contradict but serves as the basis of the fact that the eucharistic sacrifice is offered on earth on all altars at all times until the end of this aeon (and in a certain sense it continues even beyond this aeon).

On the basis of the foregoing discussion, we conclude that the Son's relation of prayer to the Father, His intercession for the world, exists also in heaven. But even though this intercession constitutes, so to speak, the particular content of this prayer, it is realized only on the basis of the general relation of the Son to the Father as to the Father and God. That is, it is realized on the basis of the Son's *praying love* for the Father.

The Son of God is *the eternal High Priest* in the Holy Trinity, offering the sacrifice of filial love to the Father; and only by virtue of this eternal high-priesthood is He our High Priest as well, interceding for the world before the Father. By virtue of this high-priesthood, *on earth as in heaven*, He offers to the Father His prayer for the world at the solemn hour when He departs the world: "now come I to thee" (John 17:13). And in this most solemn of prayers, which we call *High-priestly*, He prays for the world and for those who are faithful to Him, as well as for Himself, "that the world may know that thou hast sent me, and hast loved them, as thou hast loved me" (John 17:23). This High-priestly *prayer of the Son to the Father and God* ("that they may know thee the only true God, and Jesus Christ, whom thou hast sent" [17:3]) is pronounced in a tone of *filial* relation: "Father, the hour is come: glorify thy Son, that thy Son also may glorify thee" (17:1); "thou lovedst me before the foundation of the world" (17:24). This is not a prayer for the sake of example. And it is not only for the current moment; it is not a prayer which sounds once on earth and grows silent when Christ ascends to heaven. No! This is the eternal prayer which the Eternal High Priest offers in heaven, sitting at the right hand of the Father: "that they may be one, even as we are one: I in them, and thou in me, that they may be made perfect in one; and that the world may know that thou hast sent me, and hast loved them, as thou hast loved me. Father, I will that they also, whom thou hast given me, be with me where I am; that they may behold my glory, which thou hast given me: for thou lovedst me before the foundation of the world" (17:22-24).

If the Son is the High Priest before the Father and God (and therefore the High Priest of the New Testament priesthood, for He offers the sacrifice of Christ), what can one then say about the "Spirit of Christ," the Third hypostasis? Does the Holy Spirit remain outside this relation of prayer to God and the Father, inasmuch as His mission does not include the High-priestly ministry? Or does He present another form of the relation of prayer to the Father, in conformity with His hypostatic property? But can there be any question about this if we know that the Holy Spirit, Who eternally reposes upon the Son, has descended and reposes upon the God-Man and inspires Him? And if these inspirations are realized in unceasing prayer, is it not clear that the Spirit of inspiration is also the Spirit of prayer, that He is, so to speak, prayer itself?

But apart from this conclusion, already sufficiently convincing, we also have direct Scriptural testimony concerning this in Romans 8 and Galatians 4. The Apostle tells us that "if any man have not the Spirit of Christ, he is none of his" (Rom. 8:9), "for as many as are led by the Spirit of God, they are the sons of God" (8:14). But the sons of God must have the same relation of prayer to God and the Father as the Son, the Lord Jesus Christ, Who therefore taught us the prayer, "Our Father which art in heaven." In accordance with this idea, the apostle Paul continues his explanation of what constitutes the power of the Spirit of Christ: "ye have not received the spirit of bondage again to fear; but ye have received the Spirit of adoption, whereby we cry, Abba, Father. The Spirit itself beareth witness with our spirit, that we are the children of God" (8:15-16). And so, our Godsonhood is expressed in the invocation through the Holy Spirit, "Abba, Father!" We find the same idea in Galatians 4:6: "And because ye are sons, God hath sent forth the Spirit of his Son into your hearts, crying, Abba, Father." These words perhaps even more clearly underscore the idea that the Son's spirit of prayer in relation to the Father is the Holy Spirit Himself; for what is said here is not "Spirit of Christ" but the more general and primordial "Spirit of his Son." Further on, the idea that the Holy Spirit is the spirit of prayer is expressed in a direct and general form: "Likewise the Spirit also helpeth our infirmities: for we know not what we should pray for as we ought: but the Spirit itself maketh intercession for us with groanings which cannot be uttered. And he that searcheth the hearts knoweth what is the mind of the Spirit, because he maketh intercession for the saints according to the will of God" (Rom. 8:26-27). This passage clearly indicates the Holy Spirit's intercession by prayer; and this idea is confirmed by a mention of Christ's advocacy for us in heaven: "It is Christ that died, yea rather, that is risen again, who is even at the right hand of God, who also maketh intercession for us" (8:34).

It is thus irrefutably established that both the Son and the Holy Spirit *pray to* the Father as to Their Father and Their God (according to the usual New Testament expression); and that Their relation to the Father, besides being one of equi-divinity through generation and procession, is also one of prayer. In this relation of prayer, They are consequently united with the creaturely world, with human beings (and of course with angels as well), in crying out with them, "Our Father which art in heaven! Abba, Father!" This compels us to ask how this should be understood in the inner life of the Holy Trinity, precisely with respect to the *equi-divinity* of the three hypostases, in virtue of which it must be said about each of them that it is the true God (as the Athanasian Creed expresses it). Evidently, it is a question of a certain *nuance* in the concept of Divinity to which theologians have paid scant attention. Human language is poor and in this case insufficient, for it has only the single word and concept "prayer" to designate both creaturely prayer and divine prayer, even though the difference between the two is as great as that between God and creation.

The creature's prayer to God derives, first of all, from its consciousness of its creatureliness, of the fact that it originates in nothing and abides in nothing, in the face of God's absoluteness. This prayer is therefore the creature's praise and thanksgiving addressed to the Creator, as well as a supplication for its needs; and both aspects of this prayer are marked by the consciousness of creaturely limitedness. One can, in a certain sense, say that the very character of this prayer derives from creatureliness. It is true that, alongside this creaturely consciousness and remoteness from God, Who is "in heaven," there is also the sense of connection with God, of closeness to Him, of conformity with Him. This is in general the living sense of the image of God in man; and the creature's prayer is the realization of this connection, a "dialogue" with God.

Therefore, condescending to creaturely being in the Incarnation of Christ and in the descent of the Holy Spirit, the Son of God and the Holy Spirit *are united with us,* as it were, in our relation to God and pray together with us: "Our Father which art in heaven." They utter the same prayer that the creature uses when it prays to the Creator. But this form of prayer of the Second and Third hypostases refers only to kenotic condescension. To be sure, in the prayer of the Son and of the Holy Spirit to the Father we cannot admit any of the attributes of creaturely prayer, for it is not proper to these two equi-divine hypostases to address the Creator with *creaturely* praise and thanksgiving. Nor is supplication proper to Their divine perfection.

But there is an aspect of this Divine prayer, which, to a certain degree, is accessible to us as well, in proportion to our conformity to God. This is the aspect of the hypostatic qualification of love, which corresponds to hypostatic self-definition: "I thank thee, O Father, Lord of heaven and earth" (Matt. 11:25; Luke 10:21); "Father, I thank thee that thou hast heard me" (John 11:41). This is the aspect of Revealed and Revealing Love. The Father is God, revealing Himself in the Two revealing hypostases, divinely emptying Himself in the eternal kenosis of the Father. He is the initial hypostatic Love, the Depth that is being revealed, the unsearchable but self-manifesting Abyss, the Divine Principle, *archē*. The Dyad of the Son and the Holy Spirit is the double image of Revealing Love, and They receive Themselves from the Father and God. Their relation to the Father as either sonhood or procession does not diminish the equi-divinity of Their nature and Their hypostatic divinity, but makes them the revealing hypostases, who receive Themselves from the Father. The Father is not the "cause," for, given the equi-eternity of the hypostases, there is no place here for causal origination. The idea of eternal origination is contradictory, for origination is the appearance of something that has previously not existed, and in this sense it is a negation or limitation of the equi-eternity of the hypostases. That the Son is eternally born from the Father and the Holy Spirit eternally proceeds from the Father is not causal origination, which would necessarily introduce an ontological gradation of the hypostases, however it is formulated. Rather, it is an interrelation in eternity, an absolute interrelation. The latter possesses a supreme, divine reality. If the entire problematic of causality and origination with reference to the Holy Trinity must be excluded *a limine* [at the outset], it is incumbent upon us to adopt a more serious and responsible understanding of the principle of *hierarchism,* as the expression of the concrete interrelation of the concretely qualified hypostases. Hierarchism is the differentiation that results from the relations of the hypostases, given the recognition of their perfect ontological equality or equi-divinity.

The hierarchism of the hypostases, as their concrete qualifiedness in the Holy Trinity, results not from relations of origination but from mutual revelation, that is, from the distinction between the revealed Paternal hypostasis and the revealing hypostases, the Son and the Holy Spirit, according to the character of Their participation in the revelation. The Revealed hypostasis, the Father, is the Principle, God *par excellence, autotheos* and simply *ho Theos;* whereas the Revealing hypostases in relation to the Principle are *Theos* (as in the Prologue to the Gospel of John, 1:1). Although all the hypostases are equally divine, there exists between the revealed hypostasis and the revealing hypostases a definite hierarchical relation: the relation between the First hypostasis, the Principle, and the Second and Third hypostases (these two *not-First* hypostases). This is not an ontological subordinationism, but a qualitative and hierarchical distinction, which is expressed not only in the words, "my Father is greater than I" (John 14:28), but also in the entire relation of the Son (and then the Holy Spirit) to the Father as it is revealed in the Gospel. The two revealing hypostases are conscious of themselves in their divine life not as belonging to themselves but as the revelation of the Father. For this reason their relation to their *own* divinity is a *relation to the Father*, the source of the self-revelation of this divinity, or the Principle. And since the relation to one's own divinity in God Himself is an image of love and worship whose equivalent in the creaturely world is prayer, this worship of the Father, the most hidden Divinity, Who lives in Himself, is expressed in the relation of prayer of the Son and the Holy Spirit to *God and the Father*, or to the Father as God and to God as the Father. This prayer expresses *the love of the divine hypostases themselves for the Father*, as the hypostatic bearer of *Divinity*, which the revealing hypostases have in themselves as the revelation of the Father.

The Holy Trinity is essential Love, and its different hypostases are the image of this love. The Father loves by a self-renouncing and self-emptying love. This love cannot be expressed in prayer to Divinity, for it is impossible to pray to oneself. The Father humbles Himself in His Paternal love, extending His own life beyond Himself and revealing it in the other hypostases. By contrast, the two revealing hypostases have *before Them* the Father, Who is revealed to Them in His Divinity, not only as the Father but also as God, as the Subject of Divinity, the First hypostasis of Divinity. In a certain sense, the relation of the First hypostasis to the Second and Third hypostases consists in the distinction between *God and Divinity* (even if hypostatic); and in His love the Father proceeds into His Divinity in the Son and the Spirit, whereas this hypostatic Divinity of Theirs relates to Him *as God* in the form of praying love.

One can also say that, insofar as the self-revelation of God in His Divinity is Sophia or the Divine-humanity, which is hypostatized by the Second and Third hypostases, both of these hypostases relate to the Father out of the Divine-humanity, or Sophia. God (the Father) loves His Divinity as Sophia or the Divine-humanity, and He gives Himself to the Latter; and the Divine-humanity loves Him as Its source or principle, as God. Thus, in the Divinity itself of the Holy Trinity, there is, despite the equidivinity of the hypostases, a distinction between God as *autotheos* or *ho Theos* (the Principle of Divinity, God *par excellence*) and the Divinity that is in the two Revealing hypostases. This distinction refers to the Father as God, and it implies not a creaturely relation, not a relation to one's Creator, but the relation of the hypostases of Divinity to the hypostasis of God. This relation is qualified in the Son as the Eternal High Priest and in the Spirit as the Eternal breath of prayer.

This relation, which exists in the supra-eternal (or immanent) Trinity, is complicated in the "economic" Trinity by the kenosis of the Son and the Holy Spirit and serves as the basis for a particular relation which can be defined as a certain subordinationism.[10] Here we must confront once more the question of subordinationism, which in general has not been overcome but rather evaded in the history of dogma. In particular, we see such an evasion in Arianism and Macedonianism, to the extent they consisted in the rejection or diminution of the Divinity of the Second and Third hypostases. The ecclesial "akrivia"[11] is protected from the distortions of subordinationism by the dogma of consubstantiality, homoousianism. However, this is a victory of dogma, but not yet of theology, which remains in an indeterminate position in relation to the subordinationism that it has still not overcome.

In rejecting ontological subordinationism, we must by no means abolish the *distinction* between the forms of the self-revelation of the hypostases in the Holy Trinity, a distinction which serves as the basis of a certain *hierarchical* relationship among the hypostases. But all hierarchism, together with unity of nature or ontological equality, implies hierarchical differentiation or inequality. This hierarchism in the Holy Trinity, expressed outwardly in the *taxis* and in particular in the primacy of the Father as Principle ("the monarchy of the Father"), could not remain unnoticed in theology. But while some theologians, such as Origen, could do no more than impotently stumble around this hierarchism, others did not even notice it or associated it with relations of origination (see the commentaries on the text "my Father is greater than I" in St. Basil the Great, St. Gregory the Theologian, and others). There were also attempts to interpret this hierarchism in the sense of subordinationism, christological or economic, with reference to the human nature in the God-Man. But all this was insufficient, for hierarchism, economic and christological, has its basis in the supra-eternal being of the Holy Trinity and Its self-revelation. The Father, as the transcendent principle in Divinity, is, strictly speaking, the hypostasis of God, *God in Divinity, autotheos.* This distinction between the transcendent and the immanent principles in Divinity is covered by the relation between the Father, Who is God, and the hypostases who are co-divine with Him and reveal Him. This distinction is not a natural and ontological one, inasmuch as all the hypostases are equally divine; rather, it is a hierarchical one. It corresponds to the very nature of God as the Transcendent-immanent, self-revealing Principle, in which His entire life is

---

10. See *The Lamb of God,* pp. 309-13.
11. Akrivia is the strict and exact fulfilling of a church requirement. — Trans.

hypostatic and hypostatized. And as hypostatic life, it is not the mere automatic self-revelation of that which cannot be kept hidden, but the personal act of the mutual love of the Father and for the Father.

In other words, this self-revelation is the generation of the Son and the procession of the Spirit. The Father is the beloved Father (and not only a Transcendent and impersonal principle) for the Son Who is engendered from Him and Who is the beloved Only Begotten Son; and He is also the beloved Father for the Holy Spirit, Who, although He is not engendered from the Father, proceeds from Him and is the Father's Love. The Holy Trinity is transcendent-immanent trihypostatizedness. This corresponds to all the philosophical postulates of a consistent and comprehensive doctrine of the Absolute as a transcendent-immanent personal principle. The expression of this divine hierarchy in the Holy Trinity is precisely this praying worship in the Trinity itself which we established on the basis of Scripture. And this supra-eternal hierarchism, not of origination but of self-revelation, serves as the basis of all further — in this case economic — subordinationism manifested with reference to creation.

This hierarchism is manifested both in the creation itself and in the "economy" of the salvation of the world. The Father, as the First Will, is the Creator of the world. Volitional initiative belongs to Him, but He creates the world by the Word ("without him was not any thing made that was made" [John 1:3]) Who reveals Him; and He completes the creation by the Holy Spirit, Whom He sends to warm and quicken the primordial chaos, "the earth . . . without form and void" (Gen. 1:2). The image of the hierarchical Trinity is seen also in the Father's creation of man, who by his very creation is destined for Divine Incarnation and Godsonhood, and already bears the image of the Son; and into his body, which He formed, the Father breathes the spirit of life from the Holy Spirit. In this creation of man, we have the image of the birth of the Son and the procession of the Holy Spirit.

In the "economy" of salvation, or in relation to fallen man and the fallen world, the hierarchy of the Holy Trinity is revealed in the Father's *sending* of the Son and the Holy Spirit into the world. Hitherto, this sending has been considered only with reference to the supra-eternal origination of the hypostases and used as an argument for or against one or another doctrine of origination. The whole question has therefore received an incorrect and distorted formulation, which has deprived it of meaning; for this sending is connected not with "origination" but with the *hierarchical* interrelation of the trinitarian hypostases and, in particular, with the primacy of the Father in the Holy Trinity.

What is the nature of this sending? There is, of course, the temptation to interpret this question simplistically, to see in it an *act of volition*, by analogy with human acts of sending, which primarily have the character of commands. And to be sure, this element cannot be completely eliminated. In the sending, the Sender is characterized as the initating will, the First Will. But this will is determined by interhypostatic love; it is this love itself qualified in conformity with the image of the First hypostasis: Love-Will, the Initial and Revealed hypostasis. One must not forget that the sending is not an external but an inner, ontological relation. It corresponds to that act of the spiritual life in us in which our consciousness is awakened, our creative activity is initiated, and our self-manifestation is realized. There exists, therefore, a certain identity with respect to life-*content* between the Sender and those who are sent. The Sender conceals this content in Himself, but He reveals it by the sending. This identity of the content of the sending, as it is manifested by the relation between the Father and the Son, and then by the relation between the Father and the Holy Spirit, is the object of the express teaching of Christ, which is included in what He says about Himself and about the Father, especially in the Fourth Gospel.

The fact of the sending of the Son by the Father[12] is established just as forcefully here as this identity of thought, will, word, and deed between the One who sends and the One who is sent. "The One who sent me" becomes, as it were, the proper name of the Father on the lips of the Son. The Son says about Himself: "The Son can do nothing of himself, but what he seeth the Father do . . . for the Father loveth the Son, and sheweth him all things that himself doeth" (John 5:19-20). The will of the Father is not a command but a self-revelation in the life of love. "As the Father hath life in himself, so hath he given to the Son to have life in himself" (5:26). "The works which the Father hath given me to finish, the same works that I do, bear witness of me, that the Father hath sent me" (5:36). "I came down from heaven, not to do mine own will, but the will of him that sent me" (6:38; cf. 5:30). "The living Father hath sent me, and I live by the Father" (6:57). "Jesus knowing that the Father had given all things into his hands, and that he was come from God [= the Father], and went to God" (13:3). In general, chapters 5-8 and 10-17 of the Gospel of John contain passages on this subject.

Thus, the relation of love as sending and being sent is a certain self-identity with hypostatic distinction: "I and my Father are one" (John 10:30). The Son is not the Father, but the Father is not only revealed in the

---

12. See *The Lamb of God*, p. 311.

Son ("one"). He is also present in Him or with Him by virtue of His love ("I am not alone, because the Father is with me" [John 16:32]). This establishes the coparticipation of the Father in the Son's work and in His mission (cf. *The Lamb of God*). The sending cannot, of course, be understood as a one-sided command accompanied by inner indifference, for it is "crucifying and crucified" Love.[13] One must reject the patripassianism, condemned by the Church, which consists in directly identifying the hypostases of the Father and the Son and thus in confusing the Sender with the one who is sent. But at the same time one must remember that "God [= Father] so loved the world, that he gave his only begotten Son" (John 3:16). The Father's sacrifice when He sends His Son is just as great as the Son's (although it is different): Does the Father love the Son more or less than the Son loves the Father? If we call this patripassianism, we must remember what Christ teaches, what the Holy Gospel teaches, what our faith teaches. But with regard to the sending, we distinguish between the "God" who sends (the Father) and the Son who is sent and who calls the one who sends Him His Father and God. It is in conformity with the eternal hierarchy of the hypostases that the hierarchy of the sending in self-revelation is defined.

Not only the Second hypostasis, however, but also the Third, the Holy Spirit, is sent by the Father. And this sending too conforms with the intratrinitarian hierarchy, in which the Holy Spirit reveals the Father in the Son and the Son in the Father, is Their mysterious "One" (see John 10:30), proceeding from the Father and sent upon the Son. The Father's sending of the Holy Spirit has already been sufficiently attested by an examination of the pertinent texts. A certain complexity is introduced by the fact that the Son too participates in the Father's sending of the Holy Spirit (an imaginary victory for the Filioque party!). This participation is expressed in His breathing of the Holy Spirit upon the disciples after the Resurrection (John 20:22), in His praying to the Father that He send the Holy Spirit (14:16), in the sending itself of the Holy Spirit by the Father (15:26), and in the Father's sending of the Holy Spirit "in my name" (14:26). This does not change the fundamental fact that, when the Holy Spirit proceeds from the Father, He is sent by the Father, in conformity with the economy of the salvation. Specifically, He is sent, in the Old Testament, upon the chosen of God, i.e., of the Father; He is sent by the Father upon the Mother of God at the Annunciation-Incarnation; He is sent

---

13. This is Metropolitan Philaret's phrase from his book *On the Love of God and the Crucifixion of Christ.* — Trans.

upon the Son Himself at His baptism in order to abide upon Him; and finally, He is sent into the world after Christ's Resurrection, now with Christ's participation, through the Son, *dia tou Huiou.*

Also established here is the identity of the revelation or content of the one who sends and the one who is sent, just as in the case of the Son, according to the Son's testimony: "he [the Holy Spirit] shall receive of mine, and shall shew it unto you. All things that the Father hath are mine: therefore said I, that he shall take of mine, and shall shew it unto you" (John 16:14-15). The sending down of the Holy Spirit "through the Son" and the corresponding participation of the Son in the sending of the Holy Spirit are *economic* in nature, although they of course have a basis in the *taxis,* in the form of the Father's self-revelation not only by the Second but also by the Third hypostasis, and, moreover, by the Second *and* the Third hypostasis. This fact does not change the essence of the relation: The Father is the one who sends, whereas the Holy Spirit is one who is sent; and the two hypostases who are sent find themselves, in the order of their sending, in the following interrelation: the Holy Spirit reposes upon the Son and is sent through the Son.

Hypostatically, the Holy Spirit is the Paternal Love, by which the Father loves the Son and His (the Father's) creation. The identity of the Loving One and Love, the unity of the Father and the Holy Spirit, is self-evident, but just as obvious is their hypostatic difference, their hetero-hypostatizedness. The Father is the God Who is in heaven, whereas the Spirit is sent into the world. The Spirit is God's Love for the world, the living hypostatic connection between heaven and earth, inasmuch as He, descending into the world, also abides in heaven. The Loving One, the Father, abides in heaven, although He loves the earth. Herein lies the mystery of heavenly fatherhood for us: "Our Father which art in heaven." This invocation appears to contain a contradiction: How can the *Father* be one who abides in heaven and who therefore is *transcendent* for us? But there is a mysterious "art" here, which indicates the path of the Father's love for the world: the Holy Spirit. Likewise, the Lord's mysterious words about the *unity* of the Heavenly Father and the Son Who is on earth, the words "I and my Father are one," tacitly indicate this hypostatic bridge of love, this *Third* thing, which unites heaven and earth, as does the further unfolding of these words: "that they all may be one; as thou, Father, art in me, and I in thee" (John 17:21). This "in" as well as this "one" in God the Father and the Son, and, further, the "in them" (17:23), i.e., in the world, this is the Holy Spirit, the Spirit of the Father's love, revealing the Father's heart, afire with love for the Son.

According to this relation, the Father, the transcendent God, becomes known to us through the hypostases sent by Him, for all that we know about God in Them and through Them refers to the Father as well: "he that hath seen me hath seen the Father. . . . Believe me that I am in the Father, and the Father in me" (John 14:9, 11); and this "in" is the Holy Spirit, searching the depths of God. Through this mutual transparence of the trinitarian hypostases we know the Unknowable, see the Unseeable. The hypostases who are sent do not wish to veil and do not veil the hypostasis who sends. They themselves testify about Him that He is *the Father and God*. The Father is the Principle; the one who sends reveals Himself, as it were, in the ones who are sent. Such is the Father's love, Love-Humility, Self-renunciation. As the Father is, so is the Son, Who in Himself also shows not Himself but the Father: "he that hath seen me hath seen the Father." So also is the Holy Spirit, Who in His transparence does not exist for Himself, as it were, but shows the Son in the Father and the Father in the Son. The Holy Spirit closes the eternal ring of trihypostatic love, which, however, has an eternal Principle in the Father and God.

This concealment of the One Who is revealed *behind* Those Who reveal is the supramundane *kenosis* of the Father's love in humility; and this kenosis is accomplished also with reference to the world, which recognizes the Father not face to face but only in the Son and through the Son by the Holy Spirit. This general kenosis of the Father's love further includes the kenosis of the Son and of the Holy Spirit. The creation of the world is already in a certain sense the kenosis of the Creator, Who establishes alongside Himself the relative, creaturely, autonomous being of the world. But this world, damaged at its very foundation, is restored and "saved" by the kenosis of the Son and of the Holy Spirit, by the Divine Incarnation of the Son and the descent into the world of the Spirit, through Whom the Father is revealed and acts in the world. This action of the Father is doubly kenotic, as it were. God patiently adapts Himself to the infirmity of the world and *awaits* its salvation, His own enthronement in it, which will be accomplished after a long and tragic process: "Then cometh the end, when he [the Son] shall have delivered up the kingdom to God, even the Father . . . for he [Christ] must reign, till he hath put all enemies under his feet" (1 Cor. 15:24-25). "And when all things shall be subdued unto him, then shall the Son also himself be subject unto him that put all things under him, that God [*ho Theos* = the Father] may be all in all" (15:28), that the revelation of the Father by the Son and the Holy Spirit may be fulfilled in all things. But until this happens, God is not all in all, however He may dominate His own creation. What does this mean?

God created the world by His omnipotence and by His wisdom; and the creation is therefore perfect and "good" (cf. Gen. 1), adequate to the thought of the Creator. But the plan for the creation includes its autonomous being and self-determination, and God's will as the interaction between the Creator and creation has therefore not been fully accomplished owing to this autonomy and freedom of the world, which was contaminated by nonbeing and evil in that metaphysical event which we call original sin. That is why we pray to God: "Thy will be done in earth, as it is in heaven." God interacts with the world by His Providence, but in so doing He restrains His omnipotence in order to allow the world its freedom of action. There is no adequacy between God's will and the ways of the world, although in the final analysis God's wisdom overcomes these ways, for the world is powerless, in the end, to resist God's plan for it, and God's will is being accomplished and will be accomplished in it (otherwise vain would be the Son's prayer, which He has taught us, His brothers, the sons of God: "Thy will be done in earth, as it is in heaven"). And it is for this reason that the divinely inspired cry of amazement and prayer before the ways of God's wisdom issues from the lips of the Apostle, dumbfounded before one of the most unfathomable events, the fate of Israel, its election and rejection, its embitterment and final salvation: "O the depth of the riches both of the wisdom and knowledge of God! How unsearchable are his judgments, and his ways past finding out" (Rom. 11:33).

But until now the ways of Providence have been determined by the kenosis of God the Father, Who has restrained His omnipotence, which, of course, has lost none of its force; and that is why, for us, these ways are indicated by a series of antinomic oppositions. God provides for the world in such a way that nothing happens in it without the will of the Heavenly Father: He "knoweth what things ye have need of" (Matt. 6:8); "one of them [sparrows] shall not fall on the ground without [the will of] your Father, but the very hairs of your head are all numbered" (10:29-30); "your heavenly Father feedeth" the fowls of the air (6:26), as He does all creatures. There is in the world another will, however, another providence, an evil one, which opposes the Divine Providence actively or passively; and this is permitted by the Divine Providence. This idea is expressed with a divinely inspired clarity in the Book of Job.

God is love, but the world contains malice, struggle, and hatred. The world is full of the immeasurable suffering of creatures. Groans and wails are borne to heaven, but heaven remains mute and without answer. Such is the kenosis of the Father's Love.

God is goodness, but "the world lieth in wickedness"; and this wickedness is the law of the world, subjugated by the prince of this world. The world is suffocating in evil and malice; goodness appears to be impotent in the world — but heaven is silent. Such is the kenosis of the Father's love.

God is the source of Truth and Essential Truth itself; but the world does not desire truth. The children of the world are sons of their father, who is falsehood and the father of falsehood (John 8:44); but no limit for this falsehood is established from above, and heaven is silent. Such is the kenosis of the Father's love.

God is the source of Beauty and Essential Beauty itself; but grotesque ugliness is triumphant in the world. Even beauty itself is corrupted and corrupts. Devotion to fallen beauty poisons souls with the strongest of poisons, for heaven itself is silent. Such is the kenosis of the Father's love.

God is the King. But there is no place in the world for the Kingdom of God. It has crucified the King of kings and the Son of God; and it blasphemes against the Holy Spirit. But heaven is silent. Such is the kenosis of the Father's love.

God is Spirit and the source of inspiration, but the life of the world is foreign to spirit and inspiration. It is enmired in the service of the flesh, crawls in the lowlands of sensuality and spiritual sleep, exalts itself in frenzied atheism and blasphemous delirium, cursing all that is holy or remaining indifferent to it — and heaven is silent. Such is the kenosis of the Father's Love.

And this kenosis is so deep that the world has to pass through the gates of a kind of death to find the strength to cry out, "Lord, I believe; help thou mine unbelief" (Mark 9:24), *"Credo quia absurdum,"* in order to see — contrary to all empirical evidence or in virtue of another, higher evidence — God and the Father, Who has reconciled the world with Himself in Christ (2 Cor. 5:19).

Such is the kenosis of the Father. It consists not only in the sacrifice of love, where the Father sends into the world His Son that He redeem it with His Blood, as well as the Holy Spirit that He actualize this redemption in the struggle with the sinfulness of this world. It also consists in the sacrifice of *patience:* it consists in suffering the being of the fallen world before the face of the God of Truth, the Judge of the world, the Omnipotent God.

As we have seen, the New Testament literature is full of testimonies about the adoration of and prayer to the Father as God, in heaven and on earth; but it does not contain any *direct* testimony about a similar adoration of and prayer to the Son and the Holy Spirit. This fact should not go unnoticed. The Son and the Holy Spirit are only *included,* in one way or another, as Advocates or Intercessors in this adoration of and prayer to the Father. Jesus Christ is invariably called the *Lord, kurios,* Who reconciled us with the Father, making us His sons through the Holy Spirit. At the same time, from the early days of Christianity, the Church has prayed to the Son and the Holy Spirit as to God. This relation is so self-evident that an enormous number of church prayers and of invocations in general are addressed to our Lord and God Jesus Christ and to God the Holy Spirit.

In our prayers, we can address God in different ways: out of the depths of our creatureliness we pray to God as the Creator, and from the heights of our Godsonhood we pray to the Father of the Son, the Lord Jesus Christ, Who has sent us the Holy Spirit. When we contemplate our Creator and God in prayer, the abyss separating our creaturely being from God is so immense for us that our eyes grow blind when we try to gauge the distances in the blue of heaven: "Out of the depths have I cried unto thee, O Lord. Lord, hear my voice" (Ps. 130:1-2). For us there exists a supremely high, terrible, marvelous, unfathomable God, to Whom our soul sings its song of praise and thanksgiving, trembling before His omnipotence, the Lord of creation and the Creator of the world. (This is approximately the religious aspect of Islam, and originally of the Old Testament: the appearance of God in thunder and lightning.) This is the fear of God, awe before the *Holy* (which, in the Old Testament, is, as it were, God's proper name: the Holy of Israel). To God the Creator and the Almighty, the poor soul of creation calls out for mercy and help: "The Lord, the Lord God, merciful and gracious, longsuffering, and abundant in goodness and truth" (Exod. 34:6). This relation of prayer of man to God, as creature to Creator, is so essential and necessary that it is, so to speak, one of the fundamental "categories" of prayer, but it is not exhaustive and unique.

For the Christian world, which possesses the revelation of the Holy Trinity, essentially this very same prayer is accomplished and disclosed in the prayer addressed to the Holy Trinity as the triune God, to the *One* in *three* hypostases. The prototype of this prayer is given in the baptismal formula (Matt. 28:19) as well as in the *comma Johanneum* (1 John 5:7). Prayers to the Holy Trinity are addressed to It as to one God: "Most Holy Trinity, have mercy upon us."[14] In essence, this is the Christian prayer which the

---

14. Of the innumerable prayers of this type, I cite only one (a Vespers prayer): "I venerate You, Most Holy Trinity, consubstantial, life-giving, indivisible, Father and Son and Holy Spirit: I believe in You and I confess You. I glorify You, I praise and honor You, I exalt You, and I pray to You: have pity upon me, Your humble servant."

creature addresses to God; and this contemplation in prayer includes the dogmatic truth that Divinity has a trinitarian character. The three hypostases are, however, not distinguished here according to their particular properties and relations to the world. Rather, they are contemplated as divine hypostases in general, which manifest in their triunity the one trihypostatic God. The name of the Holy Trinity represents here the Christian name of God in general, which is therefore employed as the blessing power when the sign of the cross is made (where we bless ourselves) and in all blessings by the name of God. This veneration of the name of the Holy Trinity and the invocation of God in the Holy Trinity are proper to all Christian prayer, which explicitly expresses or tacitly implies this veneration and invocation.

But prayer addressed to the Absolute as the Creator and God does not yet exhaust or fully characterize Christian prayer. Man addresses God not only "out of the depths" of his creatureliness, insignificance, and nonbeing, but also out of His Godsonhood and Divine-humanity, not as a servant, but as a son, crying out: Abba, Father. This Christian prayer to God already manifests the distinction of the hypostases in their relation to man. To be sure, here too, the equi-divinity of the hypostases is not subject to any diminution or limitation; no Arianism or Macedonianism is permissible here. The Father is equi-divine in relation to the Son and the Holy Spirit; and therefore we pray to God the Father, and the Son, and the Holy Spirit both in the triunity of the Holy Trinity and as different hypostases. This specificity of the prayers, however, is associated with differences in the proximity to us of the different hypostases. This is the same differentiation that exists between the Paternal or Revealed hypostasis, the Principle, and the hypostases that reveal the Father in the Divine Sophia, in the Divine-humanity, in which God appears to the world not only as transcendent but also as immanent.

This general immanence is manifested through the Incarnation and the descent of the Holy Spirit. The Logos, the God-Man, is already our Friend and Brother, the Man Christ Jesus, the Advocate and Mediator ("for there is one God, and one mediator between God and men, the man Christ Jesus" [1 Tim. 2:5]); and we pray to God and the Father (a name we can never apply to the God-Man Himself) with Christ and in Him. At the same time, we also pray to Him, the Lord Jesus Christ, the Son of God, the God-Man, Who is both God and Man by the "communication of properties" and Who in His humanity has descended even down to creaturely being, is "God with us."

Likewise we pray to the Holy Spirit, Who also descended from heaven and abides in the world, in us and with us. "Omnipresent and all-accomplishing" (as the Orthodox prayer says), He comes and makes His abode in us; and in us and with us, He prays to the Father, being the breath of our prayer and the accomplishment of our sacraments. His immanence in relation to the world is other but not less than that of the God-Man. It is true that the genius of prayer, moved by the Holy Spirit, makes it so that we pray comparatively little to the Holy Spirit Himself (as is clear from the fact that the prayers addressed directly to Him are relatively few in number). Rather, we pray to the Father and the Son that They send the Holy Spirit down to us. But we shall speak about this below.

Our Lord Jesus Christ and the Holy Spirit are God for us according to Their Divinity, but They are not remote from us in heaven. They are close to us according to our divine-humanity, by virtue of the Incarnation of the Word and the descent from heaven of the Holy Spirit. They are within us as our true life. As the Apostle Paul says, "Christ liveth in me" (Gal. 2:20) and we are "the temple of the Holy Spirit" (1 Cor. 6:19). This proximity of ours to Them imparts a special character to our prayer: in praying, we strive to overcome all distance, to *embrace* the life of Christ, to *receive* the Holy Spirit, to become *one* with Them. And we know this union in our religious experience, in which we strive to commune with this divine life.

Such an expressly divine-human character is also possessed by the Christian prayer of prayers, which is, as it were, the spiritual focus of our entire life of prayer. We mean the Jesus Prayer and the analogous prayer (although not as widespread): "Comforter, Spirit of Truth, come and make Thy abode in us." Both prayers represent spiritual means for the union with Christ by virtue of and by the action of the Holy Spirit. Here, the power of the divine-human Name *Jesus* and the power of the invocation of the Holy Spirit are equivalent. These prayers represent a spiritual work which is a deification *in actu*, in which the person praying, overcoming the spiritual distance between him and God, becomes a god by grace and communes with divine life. This idea is the chief theme of the Palamite disputes about the significance of "the light of Tabor." The religious experience of Symeon the New Theologian, described by him in his *Hymns of Love*, attests to this, as does the experience of other mystics. We find the same thing in the manifestation of the power of the Holy Spirit shown by St. Seraphim of Sarov to Motovilov.[15]

Our immediate sense of prayer distinguishes here even between the

---

15. See n. 12 in chap. 5. — Trans.

Second and the Third hypostases, between Christ and the Holy Spirit, although this, of course, does not in any way diminish our belief in Their equi-divinity. The number of church prayers addressed to Christ is incomparably greater than the number of church prayers addressed to the Holy Spirit. We usually pray not so much to the Holy Spirit Himself as the Third hypostasis[16] as to God the Father or to the Lord Jesus Christ, beseeching Them to *send down* to us the grace of the Holy Spirit or His "gifts." This is a widespread and undeniable fact, which results from the very essence of our relations with God. We are close to Christ, for we ourselves are "the Body of Christ"; and by partaking of it in the sacrament of the Eucharist, we are united with Him. Despite this mysterious sacramental presence for us, however, the Ascended Christ abides in heaven, sits at the right hand of the Father, and is thus removed from us. But the Holy Spirit abides with us and in us if we do not close ourselves off from His presence by our sins. *Practically* speaking, Christ for us is the *personal* God (if one can use this expression) to a greater degree than the Holy Spirit, Who exists for us rather as a *gift*, as grace, as a power manifested in us. We pray to the Father that, having received the sacrifice of the Son on His heavenly altar, He "send down to us divine grace and the gift of the Holy Spirit."

This hierarchical interrelation which exists in the Holy Trinity is also clearly manifested in the Divine Eucharist, which is concluded by a prayer (the epiclesis) to God the Father, that He give us the Body and Blood of Christ by the action of the Holy Spirit: "Make this bread the precious body of Thy Christ, and make in this cup the precious blood of Thy Christ, by transmuting it by Thy Holy Spirit." We pray to the heavenly God and Father that He mysteriously give us Christ by the Holy Spirit, that He manifest the power of the Incarnation, that He once again send down into the world the Son and the Holy Spirit.

Thus, according to the distinction we have established, God the Father is the supramundane, transcendent God, abiding in heaven; whereas the Son and the Holy Spirit, Who also are in heaven by virtue of Their Divinity, are connected with us and with the world by virtue of the Divine-humanity. We feel this in our experience of prayer, since, for us as well, God in the proper and direct sense is precisely God the Father, Who transcendentally abides in heaven, whereas the Son and the Holy Spirit are united with us on earth. They are in the world, having a transcendental-immanent relation to it, whereas the Father transcends the world, is in

16. See my article "Prayer to the Holy Spirit" in the *Bulletin of the St. Sergius Theological Institute*, 1935, no. 6.

heaven *above* the world. What does such an idea of the Transcendent God mean for us in practical religious terms? He is, first of all, the dread Almighty Lord, before Whom all creatures tremble. He is the God of Islam and of Calvin, Whose only relation to the world is absolutely omnipotent will. This creaturely world is alien to Him; His devouring will is for us the unfathomable arbitrariness of the Absolute, which is inhuman and unworldly because it is supramundane. Besides fear and trepidation, He inspires no other feeling: the cold, airless expanses are impenetrable for the rays of love. This is a horrible metaphysical nightmare from which creation seeks to hide in its immanence. The being of the world desires to enclose itself in the world, to save itself from this icy Absolute by not recognizing it, and under the pretext of ignorance (agnosticism) to immerse itself in practical atheism, i.e., cosmotheism. This is the other side of the transcendentalism of the Absolute, its dialectical antithesis: the absolutization of the immanent and relative.

But this notion of the Transcendent God falls apart: it is full of contradictions not only from the religious but also from the philosophical point of view. As pure Transcendence, this notion is accessible only to apophatics, which pronounces all sorts of negations, the absolute NO. But the latter is mute and empty; it simply does not exist, for it is the mere resonance from some *yes*. In other words, in a purely apophatic, negative definition, the absolute is unthinkable; *it does not exist.* The icy airless expanses are ontologically void of all being; they are the *néant.* Being begins *to be* only in the presence of a definite boundary: the *apeiron* [the limitless] languishes if it does not have a *peras* [limit]. The absolute receives a certain *appearance* of being only by constantly retreating, by being repelled from all boundaries, by going into the infinite void. In this sense, it is an empty, "bad infinity," which does not know how to end, how to find closure in self-sufficiency. It is the shadow of nonbeing, the shadow of a shadow, the shadow of itself. Or, and finally one must simply say this, *it does not exist.* Being is not proper to it; and this is not at all a privilege of absoluteness but simply the limit of its extreme poverty, of its *penia,* which is nonbeing. Understood in this way, the absolute is that nothing "out of" which God created the world. But in it itself, in its emptiness, there is no creative principle; and it is not God.

And even the predicate of will, which deism (or, more precisely, deistic adogmatic atheism) ascribes to the absolute, can by no means be attributed to this *No.* Where does will come from if there is no *He* who wills, but only an *It* that wills (the evil phantom of impersonal and insane will in Schopenhauer)? If there is no He who wills, this Transcendent is, in its negativity, poorer than the immanent, which is personal. The void cannot have a personal principle; and impersonal being is not spirit, for spirit is conscious, personal being (and not the unconscious or preconscious *Urgottheit* of Eckhart and Boehme or the unconscious of Hartmann and Schopenhauer). And even if one were to admit, at the cost of contradiction, such a personal principle in the transcendent, this would be a monster of self-devouring egocentrism, absolute "I-ness." In a word, the idea of God as transcendent nonbeing abiding and concealed in heaven is contradictory and dialectically insolvent. Such an idea is a logical phantom, which in man takes the form of the trepidation of a slave in the face of religious absolutism. And the question naturally arises: Does this transcendent, inhuman deity exist and is it worthy of worship, or is the rebellion of Prometheus the only position worthy of man here?

And before this impasse of the reason, which seeks but does not find the Transcendent in the opacity of heaven, a voice resounds from there, from out of the depths of the heaven of heavens, the voice of revelation on Sinai in a cloud: "The Lord, The Lord God, merciful and gracious, long-suffering, and abundant in goodness and truth" (Exod. 34:6). And this God, Who is human in His mercy toward men and Whose voice is *heard* in the world, is revealed in the Son as God and the Father. There is nothing and can be nothing sweeter than this divine revelation, that our God is our FATHER, and we are His offspring (see Acts 17:29).

The *Father* . . . This says it all, answering all human questionings about the Transcendent, heavenly God. He is the God "Who is in heaven." His being is supramundane, above the world, transcendent, "in heaven"; but this transcendence cannot be and does not desire to be merely transcendent. Indeed, transcendent transcendence does not even exist, for it is inseparable from and identical with immanence, with self-revelation. The transcendent is the Father, from Whom all fatherhood derives and Who thus knows sonhood as well. He is correlative to sonhood, not separated from it; He is not alone in His heavenly transcendence. The Father is a person, who, as a person, is correlated with other persons; He presupposes them for Himself and for them He is the Transcendent-immanent. He is such in His own being as a congregate Person in the Holy Trinity, but He is also a Person in relation to creation, in relation to human persons. He is a Personal spirit in relation to all personal spirits. From our human I, we address Him as *Thou*, i.e., He is *co-I* for us.

He is the Father, and His relation to the world is not that of an absolute despot, but that of the *love* of the Father's heart. There is *no* cold, airless, impenetrable heaven, for heaven is permeated with the rays of the sun of Love. There is no place for the proud and frigid *No* of the Absolute in relation to the whole of creaturely being, for which only a single definition is admitted: total dissimilarity, otherness, absolute nonresemblance to this Absolute. No, the Absolute is the *Father,* from Whom all fatherhood proceeds. His image is inscribed in being: even as the Son is the image of the Father and sonhood is the revelation of Fatherhood, so the whole world is the mirror of the Father, His Image. His direct Image is inscribed in the Son and the Spirit, in the heavenly Sophia and the Divine-humanity; and His creaturely image is imprinted in the world, in the creaturely Sophia and the earthly Divine-humanity — images of images, myriads and multitudes of images of the one Image. God's world is the Father's world, the image of the Father.

The God Who is in heaven is high and remote. As heaven is for earth, He is inaccessible for this world, but He does not thereby become alien and unknown to our world. We *know* this unknown and inaccessible *heavenly* God, for we know the Son by the Holy Spirit. He does not hide, but reveals Himself in Them. He is not negated by but is identified with Their revelation. And this identification is not a cold, abstract, theoretical one; it is not an intellectual conclusion but a living reality; for it is not only a revelation through the hypostases who reveal and who are thus known to the world, but also the Divine I of the Father, Who permeates with His love all the heavens of heavens. He is *personally* present in the world and is revealed to the latter in the manner proper to Him. The hypostasis of the Father does not become incarnate and does not descend from heaven, for He only sends, but this sending, which is the Father's love for those who are sent as well as for those to whom He sends Them, is His personal presence in His love for us. He is high in heaven, but He is also terribly near by His *personal* love for every creature; He is God *and* the Father, God the Father, the Father Who is God. There is no greater essential and ontological nearness than that which exists between the Father and His children, even as there is no greater difference than that which exists between the Source and Proto-image of being and His creaturely images.

Not only is this revelation of the Father about Himself the sweetest of religious truths, but it also contains the solution to all the difficulties of philosophical speculation. The Absolute is no longer the extra-mundane, transcendent, empty *No,* totally unconnected with the world and thus not existing for it. It is now the Father, the transcendent-immanent, world-conforming unity of Proto-image and image. The transcendent Absolute stops being a bad, negative infinity, which flees from itself into the void of negations. It is now a positive infinity through the correlativeness of the absolute and the relative, of divine and creaturely being. Creaturely being is established by God in His image, which is the Divine Sophia, the Divine-humanity. The transcendent Absolute is not an impersonal and soulless objectivity, which is incapable of entering into a relation with the world of personal spirits, being, in its impersonality, poorer than they. Rather, the Absolute is the Father, the personal and absolute spirit Who actualizes Himself in His trihypostatatic sobornost and proceeds out of it and beyond it to the creaturely spirits, including them in the image of His personal and congregate being. Finally, the Transcendent Absolute is blind and mute will, fate, despotic arbitrariness. But God the Father is the Father's Love, the sun of the world, which is His heart. The following is said about Him: "That ye may be the children of your Father which is in heaven: for he maketh his sun to rise on the evil and on the good, and sendeth rain on the just and on the unjust" (Matt. 5:45). The Absolute *loves;* He is the Father. That is the idea that unites the entire absoluteness of the Heavenly God and the entire power of His revelation in the relative, for this power is *Love*. Metaphysics finds fulfillment in this divinely revealed doctrine, for it actualizes all its postulates in the latter. But this is also the only possible and true fulfillment of the postulates of the religious consciousness, which simultaneously requires that the heavenly God be remote from us and that He be near and accessible to us. These two things are harmonized in the revelation of God and the Father, heavenly by His Divinity and near to us by His Fatherhood.

All that we know and love in the Son is the Father, for as the Son is, so also is the Father. All the love and inspiration that we have in the Holy Spirit are also the Father, for as the Father is, so also is the Holy Spirit, Who proceeds from Him, His own Spirit. In loving the Son and the Holy Spirit, we love the Father, we know the Father, we contemplate His holy Person. If the Son and the Holy Spirit are Love and the revelation of Love, the Father is Love itself, the very Heart of Love and, truly, the Will of Love. We worship Him as King and God, Almighty and Creator; but in worshipping Him in fear and trembling, we love Him, the heavenly Father, the Father of heaven and earth, our Father. Together with the Apostle, we "bow [our] knees unto the Father of our Lord Jesus Christ" (Eph. 3:14), we, His creatures and His children.

And permit us, O Lord, boldly and without being judged, to invoke Thee, our Heavenly God the Father, and to say:

OUR FATHER WHICH ART IN HEAVEN!
ABBA, FATHER!

Index